Global Strategy and Management

Theory and Practice

Paul N. Gooderham
NHH Norwegian School of Economics, Norway and Middlesex University Business School, London, UK

Birgitte Grøgaard
BI Norwegian Business School, Norway

Kirsten Foss
NHH Norwegian School of Economics, Norway and Copenhagen Business School, Denmark

Edward Elgar
PUBLISHING

Cheltenham, UK • Northampton, MA, USA

© Paul N. Gooderham, Birgitte Grøgaard and Kirsten Foss 2019

All rights reserved. No part of this publication may be reproduced, stored in a retrieval system or transmitted in any form or by any means, electronic, mechanical or photocopying, recording, or otherwise without the prior permission of the publisher.

Published by
Edward Elgar Publishing Limited
The Lypiatts
15 Lansdown Road
Cheltenham
Glos GL50 2JA
UK

Edward Elgar Publishing, Inc.
William Pratt House
9 Dewey Court
Northampton
Massachusetts 01060
USA

A catalogue record for this book
is available from the British Library

Library of Congress Control Number: 2019930603

ISBN 978 1 78811 483 7 (cased)
ISBN 978 1 78811 485 1 (paperback)
ISBN 978 1 78811 484 4 (eBook)

Typeset by Servis Filmsetting Ltd, Stockport, Cheshire
Printed and bound in Great Britain by TJ International Ltd, Padstow

Contents in brief

List of authors and contributors	xvi
Acknowledgements	xviii
Introduction	xix

PART I   THE MULTINATIONAL ENTERPRISE

1	Setting the scene: The multinational enterprise	3
Case A:	What makes for an exceptional global leader? Is 'CEO disease' inevitable? The case of Carlos Ghosn *Paul N. Gooderham*	16
2	Why and how firms internationalize	27
Case B:	MTN Group Limited – subsidiary management across emerging economies *Gilbert Kofi Adarkwah*	41
Case C:	Gran Tierra Energy Inc. in Brazil *Birgitte Grøgaard, Charlene D. Miller and Vivek Shah*	55
3	International strategy and competitive advantage	75
Case D:	Uninor: Beyond local responsiveness – multidomestic MNEs at the bottom of the pyramid *Paul N. Gooderham, Svein Ulset and Frank Elter*	94
4	Strategic decisions: Operating modes	108
Case E:	BKT – IJVs and the role of effective boundary-spanning activities *Paul N. Gooderham, Michael Zhang, Atle Jordahl and Kirsten Foss*	124

PART II THE EXTERNAL CONTEXT

5 Managing external stakeholders in MNEs 141

Case F: The regulation of contract workers: A case study of LafargeHolcim and a GUF's attempt to defend workers' rights in India 153
Aranya Pakapath and Elizabeth Cotton

6 Corporate social responsibility 162

Case G: Managing CSR in supplier networks: The case of Apple 176
Kirsten Foss

Case H: Nestlé Waters and its involvement in two controversial cases regarding water extraction 181
Kirsten Foss

7 National culture 185

Case I: Danvita: Cultural diversity in a Danish MNE 206
Vasilisa Sayapina and Katya Christensen

8 The institutional context 225

Case J: Walmart in Germany 240
Kirsten Foss

PART III FUNDAMENTAL MANAGERIAL CHALLENGES

9 Social capital building and knowledge transfer 251

Case K: SFC: From multidomestic to globally integrated – when local taste matters 269
Paul N. Gooderham

10 Cross-national transfer of human resource management 289

Case L: SR-Bank: Gained in translation – the import, translation and evolution of a US sales and management concept 302
Martin Gjelsvik

11	International career development as global strategy	322
Case M:	LVMH: Career development through international mobility *Jean-Luc Cerdin*	337

Index   357

Full contents

List of authors and contributors	xvi
Acknowledgements	xviii
Introduction	xix

PART I THE MULTINATIONAL ENTERPRISE

1 Setting the scene: The multinational enterprise — 3
- 1.1 Introduction — 3
- 1.2 What is an MNE? — 3
- 1.3 The globalization of business — 6
- 1.4 Why study global strategy and management? — 8
- 1.5 What do international managers do? — 10
- 1.6 How common is top management diversity? — 12
- 1.7 Summary — 13

Case A: What makes for an exceptional global leader? Is 'CEO disease' inevitable? The case of Carlos Ghosn — 16
Paul N. Gooderham
- A.1 Introduction — 16
- A.2 The rise of Carlos Ghosn — 17
- A.3 The fall of Carlos Ghosn — 23
- Case discussion — 25

2 Why and how firms internationalize — 27
- 2.1 Introduction — 27
- 2.2 Why do firms internationalize? — 27
- 2.3 What is 'liability of foreignness'? — 29
- 2.4 Understanding MNEs' internationalization choices: A theoretical framework — 31
- 2.5 What is the process of internationalization? — 32
- 2.6 Do emerging market MNEs challenge extant theory? — 35
- 2.7 Summary — 37

Case B:	**MTN Group Limited – subsidiary management across emerging economies**	**41**
	Gilbert Kofi Adarkwah	
	B.1 Introduction	41
	B.2 About MTN	41
	B.3 MTN's products and services	42
	B.4 Strategy for expansion and long-term vision	43
	B.5 Corporate structure and organization	44
	B.6 Unique local challenges	45
	B.7 About the telecommunication industry	52
	Case discussion	53
Case C:	**Gran Tierra Energy Inc. in Brazil**	**55**
	Birgitte Grøgaard, Charlene D. Miller and Vivek Shah	
	C.1 Introduction	55
	C.2 Background of Gran Tierra	55
	C.3 Gran Tierra's strategy	56
	C.4 Gran Tierra's portfolio	61
	C.5 The decision to enter Brazil	63
	C.6 The Brazilian assets	66
	C.7 The Brazilian experience	67
	C.8 Moving forward	68
	Case discussion	74
3	**International strategy and competitive advantage**	**75**
	3.1 Introduction	75
	3.2 International strategies: The integration–responsiveness framework	75
	3.3 International strategy and competitive strategy	81
	3.4 The FSAs that enable international strategies	82
	3.5 How can we identify and assess FSAs? Drawing on mainstream strategy frameworks to determine competitive advantages	83
	3.6 The challenges of geographically distributed organizational units: The transnational solution	85
	3.7 Subsidiary roles	87
	3.8 Beyond local responsiveness: The BOP challenge	89
	3.9 Summary	91
Case D:	**Uninor: Beyond local responsiveness – multidomestic MNEs at the bottom of the pyramid**	**94**
	Paul N. Gooderham, Svein Ulset and Frank Elter	

		D.1	Introduction	94
		D.2	The failure and the turnaround of Uninor	95
		D.3	Perceived benefit and price	98
		D.4	Value delivery	99
		D.5	Global replication of BOP innovations	101
		D.6	GID	102
		D.7	GID and transfer from BOP	103
		D.8	Conclusion	104
			Case discussion	106

4 Strategic decisions: Operating modes — 108

4.1	Introduction	108
4.2	Foreign operating modes	108
4.3	Exporting	111
4.4	Licensing	112
4.5	Franchising	112
4.6	Contract manufacturing and service provision	113
4.7	Foreign direct investments (FDI)	114
4.8	International joint ventures (IJVs)	115
4.9	Wholly-owned subsidiaries	118
4.10	Summary	120

Case E: BKT – IJVs and the role of effective boundary-spanning activities — 124

Paul N. Gooderham, Michael Zhang, Atle Jordahl and Kirsten Foss

E.1	Introduction	124
E.2	Background	126
E.3	The Dalian-JV	129
E.4	The Shanghai-JV	131
E.5	The virtual boundary spanner	133
E.6	Summary	133
E.7	Conclusion	135
	Case discussion	135
	Appendix	138

PART II THE EXTERNAL CONTEXT

5 Managing external stakeholders in MNEs — 141

5.1	Introduction	141
5.2	Stakeholder theory	141
5.3	Who are the MNEs' relevant stakeholders?	143

| | | 5.4 | Unique stakeholder relations | 146 |
| | | 5.5 | Summary | 150 |

Case F:	The regulation of contract workers: A case study of LafargeHolcim and a GUF's attempt to defend workers' rights in India	153

Aranya Pakapath and Elizabeth Cotton

	F.1	Understanding the context	153
	F.2	LafargeHolcim	155
	F.3	LafargeHolcim in India	156
	F.4	Chronology of the LafargeHolcim dispute	157
	F.5	Conclusion	159
	Case discussion		160

6	Corporate social responsibility	162
	6.1 Introduction	162
	6.2 Defining CSR	162
	6.3 Stakeholder theory applied to CSR	164
	6.4 The short- and long-term benefits of CSR investments	168
	6.5 Creating 'win–win' possibilities through strategic CSR investments	169
	6.6 Internationalization strategies and the implementation of CSR in MNEs	171
	6.7 Summary	173

Case G:	Managing CSR in supplier networks: The case of Apple	176

Kirsten Foss

	G.1 About Apple	176
	G.2 The competitive situation and challenges with suppliers	176
	Case discussion	179

Case H:	Nestlé Waters and its involvement in two controversial cases regarding water extraction	181

Kirsten Foss

	H.1 Introduction	181
	H.2 Creating shared value	181
	H.3 The Bhati Dilwan case	182
	H.4 The Ontario case	183
	Case discussion	184

7	National culture	185
	7.1 Introduction	185

	7.2	Cultural distance and MNE performance	185
	7.3	The concept of culture	187
	7.4	Hofstede's four dimensions	188
	7.5	General critique of Hofstede	197
	7.6	Other dimensions of culture	202
	7.7	Summary	202

Case I:	**Danvita: Cultural diversity in a Danish MNE**		**206**
	Vasilisa Sayapina and Katya Christensen		
	I.1	Introduction	206
	I.2	Denmark and Danish	207
	I.3	Danvita and the HR challenges it is facing	208
	I.4	Cultural diversity as perceived by employees	210
	I.5	Creating the environment for cultural diversity	216
	I.6	Why workforce diversity?	219
	I.7	Two employee stories	221
		Case discussion	223

8	**The institutional context**		**225**
	8.1	Introduction	225
	8.2	Institutional distance	225
	8.3	Home country characteristics	227
	8.4	Capturing the complexities of institutional contexts	229
	8.5	Institutional voids	233
	8.6	Institutional distance versus cultural distance	236
	8.7	Summary	236

Case J:	**Walmart in Germany**		**240**
	Kirsten Foss		
	J.1	Introduction	240
	J.2	Information about Walmart	240
	J.3	Walmart's home market	241
	J.4	Germany at the time when Walmart decided to enter the market	242
	J.5	Walmart in Germany	244
	J.6	Walmart after Germany	246
		Case discussion	247

PART III FUNDAMENTAL MANAGERIAL CHALLENGES

9	**Social capital building and knowledge transfer**		**251**
	9.1	Introduction	251

9.2	The MNE as a knowledge network	251
9.3	Evolutionary theory of the MNE	253
9.4	Knowledge transfer in MNEs	254
9.5	The concept of knowledge transfer	255
9.6	Determinants of knowledge transfer	257
9.7	The external environment of the MNE	259
9.8	The role of management-initiated practices	261
9.9	Conceptual model	264
9.10	Summary	265

Case K: SFC: From multidomestic to globally integrated – when local taste matters — 269
Paul N. Gooderham

K.1	Introduction	269
K.2	Revisiting extant theory	270
K.3	Context	272
K.4	The Unification Project (2004–07)	273
K.5	Post-Unification Project	277
K.6	Programme Amalgamation (2008–10)	278
K.7	The distinctive elements of Programme Amalgamation	280
K.8	Summary	286
	Case discussion	287

10 Cross-national transfer of human resource management — 289

10.1	Introduction	289
10.2	International human resource management (IHRM)	289
10.3	The substance of cross-national HRM	290
10.4	A framework for strategic international human resource management (SIHRM)	292
10.5	Practical lessons	297
10.6	Summary	299

Case L: SR-Bank: Gained in translation – the import, translation and evolution of a US sales and management concept — 302
Martin Gjelsvik

L.1	Introduction	302
L.2	Cultural context	303
L.3	SR-Bank's strategy	304
L.4	Key financial figures	304
L.5	SESAM: The antecedents	305
L.6	SESAM: The initial steps through knowledge import	308
L.7	SESAM: The explicit face	309

		L.8	Branches and departments: The new learning communities	314
		L.9	SESAM 12 years later: Best practice in practice	315
		L.10	The issue of performance measurement	317
		L.11	Yet another transformation: The balanced scorecard	319
			Case discussion	320
11	**International career development as global strategy**			**322**
	11.1		Introduction	322
	11.2		What is expatriation and why invest in it?	322
	11.3		The importance of repatriation	324
	11.4		Enabling the expatriate	325
	11.5		Capturing the value of repatriates	327
	11.6		What can we learn from best practices?	329
	11.7		How managerial mindsets impact staffing policies	330
	11.8		Summary	333
Case M:	**LVMH: Career development through international mobility**			**337**
	Jean-Luc Cerdin			
		M.1	Introduction	337
		M.2	LVMH's history and structure	339
		M.3	Understanding international mobility through a retrospective lens	339
		M.4	HR structure	340
		M.5	Career development and international mobility	341
		M.6	Basic principles of LVMH's policy for international mobility	341
		M.7	International talents	342
		M.8	International recruitment	343
		M.9	The international transfer policy	344
		M.10	International mobility	345
		M.11	Managing benefits	350
		M.12	Logistical support	352
		M.13	Spousal support	352
		M.14	Intercultural training	352
		M.15	Repatriation	353
		M.16	The view of the future in 2001	354
			Case discussion	355
Index				357

Authors and contributors

Authors

Paul N. Gooderham is Professor of International Management and Head of the Department of Strategy & Management at NHH: Norwegian School of Economics, Bergen, Norway. He is also an Adjunct Professor at Middlesex University, London. Since 1994, he has been a member of Cranet, the world's largest and longest running comparative HRM research network spanning more than 40 countries. In addition to comparative management, his research addresses the management challenges faced by MNEs. He has published numerous articles in journals such as *Journal of World Business, Journal of Management, Journal of Management Studies, Journal of International Business Studies, Strategic Management Journal, Human Relations* and *Administrative Science Quarterly*.

Birgitte Grøgaard is an Associate Professor at BI Norwegian Business School in Oslo, Norway. Before joining BI, she worked for nine years at the University of Calgary in Canada. Her research interests include multinational firm strategies, headquarter–subsidiary relations, integration challenges in multinationals, and foreign direct investments with a particular focus on state ownership. Her work has been published in various international business journals including the *Journal of International Business Studies, Journal of World Business, International Business Review* and *Management International Review*. Prior to pursuing her PhD, Birgitte worked in a multinational oil and gas company as well as in management consulting.

Kirsten Foss is Professor of Strategy and Organization at NHH: Norwegian School of Economics, Bergen, Norway. She is also an Adjunct Professor at Copenhagen Business School, Copenhagen since 2008. In addition to international business, her research interest addresses the institutional context for businesses, strategy and economic organization of business activities. She has published in journals such as *Strategic Management Journal, Organization Studies* and *Journal of International Management*.

Contributors

Gilbert Kofi Adarkwah is a doctoral student at BI Norwegian Business School.

Jean-Luc Cerdin is a Professor of Human Resource Management at ESSEC Business School, Paris.

Katya Christensen has held various managerial roles in Scandinavian multinational companies.

Elizabeth Cotton is a Senior Lecturer at Middlesex University Business School, London.

Frank Elter is a Vice-President at Telenor Research and an Adjunct Associate Professor at NHH: Norwegian School of Economics, Bergen, Norway.

Martin Gjelsvik is Research Manager at NORCE Norwegian Research Centre AS.

Atle Jordahl was for many years a senior consultant at AFF: the Administrative Research Institute at NHH: Norwegian School of Economics. He now works as an independent leadership consultant.

Charlene D. Miller is at GFA Consulting Group, Egypt.

Aranya Pakapath is a Thai Project Coordinator for the International Federation of Chemical, Energy, Mine and General Workers Union (ICEM).

Vasilisa Sayapina is a doctoral student at NHH: Norwegian School of Economics, Bergen, Norway.

Vivek Shah is at KUFPEC, Kuwait.

Svein Ulset (1952–2015) was a Professor of Strategy at NHH: Norwegian School of Economics, Bergen, Norway.

Michael Zhang is a reader at Nottingham Trent University Business School, UK.

Acknowledgements

We wish to acknowledge that Chapter 5 draws on the work of Richard Croucher contained in Gooderham, P.N., B. Grøgaard and O. Nordhaug (2013), *International Management: Theory and Practice*, Cheltenham, UK and Northampton, MA, USA: Edward Elgar Publishing. Richard is Professor of Comparative Employment Relations at Middlesex University Business School, London.

We wish to acknowledge that Chapters 5 and 6 draw on the work of Leighton Wilks and Odd Nordhaug contained in Gooderham, P.N., B. Grøgaard and O. Nordhaug (2013), *International Management: Theory and Practice*, Cheltenham, UK and Northampton, MA, USA: Edward Elgar Publishing. Leighton is a doctoral candidate at the University of Calgary and Odd (1953–2013) was Professor in Administrative Science at NHH: Norwegian School of Economics.

We wish to acknowledge that Chapter 6 also draws on the work of Sveinung Jørgensen and Lars Jacob Tynes Pedersen contained in Gooderham, P.N., B. Grøgaard and O. Nordhaug (2013), *International Management: Theory and Practice*, Cheltenham, UK and Northampton, MA, USA: Edward Elgar Publishing. Sveinung is an Associate Professor at HIL: Lillehammer University College and Lars is an Associate Professor at NHH: Norwegian School of Economics.

Introduction

The three of us have been researching and teaching global strategy and management for 20 years. Two of us worked for multinational enterprises (MNEs) before we started our academic careers. Since then, we have all also regularly been 'inside' MNEs talking to managers about the challenges they face.

The primary audience of this text is master students undertaking courses in global strategy and management, MBAs and advanced bachelor students. However, our state-of-the art theoretical overviews of topics related to global strategy and management should also make this a useful reference book for academics. Similarly, the interaction between theory and cases makes for a text that practitioners will experience as relevant.

As we point out in Chapter 1 of this text, there has been an explosive growth in the number of MNEs. Their contribution to the global economy is such that no student of business or economics can or should avoid thinking seriously about this phenomenon. In this book, we identify some of the most crucial challenges facing managers of MNEs. We emphasize that many of these challenges are unique to MNEs because of their geographically spread organizations that have to contend with cultural and institutional distances. We chose to explore these challenges using an interactive approach whereby theory and cases are juxtaposed. A core belief underlying this book is that theory is best understood by relating it not only to short, 'tidy' cases but to 'baggy' cases that stretch the sense-making ability of the reader. Each chapter offers not only a theoretically grounded presentation of a particular aspect of global strategy and management but also a case culled from the real world of global strategy and management that serves to illustrate the theory along with case assignments that assist the student in relating the theory to the case.

The first part of the book, Chapters 1 to 4, introduces the MNE and key drivers for strategic decision-making. More specifically, Chapter 1 defines MNEs and examines the global leadership challenges facing their managers. This chapter is followed by a case study that features a once highly successful and visible global leader, Carlos Ghosn.

In Chapter 2, we discuss why and how firms choose to internationalize. We examine the role of MNEs in contemporary society and we challenge stereotypical perceptions of globalization. Based on both well-established and more recent research in international business, we discuss managerial challenges, such as the liability of foreignness, that firms face as they internationalize and enter new markets. The case studies following Chapter 2 illustrate some of the challenges MNEs face as they seek to realize their motives for internationalization.

In Chapter 3, we use the integration–responsiveness framework to reflect on international strategies in relation to external competitive pressure and introduce four generic international strategies for MNEs: simple international, global, multidomestic, and transnational. We elaborate on the links between MNEs' strategies, their competitive advantages, and the way they compete in markets. We further explore in depth some key characteristics of the transnational strategy that balances global integration and local responsiveness, and its implications for subsidiary roles and subsidiary management. Finally, we illustrate a particular kind of local adaptation: the bottom-of-the-pyramid markets. The case study for Chapter 3 illustrates the learning process that an MNE went through as it repositioned its strategy towards the bottom of the pyramid in the Indian market.

Chapter 4 provides an overview of common operating modes and ownership forms that managers choose when they decide to enter and operate in foreign markets. We also discuss the managerial challenges of each mode. The case study for this chapter gives detailed insights into the managerial challenges related to the management of an international joint venture.

The second part of the book, Chapters 5 to 8, identifies important characteristics of the external context for MNEs' international operations. Chapter 5 presents stakeholder theory as a framework to help managers identify and manage key relationships. We specifically discuss MNEs' management of stakeholder relations with non-governmental organizations (NGOs) and global union federations (GUFs), in terms of potentially adverse positions and key benefits such as information, expertise and legitimacy. The case study for this chapter provides detailed insight into the stakeholder relation between a large MNE, local unions and GUFs.

Chapter 6 focuses on the importance of operating in a socially and environmentally responsible manner – corporate social responsibility (CSR). The purpose is to provide theory and frameworks that help managers address the challenges that stem from these responsibilities. Attached to the chapter are two case studies. One provides insight into how a large MNE responded to stakeholder pressures to act responsibly in two different markets; the other illustrates the CSR challenge an MNE faces in its supply chain.

In Chapter 7, we present the concept of cultural distance and how this can be measured. This has been highly debated over the past decades and we offer an overview of the discussion and critique. The case study attached to Chapter 7 links the discussion of cultural distance with the challenges of managing a diverse workforce.

In Chapter 8, we turn our attention to the institutional context where we provide a thorough overview of two dominant strands of institutional theory rooted in economics and sociology. We discuss how insights from these strands of institutional theory help managers address the challenges that arise due to the differences they face in home and host country institutional contexts. Such challenges are also illustrated in the case study following Chapter 8.

In the final part of the book, Chapters 9 to 11 identify fundamental managerial challenges when managing knowledge and human resources across borders. Chapter 9 focuses on the challenges of transferring knowledge across organizational and national borders. We introduce a typology for classifying knowledge and present a framework for analysing knowledge transfer and sharing within MNEs. The framework highlights the importance of social capital for successful cross-border knowledge transfer. The case study following Chapter 9 illustrates how knowledge transfers are dependent on the MNE's ability to build social capital.

Chapter 10 discusses the nature of international or cross-national human resource management (HRM) as compared to domestic HRM, followed by the presentation of a model for cross-national HRM. We introduce a model for strategic international HRM that emphasizes that when MNEs design HRM systems for their subsidiaries they invariably will have to consider host country culture, socio-economic conditions and institutional constraints. In certain settings, a subsidiary may experience a pronounced tension between host country and parent company expectations. The case study attached to Chapter 10 points to the importance of institutional and cultural differences and the need to 'translate' organization and management practices when these are transferred from one institutional setting to another.

Chapter 11 deals with international career development with a particular focus on international mobility. The purpose is to provide an overview of the various roles expatriates fill and to examine factors that are associated with widespread use of international mobility. Furthermore, it deals with the importance of thorough selection and recruitment processes as well as relevant training programmes preparing the personnel selected for expatriation. We also emphasize the importance of a successful repatriation process. The case study linked to Chapter 11 illustrates how a leading global luxury brand conglomerate strategically engages in international mobility to develop its leaders and stay globally competitive.

Part I

The multinational enterprise

1
Setting the scene: The multinational enterprise

1.1 Introduction

This book is concerned with the managerial and learning challenges that multinational enterprises (MNEs) have to grapple with as they seek to develop and utilize organizational resources and capabilities that are necessary for achieving success beyond their countries of origin. The purpose of this chapter is to present a broad introduction to the MNE. We discuss MNE characteristics and provide a broad overview of the globalization of business. We address why global strategy and management is an increasingly critical area of study for business students and what distinguishes global strategy and management from domestic strategy and management. We point out that most MNEs have strong national identities and that top management is often lacking in terms of diversity. Overall, this introductory chapter provides a general overview of the MNE and the important role of global managers.

1.2 What is an MNE?

'Although many theoretical and operational definitions of the MNE have been proposed, none has become standard' (Aggarwal et al., 2011, p. 558). We can broadly divide definitions of the MNE into those with a relatively narrow scope and those whose scope is very much broader. The narrow definitions emphasize *ownership* and day-to-day *control*, whereas the broader definitions move beyond these criteria and employ *influence*. An example of the narrow definition is the working definition of the MNE used by Bartlett and Beamish (2018). They categorize firms as MNEs if they meet both of two qualifications. The first qualification specifies that for a firm to be regarded as an MNE it has to have *substantial direct investment* in foreign countries. The second stipulates that it is engaged in the *active management* of these foreign assets whether this involves the production of goods or of services. In other words, simple ownership of foreign assets is not sufficient to be classified as an MNE. Instead, entities such as hedge funds that limit themselves to ownership would be classified as investors and not as MNEs. One shortcoming of this definition is that it does not take into account that some investors are substantially more active than others in terms of their oversight and support of management. This raises the question of at what point this would count as active management. Those employing the narrow definition have no firm answers to this question.

Another shortcoming of the type of definition that Bartlett and Beamish employ is that some firms exert substantial influence over firms in other countries without having any ownership or any day-to-day management control. For example, a firm may enter into a sourcing agreement with a foreign firm and as part of that agreement insist not only on certain employment conditions, but also on the right to engage in monitoring to ensure that these conditions are being met. Or, a firm may sponsor a research agenda that it has defined at a foreign university for an extended period of time.

The reality is that MNEs are one of the main drivers of global value chains. MNEs coordinate complex international production networks, where relationships with suppliers range from arm's-length contractual relationships to direct ownership of affiliates. Participating in global value chains creates asymmetric growth opportunities for local firms depending upon how well they are integrated with MNEs. Local firms in global value chains also face an opportunity for *knowledge spillovers* from multinationals, not least because MNEs are typically at the global productivity frontier (OECD, 2015).

MNEs are often referred to as 'lead firms' because they determine the quality of inputs from suppliers with whom they may directly share knowledge, advanced technology and encourage the adoption of novel managerial practices (Buckley and Strange, 2015). Global value chains are therefore also a well-established vehicle *for productivity spillovers* to local firms (Guadalupe, Kuzmina and Thomas, 2012; Saia, Andrews and Albrizio, 2015). To take the example of Apple and its value chain of fine-sliced activities, some of which it has internalized, others that it has outsourced to locations in both developed and emerging economies:

> [l]ooking at iPhone/iPod manufacturing alone, core parts (e.g. A6 chip, audio chip, and radio frequency parts) are manufactured in the US; rare earth components (speakers, glass screens, and vibration units) are sourced from Mongolia; memory chips and batteries are produced in Taiwan; gyroscope manufacturing is outsourced to France. The parts are then shipped to one of five facilities in China and Brazil, where Foxconn and Pegatron perform the final assembly. Meanwhile, Apple has, from its inception, conducted most design and marketing activities in-house in its R&D office in Cupertino, CA. (Kano, 2018, p. 689)

This lead firm role of MNEs such as Apple has given rise to broader definitions of the MNE that go beyond ownership and day-to-day control. For example, Cantwell, Dunning and Lundan (2010, p. 569) view the MNE as:

> [. . .]a coordinated system or network of cross-border activities, some of which are carried out within the hierarchy of the firm, and some of which are carried out through informal social ties or contractual relationships. Thus an MNE is not defined solely by the extent of the foreign production facilities it owns, but by the sum total of all of its value-creating activities over which it has a significant influence. These activities may involve foreign sourcing of various intermediate inputs, including the sourcing of knowledge, as well as production, marketing and distribution activities.

Dunning and Lundan (2008, p. 8) caution that once one moves from control to influence as a criterion for determining the boundaries of a firm, 'one opens up a Pandora's box'. MNEs may not only influence suppliers, they may also exert influence on retailers and even competitors. As such, setting the boundary of the MNE becomes highly problematic. For this reason, while we acknowledge the shortcomings of the twofold *substantial foreign direct investment* (FDI) and *active management of these assets* definition of the MNE, for pragmatic reasons this is the definition we employ in this book. In other words, MNEs not only control resources in foreign operations, they also have ownership of them. Further, these foreign operations involve a significant physical presence in foreign markets including buildings and employees.

This latter aspect to our definition is now increasingly problematic. Digitally based firms can deliver services to customers and transact with partners globally with relatively low upfront expense and with little need to establish a (costly) physical presence across geographies (Brynjolfsson and McAfee, 2014). Digitally based firms like Airbnb, Facebook, Google and Uber have a much smaller proportion of their assets bound in foreign markets, compared to their foreign sales than more traditional MNEs (UNCTAD, 2017). In other words, in comparison with traditional MNEs with equivalent foreign sales, their physical presence in foreign markets is significantly smaller. In ranking the top MNEs, the United Nations Conference on Trade and Development (UNCTAD) has always based its methodology on foreign assets. However, in continuing to use this methodology, UNCTAD observes that the result is that 'some well-known global giants, such as Amazon and Facebook do not feature in the top 100' (ibid., p. 160). It is not set to get less confusing, as ultimately, we may see the rise but also possibly the dominance of globally transacting businesses, coordinated from a single location.

While the topics discussed in this book are primarily of relevance to organizations that fit our 'traditional' narrow definition of an MNE, we should be aware that taken to an extreme our definition could result in ignoring significant global enterprises.

1.3 The globalization of business

As a percentage of world GDP, the stock of FDI had risen to 35 per cent in 2015 compared to 10 per cent in 1990 (*The Economist*, 2017a). MNEs 'co-ordinate the supply chains that account for over 50 per cent of all trade. They account for a third of the value of the world's stock markets and they own the lion's share of its intellectual property – from lingerie designs to virtual-reality software and diabetes drugs' (*The Economist*, 2017b, p. 7). MNEs are particularly strong in motor vehicles, computers and soft drinks, having on a global basis 85 per cent, 70 per cent and 65 per cent of these markets, respectively.

The advantages of becoming a global player in manufacturing are more obvious than for service-based firms. In the case of the former, the value chain can be divided across many locations. Parts of the manufacturing process can be located to low-cost countries, while R&D can be located in a region with specialized competencies with its costs spread across many markets. In the case of service firms, much of the value chain has to be generated locally – that is, there is little in the way of opportunity to centralize activities to low-cost locations. To a greater or smaller degree, services have to be tailored for each client, unlike, for example, pharmaceuticals, which can be mass produced. Sharing advanced knowledge is also more problematic. In manufacturing companies, it can be made available through patented technologies or unique products. In service companies, it has to be transferred from country to country through learning processes. Nevertheless, with increasing liberalization, the share of services in FDI has risen significantly.

In most Organisation for Economic Co-operation and Development (OECD) countries (OECD, 2013), it remains the case that the importance of foreign affiliates is larger in manufacturing than in services. However, investments in services have increased. By 2017, greenfield announcements were higher in services than manufacturing (UNCTAD, 2018). This is especially the case for Central European countries, in which many Western European companies have relocated production over the past decade because of lower labour costs and the availability of a skilled workforce. Nevertheless, OECD (2013) observes that in absolute terms, foreign employment and value added are larger in services than in manufacturing in several OECD countries, owing to the importance of services in national economies but also to the growing internationalization of services during the past decade.

One conspicuous example is Accenture, the management consultancy, technology services and business process outsourcing company. In 2012, it had a staff of 240 000 employees across 54 countries (Accenture, 2012). In 2017, staffing had increased to over 435 000 employees across 55 countries (Accenture, 2017). Another is the accountancy firm PricewaterhouseCoopers (PwC). In 2012, it had around 170 000 people across 158 countries (PwC, 2012). By 2017, the headcount had increased to 236 000 (PwC, 2017). In addition, the emergence of the less conspicuous new services such as software, back-office services, call centres and data entry have also contributed to the relative growth of services in FDI.

At the start of the new millennium, the major recipients of FDI were the USA and the European Union (EU), with Germany, the United Kingdom and the Benelux countries figuring particularly strongly. During the period 1986–2000, the typical annual average FDI growth rate was in the range of 20 to 30 per cent. For 1999 and 2000, over three-quarters of global FDI inflows went to the developed world partly because of intense cross-border mergers and acquisitions activity.

Despite setbacks such as the financial crisis in 2008, the long-term flow of FDI – both inflows and outflows – has been one of significant historical increase: see Table 1.1.

Table 1.1 Selected indicators of FDI and international production

	Value at Current Prices (Billions of Dollars)			
	1990	2005–07 (pre-crisis average)	2013	2017
FDI inflows	207	1418	1427	1430
FDI outflows	243	1445	1311	1430
FDI inward stock	2077	14 500	24 533	31 524
FDI outward stock	2091	15 104	24 665	30 838
Sales of foreign affiliates	5101	20 355	31 865	30 823
Total assets of foreign affiliates	4595	40 924	95 671	103 429
Employment by foreign affiliates (thousands)	21 454	49 565	72 239	732 009

Source: UNCTAD (2016, 2018).

By the end of the first decade of the new millennium, it was apparent that the new powerhouse of FDI is the rise of emerging economies such as Brazil, India, China and Russia (often referred to as BRIC countries). By 2010, developing and transition economies attracted half of global FDI inflows (UNCTAD, 2010). Among developing economies, China was by far the most important recipient of FDI (Buckley, 2016; UNCTAD, 2018). Even when one excludes Hong Kong, in 2009 China had become the second largest FDI recipient after the US. This remains the case (UNCTAD, 2018). Since 2010, inflows of FDI into China are as large as inflows to the other three BRIC countries combined (OECD, 2016; UNCTAD, 2018). Some context is required. Between 2005 and 2014, the stock of American FDI in China trebled from about $20 billion to more than $65 billion. 'However, the value of American FDI in China pales when placed in the context of the $6 trillion worth of directly invested capital that Americans hold in all foreign economies' (Bryson and Nelson, 2015, p. 3).

1.4   Why study global strategy and management?

Unlike management of domestic companies, international management involves learning to cope and even thrive with different forms of distances. In his CAGE framework, Ghemawat (2001) distinguishes four types of distance that MNE managers have to be sensitive to: cultural, administrative, geographic and economic. Ghemawat argues that cultural and administrative distance ('C' and 'A') often have greater impact on doing business. Cultural distance is not just language. It also refers to subtler features such as social norms and values that determine how people interact with one another. A management style that works well in one culture may be unacceptable in another. Culture is also about taste and deep-seated preferences. A product that is a success in one country may be rejected in another. In 2018, when IKEA was finally able to open its first store in India, like McDonald's before it, it tweaked its offerings to appeal to local sensibilities. Instead of Swedish meatballs, diners at the new store's 1000-seat restaurant can partake of chicken or veggie balls, dal and rice, or biriyani. Textiles on sale have brighter colours and busier patterns than in IKEAs elsewhere (*Financial Times*, 2018).

Administrative distance is partly about learning to deal with being an outsider and therefore exposed to discrimination. In general, governments are patriotic and seek to protect their 'national champions'. Overcoming administrative distance is primarily about learning to deal with the institutions and legal systems in the host country. Administrative distance can be subject to sudden change. As Dunning and Rugman (1985, p. 230) once observed: 'the

MNE faces environmental uncertainty as foreign governments can change the political, cultural, and social factors which determine its economic efficiency'. Trade agreements generally reduce such distances. North (1990) refers to institutionalized constraints and regulations as the 'rules of the game'. These have to be learned.

Geographic distance ('G') refers to geographical differences that affect the costs of transportation and communication. This is of particular importance to companies that depend on a high degree of coordination and mutual understanding. Physical distances within or between countries are most often emphasized when assessing transportation costs. However, many other geographic differences are also important to consider such as differences in time zones, climate and topography.

Economic distance ('E') makes it difficult to replicate a strategy that works well in one context (e.g., a developed country) in a country where country-level economic characteristics are significantly different (e.g., at the 'bottom of the pyramid' in developing countries; Gooderham, Ulset and Elter, 2016). When Vodafone entered the Indian mobile telephony market in 2007 it was very conscious of just how challenging it would be to operate in a market where tariffs are much lower than in developed markets. Arun Sarin, Vodafone's then chief executive stated:

> [F]rankly, we are going to learn as much from India as we are going to take to India. Like we have said in the past, prices there are two and a half US cents a minute, and they make a 35 per cent margin. How do you do that? Our prices in Europe are 13, 14, 15 euro cents, and we make a 40 per cent margin. Their cost structure is very low. The question is what can we learn about how to run a scale business [with] 35m customers, and have that low a cost structure? (*Financial Times*, 2007)

One of its competitors in India, the MNE Telenor, ultimately failed to cope with this 'bottom-of-the-pyramid' challenge, and despite ratcheting up 44 million subscribers, in 2017, after eight years in India, it pulled out. Economic distances can also arise from differences in the cost and/or quality of various resources such as natural, financial or human. Differences in infrastructure and information are also key elements of economic differences that impact both transportation and communication costs.

We will discuss cultural and institutional (e.g., administrative) challenges in greater detail in Chapters 7 and 8.

1.5 What do international managers do?

MNEs depend on identifying and developing managers who have the potential to go beyond domestic leadership and who are able to exercise global leadership. Alan Bird characterizes global leaders in this way:

> Global leaders are individuals who effect significant positive change in organizations by building communities through the development of trust and the arrangement of organization structures and processes in a context involving multiple cross-boundary stakeholders, multiple sources of external cross-boundary authority, and multiple cultures under conditions of temporal, geographical and cultural complexity. (Bird in Osland et al., 2013, p. 519)

What Bird is underscoring is that global leadership is often significantly more than just domestic leadership with some additional awareness of distance.

Reiche et al. (2017) have developed a typology of global leadership roles. They distinguish two types of complexities: relationship and task. At its least complex, global leadership may involve no more than ensuring that third parties are honouring licence agreements. Relationships and tasks are relatively predictable and there are low levels of interdependence. Routinized and standardized forms of communication will suffice. At its most complex, global leadership involves coordinating and integrating interdependent activities across multiple globally distributed units. It is not just that global leadership in this context involves coping with a high number of boundaries between organizational units, it is also about coping with the diversity of the units. What is acceptable in one country context may be inappropriate, controversial or even illegal in another. Uber is uncontentious in some settings but prohibited in others such as Norway. Downsizing is less complex in the US than in France. This may lead to internal inconsistencies across the MNE. Likewise, the task environment may be highly complex. For example, finding suppliers that can deliver global solutions that take into account the particular needs of local business units may be so intricate that it is tempting to devolve purchasing and to accept internal inconsistency. Managers can only solve the complexity by undertaking sustained boundary spanning across many units in search of solutions that support MNE internal consistency. Osland et al. (2013) found that expert global leaders learned to influence multiple constituents and engaged in continuous stakeholder dialogue. This means resolving conflicts that have their roots in entirely objective interests and needs. For example, the same piece of technical equipment that managers in one location view as indispensable, managers in another location see as prohibitively expensive.

In short, international managers who are capable of exercising global leadership are change agents who are adept at developing consistency across distributed operations. Their persuasiveness depends on developing trust and common understandings across boundaries. Osland et al. (2013) investigated how 'exceptional' global leaders think about themselves and their roles. They found that while there are similarities between domestic and global leadership (e.g., self-confidence, persistence, observed high intelligence, etc.), there are also differences of degree and kind, including a particular emphasis on boundary spanning, being able to read others and to switch codes in response to dealing with high levels of diversity.

Overall, Osland et al.'s research supports previous research findings. These suggest that the primary factors in developing global leaders are expatriation; an international background; a family background involving *intercultural experiences*; *early education* involving international schools, summer camps and travel; *later education* that included exchange programmes, languages and international MBA programmes; and a *spouse and children* who are supportive, adventurous, adaptable and mobile.

However, some of the exceptional global leaders in their study had little or no cross-cultural exposure other than a diverse workplace in their home country or exposure to some form of difference. This raises the possibility of whether there are different pathways to becoming an exceptional global leader. Clearly, we should guard against overly generalizing about what makes a successful global leader. They speculate that the role of intelligence, the ability and motivation to learn, and/or the ability to deal with diversity in one's native country could constitute an alternative pathway.

In the longer term, global leadership experience is also a source of valuable management development. CEOs with substantial international assignment experience have worldviews and professional ties that help them to better manage MNEs' far-flung operations (Carpenter, Sanders and Gregersen, 2001). They are able to recognize opportunities in foreign markets, develop unique international strategies, and manage and coordinate international operations effectively, resulting in superior strategic change and overall performance of the MNE. In concrete terms, Le and Kroll (2017) found that the number of years a CEO had spent abroad had a positive effect on strategic change and firm performance, and that this was even more the case when they took into account the number of countries CEOs had worked in and the cultural distance or 'foreignness' of those countries.

1.6 How common is top management diversity?

Despite the increase in globalization, most MNEs have home bases that give them resolutely national identities. General Electric and Microsoft are clearly American just as Honda and Toyota are Japanese. In 2008, shortly after he had become chief executive of Siemens, a German conglomerate with 70 business units and 430 000 workers in 190 countries, Peter Löscher, an Austrian by birth, concluded that Siemens was, 'too white, German and male' (*Financial Times*, 2008a). However, the *Financial Times* argued that Peter Löscher's charge is 'one that could apply to most companies in continental Europe and the UK':

> Too few are good at attracting not just women and ethnic minorities but also international talent. Fixing the imbalance is not just a matter of political correctness but something vitally important for the competitiveness of the Continent. It is also a topic that brings together nearly all of the factors that will affect the long-term success of business in the Continent from demographics to skills to immigration. . . The fact that most large European countries' boards contain primarily domestic directors (or those from culturally similar countries such as Germany, Switzerland and Austria) is a big issue. (*Financial Times*, 2008b)

Little has changed. *The Economist* (2014) discussed whether anything could be done about this predisposition for promoting people of a certain type. The conclusion was not sanguine:

> Ideally, those selecting a new boss would conscientiously set aside all the stereotypes, and judge candidates purely on their merits. However, given a plethora of candidates, all with perfect CVs, selection committees continue to look for the 'X' factor and find, strangely enough, that it resides in people who look remarkably like themselves.

The alternative could be to introduce quotas for CEOs and board members. 'But the risk is that this ends in tokenism rather than a genuine equalizing of opportunity'.

However, Van Veen and Marsman's (2008) research on international executive boards of MNEs in 15 European countries indicated stark national differences. Spanish MNEs had virtually no foreigners in their top management teams, whereas Dutch MNEs had nearly 50 per cent. More recently, Davoine and Ravasi (2013) revealed similar findings. While they find that there are still clear national limits to the rise of an international market for executive labour they also found significant variations in its use. The top management teams of major Swiss firms are highly internationalized, as 64 per cent of top managers are foreigners. This was high compared to France (22 per cent), Germany (27 per cent) and even the United Kingdom (46 per cent). For Swiss firms it was not the case though that top managers were from immediate neighbours as the *Financial Times* (2008b) assumed. While Germany was the most represented country (17 per cent), UK nationals (just under 17 per cent) and US nationals (15 per cent) were nearly equally present.

But does the national diversity of top management teams matter for MNE performance? Nielsen and Nielsen (2013) found that in general the degree of the national diversity of the top management team is among the few diversity attributes that help increase firm performance. Further, this was especially the case for firms that are MNEs. More anecdotally, the CEO of the Swiss foods group, Nestlé, Paul Bulcke, a Belgian national, is a firm believer in the value of national diversity. The 13 members of the executive board come from nine different countries. National diversity is 'one of our core competencies, and a competitive advantage. In fact, we have explicitly anchored respect and openness to other cultures and traditions in our Leadership and Management Principles' (Zehnder, 2018). However, as we have indicated, Swiss MNEs are outliers in this regard.

1.7 Summary

In this chapter we have defined what we mean by an MNE – that is, actively managed substantial foreign direct investment made by firms that have a long-term commitment to operating internationally. We have thereby narrowed our scope from several prevalent forms of internationalization operating modes such as licensing and contract manufacturing. MNEs are a historically recent phenomenon whose presence is particularly evident in certain sectors. Despite local resistance, sometimes explicit and sometimes tacit, the MNE has proved itself to be a highly robust organizational form: the dramatic growth in numbers and proportions of MNEs is testimony to this. Nevertheless, the individual positions of MNEs are always under threat because of their size and geographical dispersion, factors that make communication and control problematic. Success for individual MNEs is far from guaranteed. The leadership portrait following this chapter illustrates the role that global leadership and managerial capabilities play in successful MNEs.

REFERENCES

Accenture (2012), 'Accenture fact sheet', accessed 9 July 2012 at https://newsroom.accenture.com/fact-sheet/.

Accenture (2017), 'Accenture fact sheet', accessed 26 January 2018 at https://newsroom.accenture.com/fact-sheet/.

Aggarwal, R., J. Berrill, E. Huston and C. Kearney (2011), 'What is a multinational corporation? Classifying the degree of firm-level multinationality', *International Business Review*, **20**(5), 557–77.

Bartlett, C.A. and P.W. Beamish (2018), *Transnational Management: Text and Cases in Cross-Border Management*, Cambridge, UK: Cambridge University Press.

Brynjolfsson, E. and A. McAfee (2014), *The Second Machine Age: Work, Progress, and Prosperity in a Time of Brilliant Technologies*, New York: W.W. Norton & Company.

Bryson, J.H. and E. Nelson (2015), 'How exposed is the U.S. economy to China?', Wells Fargo Securities Economics Group, Special Commentary, accessed 29 January 2018 at https://www.realclearmarkets.com/docs/2015/08/US%20Exposure%20to%20China%20_%20Aug%202015.pdf.

Buckley, P.J. (2016), 'The contribution of internalisation theory to international business: New realities and unanswered questions', *Journal of World Business*, **51**(1), 74–82.

Buckley, P. and R. Strange (2015), 'The governance of the global factory: Location and control of world economic activity', *The Academy of Management Perspectives*, **29**(2), 237–49.

Cantwell, J., J.H. Dunning and S.M. Lundan (2010), 'An evolutionary approach to understanding international business activity: The co-evolution of MNCs and the institutional environment', *Journal of International Business Studies*, **41**(4), 567–86.

Carpenter, M.A., W.G. Sanders and H.B. Gregersen (2001), 'Bundling human capital with organizational context: The impact of international assignment experience on multinational firm performance and CEO pay', *Academy of Management Journal*, **44**(3), 493–511.

Davoine, E. and C. Ravasi (2013), 'The relative stability of national career patterns in European top management careers in the age of globalisation: A comparative study in France/Germany/Great Britain and Switzerland', *European Management Journal*, **31**(2), 152–63.

Dunning, J.H. and S.M. Lundan (2008), *Multinational Enterprises and the Global Economy*, Cheltenham, UK and Northampton, MA, USA: Edward Elgar Publishing.

Dunning, J.H. and A.M. Rugman (1985), 'The influence of Hymer's dissertation on the theory of foreign direct investment', *The American Economic Review*, **75**(2), 228–32.

Financial Times (2007), 'Transcript: Arun Sarin, Vodafone chief executive', accessed 18 November 2017 at http://www.ft.com/intl/cms/s/0/04d876a2-95eb-11dc-b7ec-0000779fd2ac.html#axzz1p05lYxvK.

Financial Times (2008a), 'Siemens too white, German and male', 24 June 2008, accessed 19 January 2019 at https://www.ft.com/content/1199a7f0-4205-11dd-a5e8-0000779fd2ac.

Financial Times (2008b), 'Löscher puts his finger on a problem for Europe', 28 July 2008.

Financial Times (2018), 'Ikea finally opens in India, minus the meatballs', 13 August 2018.

Ghemawat, P. (2001), 'Distance still matters: The hard reality of global expansion', *Harvard Business Review*, **79**(8), 137–47.

Gooderham, P.N., S. Ulset and F. Elter (2016), 'Beyond local responsiveness – multi-domestic multinationals at the bottom-of-the-pyramid', in T.C. Ambos, B. Ambos and J. Birkinshaw (eds), *Perspectives on Headquarters–Subsidiary Relationships in the Contemporary MNE* (Vol. 17, pp. 3–26), Bingley, UK: Emerald Group Publishing Limited.

Guadalupe, M., O. Kuzmina and C. Thomas (2012), 'Innovation and foreign ownership', *American Economic Review*, **102**(7), 3594–627.

Kano, L. (2018), 'Global value chain governance: A relational perspective', *Journal of International Business Studies*, **49**(6), 684–705.

Le, S. and M. Kroll (2017), 'CEO international experience: Effects on strategic change and firm performance', *Journal of International Business Studies*, **48**(5), 573–95.

Nielsen, B.B. and S. Nielsen (2013), 'Top management team nationality diversity and firm performance: A multilevel study', *Strategic Management Journal*, **34**(3), 373–82.

North, D.C. (1990), *Institutions, Institutional Change, and Economic Performance*, Cambridge, UK: Cambridge University Press.
OECD (2013), 'Foreign affiliates', in *OECD Science, Technology and Industry Scoreboard 2013: Innovation for Growth*, Paris: OECD Publishing.
OECD (2015), *The Future of Productivity*, Paris: OECD Publishing.
OECD (2016), 'FDI in figures', Paris: OECD Publishing, accessed 29 January 2018 at www.oecd.org/corporate/FDI-in-Figures-April-2016.pdf.
Osland, J., G. Oddou, A. Bird and A. Osland (2013), 'Exceptional global leadership as cognitive expertise in the domain of global change', *European Journal of International Management*, 7(5), 517–34.
PwC (2012), 'Facts and figures: Geographic coverage', accessed 9 July 2012 at http://www.pwc.com/gx/en/about-pwc/facts-and-figures.jhtml.
PwC (2017), 'PWC HK: Facts and figures', accessed 26 January 2018 at https://www.pwchk.com/en/press-room/facts-and-figures.html.
Reiche, B.S., A. Bird, M.E. Mendenhall and J.S. Osland (2017), 'Contextualizing leadership: A typology of global leadership roles', *Journal of International Business Studies*, 48(5), 552–72.
Saia, A., D. Andrews and S. Albrizio (2015), 'Productivity spillovers from the global frontier and public policy: Industry-level evidence', *OECD Economics Department Working Papers*, No. 1238, Paris: OECD Publishing.
The Economist (2014), 'The look of a leader', 27 September 2014.
The Economist (2017a), 'The retreat of the global company', 28 January 2017.
The Economist (2017b), 'In retreat', 28 January 2017.
UNCTAD (2010), *Investing in a Low-carbon Economy*, New York and Geneva: UNCTAD.
UNCTAD (2016), *World Investment Report 2016*, New York and Geneva: UNCTAD.
UNCTAD (2017), *World Investment Report 2017: Investment and the Digital Economy*, New York and Geneva: UNCTAD.
UNCTAD (2018), *World Investment Report 2018: Investment and New Industrial Policies*, New York and Geneva: UNCTAD.
Van Veen, K. and I. Marsman (2008), 'How international are executive boards of MNEs? Nationality diversity in 15 European countries', *European Management Journal*, 26(3), 188–98.
Zehnder, E. (2018), 'Interview with Paul Bulcke, CEO, Nestlé S.A', *The Focus*, 14 January 2018, accessed 31 January 2018 at https://www.egonzehnder.com/the-focus-magazine/topics/the-focus-on-inclusion/leadership/interview-with-paul-bulcke-ceo-nestl-sa.html.

Case A

What makes for an exceptional global leader? Is 'CEO disease' inevitable? The case of Carlos Ghosn

Paul N. Gooderham

A.1 Introduction

In the main body of Chapter 1, we noted that Osland et al. (2013) investigated how 'exceptional' global leaders think about themselves and their roles. Overall, their findings were in line with previous research findings. Exceptional global leaders have a biography of cross-cultural experiences. However, they did identify some exceptions. The ability to engage with boundary spanning, to read others and to switch codes in response to dealing with high levels of diversity may also derive from experiences of other types of diversity. Nevertheless, our first case features a global leader who fits the profile that much of the previous research outlines. Carlos Ghosn achieved considerable fame for restructuring Renault during the 1990s and then turning round Nissan, 'winning applause from the Japanese, who celebrated his success with everything from a manga comic about his life to a bento – or packed lunchbox – in the shape of his face' (*Financial Times*, 2018a). One issue we explore in this case study is how did Carlos Ghosn become a global leader and what did he think was necessary to achieve success?

However, some wonder if hubris is inevitable among successful global leaders. On 19 November 2018, Tokyo District Prosecutors arrested Ghosn for questioning over allegations of false accounting. On the same day, Nissan chief executive Hiroto Saikawa announced at a press conference that Mr Ghosn had been dismissed from the company. Despite falling from grace, even Nissan's chief executive conceded that Mr Ghosn had 'done what not many other people could have done', especially in the first stages of Nissan's turnaround (ibid.).

As well as written material, the case study also includes suggested reading available online and lists four recommended interviews with Carlos Ghosn available on YouTube.

A.2   The rise of Carlos Ghosn

Upbringing and education

Mr Ghosn was born in 1954 in Porto Velho in Brazil to Maronite Christian Lebanese parents. Fast-forward to 2018 and 'looking fit with a sweep of black hair that shaves a decade or so off his 64 years' (*Financial Times*, 2018b) he is chair of an alliance of three carmakers, Renault, Nissan and Mitsubishi. Although he has signalled he is likely to step down as chief executive of Renault before his term ends in 2022, retirement is still some way off. Disruption, he says, 'is a huge stimulation' and he is still 'up for the challenge' (ibid.).

At the age of six, Mr Ghosn moved to Beirut to live with his grandmother, mother and sister while his father shuttled between Brazil and Lebanon. The troubles that were to engulf Lebanon still lay far in the future. He attended a Jesuit school that in addition to emphasizing discipline also encouraged competition between the students. He refers to the Jesuit order as 'the first multinational company in the world. And at the same, the Jesuits are well known for promoting intellectual freedom' (Ghosn and Riès, 2005, p. 7). He was in equal measure an exceptional but rebellious student. Because of his family's history, he learned Portuguese early and then at school in Lebanon he studied French and Arabic. 'Learning languages quickly became one of my passions. The study of language is the best way of understanding the connections between peoples and cultures' (ibid., p. 8).

At 17, Mr Ghosn moved to Paris to continue his education. Looking back, he recalls the shock of arriving in Paris. Despite speaking the language and having a French education, he found Paris enormous and the people tougher and more impersonal than Beirut. In terms of his grades, his first trimester was a disaster. 'I failed for the first time in my life. I was in complete despair. . . Instead of giving up. . . I told myself I had to make a greater effort. I was determined to go on, no matter what it took' (ibid., p. 10). Eventually, he gained admission to the prestigious École Polytechnique in Paris, graduating in 1978.

He recorded how at times he felt peculiar during his younger years. In Lebanon, no one viewed him as a 'total' Lebanese and when he went to

France, he was different there as well. 'I've never lived in a place where I could tell myself I was an integral part of the group like everyone else' (ibid., p. 12). However, he learned to surmount these difficulties in childhood so that '[o]nce you're an adult, being different isn't a problem anymore. Your defenses are already up' (ibid.).

The Michelin years

In September 1978, Mr Ghosn joined Michelin and moved out of Paris to Clermont-Ferrand. For him, a major emotional motivation for choosing to join Michelin was the prospect the company flagged of going to its operation in Brazil and being able to reconnect with his childhood. However, as it turned out, that was to be another seven years away. In the meantime, he first underwent a rigorous period of graduate training that involved a period as a factory worker cutting up rubber and putting it in moulds. In 1981, at the age of 27, he became the general manager of the Michelin factory in Le Puy-en-Velay where he had undertaken parts of his training. 'The employees were surprised to see me come back as general manager of the factory only a year and a half after serving as a shift-team leader, but it was, I think a pleasant surprise. They knew they could discuss things with me' (Ghosn and Riès, 2005, p. 24). As for his fellow managers, they were all older than he was, making for an uncomfortable situation. However, he managed to establish bonds and create a team and came to regard the learning experience in Puy as decisive for his later career.

When he finally returned to Brazil in 1985, he had with him his new wife who was Lebanese but had been studying in France. Brazil in that era was experiencing hyperinflation of more than 1000 per cent with real interest rates above 35 per cent. The Brazilian state imposed 'very finicky' regulations – price controls, financial controls, controls on imports, subsidies for exports. The Brazilian division was losing money, the company's relationship with the Brazilian state was poor and strikes were breaking out. However, Mr Ghosn viewed the major problems as internal. Inventories had to be reduced and non-core assets sold. By 1987 the division had returned to profitability and by 1989 it was in relative terms Michelin's most profitable. His next move was to the USA, but Brazil was to remain a place to return to for family vacations every Christmas for many years.

In February 1989, Mr Ghosn took charge of Michelin's North America operations. The family located to a small town in South Carolina, in the heart of the 'Bible Belt', worlds apart from Rio de Janeiro where drug-related violence was part of everyday life. The North American market was of far greater significance to Michelin than Brazil in that 35–40 per cent of total sales were made there. The contexts were very different. In Brazil, the main external challenge was the state, in the United States it was the competitiveness of the market. In 1990, the US went into recession and, in 1992, the recession spread to Europe. Things got so bad for the Michelin group that observers speculated that it would not survive. Recovery finally took place in 1995, and 1996 and 1997 were excellent years. Mr Ghosn recalled that he had 'to learn to be an American CEO, which is much different from being a Brazilian-style boss or a European CEO... The United States is a very good training school for learning about customers, and about everything to do with marketing tools and communication' (ibid., pp. 43–4). As a supplier, he also had the opportunity to observe and interact with the American automobile industry.

Le cost killer

Three of Mr Ghosn's four children were born in the United States and he and his family enjoyed the 'American way of life'. He was more than willing to stay there for a good while longer. However, in 1996, a head-hunter got in touch to sound him out about a move to Renault and the opportunity to become second-in-command. It was a chance to join a company that was not family owned and therefore ultimately family dominated. It was also a chance to work in an industry that fascinated him. However, he was moving to a company that the French state had a considerable stake in and had bailed out in the 1980s. It was now suffering a new relapse primarily because Renault's cars were simply too expensive.

In early 1997, still very much viewed as someone who was not just a newcomer to the company but one with a rather multinational persona, Mr Ghosn proposed a radical plan that aimed at cutting costs by 20 billion francs. He recalled that, '[s]ome people said, "He's off the deep end. He's raving mad"... They thought I was clueless' (ibid., p. 65). A substantial portion of the cuts aimed at improving purchasing. At Michelin, he had been a supplier to the industry. Now he was to use that knowledge and insight to reduce the prices with which suppliers operated. However, he also had to take some, for those times, socially highly controversial steps. In March 1997, Renault announced that its plant in Vilvoorde, Belgium, which employed over 3000 people, would close. The press lambasted him as 'le cost killer', a nickname that annoys him but one that has stuck (*Financial Times*, 2018b). However, the turnaround occurred quickly. By 1998, the company was recovering and the many sceptics within Renault had retreated.

The move to Japan

Midway through 1998, Renault's corporate executive committee concluded that the company by itself was too small and had to give serious thought to an alliance with another carmaker. For Mr Ghosn, Nissan was the obvious choice. It was sufficiently large and he viewed Japanese carmakers as reliable. However, Nissan had a long history of posting deficits. Renault began to negotiate with Nissan based on either a subsidiary or joint venture arrangement. Mr Ghosn 'stepped in and proposed that we set aside the legal structures and do something much more informal: set up cross-country teams' (Ghosn and Riès, 2005, p. 74). Renault bought 36.8 per cent of Nissan's stock, and Nissan vowed to buy into Renault when it was financially able. Eventually, Nissan held a 15 per cent non-voting stake in Renault while the French automaker owned 43.4 per cent of Nissan with voting rights.

Suddenly, in May 1999, Mr Ghosn was on his way to Japan with his wife and four children. The head of Renault viewed him as the natural choice to send; he had lived abroad and had experience of restructuring a company. However, it was to an unknown country and an unknown culture. After talking it through with his wife, he accepted the challenge to become chief operating officer of Nissan while remaining an executive vice-president of Renault. He was conscious that it was a risky move and he viewed failure as a 50–50 possibility. Much of the automobile industry was markedly less sanguine. Indeed, some regarded the whole business as a bottomless pit. However, with his wife on board, he leapt at the chance to go to Japan and run Nissan, not least because of cultural fascination. 'When I was studying in Beirut, Asia was very remote. But especially for me, as a fan of the car, Japan was the holy place where you could learn new approaches. So I had to go, no matter what the conditions were' (*Financial Times*, 2018b).

The disorienting reality of being new in Japan hit home very quickly. His wife realized that she understood nothing and she worried about how long it would take family life to become normal again. Her first visits to the supermarket were a demoralizing experience. For Mr Ghosn when he went to work at Nissan's headquarters for the first time he was a complete outsider. Further, the Japanese press had discovered his 'le cost killer' sobriquet. However, he was determined:

> I was bound and determined to become assimilated. When I signed on for this Japanese adventure, I told myself that Japan was going to be a part of me, just as Nissan was going to be a part of me. But assimilation doesn't mean that you have

to lose your individuality or your originality. And in any case, I knew I'd always be different here. I tried to be myself. I tried to assimilate, but without phoniness. (Ghosn and Riès, 2005, p. 83)

By the end of July 1999, Mr Ghosn had put together a team and carried out an extensive analysis of Nissan. They found that only four of Nissan's 43 models were actually making money, that Nissan effectively ignored the customer and market, that there was a lack of any sense of urgency, too much compartmentalization and no meaningful strategy. As he quickly recognized, the prophets of doom clearly had a point:

> When I arrived at Nissan in 1999, people didn't feel committed to anything; they were saying, 'I'm doing a great job and this guy next to me is not'. The company was going bankrupt and everyone was sleeping well at night. I wanted people to make a commitment, which doesn't have to reflect everything they could do but ensured that they did it. I also wanted them to express via a target what else they could do. If they don't reach their commitments, I have a problem.

It was seen as ruthless, he goes on, but 'the company went like a rocket, up in the first two years' (*Financial Times*, 2018b).

In all, he brought in 30 people from Renault, all of whom were enthusiastic about going to Japan and completely open-minded about cultural differences. He stated: 'I didn't want there to be any chance that one of my people would behave like a colonist' (Ghosn and Riès, 2005, p. 88). He communicated that it was up to them to assimilate with the Nissan people; it was not up to the Nissan people to adapt to them. However, that did not preclude frank speaking even if it meant loss of face. That July, he met with the union representatives. They were worried about the future of the company, about it simply falling apart. The meeting was frank and Mr Ghosn left it feeling they would be able to work together to get Nissan out of its hole.

The first step was to make a plan for rebuilding Nissan. At the core of the Nissan Revival Plan were nine cross-functional teams that covered the entire spectrum of the reforms. One team was to handle new products and markets, another was to focus on purchasing, and a third was to work on manufacturing and logistics. The other teams were to address R&D, sales and marketing, administration, finance, phasing out of products and organization. Overall, about 500 Nissan employees were involved in the project that lasted from July to September. By the end of this process, clearly defined and communicated goals were in place. One of these was the reduction of the headcount of 148 000 worldwide by 21 000. It was now time to move quickly and to avoid getting dragged down by Japanese traditions of consensus seeking. In April 2000, execution of the plan started.

'From the beginning', Mr Ghosn recalled, 'I knew that an important component of the plan would be cost reduction. Another would be the sale of unessential assets' (ibid., p. 108). Superfluous factories were closed and Nissan's *keiretsu* network of suppliers was dismantled. The clarity of the goals and the commitment to returning to profitability by the end of 2000 meant that there was little or no resistance within Nissan. The Japanese government stayed away, clearly preferring a return to profitability rather than a Nissan collapse. However, the press and many of the suppliers were vocal in their criticism of the Nissan Revival Plan. It was un-Japanese. Mr Ghosn knew perfectly well that taboos were being broken: 'We made a clean break with the Japanese idea that no one should win and no one should lose, the idea that a company was obligated to protect all its employees' (ibid., p. 126). In all, Mr Ghosn closed five Japanese factories, axed 21 000 jobs worldwide and halved the number of parts suppliers (*Financial Times*, 2016).

By the first half of fiscal year 2000, the balance sheet showed significant improvement. The front-page news in October was that Nissan was on its way back. The Japanese public took Mr Ghosn to its heart and 'Ghosn-mania' broke out. By 2004, the *Financial Times* ranked Nissan as one of the world's most respected companies. Eventually a Japanese superhero comic-book series chronicled his life in 'The True Story of Carlos Ghosn'.

For nearly two decades, the Nissan–Renault alliance seemed durable. Both companies became profitable and innovative: the Nissan Leaf became the world's best-selling electric car. In 2016, Mr Ghosn became chairman of a new alliance partner, Mitsubishi Motors. As chairman of all three carmakers and the alliance, Ghosn was at the helm of the world's second-largest carmaker. The investment in Mitsubishi came as the company was grappling with a fuel economy scandal. After its alliance with Nissan–Renault its fortunes improved dramatically. The company reported a 19-fold increase in annual operating profit to ¥98 billion ($889 million) in the 2017–18 fiscal year, with nearly 30 per cent of its profits generated from alliance-driven cost reduction efforts (*Financial Times*, 2018c).

Looking back

In the years following the Nissan–Renault alliance, Mr Ghosn would from time to time look back at his career. He speculated that perhaps he was fortunate to arrive in Japan at a time when after a decade of stagnation, many Japanese were calling into question its taboos. Within Nissan, he was able to abandon the system of promotion based on seniority rather than performance that was commonplace in Japan. Likewise, the guarantee of lifetime employment and the culture of working long hours and receiving overtime. He established a clear link between remuneration and individual performance. By 2005, the translators that Mr Ghosn and his team needed when they arrived in Japan are largely gone. English was the working language at executive meetings. As a non-native speaker, he saw this as simply a pragmatic rather than a cultural choice. Further, neither the French nor the Japanese had any natural superiority in using English. It was a level playing field.

In terms of being a foreigner, he could see no advantage at all:

> Being Japanese would have been an asset as a CEO – but a Japanese leader with a global vision and a good deal of experience in the industry. I felt the most important factor as that the person be someone from outside the company, given Nissan's situation. (Ghosn and Riès, 2005, pp. 137–8)

However, Mr Ghosn conceded that his not being typically Brazilian, French or any other nationality had probably been useful. 'I can't make a distinction', he said of his roots. 'I have the traditions of a Lebanese family, but I am also Brazilian, and my mother was very Francophile so the French presence was there from the day I was born. I am a mixture of the three cultures' (*Financial Times*, 2018b). What had really mattered though was his ability 'to gather a group around me and get certain things done. Whatever talent I have for managing people has been more helpful to me than my formal education' (Ghosn and Riès, 2005, p. 179). The sense of feeling comfortable everywhere was also an important feature of his success. When asked what makes a good global leader he answered: 'love the country and love the culture in which you are in. And try to learn about its strengths, don't focus on the weaknesses' (INSEAD, 2008 on YouTube).

A.3 The fall of Carlos Ghosn

The ever-present threat of hubris

On 19 November 2018, Mr Ghosn was arrested by Tokyo District Prosecutors for allegedly underreporting his pay. Nissan, the Japanese carmaker he once helped to rescue, alleged 'numerous and significant acts of misconduct, including personal use of corporate assets and understating his pay' (*Financial Times*, 2018a). Nissan said that its allegations followed several months of internal investigation following claims from a whistle-blower. Up until his arrest, Mr Ghosn was in the dark about this internal enquiry.

How can we explain Mr Ghosn's fall from grace as a global leader? It is important to bear in mind that Nissan–Renault was not a single company but an alliance of firms that owned shares in one another in a structure designed almost 20 years previously. Although Nissan was the junior partner, by 2018 it had become the more profitable performer – indeed, in 2018 it was the larger company, with annual revenues almost 60 per cent higher than Renault. Despite this imbalance, Mr Ghosn had been planning a merger between Renault and Nissan before his arrest that would have made the partnership 'irreversible'. This was a deal that the Japanese carmaker's board opposed and was looking for ways to block (*Financial Times*, 2018d). However, these tensions do not invalidate the allegations.

Nissan's chief executive, Hiroto Saikawa, proffered one explanation of Mr Ghosn's fall: 'Too much authority was given to one person in terms of governance. I have to say that this is a dark side of the Ghosn era which lasted for a long time' (*Mail Online*, 2018). In other words, corporate governance was wanting.

Another explanation was suggested by Bob Lutz, former General Motors vice-chairman who had known Mr Ghosn for many years. He commented to CNBC (2018) that:

> I'm both surprised but in a way not too surprised because Carlos since I've first known him is a highly capable person of very high intelligence but also extremely aware of his own capabilities and his own importance. That type of personality can flip into borderline behaviour. . . No CEO is immune to 'CEO disease'. Think about it. Everywhere he [i.e., Ghosn] goes in all three corporations there is nothing but admiration and adulation. 'Yes boss' etc. etc. So [unlike the President of the USA] you get no negative feedback ever. . . A CEO never gets any. So CEOs tend to develop this. . . 'Oh, I'm God's gift to leadership and everybody loves me and I'm fabulous'. And over a while they tend to believe that they're above the rules and above the law and then they start misbehaving.

In addition to insufficient corporate governance and narcissism, the editorial board of the *Financial Times* (2018a) pointed to the bubble-like existence of CEOs:

> The strains of doing business across continents are alleviated by high pay and privileges, such as use of private jets and luxury accommodation. Dangers arise

when leaders start to take those perks for granted. They untether from the communities where their companies are located, and float off in a gilded bubble with other similarly cocooned magnates. When the bubble bursts, the fall is particularly hard for those chief executives who were merely hired hands, such as Mr Ghosn, rather than entrepreneurs or founders. Like political lives, many executives' careers end in failure. Those who over-extend their tenure are often prone to stumble in their last years in office. The intense focus on pay – a lightning rod for criticism of Mr Ghosn – adds pressure for listed company executives to perform. Mr Ghosn seemed to be doing some of the right things to cushion a hard exit. He had handed over to Mr Saikawa at Nissan, and this year appointed a chief operating officer at Renault to allow him to concentrate on managing the alliance with Nissan and Mitsubishi. In the end, though, Icarus-like, he may have flown his corporate jet too close to the sun. For chief executives who move in the same circles and who seem never to touch down, Mr Ghosn's fate sends an important warning that they had better come down to earth.

As time passes, new insights will undoubtedly emerge. The information contained in this case is by no means the final word or any attempt at assessing the validity of the allegations against Mr Ghosn. We encourage you to update the case as the case of Mr Ghosn unfolds.

CASE DISCUSSION

1 In what ways does global leadership differ from domestic leadership?
2 From an early age, Carlos Ghosn was exposed to a variety of cross-cultural experiences. What other types of experience could substitute for these?
3 Is 'CEO disease' inevitable or can it be counteracted?

REFERENCES

Financial Times (2016), 'Carlos Ghosn stakes his reputation on Mitsubishi', 20 October 2016.
Financial Times (2018a), 'Hubris is an ever-present risk for high-flying chief executives', 19 November 2018, accessed 20 November 2018 at https://www.ft.com/content/69343192-ebf0-11e8-8180-9cf212677a57.
Financial Times (2018b), '"Le cost killer": The relentless drive of Carlos Ghosn', 15 June 2018, accessed 20 August 2018 at https://www.ft.com/content/e3acccf2-6e20-11e8-92d3-6c13e5c92914.
Financial Times (2018c), 'Mitsubishi turn-around raises questions for Nissan–Renault', 8 July 2018.
Financial Times (2018d), 'Carlos Ghosn was planning Nissan–Renault merger before arrest', 20 November 2018.
Ghosn, C. and P. Riès (2005), *Shift: Inside Nissan's Historic Revival*, New York: Currency Books.
Mail Online (2018), '£14 million of Nissan cash was used to buy homes in Paris, Beirut, Rio de Janeiro and Amsterdam', accessed 20 November 2018 at https://www.dailymail.co.uk/news/article-6408931/Nissan-shares-plunge-arrest-chairman-Carlos-Ghosn.html.
Osland, J., G. Oddou, A. Bird and A. Osland (2013), 'Exceptional global leadership as cognitive expertise in the domain of global change', *European Journal of International Management*, 7(5), 517–34.

RECOMMENDED YOUTUBE INTERVIEWS

CNBC (2018), 'GM's Bob Lutz on Carlos Ghosn: No CEO is immune to CEO disease', 19 November 2018, accessed 20 November 2018 at https://www.webpronews.com/gm-bob-lutz-nissan-carlos-ghosn-arrest/.

INSEAD (2008), 'The transcultural leader: Carlos Ghosn', 9 May 2008, accessed 29 August 2018 at https://www.youtube.com/watch?v=SF3W2vCH9dU.

Stanford Graduate School of Business (2010), 'Carlos Ghosn of Nissan/Renault: Look ahead, don't stand still', 4 February 2010, accessed 20 January 2019 at https://www.youtube.com/watch?v=yChtop17sd8.

Stanford Graduate School of Business (2014), 'CEO Carlos Ghosn of Renault–Nissan alliance on innovation', 21 January 2014, accessed 20 January 2019 at https://www.youtube.com/watch?v=r2gZ_23z92o.

2
Why and how firms internationalize

2.1 Introduction

In this chapter, we address *why* firms internationalize. We follow this with a discussion of the liabilities of foreignness that face MNEs and the implications these have for *how* firms internationalize. We also address the rise of MNEs from emerging economies. This chapter emphasizes that MNEs are far from guaranteed success. They are 'playing away from home' where they must overcome various 'liabilities of foreignness'. A firm may well have superior technological assets and still struggle to succeed.

2.2 Why do firms internationalize?

Over 50 years ago, Hymer raised the firm-based question of why MNEs existed at all, given that they are playing away from home both in national and cultural terms. After all, domestic companies, he observed, have 'the general advantage of better information about their country: its economy, its language, its laws and its politics' (Hymer, 1960 [1976], p. 34). He was writing at a time when MNEs were still relatively marginal phenomena. Worldwide, in 1969 there were only 7 000 MNEs. The major turning point for the growth of the MNE as a significant organizational phenomenon was roughly 1990. After adjusting for inflation, 85 per cent of the global stock of MNE investment was created after 1990 (*The Economist*, 2017a). The number of MNEs soared from 37 000 in 1992, to 82 000 in 2008. In 2016, there were over 100 000 (UNCTAD, 2010, 2017). These 100 000 MNEs had some 860 000 foreign affiliates (UNCTAD, 2017). Employment by foreign affiliates rose from 21 million in 1990, to 50 million in 2006 and 82 million in 2016 (ibid.).

Hymer's (1960 [1976], p. 25) explanation of the existence of MNEs as primarily driven by relatively powerful firms wanting to 'remove competition between (them) and enterprises in other countries' in order to achieve monopolistic power is now regarded as too fearful and too crude.

Firms' motives to internationalize are now most frequently grouped into four categories: market seeking, resource seeking, efficiency seeking and strategic asset seeking (Dunning, 2009):

- Firms with *market-seeking* motives have identified a need to expand the market for the company's products or services by capitalizing on its idiosyncratic strategic assets through their application in foreign markets. This has been particularly important for firms with small home markets such as Nestlé of Switzerland and Nokia of Finland.
- *Resource-seeking* motives are common among firms that are dependent on having a reliable supply of raw materials that can only be accessed in foreign locations. For example, European tire companies established rubber plantations in Malaysia and South America while aluminium companies established smelters where cheap energy was available. Internalizing transactions provide firms with a supply that may be less vulnerable and therefore, in the long run, cheaper than market solutions.
- *Efficiency-seeking* motives became more common from the 1960s onwards. As tariffs declined, firms located in the US and Europe found themselves at a competitive disadvantage because of their relatively high labour costs. As a result, a third motive for establishing foreign operations emerged, accessing low-cost labour. An added incentive to relocate production has been the willingness of some host governments to provide direct or indirect subsidies in the form of low levels of corporate taxation. MNEs are then able to spread their activities across multiple countries to optimize their value chains. Each link in the value chain is located in a country where the associated costs are the lowest. Production is moved to more favourable locations in accordance with changing wage rates, interest rates and costs of input factors.
- The *strategic asset-seeking* motive is driven by an increasing dependence among MNEs on knowledge-related assets. Many MNEs choose to acquire a local firm that either has valuable knowledge internally or is embedded in a local cluster of knowledge. By acquiring a foreign firm, the MNE immediately gains access to the desired knowledge and becomes an 'insider' of a knowledge cluster that may otherwise be difficult to tap into. Market entry through mergers and acquisitions (M&As) are often preferred to greenfield investments for MNEs with strategic asset-seeking motives to ensure that the MNE actually does gain access to the desired knowledge in a timely manner. Successful MNEs with strategic asset-seeking motives typically engage actively in the local market.

2.3 What is 'liability of foreignness'?

MNEs have a number of advantages over local companies. In addition to the general location-specific advantages derived from their country of origin they carry with them the firm-specific advantages and strategic assets that enabled them to succeed in their home market. Furthermore, their size provides them with the opportunity to achieve economies of scale in manufacturing and product development while their global presence exposes them to new ideas and opportunities regardless of where they occur. Additionally, their location in many countries can be used as a bargaining chip in obtaining favourable conditions from governments anxious to preserve inward investment and jobs.

However, despite all their advantages, MNEs are also exposed to a potential 'liability of foreignness' (LoF) (Zaheer, 1995). Foreign firms face a 'liability' that is derived from their lack of experience and knowledge about the culture and the 'rules of the game' of the host environment relative to local firms. They face further liabilities in lacking local business networks and being exposed to discriminatory hazards. None of these are necessarily always well understood or anticipated, particularly in the initial entry phase. MNEs are therefore not necessarily successful when internationalizing. One classic investigation, the *Templeton Global Performance Index* (Gestrin, Knight and Rugman, 2000, 2001), revealed that in 1998 while the foreign activities of the world's largest MNEs accounted on average for 36 per cent of their assets and 39 per cent of revenues, these activities only generated 27 per cent of their profits. Over 60 per cent of these companies achieved lower profitability abroad than at home. More recently, *The Economist* (2017b, p. 7) observes a falling share of global profits accounted for by MNEs as '[l]ocal firms have become more sophisticated. They can steal, copy or displace global firms' innovations without building costly offices and factories abroad'. For American MNEs, returns are now 30 percent higher at home than abroad. Let us consider LoF in some detail.

LoF is not a new concept. As we observed above, Hymer (1960 [1976]) was highly conscious of it. One aspect of LoF is that MNEs may be competing head on with domestic companies that have a number of natural advantages. First, domestic companies have a customer base they have cultivated and that is familiar with their brands. Second, local firms will also have developed supply chain relations that may involve long-term contractual relationships that effectively preclude newcomers. This has been a formidable barrier for companies entering the Japanese market.

Another LoF is that national regulators will tend to discriminate against foreign subsidiaries. Except when they are so locally embedded that they are perceived as domestic, foreign firms will be significantly more investigated, audited, and prosecuted than their domestic counterparts (Vernon, 1998).

To take China, there have been periods of outspoken criticism of its business environment from foreign investors in numerous sectors and from a broad range of countries. These companies point to a wide range of discriminatory government practices and regulatory barriers to foreign investment, government procurement rules that favour domestic companies and the country's lack of a transparent and independent legal system (*Financial Times*, 2010; *The Economist*, 2017a).

However, discrimination of foreign companies is by no means unique to China. Even in the United States, officially committed to applying the same 'national treatment' to the offspring of foreign companies that they give to their own companies, it has been empirically documented that 'foreign subsidiaries face more labor lawsuit judgments than their domestic counterparts' (Mezias, 2002, p. 239). In 1990, a group of foreign MNEs operating in the US including Nestlé, Sony, and Unilever, banded together to form the Organization for International Investment (OFII), a body that monitors and responds to discrimination. Membership has expanded to over 200 subsidiaries of foreign-based MNEs and OFII's primary task is to remain on alert for discrimination. OFII advocates for fair, non-discriminatory treatment of foreign-based companies and promotes policies that will encourage them to establish U.S. operations, which in turn increases American employment and U.S. economic growth (OFII, 2019). However, it remains the case that 'in America...foreign companies feel they are at a competitive disadvantage' (*The Economist*, 2017c, p. 58).

A third aspect of LoF concerns the lack of institutional and cultural insight, where firms fail to identify and overcome the cultural and administrative distances, as discussed in Chapter 1. When Walmart moved into Germany in 1998 it had little feel for German shoppers, who care more about price than having their bags packed, or German staff, who hid in the toilets to escape the morning Walmart cheer. Added to that were the inflexibility of local suppliers, the entrenched position of local discounters such as Aldi, but also the strength of trade unions. In the wake of losses of $300 million a year, John Menzer, head of Walmart International, admitted, 'We screwed up in Germany' (*The Economist*, 2001). Walmart withdrew from Germany in 2006.

However, '[as] the firm becomes more of an insider in a particular host society...developing linkages and aligning its values and actions to the institutional requirements of the host environment, its LoF should decline and perhaps even disappear' (Zaheer, 2002, p. 353).

2.4 Understanding MNEs' internationalization choices: A theoretical framework

In an effort to meld theoretical perspectives, Dunning (1981, 2009) developed the OLI framework (also referred to as the eclectic paradigm) to understand firms' internationalization choices. The OLI framework can be seen as an umbrella for issues to consider when selecting an operating mode. It proposes that firms will seek operational control of assets abroad, that is, engage in foreign direct investment (FDI), when three conditions are met. The first is that of 'ownership advantages' ('O'): the firm has superior assets (e.g., technology, managerial competence, marketing capabilities or privileged access to resources) that can be exploited. These advantages are also often termed firm-specific advantages (FSAs).

The second condition is referred to as 'location advantages' ('L'): the firm benefits from localizing certain activities in the foreign market. Firms may, for instance, prefer to locate production outside the home country to realize lower factor costs. We refer to this as 'vertical expansion'. The comparative location advantage 'typically has to do with the prices or productivities of production factors such as capital, labor, or land. For instance, a clothing firm may consider production abroad to take advantage of lower labor costs' (Hernandez and Guillén, 2018, p. 25). However, in other cases firms may be driven by tariff barriers, high transportation barriers or the need to adapt their products to local tastes to expand horizontally. The firm 'sets up a plant or service delivery facility in a foreign location with the goal of selling in that market without abandoning production of the good or service in its home country' (ibid.). Thus, in the original version of OLI, vertical expansion is driven by efficiency seeking or natural resource seeking, while horizontal expansion is driven by market seeking. However, as Dunning himself indicated, by the 1990s, the 'L' of OLI needed to be supplemented because:

> [...]increasingly, firms are investing abroad to protect or augment their core competencies. In such cases, they are 'buying into' foreign created assets (notably technological capacity, information, human creativity, and markets) some of which are proprietary to particular foreign firms [hence the pronounced trend towards acquisition of foreign firms, rather than greenfield investment] and others that are more generally accessible to corporations, but immobile across geographical space. (Dunning, 1997, p. 64 [with our insertion])

Arguably, these 'asset-seeking' investments are a prime motivation of emerging market MNEs as well as MNEs from developed economies (Hernandez and Guillén, 2018).

The third condition that must be met for a firm to engage in FDI is that it must perceive 'internalization' ('I') of assets as the most advantageous organizational form. The 'I' of OLI 'avows that the greater the net benefits of internalizing cross-border intermediate product markets, the more likely a firm will prefer to engage in foreign production itself, rather than license the right to do so, e.g. by a technical service or franchise agreement, to a foreign firm' (Dunning, 2000, p. 164). In other words, after a cost–benefit calculus (Buckley, 2016), the firm concludes that it prefers to set up and own a foreign subsidiary rather than relying on a contractual agreement with a foreign firm. Thus, assets, not least intangible assets such as knowledge or technology, are transferred across national boundaries within the firm's own organizations rather than through contractual agreements with foreign-based enterprises. The cost–benefit calculus that firms make will involve trying to calculate different forms of opportunism. On the one hand, for a firm to establish external contracts it can be both challenging and costly in terms of negotiations and monitoring in order to ensure that commitments are fulfilled. Can the firm trust a contractual partner with, for example, its technology? On the other hand, does the firm have the resources to meet the governance costs involved in running a foreign subsidiary? One particular governance cost is that of measuring the performance of the foreign unit.

When company headquarters have problems in evaluating the performance of the foreign unit, they incur measurement costs. Such costs can manifest themselves as time spent on controlling delivered services from the foreign subsidiary, time and money spent on accounting issues, and extra travel expenses to control working effort (Tomassen and Benito, 2009, p. 294). Another example of a governance cost is the 'bonding' cost. Time and resources have to be spent on developing personal ties with the foreign unit and on developing a common company culture. The choice of organizing the assets through markets, hierarchies or some combination of the two is thus based on an attempt to optimize anticipated costs.

2.5 What is the process of internationalization?

As we have indicated above, OLI concerns itself with the question of *why* firms acquire foreign operations. The Uppsala internationalization process model of the firm is a reaction to the challenge of LoF – which they refer to as 'psychic distance' – and a response to the issue of *how* firms evolve into

MNEs. The model emerged inductively from observing how Swedish firms developed into MNEs. It argues that firms internationalize incrementally, with firms initially beginning with ad hoc exporting. As foreign market knowledge increases through learning-by-doing, sales agents are replaced by operational modes that involve a stronger commitment such as foreign sales organizations followed by production in wholly-owned subsidiaries. The Uppsala model further argues that firms prefer to start their internationalization in culturally proximate markets where the psychic distance is low (e.g., low perceived difficulties in understanding the foreign market). Firms enter foreign markets that resemble their domestic markets and that are therefore more easily understood. Moving beyond neighbouring markets is gradual (Johanson and Vahlne, 1977, 2009; Vahlne and Johanson, 2017). The implication of the Uppsala model is that most MNEs are regional rather than global.

Focusing on global sales penetration rather than sourcing or production, Rugman (2001) also argues that most MNEs are region bound. His starting point is that the 'triad' economies, the EU, the USA and Japan, have long accounted for the bulk of global FDI. Rugman's (2001) analysis indicated that of the world's largest 500 MNEs in 1999, 434 were from the triad and that this percentage had remained fairly constant over the past decades.

Rugman and Verbeke (2004) argue that the problem faced by many MNEs is that they sell innovative products that stem from high investments not least in knowledge development. Although patents and brand names protect these products, in reality rivals in other parts of the triad create equivalent products more rapidly than they can develop distribution capabilities throughout the triad. Consequently, most MNEs trade within their respective immediate region, the North American Free Trade Agreement (NAFTA), the expanded EU and Asia. Rugman and Verbeke (2004, pp. 6–7) were only able to identify nine MNEs in the Fortune 500 that were 'unambiguously "global", with at least 20% of their sales in all three regions of the triad, but less than 50% in any one region'. The exceptions were IBM, Sony, Philips, Nokia, Intel, Canon, Coca-Cola, Flextronics and LVMH. Although they identified a number of bi-regional MNEs, such as McDonald's, Toyota and Unilever, nearly 90 per cent of MNEs are home region oriented. They further observed that most large MNEs average 80 per cent of their sales in their home region. Furthermore, MNEs generally have large portfolios of purely domestic assets. They noted that even the largest MNEs have on average nearly half of their total assets in domestic assets (in more recent years this has decreased to just under 40 per cent; UNCTAD, 2016). For many smaller MNEs, the proportion is substantially larger. In the final analysis, 'if firms have exhausted their growth in their home region of the triad and still go into other regions, they then face (inter-regional) foreignness and other additional risks by this global expansion' (Rugman, 2005, p. 1). As few firms are capable and willing to bear these costs and risks, they are destined to compete within their home regions. Rugman (2001, p. 10) concludes:

> There is no evidence for globalization, that is, of a system of free trade with fully integrated world markets. Instead the evidence on the performance and activities of multinational enterprises demonstrates that international business is triad-based and triad-related... European, North American and Asian manufacturing and service companies compete viciously for market share, lobbying their governments for shelter and subsidies.

Proponents of the regionalization thesis thus argue that the world's largest MNEs operate mostly within their home regions, that very few are global, that the global strategy is a myth (Collinson and Rugman, 2008) and that the CEOs of MNEs should, 'encourage all [of their] managers to think regional, act local – and forget global' (Rugman and Hodgetts, 2001, p. 341).

However, the regionalization thesis has had its critics. For example, Osegowitsch and Sammartino (2008) agree that sales are the decisive indicator of firm-specific advantages: international sales reflect international customers' judgement about the attractiveness of the firm's goods services and ultimately the strength of the FSAs. However, they view the thresholds used by Rugman and co-authors as arbitrary. Why, they ask, set the home region threshold to 50 per cent? They re-test Rugman's data using different cut-offs and find that the conclusions are far from robust, with a significant share of firms attaining bi-regional or global status. They also observe that longitudinal analysis shows that large firms are increasingly extending their sales beyond the home region. Aggarwal et al. (2011) are even more critical. They employ a classification system that goes beyond triad countries to include all countries in the world, which does not apply activity thresholds and which supplements sales with subsidiaries. Their findings indicate that the vast majority of the 100 largest G7 firms operate beyond their home regions. Nevertheless, while most are trans-regional, only 3 per cent of these firms have truly global sales, although 13 per cent have global subsidiaries.

A different type of challenge to the regionalization thesis is the revisited version of the Uppsala model. Johanson and Vahlne (2009) argue that regional bias in firm internationalization has weakened significantly. Increasingly it is not psychic distance or LoF that matters, but outsidership in relation to relevant networks. Insidership in networks of business relationships provides a firm with an extended knowledge base, thereby enabling it to identify opportunities and to overcome the liability of outsidership (LoO). Thus, the key challenge for internationalizing firms is to overcome their lack of relevant business networks in new local contexts. In this revised version of the Uppsala model of how firms internationalize, firms go abroad based on their relationships with important partners who are committed to developing the business relationship and this may take them to much more distant markets than assumed by the original Uppsala model. Hence:

> We do believe that the correlation between the order in which a company enters foreign markets and psychic distance has weakened. Some companies and individuals have acquired more general knowledge of foreign environments, and perhaps this instils in them greater confidence in their ability to cope with psychic distance. (Johanson and Vahlne, 2009, p. 1421)

One obvious indicator of weakening regionalization is the increased share of global inward FDI experienced by emerging economies, and not least China. While a considerable proportion of goods produced by MNEs in China are destined for other markets, about 50 per cent of its exports are produced by the subsidiaries or joint ventures of MNEs (Park and Vanhonacker, 2007; *The Economist*, 2017a). US and EU MNEs are increasingly 'lured by these countries' fast-growing markets as much as lower wages' (*The Economist*, 2011). For example, automakers have recognized that producing locally and thereby avoiding import tariff and non-tariff barriers unlocks significant value. Local production means that they can sell vehicles at much lower prices and therefore target a much larger pool of potential customers. In 2013, China accounted for 25 per cent of global vehicle sales (Forbes, 2014). Similarly, Apple, which uses a locally based Taiwanese manufacturing partner, Foxconn, generates nearly a quarter of its revenues from sales in China (Barboza, 2016).

2.6 Do emerging market MNEs challenge extant theory?

The relative dominance of MNEs from the triad is in decline. Nearly one-third (164) of the Fortune Global 500 firms in 2017 came from emerging markets; in 1995 it was 4 per cent (*The Economist*, 2011). Of these, firms from the BRIC economies (Brazil, Russia, India and China) dominate. In 2010, 67 companies from BRIC countries were on Fortune's Global 500 list (*Financial Times*, 2011); by 2017, this had risen to 128. More broadly, while more than 90 per cent of all MNEs were headquartered in developed countries in the early 1990s, parent MNEs from developing and transition economies accounted for more than a quarter of MNEs in 2008 (UNCTAD, 2010) and around 30 per cent by 2017 (Luo and Tung, 2018). Among emerging market MNEs (EMNEs), Chinese firms dominate. In 2017, China had 109 firms on the Fortune Global 500 list, whereas Brazil had seven, India seven and Russia five. Only the USA had more (133). It is noteworthy that 70 per cent of Chinese outward FDI is accounted for by state-owned enterprises (SOEs) (Ramamurti and Hillemann, 2018, p. 36).

Luo and Tung (2007) developed a 'springboard perspective' to describe the internationalization strategy of EMNEs. This strategy aims at catching up 'with established and powerful rivals in a relatively rapid fashion through aggressive strategic asset and opportunity seeking, and by benefitting from favorable institutions in foreign countries' (Luo and Tung, 2018, p. 130). In general, EMNEs follow dual paths, simultaneously expanding into both developing and developed economies. The former is driven by market-seeking and resource-seeking motives. The latter is motivated by knowledge seeking, that is, access to brands, new technology, research and development, and managerial and operational expertise (UNCTAD, 2017).

This latter form of expansion is potentially a challenge to 'OLI' and its assumption as discussed above of firm 'ownership advantages' ('O'). One response is that while EMNES are apparently lacking in 'O', they, and particularly Chinese SOEs, may have access to resources such as capital that is available at below-market rates for a considerable period of time. Buckley et al. (2007) propose that state ownership could be considered a firm-specific advantage ('O') for many Chinese MNEs. Hennart (2012) disagrees, arguing that in reality most EMNEs that acquire knowledge-rich firms in developed countries have few if any proprietary firm-specific advantages. Similarly, Ramamurti and Hillemann (2018, p. 44) argue that 'government-created advantage (rather than firm ownership advantage), is the secret sauce that explains the rapid expansion of Chinese MNEs'. What they possess are country-specific advantages available to all firms. Thus, Hennart views the OLI model as unable to explain this form of FDI. The debate is set to continue.

EMNEs also pose a challenge for the Uppsala model and the related regionalization thesis. Satta, Parola and Persico (2014) find that the effect of psychic distance is negligible for EMNEs. Further, as the notion of the springboard perspective suggests, EMNEs do not proceed incrementally. Indeed, a distinguishing feature of EMNEs is their willingness to enter risky countries (Buckley et al., 2018). However, a considerable proportion of FDI from emerging market economies is relatively local. In the case of China, which increased its outward FDI from about $15 billion in 2004 to more than $220 billion by 2010, much of this is very local. Hong Kong accounts for nearly 70 per cent of mainland China's outward FDI stock and other parts of Asia for about 9 per cent. Europe and North America account for a mere 6 per cent of its stock (Peng, 2011). Peng (2011, pp. 8–9) concludes that any notion 'that China is "buying up the world" . . . is disconnected from reality and unsubstantiated by facts'. We revisit the issue of EMNEs in Chapter 8.

Despite the various challenges to the Uppsala model and the thesis of regionalization, our view is that these perspectives are powerful antidotes to naive notions of the geographical scope of most MNEs. As Osegowitsch and Sammartino (2008) acknowledge, it is clear that the world will remain in a state of 'semi-globalization' (Ghemawat, 2003) for the near future. In general, the regionally integrated MNE remains more the rule than the exception (Oh and Rugman, 2012). Tellingly, despite revising their model to account for a weakening of the correlation between the order in which a company enters foreign markets and psychic distance, Vahlne and Johanson (2017, p. 8) remain of the view that generally 'firms expand predominantly in markets similar – or adjacent – to the home market'.

2.7 Summary

In this chapter, we identify why and how MNEs internationalize. We further highlight some of the challenges involved in creating and sustaining the necessary organizational capabilities that in turn enable the MNE to harness its firm-specific advantages. Let us further develop this argument. To outweigh and overcome LoF, MNEs must possess some strategic capability that gives them a competitive advantage, whether it is advanced technological expertise, marketing competencies or scale economies. These capabilities and the costs associated with developing them must not be taken for granted. Increasingly, managing the knowledge base of the MNE has become one of the most important organizational capabilities. This comprises not only the transfer of knowledge between the various parts of the MNE, but also the creation of new forms of knowledge by combining knowledge located transnationally both within and beyond the MNE.

Much of the focus in the remainder of this book is on the managerial and learning challenges that MNEs have to confront in order to create these organizational capabilities. Despite their strengths, globally dispersed companies can easily become bureaucratic and therefore non-entrepreneurial and insensitive to the many different environments in which they operate (Birkinshaw, 2000). Indeed, some researchers claim that there is a nonlinear inverted U-shaped relationship between international diversification and performance (e.g., Geringer, Beamish and daCosta, 1989; Hitt,

Hoskisson and Kim, 1997). Beyond a threshold of international expansion, returns diminish due to the limits of the firm and its management. That is, at some point the transaction costs involved in co-coordinating and controlling geographically dispersed units outweigh the benefits of international diversification. Other researchers are less sure. In an extensive review of research articles measuring performance effects of international diversification, Hennart (2011) found no clear theoretical rationale to support performance effects. However, what is clear is that being an MNE does not guarantee success. The two case studies accompanying this chapter exemplify different internationalization motives and illustrate how firms overcome LoFs. The case studies can also be used to illustrate the CAGE framework, as discussed in Chapter 1.

REFERENCES

Aggarwal, R., J. Berrill, E. Huston and C. Kearney (2011), 'What is a multinational corporation? Classifying the degree of firm-level multinationality', *International Business Review*, **20**(5), 557–77.

Barboza, D. (2016), 'How China built "iPhone City" with billions in perks for Apple's partner', *New York Times*, 29 December 2016, accessed 29 January 2018 at https://www.nytimes.com/2016/12/29/technology/apple-iphone-china-foxconn.html.

Birkinshaw, J. (2000), 'Mastering Management 10: The structures behind global companies', *Financial Times*, 4 December 2000.

Buckley, P.J. (2016), 'The contribution of internalisation theory to international business: New realities and unanswered questions', *Journal of World Business*, **51**(1), 74–82.

Buckley, P.J., L. Chen, L.J. Clegg and H. Voss (2018), 'Risk propensity in the foreign direct investment location decision of emerging multinationals', *Journal of International Business Studies*, **49**(2), 153–71.

Buckley, P.J., L.J. Clegg and A.R. Cross et al. (2007), 'The determinants of Chinese outward foreign direct investment', *Journal of International Business Studies*, **38**(4), 499–518.

Collinson, S. and A. Rugman (2008), 'The regional nature of Japanese multinational business', *Journal of International Business Studies*, **39**(2), 215–30.

Dunning, J.H. (1981), *International Production and the Multinational Enterprise*, London: George Allen & Unwin.

Dunning, J.H. (1997), 'The sourcing of technological advantage by multinational enterprises', in K. Macharzina, M.J. Oesterle and J. Wolf (eds), *Global Business in the Information Age* (pp. 63–101), proceedings of the 23rd Annual EIBA Conference, Stuttgart.

Dunning, J.H. (2000), 'The eclectic paradigm as an envelope for economic and business theories of MNE activity', *International Business Review*, **9**(2), 163–90.

Dunning, J.H. (2009), 'Location and the multinational enterprise: A neglected factor?', *Journal of International Business Studies*, **40**(1), 5–19.

Financial Times (2010), 'China vows to treat foreign business fairly', 7 September 2010, accessed 20 January 2019 at http://www.ft.com/intl/cms/s/2/0880387e-ba34-11df-8804-00144feabdc0.html#axzz1pekxjzEs.

Financial Times (2011), 'Infosys: Include the poor in development, or face the consequences', 30 November 2011, accessed 20 January 2019 at http://blogs.ft.com/beyond-brics/2011/11/30/infosys-include-the-poor-in-development-or-face-the-consequences/#axzz1pf3geUCg.

Forbes (2014), 'Moving production share to emerging markets can unlock substantial value for automakers', 22 May 2014, accessed 29 January 2018 at https://www.forbes.com/sites/greatspeculations/2014/05/22/moving-production-share-to-emerging-markets-can-unlock-substantial-value-for-automakers/.

Geringer, J.M., P.W. Beamish and R.C. daCosta (1989), 'Diversification strategy and internationalization: Implications for MNE performance', *Strategic Management Journal*, **10**(2), 109–19.

Gestrin, M., R.F. Knight and A.M. Rugman (2000), *Templeton Global Performance Index*, Oxford: Templeton College, University of Oxford.

Gestrin, M., R.F. Knight and A.M. Rugman (2001), *Templeton Global Performance Index*, Oxford: Templeton College, University of Oxford.

Ghemawat, P. (2003), 'Semiglobalization and international business strategy', *Journal of International Business Studies*, **34**(2), 138–52.

Hennart, J.F. (2011), 'A theoretical assessment of the empirical literature on the impact of multinationality on performance', *Global Strategy Journal*, **1**(1), 135–51.

Hennart, J.F. (2012), 'Emerging market multinationals and the theory of the multinational enterprise', *Global Strategy Journal*, **2**(3), 168–87.

Hernandez, E. and M.F. Guillén (2018), 'What's theoretically novel about emerging-market multinationals?', *Journal of International Business Studies*, **49**(1), 24–33.

Hitt, M.A., R.E. Hoskisson and H. Kim (1997), 'International diversification: Effects on innovation and firm performance in product-diversified firms', *Academy of Management Journal*, **40**(4), 767–98.

Hymer, S.H. (1960 [1976]), *The International Operations of National Firms: A Study of Direct Foreign Investment*, Cambridge, MA: MIT Press.

Johanson, J. and J.E. Vahlne (1977), 'The internationalization of process of the firm: A model of knowledge development and increasing market commitments', *Journal of International Business*, **8**(1), 23–32.

Johanson, J. and J.E. Vahlne (2009), 'The Uppsala internationalization process model revisited: From liability of foreignness to liability of outsidership', *Journal of International Business Studies*, **40**, 1411–31.

Luo, Y. and R.L. Tung (2007), 'International expansion of emerging market enterprises: A springboard perspective', *Journal of International Business Studies*, **38**(4), 481–98.

Luo, Y. and R.L. Tung (2018), 'A general theory of springboard MNEs', *Journal of International Business Studies*, **49**(2), 129–52.

Mezias, J.M. (2002), 'Identifying liabilities of foreignness and strategies to minimize their effects: The case of labor lawsuit judgments as liabilities of foreignness', *Strategic Management Journal*, **23**(3), 229–44.

OFII (2019), Organization for International Investment Companies [website], accessed 18 April, 2019 at https://ofii.org/about-us.

Oh, C.H. and A. Rugman (2012), 'Regional integration and the international strategies of large European firms', *International Business Review*, **21**(3), 493–507.

Osegowitsch, T. and A. Sammartino (2008), 'Reassessing (home-)regionalization', *Journal of International Business Studies*, **39**(2), 184–96.

Park, S.H. and W.R. Vanhonacker (2007), 'The challenge for multinational corporations in China: Think local, act global', *MIT Sloan Management Review*, **48**(4), accessed 20 January 2019 at https://sloanreview.mit.edu/article/the-challenge-for-multinational-corporations-in-china-think-local-act-global/.

Peng, M.W. (2011), 'The social responsibility of international business scholars: The case of China', *AIB Insights*, **11**(4), 8–10.

Ramamurti, R. and J. Hillemann (2018), 'What is "Chinese" about Chinese multinationals?', *Journal of International Business Studies*, **49**(1), 34–48.

Rugman, A. (2001), 'Mastering Management 13: The illusion of the global company', *Financial Times*, 8 January 2001.

Rugman, A. (2005), *The Regional Multinationals: MNCs and 'Global' Strategic Management*, Cambridge, UK: Cambridge University Press.

Rugman, A. and R. Hodgetts (2001), 'The end of global strategy', *European Management Journal*, **19**(4), 333–43.

Rugman, A. and A. Verbeke (2004), 'Regional and global strategies of MNCs', *Journal of International Business*, **35**(1), 3–18.

Satta, G., F. Parola and L. Persico (2014), 'Temporal and spatial constructs in service firms' internationalization patterns: The determinants of the accelerated growth of emerging MNEs', *Journal of International Management*, **20**(4), 421–35.

The Economist (2001), 'Wal-Mart: Wal around the world', 6 December 2001, accessed 20 January 2019 at http://www.economist.com/node/895888.

The Economist (2011), 'Why the tail wags the dog', 6 August 2011.

The Economist (2017a), 'The retreat of the global company', 28 January 2017.

The Economist (2017b), 'In retreat', 28 January 2017.

The Economist (2017c), 'Schumpeter: They've lost that loving feeling', 14 January 2017.

Tomassen, S. and S.R.G. Benito (2009), 'The costs of governance in international companies', *International Business Review*, **18**(3), 292–304.

UNCTAD (2010), *Investing in a Low-carbon Economy*, New York and Geneva: UNCTAD.

UNCTAD (2016), *World Investment Report 2016*, New York and Geneva: UNCTAD.

UNCTAD (2017), *World Investment Report 2017: Investment and the Digital Economy*, New York and Geneva: UNCTAD.

Vahlne, J.E. and J. Johanson (2017), 'From internationalization to evolution: The Uppsala model at 40 years', *Journal of International Business Studies*, **48**(9), 1087–102.

Vernon, R. (1998), *In the Hurricane's Eye: The Troubled Prospects of Multinational Enterprises*, Cambridge, MA: Harvard University Press.

Zaheer, S. (1995), 'Overcoming the liability of foreignness', *Academy of Management Journal*, **38**(2), 341–63.

Zaheer, S. (2002), 'The liability of foreignness, redux: A commentary', *Journal of International Management*, **8**, 351–8.

Case B
MTN Group Limited – subsidiary management across emerging economies

Gilbert Kofi Adarkwah

B.1 Introduction

In a recent shareholders meeting, Mr Phuthuma Nhleko, group president and CEO of MTN, affirmed MTN's goal to be the number one telecommunication company in its segments in every country in which MTN operates. To achieve this goal, MTN has made it a point to be responsive to its local customer needs as well as the needs of the local communities. MTN became one of Africa's most successful MNEs by entering markets that had been overlooked by Western companies. But, after losses in its second largest markets, and the subsequent effect on its profit and stock performance, management at headquarters are reconsidering how to manage the subsidiaries in West Africa and beyond. In this case, we examine MTN's structure, its operations, as well as the management of its subsidiaries across the diverse emerging markets in which it operates.

B.2 About MTN

MTN Group Limited (MTN) is the largest telecommunication company ever to originate from the continent of Africa. MTN was incorporated in South Africa in 1994. Since its incorporation, MTN has enjoyed tremendous success, the likes of which few African multinational companies can only dream of. From a humble beginning from its headquarters in Johannesburg, MTN has grown from a one-country operation to an MNE with operations in 22 countries across Africa, Europe and Asia (Table B.1).

MTN Group has over 230 million subscribers across its operating subsidiaries and joint ventures (MTN Group, 2018c). It employs over 20 000 people comprising 45 different nationalities. As an emerging markets

Table B.1 MTN geographical locations

Founded	Market	MTN Ownership (%)
1994	South Africa	100
1996	Ghana	98
1998	Côte d'Ivoire	59
1998	Benin	75
1998	Guinea	75
1998	Republic of the Congo	100
1998	Uganda	96
1998	Rwanda	80
1998	Zambia	86
2000	Cameroon	70
2001	Liberia	60
2001	Guinea-Bissau	100
2001	Nigeria	79
2002	Syria	75
2002	Sudan	85
2002	Yemen	83
2002	Afghanistan	100
2004	Cyprus	100
2005	South Sudan	100
2005	Botswana	53
2005	Swaziland	30
2006	Iran	49

Source: MTN Ghana (2018b).

mobile telecommunications operator at the forefront of technological and digital changes, MTN is unique. It has a market capitalization of $16.3 billion (MTN Group, 2018b). Since 2013, MTN has been selected among the group of emerging market companies classified as 'global challengers' by the Boston Consulting Group (BCG, 2018).

B.3 MTN's products and services

MTN's products and services include traditional phone lines, mobile and voice, data, security as a service, managed networks, cloud services, software as a service, enterprise mobility as well as mobile money and entertainment, segmented between personal customers, business customers, and digital services (see Table B.2). Besides offering communications products and services, MTN also offers financial services in the form of mobile payments as well as enterprise solutions to corporate and public sector customers.

Table B.2 A cross-section of MTN products and services

Personal Customers	Business Customers	Digital Services
Traditional phone lines	Unified communications	Mobile money
Mobile and voice	Security as a service	Entertainment:
Data	Managed networks	– MTN Music
Digital	Cloud services	– MTN Play
	Software as a service	
	Enterprise mobility	

Source: MTN Ghana (2018b).

B.4 Strategy for expansion and long-term vision

Operating a telecommunication company across emerging economies is more complicated than most industries. First, firms must secure a concession and/or licence from the host country authorities. Afterward, they must go through the capital-intensive process of building and installing cell site and fibre optic cable infrastructures. Because of this, the decision on which markets to expand into is a challenging one for telecommunication companies. MTN has a long-term vision of being a leading telecommunications provider in the emerging world by leading the delivery of a bold, new digital world to its customers. This vision is supported by five key strategic themes, namely (1) creating and managing stakeholder value; (2) creating a distinct customer experience; (3) driving sustainable growth; (4) transforming its operating model; and (5) continuous innovation and best practice.

MTN's international expansion strategy is based on supporting its vision of being a leading telecommunications provider in emerging economies. From the start, MTN pursued an aggressive internationalization strategy, moving from a one-country operation in 1997 to a 22-country operation in 2017, utilizing the combination of greenfield organic operations, strategic alliances such as international joint ventures (IJVs) as well as targeted acquisitions depending on the regulatory and licensing regime in the host country. This strategy has helped MTN expand its network coverage to many countries.

Although emerging markets share a number of similarities, they remain a very diverse group of countries, with a diverse population, local requirements, competition and so on. The management of the MTN Group understands that to succeed in these markets, they need to be responsive to their local environment. In 2017, MTN adopted a customer-focused strategy to respond proactively to its customers' needs. Aside from the need to further expand geographically, management has highlighted improvement in customer care as a key strategic objective. To achieve this, MTN plans to build more local customer call centres across its markets. It also plans to appoint a senior executive for managing customer care operations who reports directly to the president and CEO. To achieve its goals, MTN has reorganized its operating structure to enhance customer service to strengthen operational oversight, leadership, governance and regulatory compliance across its 22 markets.

B.5 Corporate structure and organization

To ensure robust operational oversight across its 22 operations, MTN organizes the management of its subsidiaries in groups: Southern, East Africa & Ghana (SEAGHA), West and Central Africa (WECA), the Middle East and North Africa (MENA), South Africa, and Nigeria (MTN Ghana, 2018b; see also Table B.3):

Table B.3 Group structure – revenue (2017)

Region	Percentage of Total Revenue of Rand133 Billion
South Africa	32.20
Nigeria	27.20
SEAGHA	15.10
WECA	15.90
MENA	9.60

Source: MTN Group (2017).

- **Southern, East Africa & Ghana**   MTN Group's Southern, East Africa & Ghana (SEAGHA) region encompasses seven operations: MTN Ghana, MTN Uganda, MTN Rwanda, MTN Zambia, MTN South Sudan, Mascom Botswana (joint venture) and MTN Swaziland (joint venture). SEAGHA represents 15 percent of MTN Group total revenue.
- **West and Central Africa**   West and Central Africa (WECA) sub-category consists of seven operations. They are MTN Cameroon, MTN Ivory Coast, MTN Benin, MTN Guinea Conakry, MTN Congo-Brazzaville, Lonestar Cell MTN in Liberia and MTN Guinea-Bissau. WECA represents 16 percent of MTN Group total revenue.
- **Middle East and North Africa**   MTN's Middle East and North Africa (MENA) region is made up of Irancell Telecommunication Services (Proprietary) Limited (in which the Group owns 49 percent), MTN Syria, MTN Sudan, MTN Yemen, MTN Afghanistan and MTN Cyprus.

The MTN office in Dubai hosts the Group's network technology and operations process group along with the region's functional units. MENA represents 10 percent of MTN Group total revenue.
- **South Africa and Nigeria**   South Africa and Nigeria represent 32 percent and 27 percent respectively.

Since the establishment of MTN International in 1996, MTN has distinguished between operational structure and ownership structure. Operating structure involves the day-to-day management of MTN while ownership structure is about the legal ownership of the subsidiaries. Concerning ownership, except the South African operation, all other MTN subsidiaries are organized under MTN International. MTN International has three subsidiaries: MTN Swaziland, MTN Dubai and MTN Mauritius. MTN Dubai is the legal parent company for all MTN subsidiaries in Guinea, Benin, Ghana, Guinea-Bissau, Liberia, Syria, Yemen, Cyprus, Sudan, and Afghanistan. MTN Dubai also controls the ownership of MTN international carrier services, the unit responsible for international roaming services. MTN Mauritius is the legal parent company for MTN in Cameroon, Uganda, Congo, Botswana, Nigeria, Rwanda, Côte d'Ivoire, Zambia, and Iran.

As shown in Figure B.1 and Table B.4, MTN operates in a diverse group of countries, with diverse institutional development – measured by the World Bank's Worldwide Governance Indicators (Kaufmann, Kraay and Mastruzzi, 2018). The Governance Indicators track and report on six broad dimensions of governance for over 200 countries and territories. Most of the MTN subsidiaries are in countries with more volatile institutions than its home country, that is, South Africa.

B.6   Unique local challenges

Below, we examine MTN operations in two of its most important markets, Ghana and Nigeria.

MTN in Ghana

MTN's history in Ghana can be traced to 1994 when a small company called Scancom Limited was awarded a licence to operate a global system for mobile communications (GSM) in Ghana. After two years of preparations, Scancom was acquired by the MTN Group. After the acquisition, MTN quickly expanded its network coverage across all major cities in Ghana. By 1999, MTN was the only cellular company with coverage in Accra, Tema, Kumasi, Obuasi, Takoradi, Bibiani, Tarkwa and Cape Coast. By 2006, MTN was the

46 • Global strategy and management

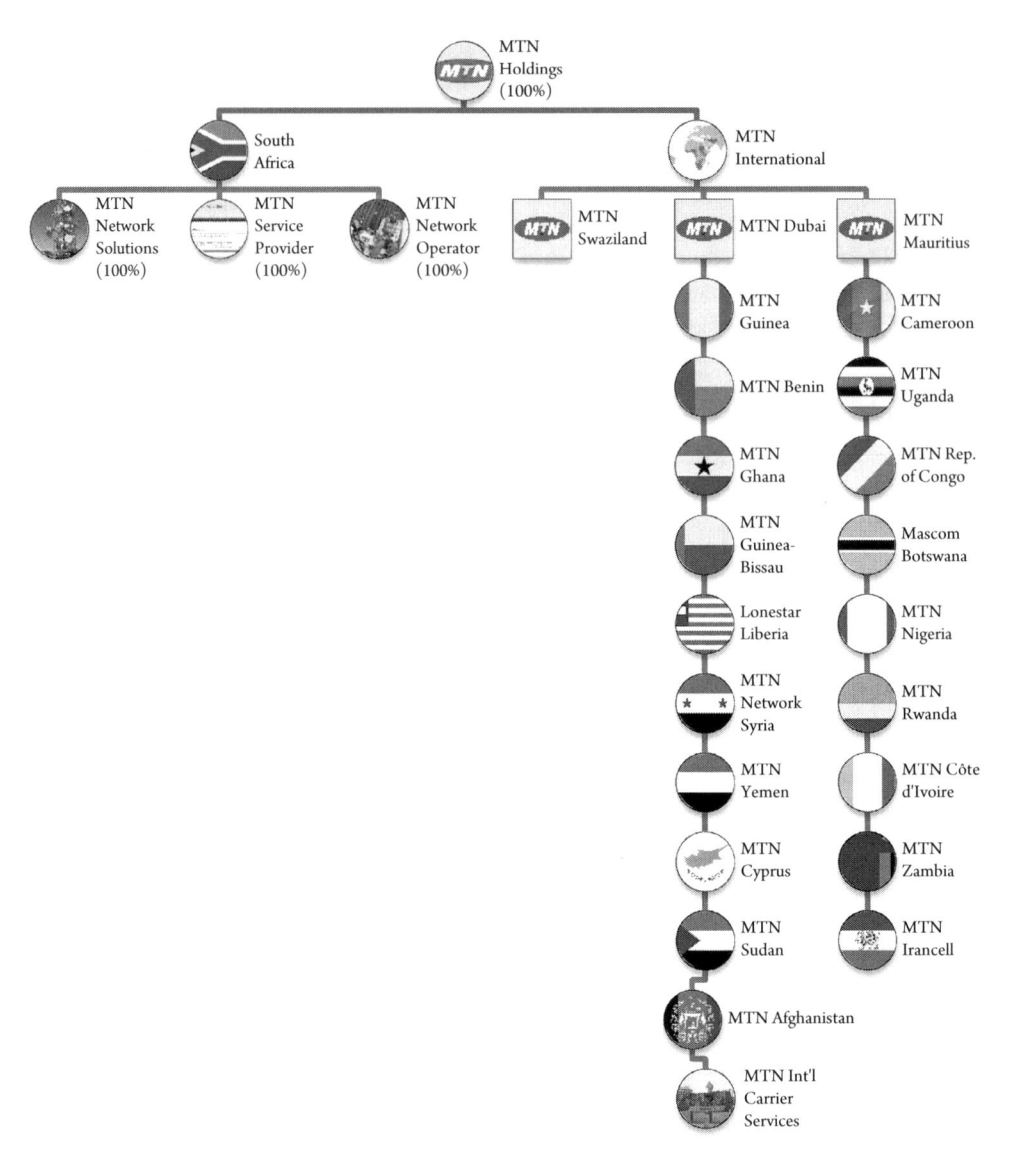

Source: MTN Group (2017).

Figure B.1 MTN Group organization structure

market leader in Ghana with a nationwide coverage and a record of eight million subscribers (Zaney, 2014). Before MTN entered into the Ghanaian market, there were two main telecommunication companies in the country: the state-run Ghana Telecom (which was later acquired by Vodafone), and Tigo, operated by Millicom International Cellular (Samuel, 2018). Today, MTN has overtaken both, and it is the number one carrier in Ghana with

Table B.4 Institutional development of MTN markets, 2016 (0 to 100, with higher values corresponding to better institutions)

	Voice & Accountability	Political Stability & Absence of Violence	Government Effectiveness	Regulatory Quality	Rule of Law	Control of Corruption	Corporate Tax Rate (%)
South Africa	68.0	42.4	64.9	62.0	58.2	60.1	28
Ghana	67.5	40.0	46.2	45.7	54.8	51.0	25
Côte d'Ivoire	36.5	16.2	26.9	39.9	28.4	33.7	25
Benin	63.1	48.6	33.2	30.3	29.3	36.5	30
Guinea	26.1	31.0	14.9	19.2	8.7	14.9	35
Republic of the Congo	17.2	25.2	12.0	10.6	14.4	9.6	34
Uganda	27.1	21.4	32.2	46.2	45.7	13.0	30
Rwanda	14.8	45.7	58.2	57.7	57.7	74.5	30
Zambia	35.5	52.9	27.4	32.7	43.3	42.3	35
Cameroon	21.7	14.8	22.1	23.1	15.4	11.1	33
Liberia	43.3	25.7	8.2	15.9	17.8	26.4	25
Guinea-Bissau	27.6	28.1	4.3	8.7	6.3	3.8	25
Syria	1.5	0.0	1.9	3.8	1.0	2.4	28
Sudan	3.4	2.4	7.2	4.8	9.1	1.4	35
Yemen	5.9	0.5	2.4	5.3	4.8	1.0	20
Afghanistan	21.2	1.0	9.6	7.2	3.8	3.4	20
Cyprus	82.8	65.7	78.4	82.7	75.5	77.9	12.5
Sudan	5.4	1.9	0.0	2.9	2.9	1.9	35
Botswana	59.1	90.0	70.7	70.2	70.7	80.3	22
Swaziland	9.4	29.5	33.7	29.3	40.9	39.4	27.5
Nigeria	36.0	6.7	12.5	18.3	13.9	13.5	30
Iran	11.3	20.5	45.7	9.1	26.0	26.0	25
Average for subsidiaries	29.3	27.0	26.1	26.8	27.2	26.9	27.7

Source: Kaufmann et al. (2018).

Source: GSMA (2018).

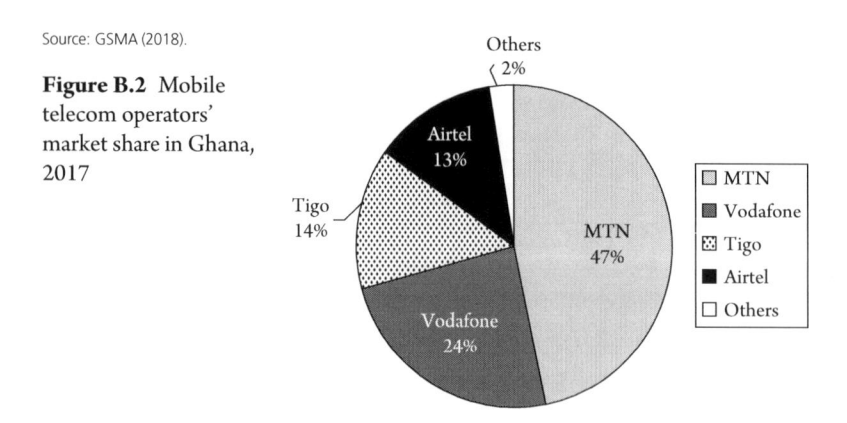

Figure B.2 Mobile telecom operators' market share in Ghana, 2017

- MTN 47%
- Vodafone 24%
- Tigo 14%
- Airtel 13%
- Others 2%

over 12 million subscribers, and 47 percent of the total subscriber market share (Figure B.2).

MTN Ghana's mission is to be a vehicle for Ghana's economic growth and development, helping to promote Ghana's strong development potential from the provision of world-class telecommunications products and services, through innovative and sustainable corporate social investment initiatives (MTN Ghana, 2018a). Since entering Ghana, MTN has invested over US$2.5 billion into its infrastructure and network in Ghana, making it the telecommunication company with the most extensive network coverage in the country covering all ten regions. To stay ahead of its competitors MTN has introduced exciting products and services including 3.5G technology, DStv Mobile, Seamless Roaming, Mobile Money, MTN e-Selfcare, MTN fonm@il, as well as BlackBerry phones and services into the Ghanaian market. Other unique services introduced in Ghana include Call Me Back, MTN Me2U, Voice SMS, and MTN Zone. Later this year, MTN plans to roll out additional unique services such as Pay4me, Phone Backup service, Life Insurance, Vehicle Tracking service, and audio conferencing, all tailored for the Ghanaian market (ibid.).

Aside from its core business, MTN Ghana has established relationships with governments and community groups for partnerships that are geared towards making a meaningful impact on the lives of people and communities in Ghana. It has established the MTN Foundation where a proportion (1 percent) of the Ghana operating unit's profit after tax is dedicated to undertaking corporate social investment (CSI) initiatives for local communities. The Foundation aims to achieve a broad community impact by supporting national development priorities around health, education and economic empowerment. So far, it has invested over $4 million in more than 83 projects across Ghana, impacting over 2.5 million Ghanaians (ibid.). MTN has also instituted '21 days of Y'ello Care' where staff may volunteer to serve their communities for 21 days in the month of June every year paid for by the company.

Through local CSI initiatives, MTN has built a strong loyal customer base and has won the admiration of many Ghanaians. In 2017, it was voted the best Customer Experience Company; CSR Company of the Year; Data Service Provider of the Year; Mobile Money Service of the Year; Mobile Operator of the Year; as well as the Telecoms Hall of Fame award (Citinews, 2018). Ghana is MTN's third largest market in Africa. In 2017, the CEO of MTN Ghana, Mr Ebenezer Asante, announced that MTN Ghana would launch a historic initial public offering (IPO) in Ghana in 2018 (Kazeem, 2017), making the Ghana subsidiary the only publicly traded subsidiary of the MTN Group.

MTN Nigeria – local fine leads to global annual loss

Nigeria is MTN's second largest market globally. MTN has 62.8 million subscribers and 43 percent of the total market share in Nigeria. MTN Nigeria represents 27 percent of the MTN Group's total revenue. However, Nigeria is one of the most difficult markets for MTN to operate in. For instance, a $5.2 billion fine by the local authorities led to MTN Group's first ever loss in 2016 (see Figure B.3).

Between 2009 and 2016, the militant group, Boko Haram, killed over 10 000 people in Nigeria and forced many young children to become soldiers

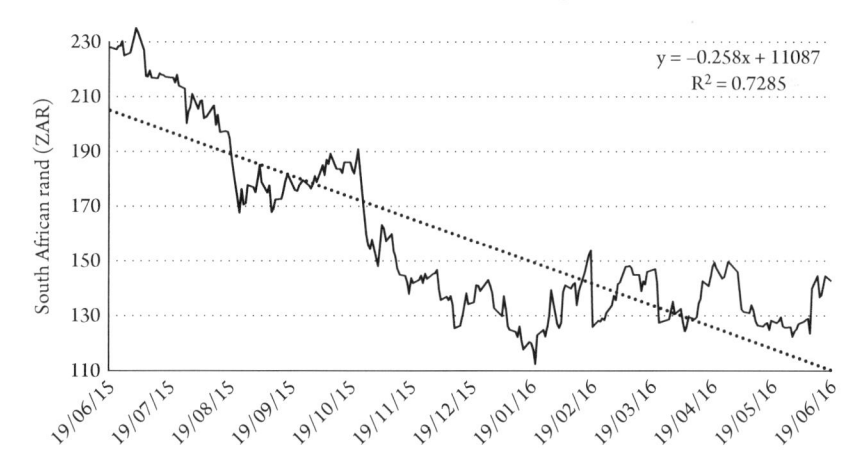

Source: Bloomberg (2018).

Figure B.3 MTN Group one-year share price June 2015–June 2016

(Hinshaw and Parkinson, 2016). To combat the spread of the militant group across the country, the federal government of Nigeria in 2011 compelled all telecommunication companies to register SIM cards purchased. This registration involved obtaining biometric information, identity documents, photographs, and other information on each subscriber. In addition to combating insurgencies, the government saw the registration of SIM cards as an opportunity to track and curb criminal activities carried out over mobile networks. Other African countries had introduced similar rules to help thwart fraudsters and even terrorist plots.

Telecommunication companies in Nigeria were required to disconnect already active SIM cards whose owners refuse to register their phone numbers within the set deadline. The CEOs of all telecommunication operators in Nigeria were in addition summoned to a meeting with heads of the main security agencies in the country. During the meeting, the CEOs were informed that the government saw the deactivation of unregistered SIM cards as a national security priority and that non-compliance could lead to a huge fine and/or a revocation of operating licences.

All the other telecommunication companies in Nigeria complied, except for MTN Nigeria. In response, the Nigerian government through the Nigerian Communications Commission (NCC) fined MTN $5.2 billion for failing to disconnect the unregistered SIM cards (Wexler, 2015). For each SIM card, MTN was fined 200 000 naira ($1 000), totalling 1.04 trillion naira or $5.2 billion. To put it in perspective, the $5.2 billion fine is equivalent to 37 percent of MTN's total revenue and more than double the Group's annual profits the year the fine was imposed. When Headquarters received the news of the massive fine, it quickly sent out a press statement to its stockholders, informing them that MTN was in discussions with the NCC to resolve the matter (ibid.). Analysts saw the Nigeria fine as a huge blow to MTN's operations and that it indicated a huge level of hostility from the government (England and Wallis, 2015), a sign of political risk. MTN lost about 25 percent of its market value (Shapshak, 2015).

MTN Group owns 79 percent of MTN Nigeria. The remaining 21 percent is held by other investors both local and foreign. The expansion into Nigeria helped propel MTN to become one of the world's top emerging market operators (*Financial Times*, 2018). However, in the past year, MTN has been experiencing a declining revenue per user in Nigeria, and it is facing increasing pressure from competitors (Figures B.4, B.5 and B.6).

MTN Group Limited – subsidiary management · 51

Source: Tshabalala (2015).

Figure B.4 MTN Nigeria's average revenue per user

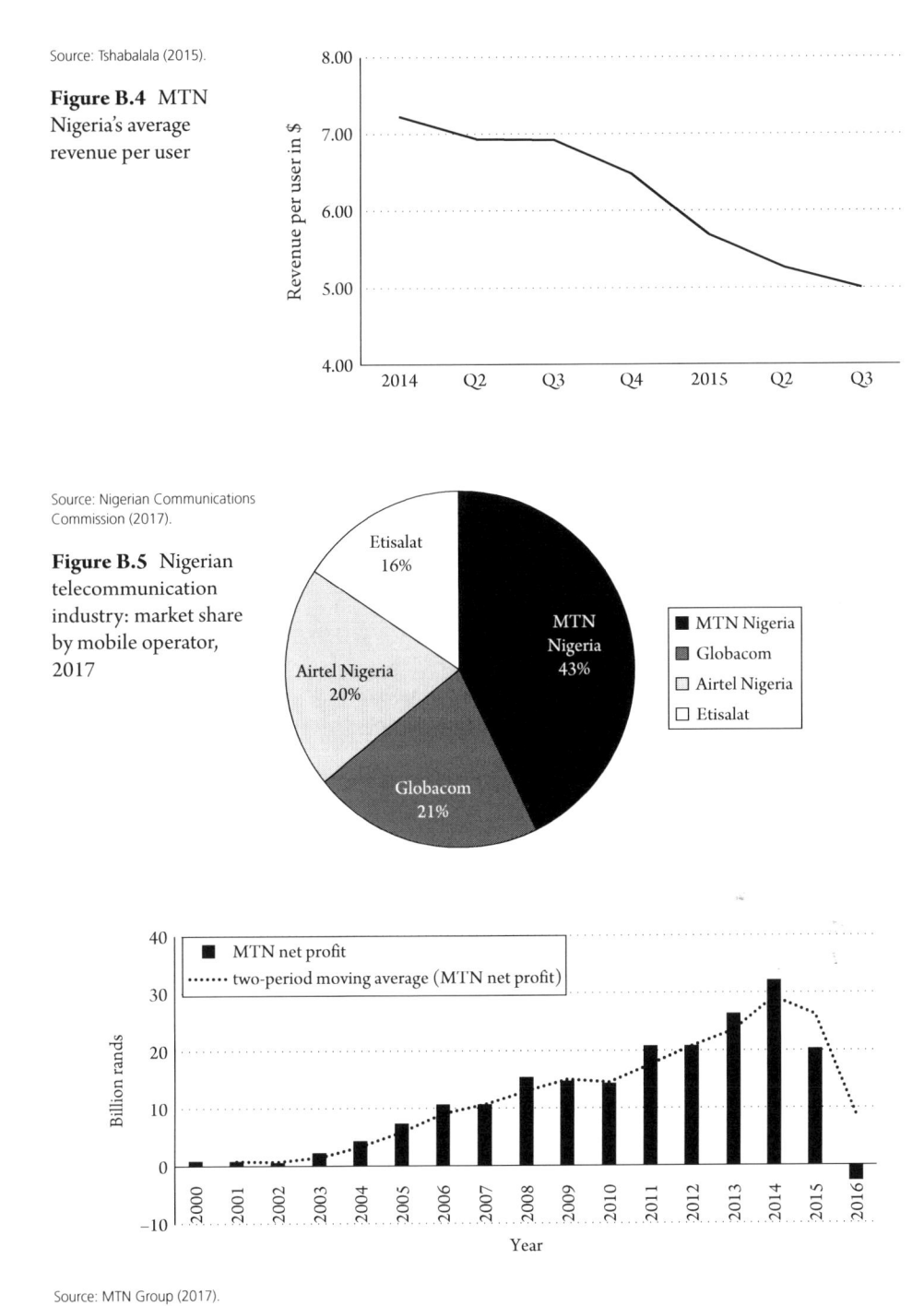

Source: Nigerian Communications Commission (2017).

Figure B.5 Nigerian telecommunication industry: market share by mobile operator, 2017

Source: MTN Group (2017).

Figure B.6 MTN Group recorded first ever loss after a fine of $5.2 billion by Nigeria

In 2018, MTN announced the sale of its Cyprus unit for $305 million to Monaco Telecom (MTN Group, 2018a), although Cyprus has been a very profitable business for MTN. MTN Group owned 100 per cent of the operation in Cyprus. Cyprus has a mobile penetration of 115 percent, with MTN as the market leader with a market share of approximately 42 percent.

B.7 About the telecommunication industry

The telecommunication industry is a fast-growing industry globally. Advances in fibre optics, wireless, and other signal-processing technologies have created new markets and made new network infrastructure far more affordable. Globally, cellular subscriptions have overtaken traditional telephony, with the number of unique mobile subscribers expected to reach 5.9 billion by 2025, equivalent to 71 percent of the world's population, driven by emerging markets countries, particularly India, China, Pakistan, Indonesia and Bangladesh, as well as Sub-Saharan Africa and Latin America (GSMA, 2018).

Mobile subscriber growth in emerging markets remains the fastest in the world. In the last ten-year period, the African market has enjoyed penetration growth and profitability far above the global averages (Boniecki et al., 2016). However, the growing market in emerging economies is facing a turning point. It is expected that growth will be maturing and could saturate in the medium term in some markets if coverage in rural areas does not increase. Voice still represents the lion's share of revenues by a large margin in emerging markets. However, it is expected to decline through competition. In addition, regulations such as special taxation on telecommunication services are expected to increase across emerging economies in the coming years, adding pressure to pricing and revenue. The telecommunications industry in emerging economies is a place for the brave (Deloitte, 2014). The market is far from homogeneous – it comprises 1.4 billion people living in countries as poor as Niger, with $441 GDP per capita, or as wealthy as Qatar, with $93 000 GDP per capita. Mobile penetration is as low as 25 percent in Ethiopia and as high as 180 percent in Kuwait. Companies that have entered these markets have enjoyed tremendous growth and profitability. The outlook for the industry is very strong, as consumer demand for data transmission, entertainment, applications, and services continues to grow exponentially. In the coming years, investors are still expected to invest capital in the sector. The key question for management of telecommunications companies in emerging economies is, how best to manage subsidiaries to take advantage of this boom to increase growth.

CASE DISCUSSION

1. What kind of motives presented in Chapter 2 best describe MTN's internationalization?
2. Using the CAGE framework from Chapter 1, identify key cultural, administrative, geographic and economic differences across MTN's markets.
3. Describe the managerial challenges that MTN faces as a foreign firm in Ghana and Nigeria.
4. Discuss the way in which MTN deals with this challenge.
5. How does the corporate structure and organization of MTN reflect its goals and challenges?

REFERENCES

BCG (2018), *Global Challengers: Digital Leapfrogs*, accessed 20 January 2019 at https://www.bcg.com/Images/BCG-Digital-Leapfrogs-May-2018-revised_tcm9-195110.pdf.

Bloomberg (2018), 'Company overview of MTN Ghana Ltd', accessed 11 February 2019 at https://www.bloomberg.com/research/stocks/private/people.asp?privcapId=25614046.

Boniecki, D., C. Marcati and W. Abou-Zahr et al. (2016), *Middle East and Africa Telecommunications Industry at Cliff's Edge: Time for Bold Decisions*, McKinsey & Company.

Citinews (2018), 'MTN Ghana receives 12 awards at 2018 GIITA', accessed 21 January 2019 at http://citibusinessnews.com/index.php/2018/07/04/mtn-ghana-receives-12-awards-at-2018-giita/.

Deloitte (2014), *The Future of Telecoms in Africa: The 'Blueprint for the Brave'*, accessed 21 January 2019 at https://www2.deloitte.com/content/dam/Deloitte/fpc/Documents/secteurs/technologies-medias-et-telecommunications/deloitte_the-future-of-telecoms-in-africa_2014.pdf.

England, A. and W. Wallis (2015), 'MTN shares plunge after $5.2bn fine by Nigerian regulators', *Financial Times*, 26 October 2015, accessed 21 January 2019 at https://www.ft.com/content/ef26f4b2-7bfd-11e5-98fb-5a6d4728f74e.

Financial Times (2018), 'MTN shares plunge after $5.2bn fine by Nigerian regulators', *The Financial Times*. Retrieved from https://www.ft.com/content/ef26f4b2-7bfd-11e5-98fb-5a6d4728f74e.

GSMA (2018), *The Mobile Economy 2018*, accessed 21 January 2019 at https://www.gsma.com/mobileeconomy/wp-content/uploads/2018/02/The-Mobile-Economy-Global-2018.pdf.

Hinshaw, D. and J. Parkinson (2016), 'The 10,000 kidnapped boys of Boko Haram', *The Wall Street Journal*, 12 August 2016, accessed 21 January 2019 at https://www.wsj.com/articles/the-kidnapped-boys-of-boko-haram-1471013062.

Kaufmann, D., A. Kraay and M. Mastruzzi (2018), 'The Worldwide Governance Indicators: Methodology and analytical issues', *Hague Journal on the Rule of Law*, 3(2), 220–46.

Kazeem, Y. (2017), 'Africa's largest telecoms operator is betting on mobile money for a historic Ghana IPO', *Quartz Africa*, 4 June 2018, accessed 21 January 2019 at https://qz.com/africa/1295791/mtn-ghana-ipo-uses-mobile-money/.

MTN Ghana (2018a), 'About us', accessed 21 January 2019 at https://www.mtn.com.gh/about-mtn/about-us.

MTN Ghana (2018b), *Initial Public Offering Prospectus*, accessed 20 January 2019 at https://drive.google.com/file/d/1uAgEzEmKbpP0GTFKqDXUL_3nAIu5Y_L/view.

MTN Group (2017), 'Integrated reports', accessed 11 February 2019 at https://www.mtn.com/en/investors/financial-reporting/integrated-reports/Pages/default.aspx.

MTN Group (2018a), 'MTN GROUP LIMITED – MTN sells 100% of MTN Cyprus to Monaco Telecom for approximately R4,1bn', press release, 16 July 2018, accessed 21 January 2019 at https://www.sharenet.co.za/v3/sens_display.php?tdate=20180716073000&seq=3&scode=MTN.

MTN Group (2018b), 'Our belief, vision, purpose and strategy', accessed 20 January 2019 at https://www.mtn.com/en/mtn-group/about-us/our-story/Pages/vision-and-strategy.aspx.

MTN Group (2018c), 'What we do', accessed 20 January 2019 at https://www.mtn.com/en/what-we-do/Pages/default.aspx.
Nigerian Communications Commission (2017), 'Subscriber statistics', accessed 11 February 2019 at https://www.ncc.gov.ng/stakeholder/statistics-reports/subscriber-data#quarterly-subscriber-operator-data.
Samuel, B. (2018), 'Telecom map: Ghana's telecom operators by market share', *Bandspur*, 1 May 2018, accessed 20 January 2019 at https://brandspurng.com/telecom-map-ghanas-telecom-operators-by-market-share/.
Shapshak, T. (2015), 'The curious case of MTN's whopping $5bn fine in Nigeria', *Forbes.com*, 4 December 2015, accessed 21 January 2019 at https://www.forbes.com/sites/tobyshapshak/2015/12/04/the-curious-case-of-mtns-whopping-5bn-fine-in-nigeria/#15548a814095.
Tshabalala, S. (2015), 'MTN Nigeria's declining average revenue per user (ARPU)', *Quartz*, accessed 11 February 2019 at https://www.theatlas.com/charts/Ny9qxEDWe.
Wexler, A. (2015), 'Nigeria reduces MTN Group fine by $1.8 billion', *The Wall Street Journal*, 3 December 2015, accessed 21 January 2019 at https://www.wsj.com/articles/nigeria-reduces-mtn-group-fine-by-1-8-billion-1449126497.
Zaney, G.D. (2014), 'MTN Ghana launches 20th anniversary celebrations', accessed 20 January 2019 at http://www.ghana.gov.gh/index.php/media-center/news/2733-mobile-telecommunications-network-mtn-ghana-launches-20th-anniversary-celebrations.

Case C

Gran Tierra Energy Inc. in Brazil*

Birgitte Grøgaard, Charlene D. Miller and Vivek Shah

IVEY | Publishing

C.1 Introduction

During the first week of June 2013, Dana Coffield, the CEO of Gran Tierra Energy Inc. (Gran Tierra), pored over the company's latest progress reports. He was preparing for the upcoming strategy session with senior executives and business unit presidents. Gran Tierra's investments in Peru looked promising, as recent exploration well tests indicated large oil reserves with significant production potential that could transform the company. However, the company's Brazil operations continued to encounter challenges. Coffield had high hopes when Gran Tierra entered Brazil in 2009 and thought that he and his team had carefully considered the risks. Given the increasingly positive developments in Peru, was dedicating Gran Tierra's resources to the Brazil operations still worth the risk? Could Gran Tierra turn the situation around or should Coffield recommend a divestment of the Brazilian assets?

C.2 Background of Gran Tierra

Gran Tierra, based in Calgary, Canada, was formed in 2005 by three senior-level executives – a geologist, an engineer and a finance expert – with proven track records in international upstream oil and gas who joined forces with three founding entrepreneurial directors with decades of broad international experience in the upstream and oil services industry. This executive team envisioned an international oil and gas company that could swiftly identify and capitalize on undervalued and overlooked opportunities in the energy industry.

The conception of the company came at a time when several South American countries were making political, legal and fiscal changes in their national frameworks to attract more foreign investment. The management team had extensive experience in this region and knew of several opportunities to access assets that were undervalued and underdeveloped. With the support of a small community of Calgary-based entrepreneurial investors, Gran Tierra was able to attract the initial seed funding that allowed the team to begin pursuing these opportunities. Two subsequent financings from the broader financial community in Canada, the United States and Europe allowed Gran Tierra to capture a small set of assets and operations in Argentina, and then move into Colombia and Peru over the next 18 months.

From 2007 onward, Gran Tierra strengthened the executive team through the addition of seasoned managers with extensive international experience, including Martin Eden as chief financial officer (CFO) in 2007, Shane O'Leary as chief operating officer (COO) in 2009 and David Hardy as vice-president of legal, secretary and general counsel in 2010. Eden was a Chartered Accountant with over 26 years of industry experience both in Canada and overseas. O'Leary was a professional engineer with an MBA degree and over 17 years of experience from various international positions in integrated oil and gas companies. O'Leary had previously worked as the vice-president of Encana's Brazil Business Unit. Hardy had over 20 years of experience in the legal profession, including extensive international experience in the oil and gas industry. Table C.1 gives an overview of the new executive team.

Within a few years, the executive team had established a solid South American platform. The company's oil exploration and subsequent development successes exceeded expectations and provided Gran Tierra with enough of a financial cushion to explore new, possibly riskier opportunities. This led Gran Tierra to enter Brazil in 2009, where the company saw significant opportunities.

C.3   Gran Tierra's strategy

Gran Tierra began as an international oil and gas company with an initial focus on select countries in South America. The aim was to build the company through a two-stage approach to growth. First, establish a base of production by selective acquisitions; and second, achieve future growth through exploration and the development of new fields. This business model would be replicated in other areas as opportunities arose.

Table C.1 The new executive team's global experience

	President and CEO (Dana Coffield)	CFO (Martin Eden)	VP Operations (Shane O'Leary)	VP Legal, Secretary and General Counsel (David Hardy)
Educational background	Geologist (PhD)	Economics Business administration (MBA)	Chemical engineering Business administration (MBA)	Juris Doctor degree
Range of previous experience (list not exhaustive)	Business development Exploration & development operations Commercial evaluations Government and partner relations Planning and budgeting Environment/health/safety Security Operations management	Accounting Finance Auditing Business analysis Treasurer Corporate acquisitions	Reservoir engineering Project management Business development and international new ventures Operations management Government and partner relations	General legal services Legal and commercial negotiations Regulatory services Corporate relations Legal counsel for new ventures, dispositions and operations
Experience from geographical areas	Africa Asia Middle East South America North America	Africa Asia Europe Middle East North America	Africa Europe Middle East North America South America The Caspian	Africa Australia North America South America
Examples of organizations previously worked for	Encana ARCO International	Nexen Coopers & Lybrand Several junior companies	Encana BP/Amoco First Calgary Petroleums	Encana Private practice

Source: Gran Tierra Energy Inc., www.grantierra.com, accessed September 2014.

To maximize the chance of success and return on investment, the team planned to pursue opportunities in countries with:

- proven petroleum/hydrocarbon systems;
- attractive fiscal terms (e.g., for royalties and taxation);
- stable legal systems;
- deal flow (i.e., the ability to acquire assets and/or enter into partnerships);
- the ability to become the operator; and
- necessary infrastructure in place (e.g., pipelines and roads).

Gran Tierra recognized that laws and legal systems might change, but tried to focus on countries with some measure of stability and avoid countries with a higher potential for arbitrary changes. A key aspect of Gran Tierra's business plan was positioning – being in the right place at the right time with the right resources. This involved:

- entering countries with assets that Gran Tierra saw as being previously ignored or undervalued and that welcomed foreign investment, as evidenced by the offer of attractive fiscal terms;
- building a diverse portfolio of drilling opportunities, including exploration, development and production assets;
- engaging qualified and experienced professionals locally;
- establishing an effective local presence; and
- assessing and acting upon opportunities expeditiously.

This approach provided a balanced portfolio that mixed a lower-risk predictable production base and cash flow with higher-risk exploration that could provide better rewards and growth opportunities. Gran Tierra did not invest directly in research and development. Rather, the company made use of existing technologies and processes that were available 'off the shelf'. The oil and gas industry was highly competitive. Competitors ranged from local companies, to smaller international independent companies such as Pacific Rubiales, to major international oil and gas companies such as BP and ConocoPhillips. The industry players primarily competed to access acreage licences for land to explore and develop, secure contracts with service companies to conduct work, and attract highly qualified personnel. Please see Box C.1 for a brief overview of the different market players in the international oil and gas industry.

Gran Tierra also had a unique approach in terms of how the organization established a presence in local jurisdictions. The executive team made a point of hiring as many local staff as possible, and only using expatriates

Box C.1

BACKGROUND ON THE INTERNATIONAL OIL AND GAS INDUSTRY

The oil and gas industry (also referred to simply as the energy industry) is inherently uncertain. The industry operates in cycles, where profitability can be extremely high for periods of time – even years – yet it must be understood that large profit margins tend not to last. A long-term approach to investment in the industry is essential, where producers cannot control the price of the commodity that they extract and sell, and can only control their own cost efficiency with the hopes of greater returns despite unpredictable fluctuating energy prices on the global market. Energy firms primarily compete on access to quality land, resources and finances, the ability to develop strong relationships with firms with complementary resources such as firms in the service industry (e.g., technology and processes), and attracting qualified personnel.

Oil and gas companies track reserve replacement as one of their key measures of success for long-term sustainable operations – that is, the number of reserves added through exploration every year that replace the current year's production to sustain a company's current production levels with its booked reserves.[a] Reserve replacement can be achieved through organic growth (exploration) or inorganic growth (acquisition). The price of oil depends on its quality characteristics such as density and sulphur content. Oil that is characterized as sweet (low sulphur content) and light (higher API gravity, or lower density) typically trades at a higher price than sour and heavy oil.[b]

According to industry standards, reserves are categorized as proved, probable and possible. Proved reserves can with reasonable certainty be produced from a known reservoir at a given date based on thorough analysis of geoscience, engineering and economic data. The economic viability and quantities of probable reserves are less certain and are just as likely not to be recovered, but there should be at least a 50 per cent probability that the quantities recovered will equal or exceed estimates. Possible reserves are even less certain to be recovered. For reserves to be classified as possible, there should be at least a 10 per cent probability that these reserves will equal or exceed estimates. Industry actors communicate this categorization as:

1P = total proved reserves
2P = total proved plus probable reserves
3P = total proved plus probable plus possible reserves

There were a variety of national and international players competing for resources. These included the following:

- National oil companies (NOCs) are partially or fully owned by a national government, usually formed to manage the country's hydrocarbon resources. NOCs can have many different governance forms. Some are extended arms of a government while others are run similarly to privately held organizations. Several NOCs have portions of their

➡

ownership listed on stock exchanges (e.g., Gazprom, Petrobras and Statoil[c]) and function as any other publicly traded organization. Other NOCs are 100 per cent state-owned but are nevertheless managed similarly to firms with private ownership (e.g., Petronas). Some NOCs operate primarily in their home countries (e.g., the National Iranian Oil Company and PEMEX), while others have extensive global operations (e.g., Petrobras and Statoil).
- Integrated oil and gas companies (IOCs) compete internationally in upstream, midstream, downstream and even petrochemicals. IOC usually refers to large oil and gas companies such as Chevron, ConocoPhillips, ExxonMobil, Shell and Total. These companies often partner with NOCs in NOCs' home countries. IOCs are sometimes also referred to as oil majors.
- Super majors: the largest IOCs/oil majors (e.g., BP, Chevron, ConocoPhillips, ExxonMobil, Shell and Total).
- Independents: smaller firms that typically focus on one or a few parts of the values chain (such as exploration and production). Independent oil and gas firms come in various sizes. Firms with production under 10 000 boe/day[d] are often referred to as junior companies.

The combination of interests of the above players – including national interests and financial accountability to private investors – creates a highly complex, competitive environment. By 2013, more than 90 per cent of the world's resources was controlled by NOCs; however, this does not mean that they necessarily confined themselves to operations in their home countries. NOCs were growing increasingly large and global, creating issues of governance and ownership that were blurring the distinction between IOCs and NOCs. CNOOC's (the Chinese National Offshore Oil Corporation) acquisition of Nexen (Canadian IOC) in 2012, exemplified this complexity.

The activities in which these companies engage vary across the value chain, known as upstream (exploration and production), midstream (transportation and trading) and downstream (refining and marketing). Firms may engage in all these activities (particularly the super majors and the IOCs) or can specialize in any one component of these activities. There are also firms in supporting industries (often referred to as service companies) that specialize in delivering specific activities and services such as well services, rigs and so on. Within the past 15 to 20 years, access to resources had become increasingly difficult, with new technologies continuously evolving to try to extract every last drop from existing wells, often triggering debate about environmental and social impacts and liabilities.

Many investments in the energy industry are long term and capital intensive, with high uncertainty around their economic viability. Although investment levels often fluctuate with changes in oil and gas prices, many capital investments require patience and a willingness to take on risk for an extended period of time before an income stream is realized. The ability and willingness to take risk varies among the market actors. Smaller companies in particular may be more vulnerable to high levels of risk than NOCs and IOCs.

Notes:
a   Inkpen, A. and M.H. Moffett (2011), *The Global Oil & Gas Industry: Management, Strategy & Finance*, Tulsa, OK: PennWell Corp.
b   U.S. Energy Information Administration (2012), 'Crude oils have different quality characteristics', 16 July, accessed 2 September 2014 at www.eia.gov/todayinenergy/detail.cfm?id=7110.
c   Statoil's company name was changed to Equinor on 15 May, 2018.
d   Barrels of oil equivalents per day.

Source: Inkpen, A. and M.H. Moffett (2011), *The Global Oil & Gas Industry: Management, Strategy & Finance*, Tulsa, OK: PennWell Corp.

for limited or short-term technical assignments to fill critical gaps when local talent was unavailable. The local business units took ownership of the day-to-day operations of the company, while staff in the Calgary office were responsible for the overall strategy, business development, technical support, consolidating of operating results, and reporting to stock exchange regulators and shareholders (Gran Tierra was listed on both the Canadian TSX and American NYSE stock exchanges). Gran Tierra also made significant community investments related to health, education and infrastructure. Local projects that benefitted communities included maintaining roads and drainage, sponsoring agriculture and fishery initiatives, sponsoring medical and dental brigades,[1] sponsoring education initiatives by providing school materials and scholarships, and many other projects specific to the needs of the local communities near each operation.

C.4 Gran Tierra's portfolio

When the founders had raised an initial $2 million[2] in seed money from private investors, the newly formed team targeted Colombia, Peru and Argentina, and initially identified Argentinian assets with some production to provide the company with enough cash flow to cover expenses and fund further growth. Rafael Orunesu, an Argentine national, was hired as country manager. He had over 20 years of experience in the oil and gas sector in Argentina and the greater region, including the Peruvian Amazon jungle. Orunesu was a trained geologist, had strong business relationships and spoke Spanish, which facilitated Gran Tierra's initial movement into the region. He played a pivotal role in developing the local office in Buenos Aires to manage all functions necessary to support local operations, as well as the greater region. This became the basic model for Gran Tierra's other business units.

Within one year of establishing the Argentine base, Gran Tierra had purchased interests in eight producing and non-producing properties in Argentina's Noroeste basin. These initial properties were profitable enough to provide cash flow and cover overheads in the company's early stages and effectively establish Argentina as Gran Tierra's South American base with a trusted, knowledgeable team in place.

Despite the good fit with Gran Tierra's decision criteria upon market entry, operations in Argentina had their challenges. The country was prone to political and economic instability, with the government of Argentina showing a tendency to change the regulatory and commercial rules more frequently than expected. There were also price caps on oil that brought less return on investment. Although the seed money had helped Gran Tierra solidify its position in Argentina, the long-term potential for Gran Tierra to grow in the Argentine market did not look particularly lucrative. The team agreed that it was time to continue looking at Colombia and Peru for growth.

After having raised an additional $90 million from US, Canadian and European investment markets in 2005–06, the team looked seriously at Colombia for further expansion. Under President Álvaro Uribe's reforms, Colombia had become one of the best places for a small foreign exploration and production company to do business. The legal and fiscal regimes were attractive and stable, and the country had a solid history of oil and gas production, with an immense amount of untapped resources. The government licensed large areas of the country for exploration and offered tax breaks to investors. The reforms had opened competition between foreign companies and the state-owned enterprise (SOE) Ecopetrol. These changes were also coupled with improvements in national security. Social conflicts and associated high security risks had limited or stalled the industry during the past 40 years with disruptions in operations due to attacks on plants, pipelines and personnel. Local communities had not yet visibly benefitted from the many years of natural resource extraction in Colombia, an inequality that Colombian terrorist groups had previously played on. Coffield and his team wanted to create value for all stakeholders by maintaining a strong local presence, training personnel and contributing to the development of local communities. The executive team saw an opportunity for entry and seized it through the acquisition of Argosy Energy International, a company that had long existed but had not fully realized its potential because of historical conflicts in the region.

Gran Tierra had extraordinary success and discovered the largest and second-largest light oil fields in Colombia in 20 years. As the rest of the world began to catch up to the fact that Colombia had become a more attractive country in which to invest, competition and prices increased for land and concessions. In parallel, the attractiveness of available land decreased over time, as the early entrants (including Gran Tierra) had captured the best acreage. Access to new quality assets to continue Gran Tierra's growth trajectory became increasingly difficult, making it much more difficult for the company to continue growing. This pushed Gran Tierra to once again look at new countries for further growth.

In 2006, Gran Tierra acquired two exploration blocks in the Marañon basin in Northern Peru. Peru's geology in this area was similar to Colombia's, but with greater prospects, and seemed to be the most natural move for the company. The Peruvian operations were managed by the Argentinian office until a local country manager was hired in 2011 as a result of a local acquisition.

Located in the Amazon, the Marañon basin in Peru was an extremely environmentally sensitive and relatively remote and unexplored area that was home to indigenous populations. This made it challenging to obtain permits for oil and gas exploration and production activities. If Gran Tierra had a successful discovery, the upside potential for such a small company could be transformational. Peru also had extremely good fiscal terms that could ultimately pay off when a discovery was made, but due to the extensive environmental risk and consequent regulation, the executive team knew it could take years to reap the gains.

Each of the markets Gran Tierra had entered in its early years had been beneficial to the company's growth in different ways. Argentina was an effective base for smaller-scale production and for Gran Tierra to initially use as its main operating base in South America. The company had been successful in Colombia, which had been transformational in terms of finding reserves, growing production quickly and generating cash flow to fund future growth opportunities. The Colombian market was now of interest to SOEs, majors and independents alike, and the executive team realized that the quick growth that Gran Tierra had previously experienced in Colombia could not be easily repeated due to increased competition for lower-quality land. Peru had vast, untapped oil and gas reserves, but growth there was sure to be slow because of the environmental sensitivities and lengthy permit process. See Table C.2 for a summary of Gran Tierra's initial markets.

The executive team set out again to explore other potential avenues for Gran Tierra's future growth. If Gran Tierra wanted to continue to strengthen its South American platform, the executive team saw few countries left that would meet the criteria: the political climates in Bolivia, Ecuador and Venezuela were not welcoming to a public energy company due to harsh fiscal terms and a lack of contract sanctity, and Chile simply did not have the potential hydrocarbon resources. This left only Brazil, which, based on the team's previous experience in the region, had great potential in terms of untapped hydrocarbon resources.

C.5 The decision to enter Brazil

Brazil offered several opportunities for farm-ins,[3] bid rounds and M&A transactions. Although Petrobras, a Brazilian SOE, had historically dominated the Brazilian oil and gas industry, regulatory changes in the mid-1990s opened the Brazilian market to competition. As a result, foreign companies were increasingly entering Brazil. While there were more than 20 proven basins in the country, other opportunities both onshore and offshore seemed

Table C.2 Gran Tierra's initial markets

	Argentina	Colombia	Peru
Initial market entry	2005	2006	2006
Country characteristics	Access to small assets with limited funds. Assets with production	Considered one of the best countries for small businesses, as the government encouraged foreign direct investment Long history of oil and gas, but also an immense amount of untapped resources due to stalled activity from 40 years of civil strife Large areas for exploration & production were licensed Tax breaks, new attractive fiscal terms Improvements in national security	Long-term potential in relatively unexplored areas Potential exploration success could be transformational for smaller companies The region had previously suffered from environmental damage and a lack of consideration for indigenous issues Good fiscal conditions
Entry/operating mode	Initial participation through joint ventures operated by other companies Acquired individual assets and set up a local organization to manage these assets	Acquired a fully operational local organization (18 years since initially established) with assets in three geographical regions Later (2008) also acquired a joint venture partner, thereby increasing assets in existing and new areas	Signed licences for two exploration blocks Acquired working interests in five additional blocks after relinquishing the initial two blocks
Portfolio characteristics	Cash flow to cover expenses and provide opportunity to grow	Five producing properties operated by Gran Tierra provided cash flow Upside potential in exploration assets	Highly uncertain but lucrative long-term potential ('elephant hunting')
Operational statistics by year-end 2012	11 blocks 0.6 million net acres (net after royalties, NAR) Production level at 3474 barrels of oil equivalent per day (boe/day) NAR	23 blocks 3.7 million acres (NAR) Production level at 13 146 boe/day NAR	5 blocks 6.4 million acres (NAR) No production by year-end 2012

	Argentina	Colombia	Peru
Country manager	Native Argentinian with over 20 years of experience from oil and gas sector in Argentina and Peru Geologist, operations Strong local business relationships	Foreign national with extensive international industry experience in many geographical regions (including headquarters experience from integrated oil and gas companies) Geologist	Initially managed from Argentina Local country manager position established in 2011 after an acquisition (the new country manager had held the same position in the acquired company since 2005) Peruvian national with over 30 years of industry experience Geologist with a management degree
Characteristics of local organization	The local organization had the functions necessary to support local operations Recruited local managers for operations, geologists, finance and administration	Included 17 office staff and 68 field staff when acquired by Gran Tierra Maintaining a strong local presence was important	The Argentina and Calgary employees focused on strategic planning, as well as support and quality control of the seismic and technical work conducted in Peru Transitioning to more local Peru talent
Experiences after the initial entry into the country	Politically and economically unstable The Argentinian government had shown a tendency to change the fiscal rules frequently and negatively The ability to do business there was notoriously unpredictable Price caps on the price of oil	Security threat from revolutionary paramilitary groups such as FARC (Revolutionary Armed Forces of Colombia) and ELN (National Liberation Army) The acquired company had experienced attacks on facilities and pipelines The price of assets rising Increased competition Increasingly difficult to grow further in Colombia due to increasingly limited subsurface potential	The state-owned enterprise Perupetro dominated the industry Environmentally sensitive area – challenging to obtain permits Locals less skilled and knowledgeable about oil and gas production
Situational analysis in June 2013	The long-term growth potential was uncertain due to political risk		Recent well tests seemed promising with the potential for exponential growth in reserves (estimated 2P over 55 000 million boe NAR)

Source: Gran Tierra Energy Inc. annual reports 2005–13.

underdeveloped. The country had a stable legal system with established regulatory jurisdictions and attractive fiscal terms. In contrast to Colombia, the operating environment was also much safer. Coffield saw potential for leveraging Gran Tierra's capabilities generally, and O'Leary's experience specifically, in this new territory.

Soon thereafter, Gran Tierra expanded its geographical focus and opened a business development office in Rio de Janeiro, Brazil, in September 2009. Julio Moreira, a local with over 25 years of experience working for international oil and gas companies, was hired as president of the Brazilian business unit. In his previous position as country manager for Encana in Brazil, Moreira had already developed a strong relationship with O'Leary. A dedicated technical team with Brazil experience was also established in Calgary to support the local efforts to evaluate opportunities in Brazil.

C.6 The Brazilian assets

In August 2010, as a first step to establishing Brazilian operations, Gran Tierra acquired a 70 per cent interest in four onshore blocks in the Recôncavo basin. The Recôncavo basin was a mature area with conventional production that was slowly declining. An advantage to Gran Tierra was that there was already substantial infrastructure in the area. The blocks provided Gran Tierra with production as well as exploration upsides that could serve as a strong initial platform for further expansion in Brazil. There was also the potential to introduce North American technology such as horizontal drilling and multi-stage fracturing stimulation that was not used onshore in Brazil. There were strong similarities between the Recôncavo basin and basins in North America such as Bakken and Eagle Ford,[4] where activities were booming as a result of the implementation of these technologies. While Gran Tierra did not have the technical expertise in-house to perform these tasks, it expected these services could be transferred to the Brazil market through contracts with service companies.

The team's strategy was to reverse declining production by exploiting new technology. By generating increased activity for existing fields, it would also contribute to the creation of new jobs in local communities. However, its success ultimately relied on Petrobras granting it access to infrastructure and marketing the final products. This was not seen as a major obstacle, since the team assumed that Petrobras would also find these opportunities attractive, especially when the economy was still recovering from the 2008 financial crash and the downturn that the industry had experienced due to the decline in the average price of crude oil in 2008–09.

In September 2011, Gran Tierra had two offshore farm-in opportunities in shallow water – partnering with the Norwegian SOE Statoil and Petrobras. Statoil was the operator of one agreement, while Petrobras was the operator of another. These were high-risk opportunities for Gran Tierra, with an estimated one-in-six chance of success. But if successful, the company would be transformed due to the huge potential of the prospects. Despite the high risk, these opportunities were very attractive, given that Brazilian offshore resources were considered to be among the most promising areas globally. Although shallow water operations were comparable to areas where the executive team had similar offshore experience, Gran Tierra's current portfolio was entirely onshore and the company relied on the extensive experience of the two much larger integrated (and partly state-owned) oil and gas companies. Gran Tierra entered the offshore agreements as a non-operating partner with modest 10 per cent and 15 per cent working interests, respectively, due to the high costs expected from offshore operations.

C.7 The Brazilian experience

The challenges in Brazil became increasingly evident after the initial investments and onshore operations moved slower than anticipated. The team began to sense that it had not fully taken into account the uncertainty of Petrobras's priorities. The management team had known that Brazil was considered very relationship based in its approach to doing business, but Gran Tierra saw its ability to develop and manage business relationships as one of its main strengths as a company. It consequently had not anticipated the slow progress in convincing Petrobras of the benefits of applying new technology. Gran Tierra's strategy in Brazil depended on its ability to partner with other firms to exploit new technologies. Since horizontal drilling and multi-stage fracture stimulation were not used onshore in Brazil, the service providers lacked the 'critical mass' to develop strong expertise, and the lack of scale led to high costs. As a result, the desired services were offered at lower quality and higher prices than the same services in North America, and operations took longer to execute and ultimately had poorer results.

The reality of these challenges led the management team to question how great a commitment it was prepared to make in Brazil. Its own uncertainty about the scale and scope of activities made it difficult to convince service companies from North America with the necessary technical expertise to get involved in potentially short-term, highly cost-intensive projects in Brazil with little certainty of a payoff.

Furthermore, Gran Tierra's high-risk offshore activities were not as successful as initially hoped. By the end of 2011, Statoil had drilled an unsuccessful offshore well, which was disappointing but not altogether unexpected. The progress on the second offshore well, operated by Petrobras, was delayed indefinitely. These activities were capital intensive with high technical risk and, as a minor player, Gran Tierra was only able to participate as a passive investor in these risky ventures.

C.8 Moving forward

Only a few years ago, Coffield had looked to Brazil as one of the most promising markets for new opportunities. He had been prepared to allocate the necessary resources to ensure that Brazil operations could continue to grow. The slow progress onshore and disappointing results offshore in past years made him less certain. While Gran Tierra had anticipated challenges in Brazil, Coffield wondered if the management team had underestimated the impact these would have on the progress and success rate of activities. With its early successes, Gran Tierra had enjoyed the flexibility of funding its growth from its operations without the need to approach investors for additional funds. This had also required a fiscally conservative approach where Gran Tierra continuously assessed its current operations and growth prospects to determine if they aligned with the company's strategy and desire to maintain and develop a robust portfolio of assets. See Tables C.3 and C.4 for an overview of Gran Tierra's financial situation.

Coffield continued to read through the progress reports from May 2013. The organization had grown exponentially over the past years. By the end of 2012, Gran Tierra's portfolio had grown to 44 blocks with 40.6 million boe[5] total proved reserves net after royalties (NAR), and production levels had grown to over 17 000 boe/day NAR,[6] as illustrated in Figures C.1–C.3. The organization now employed a total of 485 people full time, as illustrated in Figure C.4. Things were starting to look up in several markets and Coffield felt the need to prioritize the allocation of resources more clearly. While opportunities in Peru and Brazil potentially represented more transformational changes for the growth of the company, there were also undeveloped potential reserves and exploration opportunities in Colombia that needed to be considered. Argentine reserves were also becoming more attractive due to an ease of the existing price cap on oil.

A conversation Coffield had with O'Leary and Eden earlier during the day indicated that the capital allocation budget needed revisiting (an overview of Gran Tierra's capital expenditures can be found in Table C.5). Gran Tierra

Table C.3 Key financials from Gran Tierra's balance sheet (thousands of US$)

	Year ended 31 December, US$ (000)				
	2012	2011	2010	2009	2008
Assets					
Total current assets	413 853	457 929	418 148	320 757	195 045
Oil and gas properties	1 196 661	1 036 850	721 157	709 568	765 050
Other property plant and equipment	8 765	7 992	5 867	3 175	2 502
Total property plant and equipment (including oil and gas properties)	1 205 426	1 044 842	727 024	712 743	767 552
Total other long-term assets	113 596	124 009	104 082	110 308	110 028
Total assets	1 732 875	1 626 780	1 249 254	1 143 808	1 072 625
Liabilities and shareholders' equity					
Total current liabilities	191 385	244 829	152 313	105 596	62 238
Total long-term liabilities	250 059	207 633	210 075	221 786	218 461
Total shareholders' equity	1 291 431	1 174 318	886 866	816 426	791 926
Total liabilities and shareholders' equity	1 732 875	1 626 780	1 249 254	1 143 808	1 072 625

Source: Gran Tierra Energy Inc. annual reports 2008–13.

had revised its original capital expenditure budget for 2013 from $363 million to $424 million due to the scale of the successful exploration success in Peru (see Table C.6). Despite this increase, Gran Tierra still expected to fund its capital budget through cash on hand, cash flows from current operations and the occasional use of credit if required. In the revised 2013 capital budget, a total of $218 million was allocated for drilling, $73 million for facilities, equipment and pipelines, $130 million for geological and geophysical expenditures and $3 million for corporate activities. The planned drilling activities were split roughly as 50 per cent for development and appraisal drilling and 50 per cent for exploration drilling.[7]

A successful bid round in Brazil in May 2013 had opened the potential for Gran Tierra to explore familiar areas in the Recôncavo basin, where the company had so far successfully developed the Tiê conventional oil discovery. The additional three blocks (20 658 gross acres of land) acquired in the bid round, adjacent to the existing acreage, would allow Gran Tierra to leverage its growing knowledge of this basin. As a result of recent bid rounds, other junior companies were increasingly entering the Brazilian market, which could potentially impact the availability, quality and price of the service

Table C.4 Key financials from Gran Tierra's consolidated statements of cash flows (thousands of US$)

	Year ended 31 December, US$ (000)				
	2012	2011	2010	2009	2008
Operating activities					
Net income	99 659	126 917	37 172	13 941	23 495
Net cash provided by operating activities	156 319	353 752	203 782	165 453	109 737
Investing activities					
Net cash provided by (used in) investing activities	(299 720)	(308 515)	(143 925)	(76 356)	27 141
Financing activities					
Net cash provided by financing activities	4 340	(48 980)	24 785	4 935	21 687
Net increase (decrease) in cash and cash equivalents	(139 061)	(3 743)	84 642	94 032	158 565
Cash and cash equivalents, end of year	216 624	351 685	355 428	270 786	176 754
Total liabilities and shareholders' equity	1 732 875	1 626 780	1 249 254	1 143 808	1 072 625

Source: Gran Tierra Energy Inc. annual reports 2008–13.

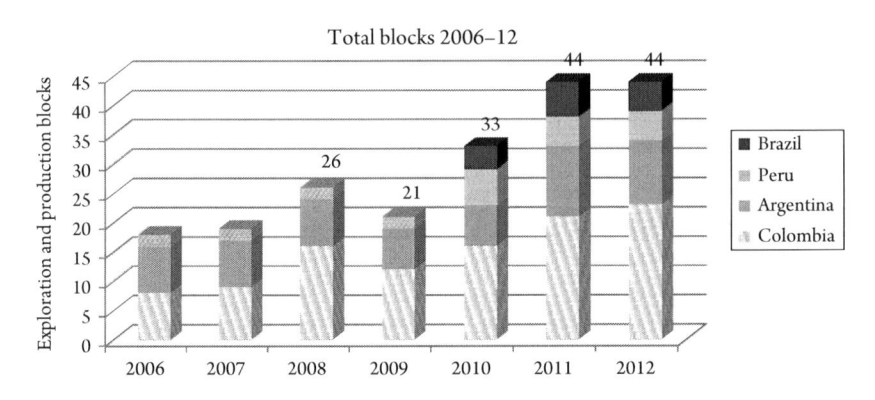

Source: Gran Tierra Energy Inc. annual reports 2006–13.

Figure C.1 Gran Tierra's portfolio of assets

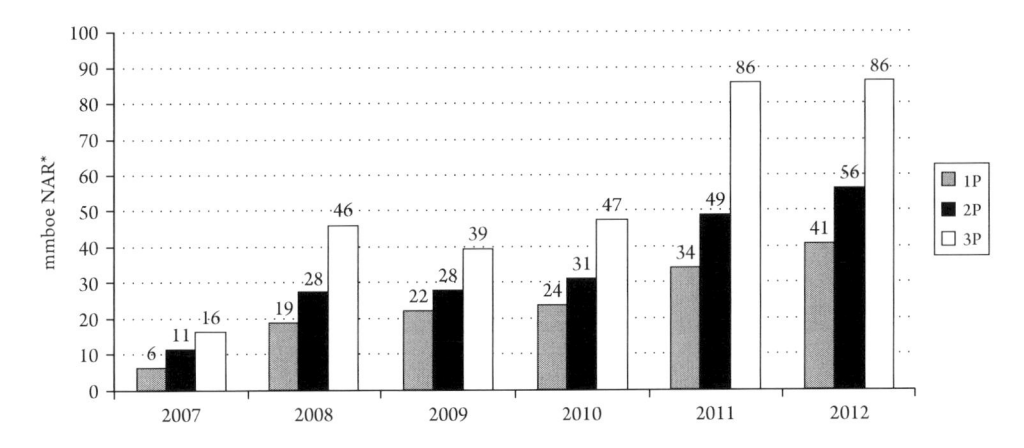

Note: * Million barrels of oil equivalents NAR (net after royalties).
Source: Gran Tierra Energy Inc. annual reports 2007–13.

Figure C.2 Gran Tierra's total reserves, 2007–12

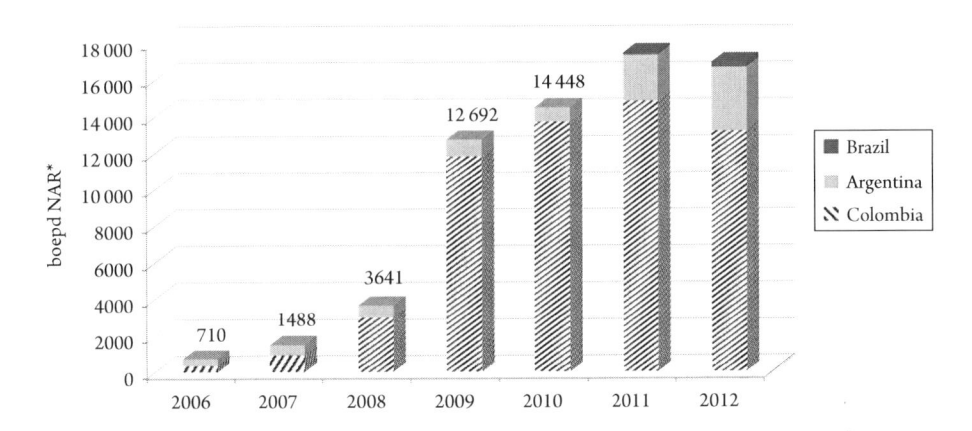

Note: *Barrels of oil equivalents per day NAR (net after royalties).
Source: Gran Tierra Energy Inc. annual reports 2007–13.

Figure C.3 Gran Tierra's average daily production, 2006–12

industry. The Brazilian government was also pleased to see its efforts to attract foreign direct investment were paying off.

However, preliminary results from Peru put additional pressures on Gran Tierra's resource allocation. Gran Tierra currently held operatorship and 100 per cent working interests in five blocks in Peru. Of these, the main focus was on the Bretaña oil discovery, which showed enormous potential. The results from recent tests were beyond expectations and indicated significant resources of high-quality oil (i.e., low in sulphur and density). Although there

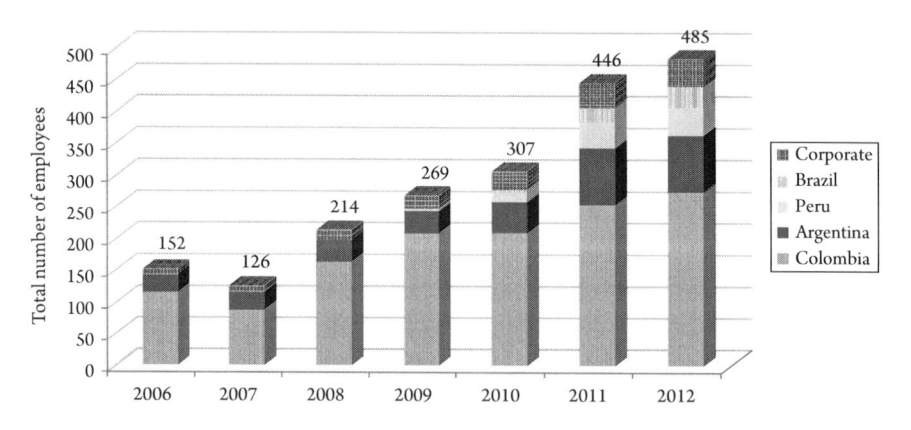

Source: Gran Tierra Energy Inc. annual reports 2007–13.

Figure C.4 Gran Tierra's organization (total employees 2006–12)

Table C.5 Gran Tierra's capital expenditures (US$ million) 2006–12

	2006	2007	2008	2009	2010	2011	2012
Argentina	14	2	12	5	34	36	41
Brazil					12	51	55
Colombia	34	14	32	81	106	202	153
Peru					23	46	63
Corporate*		1	3	2	2	2	2
Total	48	17	47	88	177	337	314

Note: *Corporate figures include Peru and Brazil until 2009.

Source: Gran Tierra Energy Inc. annual reports 2006–13.

Table C.6 Gran Tierra's original capital expenditure budget for 2013 (US$ million)

	Argentina	Brazil	Colombia	Peru	Total
Drilling	19	43	119	21	202
Geological & geophysical expenditures	4	6	66	17	93
Facilities, equipment & pipelines	10	18	39	–	67
Corporate activities					3

Source: Gran Tierra Energy Inc.

was still uncertainty around the project's economic viability, the sheer size of the Bretaña asset plus additional exploration potential on Gran Tierra's land could lead to exponential growth for many years. However, this would take considerable investments over the next several years, larger than any of Gran

Tierra's current operations. Gran Tierra had initially allocated $38 million in capital spending for activities in Peru during 2013. Based on the success of the ongoing well tests in the Bretaña field, the capital needed to increase approximately $70 million. Coffield had to consider if Gran Tierra was willing and able to commit these resources.

Recent investor reports did not fully reflect opportunities in Brazil or Peru. While Gran Tierra's current stock price at approximately $6.11 per share was slightly higher than its base net asset value, the potential in 2P reserves (total proved plus probable reserves) was not taken into account. A recent report from one of the leading investment firms estimated a target share price of approximately $8.20 for the coming year if current opportunities proved successful. See Table C.7 for a sample analysis of Gran Tierra's value in May 2013.

Some of the investors had also questioned whether a smaller firm such as Gran Tierra should engage in capital-intensive, high-risk offshore activities in Brazil or even take on a first-mover role in utilizing unconventional technology onshore in Brazil. It would take years for the service industry to develop the scale and scope necessary to make these types of activities as financially attractive as operations in similar basins in North America. If Petrobras was not aligned with Gran Tierra's plans for the onshore activities, it could be difficult for Gran Tierra, as a much smaller foreign firm, to convince the large domestic giant to implement any changes. Despite its enormous growth since inception, Gran Tierra was still a small player on a global scale with limited resources. Though it is considered financially stable today, did Gran Tierra and the company's investors have the patience and financial strength to get involved in such large-scale and/or long-term investments?

Table C.7 Example of a potential asset valuation summary from May 2013

Asset	Risked value per share (US$/share)
Total producing assets (excl. Brazil)	4.78
Total producing assets in Brazil	0.15
Cash and other financial items	1.06
Base net asset value	5.99
Unbooked exploration and development upside in Colombia	1.75
Unbooked exploration upside Peru	0.46
Unbooked value	2.21
Potential asset value	8.20

Source: Modified reproduction of investor report.

For a small company, Coffield felt he had much to consider. With the approaching strategy session, Coffield wanted to have a clear understanding of where he saw the company moving in the future.

CASE DISCUSSION

1. What is Gran Tierra's international strategy?
2. Have Gran Tierra's previous internationalization decisions been aligned with the firm's strategy? Was the decision to enter Brazil aligned with the firm's strategy?
3. What are Gran Tierra's firm-specific advantages? How does the firm leverage these advantages when entering new markets?
4. Identify relevant location advantages. How do these impact the internationalization of Gran Tierra? What makes Brazil attractive for Gran Tierra?
5. How different or similar is the Brazilian market compared to other host markets where Gran Tierra is already operating?
6. Discuss why Gran Tierra has chosen its current operating methods. Are these feasible if the growth opportunities in Peru become economically viable?

NOTES

* This case was first published in 2014 (Ivey case 9B16M071). Birgitte Grøgaard, Charlene D. Miller and Vivek Shah wrote this case solely to provide material for class discussion. The authors do not intend to illustrate either effective or ineffective handling of a managerial situation. The authors may have disguised certain names and other identifying information to protect confidentiality. This publication may not be transmitted, photocopied, digitized or otherwise reproduced in any form or by any means without the permission of the copyright holder. Reproduction of this material is not covered under authorization by any reproduction rights organization. To order copies or request permission to reproduce materials, contact Ivey Publishing, Ivey Business School, Western University, London, Ontario, Canada, N6G 0N1; (t) 519.661.3208; (e) cases@ivey.ca; (w) www.iveycases.com.

1. International movement of students and medical professionals working alongside local communities to implement sustainable health systems.
2. All currencies in US$ unless otherwise stated.
3. An arrangement whereby an operator buys in or acquires an interest in a lease owned by another operator on which oil or gas has been discovered or is being produced. Often, farm-ins are negotiated to help the original owner with development costs and to secure for the buyer a source of oil or natural gas (MineralWise, accessed 23 January 2019 at https://www.mineralweb.com/library/oil-and-gas-terms/farm-in-definition/).
4. 'US Gulf Coast: New crudes', Platts, McGraw Hill Financial, 31 January 2013, accessed 2 September 2014 at www.platts.com/news-feature/2013/oil/gulfcrude/index.
5. Production is measured according to the industry standard of barrels of oil equivalents per day (boe/day). The size of a barrel of oil equals approximately 159 litres of oil. Natural gas is typically converted as roughly 6000 cubic feet of natural gas per boe.
6. Gran Tierra Energy Inc. (2013), 'Gran Tierra Energy Inc. announces fourth quarter and 2012 year-end results', 26 February 2013.
7. Gran Tierra Energy Inc. (2012), 'Gran Tierra announces $363 million USD capital program for 2013 and operations update', 14 December 2012.

REFERENCE

Gran Tierra Energy Inc. 2005–2013 Annual Reports, accessed 19 April 2019 at https://sedar.com/DisplayCompanyDocuments.do?lang=EN&issuerNo=00026590.

3
International strategy and competitive advantage

3.1 Introduction

In this chapter, we use the integration–responsiveness framework to reflect over international strategies in relation to external competitive pressures and introduce four generic international strategies for MNEs with international operations: simple international, global, multidomestic and transnational. We then elaborate on the differences in underlying firm-specific advantages (FSAs) that enable firms to pursue different strategies, and tools for assessing such FSAs. We further explore in depth some key characteristics of the transnational strategy that balances global integration and local responsiveness, and its implications for subsidiary roles and subsidiary management. Finally, we contrast the international strategy literature with key strategic management frameworks to understand how key concepts interrelate and/or differ and illustrate a particular kind of local adaptation: the bottom-of-the-pyramid (BOP) markets.

3.2 International strategies: The integration–responsiveness framework

While there are multiple frameworks to guide MNEs in selecting an appropriate strategy for their foreign operations, the integration–responsiveness framework has persisted as one of the most influential international strategy frameworks over the past decades (Kostova, Marano and Tallman, 2016). The integration–responsiveness framework identifies four international strategy archetypes that illustrate the MNE's competitive positioning. In practice, it is widely recognized that most MNEs experience competitive pressures for both global integration and local responsiveness. However, it is vital that MNEs understand their 'dominant logic' to ensure that transferrable or location-bound FSAs are developed and leveraged appropriately. The integration–responsiveness framework is thus largely a reflection of the

Figure 3.1 Four international strategies

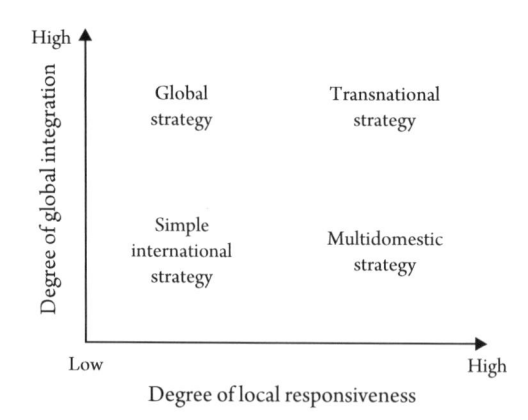

	Low — Degree of local responsiveness — High
High Degree of global integration	Global strategy / Transnational strategy
Low	Simple international strategy / Multidomestic strategy

degree of global integration the MNE chooses to exercise over its subsidiaries and the recognized need for subsidiaries to be flexible and responsive in regard to their local environments, as illustrated in Figure 3.1. Each of the four international strategy archetypes is discussed in greater detail below.

The simple international strategy

Foreign operations in MNEs with simple international strategies are characterized by having an adjunct or peripheral function. Although headquarters is directly involved in decision making or through the use of expatriates, foreign subsidiaries are not integrated into the daily activities of the company's other business units. These types of international activities often indicate an MNE in its infant stages or that decisions to internationalize may be based on isolated opportunities that arise.

Another trait of MNEs with simple international strategies is that foreign subsidiaries lack the resources and mandate to adapt, let alone develop, the product to any significant extent. There is a one-way transference of technology and knowledge from the parent company to its foreign subsidiaries, resulting in a low degree of local responsiveness. The approach is to exploit home-country FSAs (e.g., innovations) in order to achieve incremental sales rather than to develop flexible or large-scale operations. In their early days, this was how Colgate-Palmolive and many other American companies, such as Kraft and Procter & Gamble, operated in Europe. This type of international organization is essentially a transitory phase for firms in the early stages of internationalization that precedes a more globally integrated form of organization or foreign subsidiaries with greater autonomy.

The global strategy

In the early 1980s, the emphasis on global strategy increased dramatically and by some, including the influential scholar Theodore Levitt (1983), it was almost regarded as mandatory for competitive advantage. During this time period, tariffs decreased and product life cycles became dramatically shorter. This escalated research and development (R&D) costs and increased competitive pressures. The ability to operate under such a cost burden entailed an expanded scale of production over and above what a firm's domestic market was capable of absorbing. As such, foreign markets had to be sought out just in order to 'enter the game'. A further reason to seek out foreign markets was that without a presence in every market, competitors could achieve dominant positions that granted high profit margins. Dominance and strong profitability in one or more markets could then be surreptitiously used to subsidize loss-making entries into other markets.

Companies such as Sony epitomize MNEs with global strategies. Sony makes most of its value-added high-tech products, such as chips and personal computers in Japan, where it can monitor quality and where it has location-bound advantages not least in terms of research and development. When products have become highly standardized, their production is transferred to other locations, either to lower costs or to improve market entry. In relation to Europe, Sony has transferred production of audio-visual products, such as televisions and computer displays, to purpose-built greenfield sites that have been managed largely according to Sony's management principles. The standardized capabilities involved are easily transferred through training programmes.

The mentality underlying the global strategy is, of course, far from exclusively Japanese. IKEA's history is one of having ignored local taste and bucking fragmented furniture markets by producing scale-intensive globally standardized furniture. Despite serving a range of markets from Russia to North America, purchasing, distribution and design functions remain centrally controlled and served by Swedes. Although IKEA has increasingly allowed for market adaptations, such as adapting the size of its beds sold in the North American markets, these adaptations are mainly linked to their downstream activities. Similarly, General Electric functions on the basis of a distinctly uniform corporate mentality although this does not preclude non-Americans. Its businesses are global businesses each with its own president who coordinates and integrates activities worldwide.

The multidomestic strategy

This strategy has historically been a particular feature of European firms operating subsidiaries in other European countries. Large national differences in consumer preferences between European countries, logistical barriers and, at one point, high tariff barriers, all contributed to favouring a strategy involving high local responsiveness. However, as technology has changed information flows and the ease of transportation, markets are increasingly blurring. This has made it increasingly challenging to remain competitive as a purely localized MNE and has also resulted in a wave of new market actors and increased cross-border competitive pressures (Hitt, Li and Xu, 2016). As a result, many MNEs that originated as pure multidomestic firms are reconsidering the extent that they can be locally responsive.

Nestlé's early phases of international expansion illustrates the shift from a multidomestic to a global strategy. Its motive for expansion outside of Switzerland was entirely different from that underlying the simple international strategy. With a small domestic market, expansion could only come from establishing operations abroad. In other words, foreign activities were never viewed as purely incremental and this has influenced the way it has traditionally structured its operations. Founded in 1866, by the early 1900s it had operations in Britain, Germany, Spain and the United States. By 2018, Nestlé's products were sold in 189 countries, where international sales account for over 98 per cent of Nestlé's sales of EUR 80 690 million. It had also located factories in over 80 countries (Nestlé, 2018). Its expansion has been accompanied by a profound recognition that as tastes in human foodstuffs vary enormously from country to country, centralization was to be kept to a minimum. From its earliest days, Nestlé delegated brand management authority to country managers who independently adjusted the marketing and manufacturing strategies in accordance with local tastes and preferences. Nearly a century after its initial internationalization, only 750 of its 8 000 brands were registered in more than one country. As such Nestlé was for many years a multidomestic company characterized by relatively weak global integration and pronounced local responsiveness.

When Peter Brabeck became CEO in 1997, he wanted to keep Nestlé's commitment to decentralization, seen as the best way to cater to local taste and to establish emotional links with clients in far-flung places. However, after a couple of years in the job, Mr Brabeck abruptly switched tack. By the end of his tenure as CEO in 2008, Nestlé had become significantly less of a collection of fiefdoms. First, Mr Brabeck made production more regional. For example, Nestlé's operations in New Zealand had been run as a local company with four factories and very few imports and exports. Nestlé's operations in New Zealand were pooled with those of Australia and the Pacific Islands by consolidating accounting, administration, sales and payroll. It was not a popular decision with the Australians (*The Economist*, 2004). Overall, between 1998 and 2002, Nestlé was able to close or sell about half of its factories.

Purchasing is another area Nestlé has attempted to integrate, yet making the most of purchasing data is not easy. The first step was to improve the accuracy of the information. Nestlé, for example, was selling more than 100 000 products in 200 countries, using 550 000 suppliers, but the company was not using its huge buying power effectively because its databases were a mess. On examination, it found that of its 9 million records of vendors, customers and materials around half were obsolete or duplicated, and of the remainder about one-third was inaccurate or incomplete. The name of a vendor might be abbreviated in one record but spelled out in another, leading to double counting.

Since Mr Brabeck changed strategic direction, Nestlé has been overhauling its IT system, using SAP software, and improving the quality of its data. This has enabled Nestlé to become more efficient. For just one ingredient, vanilla, its American operation was able to reduce the number of specifications and use fewer suppliers, saving $30 million a year. Overall, such operational improvements have saved more than $1 billion annually (*The Economist*, 2010).

However, there are limits to how globally integrated Nestlé can become without losing the ability to adapt its products to local tastes and traditions. As CEO, Mr Brabeck was always conscious that there is no global consumer. For instance, Nestlé produces 200 different varieties of Nescafé, its instant coffee brand, to cater to local palates. Russians prefer their coffee thick, strong and sweet mixed with milk powder. This would not go down well with Western Europeans. KitKat in Japan comes in flavours such as lemon cheesecake, sushi, and mustard wasabi (Iyengar, 2018), utterly different from the KitKat sold in Britain. As a rule, the simpler the wares, the more they need to be adapted to local preferences. Sophisticated products such as milk powder for premature babies, on the other hand, are the same everywhere (*The Economist*, 2004).

The lesson is that integrating multidomestic MNEs involves considerable effort and is time consuming. Over time, local subsidiary managers develop a fiefdom mentality that does not incline them to favour any form of MNE-wide integration that may involve a loss of strategic or operational discretion. Furthermore, a substantial proportion of the knowledge that is developed in multidomestic MNEs is locally developed and locally embedded. Typically, these MNEs have little in the way of MNE-wide social networks that enable the pooling and integration of such knowledge. The lack of social networks also means that there is no common vision across the MNE and trust is underdeveloped. Finally, there are often limitations to how integrated a multidomestic MNE should become. The challenges involved in the integration of multidomestic MNEs is an important feature of Case K that accompanies Chapter 9.

The transnational strategy

At the end of the 1980s, it was argued by, for example, Bartlett and Ghoshal (1998) that important as the global integration dimension is, there is also an increasing need to achieve close proximity to local markets or customers to be able to adapt products to local tastes. The ability to balance the two strategic challenges requires a focus on worldwide learning in MNEs. Customers are no longer prepared to accept a 'one-size-fits-all' product strategy. Furthermore, not only do customers have their idiosyncratic national preferences, host governments also increasingly expect both local content and transference of FSAs (e.g., technology). In terms of this perspective, subsidiary management increasingly involves an ability to balance integration with the ability to adapt and enhance products and services in line with local market demands.

According to Bartlett and Ghoshal, the requirements for global integration, local responsiveness and worldwide learning, meant that a new MNE strategy, the transnational, was emerging:

> While some products and processes must still be developed centrally for worldwide use and others must be created locally in each environment to meet purely local demands, MNCs must increasingly use their access to multiple centres of technologies and familiarity with diverse customer preferences in different countries to create truly transnational innovations. (Bartlett and Ghoshal, 1995, p. 127)

The introduction of a transnational strategy recognized that for many MNEs the choice is not whether to globally integrate or adapt to local needs, but rather how to address multiple pressures from geographically dispersed subsidiaries. One of the key aspects of a successful transnational strategy is the ability to develop organizational flexibility and continuous learning. This requires an organizational structure that allows for differentiated management of organizational units and capabilities to sense needs for integration and local responsiveness as well as the ability to seize such opportunities and recombine FSAs as needed. One of the main challenges with a transnational strategy is the coordination complexities. Some critics even argue that the transnational strategy is more of an 'ideal' to strive for, while most companies are far from transnational in practice.

3.3 International strategy and competitive strategy

The MNE's internationalization strategy reflects the dominant way in which it competes in markets. The positioning school argues that firms consistently earn above average returns compared to competing firms if they are able to position themselves against the five competitive forces of:

- rivalry on prices and product quality within an industry;
- bargaining power of buyers;
- bargaining power of suppliers;
- threats of entry from close competitors;
- threats of entry from firms that produce substitute products or services.

When MNEs establish production units in international markets they often face aggressive competition from incumbent firms. The lack of knowledge of the precise form this opposition will take is a dimension of the liability of foreignness. The effectiveness of any deterrence that the subsidiary faces depends on whether it has competitive advantages relative to competitors that enable it to position itself against competitive forces.

In general, firms can implement two types of generic positioning strategies: (1) *cost leadership:* cost leaders have lower production cost than competitors and potential entrants/potential substitutes; and (2) *differentiation:* differentiators offer specialized products/services to groups of customers who have a high willingness to pay.

MNEs that mainly compete based on cost leadership need to seek economies of scale and they therefore often follow a global integration strategy. MNEs that mainly pursue a differentiation strategy may also follow a global integration strategy. However, in this case, it is to achieve economies of scope across different product lines.

Globally integrated MNEs often organize their activities as global product divisions. The major line of authority lies with product managers who have a global responsibility for their product lines. These MNEs typically have highly centralized scale-intensive manufacturing and R&D operations, with very little latitude for foreign subsidiaries to respond actively to local market demands.

Not all MNEs sell the same kind of products across all markets. MNEs may seek to exploit their sources of competitive advantage in markets where customers have idiosyncratic needs and preferences and MNEs have to develop local responsiveness and become multidomestics. MNEs that emphasize local responsiveness often structure their subsidiaries as loose federations of relatively small, decentralized subsidiaries with local activities. Subsidiaries of these MNEs have significant latitude to adapt products in accordance with local preferences. Typically, this local focus means that they are lacking in interest for cross-subsidiary synergies. Indeed, the loose federation structure can be a significant hindrance for the transfer of knowledge across subsidiaries (see Case K that follows Chapter 9).

MNEs that pursue local adaptation do not rely on economies of scale and scope to the same extent as MNEs that pursue price leadership or MNEs that only differentiate in terms of product lines. However, they may pursue economies of scale in functional areas such as purchasing, or in human resource management (HRM) practices. MNEs that address multiple pressures for global integration and local responsiveness compete in terms of both transferrable and non-transferrable FSAs may attempt to organize their activities as networks or matrix organizations in order to increase their flexibility and enhance knowledge sharing. While there is not one 'right' way to organize, aligning strategy with structure certainly helps facilitate FSA recombination and knowledge transfer.

3.4 The FSAs that enable international strategies

As a result of geographically spread organizational units, MNEs experience multiple and sometimes conflicting competitive pressures. On the one hand, one of the main competitive advantages of an MNE is rooted in its ability to leverage its FSAs such as technology, brands, and processes across geographical markets. To achieve such competitive advantages, MNEs rely on control and coordination of resources and activities across organizational units to ensure successful transfer of FSAs. On the other hand, host markets may have unique needs that pressure MNEs to be locally responsive and adapt to the local context. Local responsiveness inherently limits the ability to create value with transferable FSAs. MNEs can address this by recombining transferable FSAs with local resources and/or activities to better suit local needs and by ensuring that location-bound FSAs are either developed internally or accessed through a local partner (Rugman and Verbeke, 2001; Rugman,

Verbeke and Nguyen, 2011). In most contexts, MNEs need both transferrable and location-bound FSAs to compete successfully in foreign markets.

To achieve global integration, MNEs rely on FSAs that are transferrable, that is, that create value across multiple markets. Examples of transferable FSAs include technology and standardized processes. Transferring technology or other proprietary knowledge is particularly valuable for MNEs that invest in R&D so that costs are spread across several markets. Transferring FSAs can also enable MNEs to offer high-quality products and services in multiple markets, increase efficiencies and reduce costs through economies of scale.

MNEs typically use multiple control and coordination mechanisms to achieve integration. These control and coordination mechanisms are often grouped into three broad categories: (1) centralization of decision making; (2) standardization of processes (also referred to as formalization); and (3) socialization of organizational members to achieve shared values and a culture that encourages knowledge transfer (Keupp, Palmié and Gassmann, 2011; Kim, Park and Prescott, 2003; Zeng, Grøgaard and Steel, 2018). Expatriation, as discussed in Chapter 11, is also frequently used to facilitate integration and transfer of FSAs.

However, transferable FSAs may not create value in markets with unique needs, where multidomestic strategies are preferred. Firms with multidomestic strategies compete based on locally adapted products, services and ways of doing business. This requires local knowledge and local resources, referred to as location-bound FSAs, that are not transferrable across markets. Examples of location-bound FSAs include local business networks, local ways of conducting business, and physical assets that are tied to a specific location such as real estate (Rugman and Verbeke, 2001; Verbeke, 2013).

Competing based on both transferrable and non-transferrable FSAs, characterized by the transnational strategy, requires the orchestration, also referred to as recombination, of diverse location-bound and non-location-bound resources and assets (Verbeke and Asmussen, 2016; Verbeke and Kano, 2016).

3.5 How can we identify and assess FSAs? Drawing on mainstream strategy frameworks to determine competitive advantages

FSAs are central for both the OLI (ownership, location and internalization; see Chapter 2) and integration–responsiveness frameworks. For instance,

OLI holds that firms become multinationals because they seek advantages and/or because they want to exploit their FSAs. The OLI framework does not explain in any depth the sources of the advantages that firms exploit internationally and for that reason we turn to the field of strategy. The main question within the field of strategy is why some firms are consistently more successful compared to their competitors. We use strategy theory to address the issue of what constitutes the FSAs that allow firms to compete internationally. The resource-based theory of strategy seeks to answer this question by pointing to the characteristics of the resources that firms possess. Resources that can be sources of long-lasting competitive advantage must have certain characteristics: they have to be valuable, rare, inimitable and organized (VRIO):

- **Valuable resources** Resources are valuable to a firm when they allow the firm to respond to environmental threats or opportunities. This means that these resources are critical for the cost of production or for determining how willing customers are to pay for the firm's services and products. A firm may possess valuable resources but it may not be able to exploit its advantages internationally because the value of the resources is location bound. For example, a restaurant with a competitive advantage based on its unique location cannot exploit these sources of its advantage internationally. Many MNEs have experienced success in some markets and failure in other markets. For example, Uber had success in the US as well as in many other Western countries but failed in China. Part of the reason is that the resources that constituted Uber's competitive advantage were partly location bound. For example, Uber found that it could not tap into the same complementary resources such as internet, credit and GPS services in China as it had been able to in other countries. In many respects, the CAGE framework (cultural, administrative, geographic and economic distance; see Chapter 1) provides a powerful guide to how 'easy' it is for a firm to exploit its source of competitive advantage in a particular foreign location.
- **Rare resources** Resources have to be rare, meaning that competing firms do not possess them and therefore do not have the same advantages in the competition for customers. Many scholars have argued that knowledge-based types of resources are those that are most likely to be rare. There are two reasons for this. First, knowledge-based resources such as reputation, innovativeness and culture are often accumulated within firms and are therefore unique to the firm. Second, it is difficult to specify the content of these resources in contracts and therefore they are difficult to transfer to other firms by means of market transactions (in Chapter 4 we refer to this as 'market failure'). Firms may have resources

that are rare in their home market but when they internationalize they meet international competitors that have similar (or even more valuable) resources to their own. Lack of knowledge of competitors is one of the reasons why firms experience liability of foreignness.
- **Inimitable resources** For a firm to have long-lasting competitive advantages it is important that competing firms cannot imitate the valuable and rare resources they possess. Patents and trademark protection are an established means of protecting resources from imitation. Patent protection requires that a resource (e.g., valuable knowledge) is able to meet a number of statutory requirements including novelty and non-obviousness. Patents do not work equally well in all industries or in all countries. Resources that cannot be effectively protected by patents can still be difficult to imitate by competitors. Scholars within the resource-based perspective have identified other barriers to resource imitation. One set of barriers pertains to the historic circumstances and the path-dependent process of knowledge accumulation. For example, a firm's reputation as a reliable supplier is based on historically accumulated experience from buyers and therefore competitors cannot 'acquire' reputation instantly (Dierickx and Cool, 1989). Another source of difficulty for competitors trying to imitate is that they often find it difficult to understand how specific valuable resources combine to contribute to competitive advantage. Such causal ambiguity protects competitive advantage. However, sometimes the 'system' is not even fully understood by managers in the focal firm. This is clearly a disadvantage for a firm that wants to exploit its advantages internationally and a firm that internationalizes without having fully understood its source of competitive advantage will most likely embark on a process of learning by failing in foreign markets.
- **Organized resources** In order to realize its competitive advantage a firm needs complementary resources (or capabilities) to organize the exploitation of its resources. These include formal structures, management systems, HRM practices and knowledge transfer systems. When a firm makes a choice as to whether it wants to exploit its sources of competitive advantage through market contracts or within the firm, it implicitly also chooses whether it should control its complementary assets or whether these are to be controlled by a contracting partner. We discuss this choice in more detail in Chapter 4.

3.6 The challenges of geographically distributed organizational units: The transnational solution

The integration–responsiveness framework captures the challenges that managers face in catering to the pressure to adapt to local needs and preferences. However, some MNEs have a high degree of geographic distribution of organizational units and they experience various competitive pressures simultaneously, also referred to as 'multiple embeddedness' (Meyer, Mudambi and Narula, 2011). On one hand, parent organizations see the benefits of transferring and utilizing FSAs across borders, creating pressures for global integration. On the other hand, local host countries often have unique needs due to differences in institutions and culture. A location may also have unique country-specific (dis)advantages that are particularly valuable for the MNE to tap into or avoid. These country-specific (dis)advantages also affect the development of firm-level knowledge and capabilities and can create tension between pressures for global integration and local responsiveness in the MNE.

In the 1990s, international managers and scholars in international business increasingly focused on how MNEs could benefit from worldwide learning as well as from combining global integration and local responsiveness. The transnational strategy was proposed as a way for MNEs to address multiple competitive pressures. Bartlett and Ghoshal (1986, 1998) argued that MNEs should build flexible organizations through use of multiple control and coordination mechanisms, diversity of management groups, and socialization processes to develop shared values and aligned goals. According to Kostova et al. (2016), transnational MNEs are characterized by network organizations of units with differentiated needs, roles, and responsibilities. In other words, the transnational 'solution' proposes that MNEs move away from traditional hierarchies towards networks that foster organizational flexibility and worldwide learning (Bartlett and Ghoshal, 1998; Nohria and Ghoshal, 1994).

ABB, an engineering MNE with Swedish-Swiss roots, was often used by scholars as an illustration of the transnational MNE. By the late 1990s, ABB had implemented a balanced global matrix for its 1300 separate operating companies. Each operating manager was responsible for creating and pursuing entrepreneurial opportunities. Each of these front-line managers reported to a country manager, who was typically responsible for all the operating companies within a specific country, and to a business area manager who was responsible for developing worldwide product and technology strategies. In turn, each business area manager reported to one of 11 executive vice-presidents. These vice-presidents were the lynchpins of the matrix system in that they were responsible for an interrelated set of business areas as well as for several regions. They constituted the executive committee that defined overall strategy and broad performance targets. Significantly, of ABB's 215 000 employees only 100 were located at corporate headquarters in Zurich.

ABB combined a centralized reporting system with the decentralization of assets and responsibilities to local operating units. Managers of the local operating units had a mandate to build their businesses as if they owned them. They also inherited their results. Top management in ABB pursued global integration when they designed the mandate of the business area manager to facilitate horizontal integration between units in respect to knowledge, export markets and production facilities. In addition to the objective structural features, the development of a structure of shared values at ABB, a 'common organizational psychology', was according to Bartlett and Ghoshal (1995) of even greater significance. This concept of 'common organizational psychology' has much in common with aspects of 'social capital' that we discuss in Chapter 9.

After a few years of operating more or less as a transnational, ABB reorganized its structure of operation and in so doing dropped its transnational aspirations. Although the ABB case functioned as a source of scholarly insights on how to address multiple competitive pressures (Bartlett and Ghoshal, 1986, 1998; Prahalad and Doz, 1987), the interest in ABB in particular and the transnational in general has faded. Indeed, scholars have challenged the original scholarly insights (Gooderham and Ulset, 2002; Kostova et al., 2016). Currently, the transnational strategy is often considered to be too idealistic and too complex (Kostova et al., 2016). However, there are still some scholars who continue to employ the concept (e.g., Lessard, Teece and Leih, 2016; Meyer and Su, 2015; Teece, 2014). We view the transnational concept as a useful ideal-type rather than the empirical reality of global and multidomestic MNEs.

3.7 Subsidiary roles

The multiple embeddedness of MNEs can make it difficult to manage foreign subsidiaries in a uniform manner. Some subsidiaries may require more autonomy than other subsidiaries. Simply granting autonomy to all subsidiaries may result in the loss of valuable synergies and the ability to leverage economies of scale. Equally, while imposing close control on all subsidiaries may facilitate knowledge transfer and cost efficiencies, subsidiaries operating in local environments with unique needs may suffer (Bartlett and Ghoshal, 1986; Rugman and Verbeke, 2001; Verbeke and Greidanus, 2009). In short, MNEs must often manage their foreign subsidiaries in differentiated ways.

Research on subsidiary roles took off from the mid-1990s, with increased attention on subsidiary specific challenges (Kostova et al., 2016). The literature on subsidiary roles recognized that subsidiaries could develop key FSAs that could also be used in other parts of the MNE and that the knowledge transferred in MNEs was not unidirectional from headquarters to subsidiaries (Paterson and Brock, 2002). While studies on subsidiary roles have generated many different frameworks and subsidiary role typologies, we will focus particularly on the roles proposed by Bartlett and Ghoshal since these align well with our previous discussions of MNE strategies.

Bartlett and Ghoshal (1986) originally proposed that foreign subsidiaries in differentiated MNE networks can be clustered into four main categories: black holes, implementers, contributors and strategic leaders. The subsidiary role is determined both by the competence of the subsidiary (e.g., the strength of FSAs) and the strategic importance of the local environment. Subsidiaries that are strategic leaders have strong FSAs and are located in strategically important markets, similar to what other frameworks refer to as centres of excellence or world product mandates (Frost, Birkinshaw and Ensign, 2002; Moore and Birkinshaw, 1998; Paterson and Brock, 2002; White and Poynter, 1984). Strategic leaders are developers of technology and knowledge based on their presence in foreign locations and thus play an important role for the development of new FSAs. However, for an MNE to benefit from strategic leaders, it needs to create internationally coordinated learning processes to leverage their knowledge. This is particularly the case in regards to technologically intensive industries such as pharmaceuticals and electronics, where levels of sophistication make labour costs increasingly less of an issue than skills and creativity.

However, although strategic leaders have an important role to play, most MNEs need different types of subsidiaries to remain competitive. Implementer subsidiaries represent subsidiaries with low specialized competence levels (FSAs) that are located in markets that have low strategic importance. While this may initially sound unattractive, subsidiaries that produce standardized goods efficiently are often the 'cash cows' of MNEs. Scholars have pointed out that by overlooking that a market can be strategically important in multiple ways, Bartlett and Ghoshal's (1986) subsidiary role framework does not sufficiently nuance the importance of implementer subsidiaries to the MNE (Verbeke, 2013). In practice, most foreign subsidiaries fall into the category of implementers.

The last two subsidiary roles reflect positions that subsidiaries may not wish to hold in the long term, but these roles contribute to the continued development of the MNE and to entrepreneurial activities in subsidiaries. Contributor subsidiaries typically hold strong FSAs but headquarters and other MNE units have not yet recognized their FSAs. We can expect subsidiaries in this position to actively engage in subsidiary initiatives to leverage their strengths, gain increased headquarter attention, and influence the MNE (Birkinshaw, 2000, 2014). Black holes are subsidiaries that are located in strategically important markets but currently lack the necessary FSAs to succeed in this market. Such subsidiaries need to engage in entrepreneurial activities to tap into valuable knowledge in the local market network. While a subsidiary may initially be a black hole, MNEs can make investments that enable it to develop into a strategic leader. For example, nearly all of the big European pharmaceutical companies have established an R&D presence in the United States, particularly in high-technology clusters such as Boston and San Diego. Likewise, American pharmaceutical companies, such as Pfizer, have European research facilities. These subsidiaries have become strategic leaders in the MNE for particular products and technologies (Birkinshaw, 1997).

The above discussion indicates that subsidiary roles are not static. A subsidiary may change its role in the MNE as headquarters invest in it or as it develops competencies from its engagement in local networks or clusters. However, external competitive pressures and risk exposure also influence subsidiaries' roles and how MNEs manage their subsidiaries. All firms are exposed to some form of risk but cross-border activities generate 'new' and different risks such as exposure to fluctuating exchange rates or changes in regulations and economic conditions that are not aligned across borders. Moreover, MNEs that have high levels of FDI in environments with higher cultural and institutional distances need to manage the risks that arise. For instance, subsidiaries in locations with high economic or political risk (e.g., inflation or expropriation risk) may have greater autonomy to shield the rest of the MNE from volatile changes. In contrast, subsidiaries in locations with high levels of corruption, low legal protection of proprietary information and reputation risks may experience more headquarter involvement to increase control to mitigate unwanted exposure.

In the following section, we turn to MNEs that have subsidiaries that operate in 'bottom-of-the-pyramid' (BOP) markets. The roles of these subsidiaries involve considerable latitude to respond to local market conditions.

3.8 Beyond local responsiveness: The BOP challenge

In this section, we examine a particular kind of local adaptation that arises not just because of substantial economic distance between the MNE headquarters and the foreign market, but also between potential customer groups in the foreign market. Examples of such foreign markets include India and parts of Sub-Saharan Africa where average levels of income and wealth conceal substantial within-country variations. Operating in these locations has become known as the BOP challenge. BOP markets require local adaptation that go beyond minor adaptations to products and services, and challenge MNEs to rethink how to create value in a foreign market and how to organize its activities.

Since 1995, annual flows of FDI into emerging economies have increased from about $100 billion to nearly $800 billion (UNCTAD, 2014, p.2). However, Prahalad and Lieberthal (2003) observe that MNEs have tended to bring their existing products and marketing strategies to emerging markets and generally fail to consider consumers beyond the wealthy elite at the top of the economic pyramid. A common assumption has been that emerging markets are at an earlier stage of the same developmental path followed by developed economies and that it is sufficient to operate with locally adapted versions of the products and business models used in the developed world (Arnold and Quelch, 1998). The outcome has been a failure by MNEs to tap into the potential in tiers of consumers beneath the elites at the very top of the pyramid (Hart and Christensen, 2002).

By way of reaction to this, a BOP approach has emerged whereby 'poor people are identified as potential customers who can be served if companies learn to fundamentally rethink their existing strategies and business models. This involves acquiring and building new resources and capabilities and forging a multitude of local partnerships' (Seelos and Mair, 2007, p.49). By business models, we mean the 'economic logic' of how to organize activities, resources, and relationships to create value for the MNE. An important implication of the BOP approach is that there is a need to develop business models anew for BOP markets, thus limiting the ability to leverage existing models.

Plainly, radical business model innovation in BOP settings will sit uncomfortably with 'global' MNEs, that is, MNEs that pursue global standardization supported by a centralized hub organization. However, BOP business model innovation is also a testing challenge for the other main generic MNE, the 'multidomestic'. Even though multidomestic MNEs are decentralized federation organizations characterized by considerable local autonomy that compete by customizing products to the local market (Bartlett and Ghoshal, 1998; Roth, 1992; Yip, 1989), London and Hart (2004) argue that the idea of adapting pre-existing solutions to BOP conditions is wholly inadequate. Furthermore, they argue, the local responsiveness heritage of multidomestics may be a liability in confronting the need to engage with BOP business model innovation.

In broad terms, London and Hart (2004) propose that the successful pursuit of low-income markets in emerging economies requires MNEs in general to rethink their business models in fundamental ways. One aspect of their critique is particularly relevant for multidomestic MNEs: London and Hart (2004) argue that in pursuing low-income markets in developing countries, MNEs must go far beyond the traditional idea of local responsiveness. Thus, when entering BOP pyramid markets, the specific reliance by multidomestic MNEs on their traditional capability of local responsiveness is wholly inadequate. Indeed, it might actually inhibit effectiveness to such an extent that performance is critically undermined.

London and Hart (2004) propose that what characterizes successful MNEs in BOP markets is the capability to value and facilitate bottom-up co-invention of locally appropriate solutions by a diversity of partners. These solutions involve investing resources to develop capacity beyond the defensive boundaries of the firm. They refer to this capability as 'social embeddedness' and define it as 'the ability to create competitive advantage based on a deep understanding of and integration with the local environment. This capability involves the ability to create a web of trusted connections with a diversity of organizations and institutions, generate bottom-up development, and understand, leverage, and build on the existing social infrastructure' (London and Hart, 2004, p. 364).

3.9 Summary

In this chapter, we introduce a framework to discuss international strategies and reflect on the underlying competitive advantages needed for the various strategies. We emphasize that the geographically distributed nature of MNEs results in multiple embeddedness that can generate tensions in pressures for global integration and local responsiveness. We further highlight the link between internationalization strategies and mainstream strategy literature. The case study that follows this chapter shows the entry of Norwegian MNE Telenor's subsidiary, Uninor, into India. Despite a significant record of achieving competitive advantage in neighbouring countries, it soon became clear that Telenor had to learn how to develop a BOP operation.

REFERENCES

Arnold, D.J. and J.A. Quelch (1998), 'New strategies in emerging markets', *Sloan Management Review*, **40**(1), 7–20.

Bartlett, C.A. and S. Ghoshal (1986), 'Tap your subsidiaries for global reach', *Harvard Business Review*, **64**(6), 87–94.

Bartlett, C.A. and S. Ghoshal (1995), *Transnational Management: Text, Cases, and Readings in Cross-Border Management*, 2nd edition, Chicago, IL: Irwin.

Bartlett, C.A. and S. Ghoshal (1998), *Managing Across Borders: The Transnational Solution*, 2nd edition, Boston, MA: Harvard Business School Press.

Birkinshaw, J. (1997), 'Entrepreneurship in multinational corporations: The characteristics of subsidiary initiatives', *Strategic Management Journal*, **18**(3), 207–29.

Birkinshaw, J. (2000), *Entrepreneurship in the Global Firm*, London: Sage.

Birkinshaw, J. (2014), 'Subsidiary initiative in the modern multinational corporation', in J. Boddewyn (ed.), *Multidisciplinary Insights from New AIB Fellows*, Bingley, UK: Emerald Group Publishing Ltd.

Dierickx, I. and K. Cool (1989), 'Asset stock accumulation and sustainability of competitive advantage', *Management Science*, **35**, 1504–11.

Frost, T.S., J.M. Birkinshaw and P.C. Ensign (2002), 'Centers of excellence in multinational corporations', *Strategic Management Journal*, **23**(11), 997–1018.

Gooderham, P.N. and S. Ulset (2002), '"Beyond the M-form": Towards a critical test of the new form', *International Journal of the Economics of Business*, **9**(1), 117–38.

Hart, S.L. and C.M. Christensen (2002), 'The great leap: Driving innovation from the base of the pyramid', *Sloan Management Review*, **41**(1), 51–6.

Hitt, M.A., D. Li and K. Xu (2016), 'International strategy: From local to global and beyond', *Journal of World Business*, **51**(1), 58–73.

Iyengar, R. (2018), 'Nestle is making a pink KitKat from ruby chocolate', *CNN Business*, 18 January 2018, accessed 20 August 2018 at https://money.cnn.com/2018/01/18/news/companies/pink-kitkat-ruby-chocolate-nestle-japan-korea/index.html.

Keupp, M.M., M. Palmié and O. Gassmann (2011), 'Achieving subsidiary integration in international innovation by managerial "tools"', *Management International Review*, **51**(2), 213–39.

Kim, K., J.H. Park and J.E. Prescott (2003), 'The global integration of business functions: A study of multinational businesses in integrated global industries', *Journal of International Business Studies*, **34**(4), 327–44.

Kostova, T., V. Marano and S. Tallman (2016), 'Headquarters–subsidiary relationships in MNCs: Fifty years of evolving research', *Journal of World Business*, **51**(1), 176–84.

Lessard, D., D.J. Teece and S. Leih (2016), 'The dynamic capabilities of meta-multinationals', *Global Strategy Journal*, **6**(3), 211–24.

Levitt, T. (1983), 'The globalization of markets', *Harvard Business Review*, **61**(3), 92–102.

London, T. and S.L. Hart (2004), 'Reinventing strategies for emerging markets: Beyond the transnational model', *Journal of International Business Studies*, **35**(5), 350–70.

Meyer, K.E. and Y.-S. Su (2015), 'Integration and responsiveness in subsidiaries in emerging economies', *Journal of World Business*, **50**(1), 149–58.

Meyer, K.E., R. Mudambi and R. Narula (2011), 'Multinational enterprises and local contexts: The opportunities and challenges of multiple embeddedness', *Journal of Management Studies*, **48**(2), 235–52.

Moore, K.J. and J.M. Birkinshaw (1998), 'Managing knowledge in global service firms: Centers of excellence', *Academy of Management Executive*, **12**(4), 81–92.

Nestlé (2018), *Annual Report 2017*, accessed 20 August 2018 at https://www.nestle.com/investors/annual-report.

Nohria, N. and S. Ghoshal (1994), 'Differentiated fit and shared values: Alternatives for managing headquarters–subsidiary relations', *Strategic Management Journal*, **15**(6), 491–502.

Paterson, S.L. and D.M. Brock (2002), 'The development of subsidiary-management research: Review and theoretical analysis', *International Business Review*, **11**(2), 139–63.

Prahalad, C.K. and Y. Doz (1987), *The Multinational Mission: Balancing Local Demands and Global Vision*, New York: Free Press.

Prahalad, C.K. and K. Lieberthal (2003), 'The end of corporate imperialism', *Harvard Business Review*, **81**(8), 109–17.

Roth, K. (1992), 'Implementing international strategy at the subsidiary level: The role of managerial decision-making characteristics', *Journal of Management*, **18**(4), 769–89.

Rugman, A.M. and A. Verbeke (2001), 'Subsidiary-specific advantages in multinational enterprises', *Strategic Management Journal*, **22**(3), 237–50.

Rugman, A.M., A. Verbeke and Q.T.K. Nguyen (2011), 'Fifty years of international business theory and beyond', *Management International Review*, **51**(6), 755–86.

Seelos, C. and J. Mair (2007), 'Profitable business models and market creation in the context of deep poverty: A strategic view', *The Academy of Management Perspectives*, **21**(4), 49–63.

Teece, D.J. (2014), 'A dynamic capabilities-based entrepreneurial theory of the multinational enterprise', *Journal of International Business Studies*, **45**(1), 8–37.

The Economist (2004), 'Daring, defying, to grow', 5 August 2004.

The Economist (2010), 'A different game', 25 February 2010.

UNCTAD (2014), *World Investment Report, 2014: Investing in the SDGs: An Action Plan*, New York and Geneva: UNCTAD.

Verbeke, A. (2013), *International Business Strategy*, 2nd edition, Cambridge, UK: Cambridge University Press.

Verbeke, A. and C.G. Asmussen (2016), 'Global, local, or regional? The locus of MNE strategies', *Journal of Management Studies*, **53**(6), 1051–75.

Verbeke, A. and N.S. Greidanus (2009), 'The end of the opportunism vs trust debate: Bounded reliability as a new envelope concept in research on MNE governance', *Journal of International Business Studies*, **40**(9), 1471–95.

Verbeke, A. and L. Kano (2016), 'An internalization theory perspective on the global and regional strategies of multinational enterprises', *Journal of World Business*, **51**(1), 83–92.

White, R.E. and T.A. Poynter (1984), 'Strategies for foreign-owned subsidiaries in Canada', *Business Quarterly*, **49**(2), 59–69.

Yip, G. (1989), 'Global strategy – in a world of nations?', *Sloan Management Review*, **31**(1), 29–41.

Zeng, R., B. Grøgaard and P. Steel (2018), 'Complements or substitutes? A meta-analysis of the role of integration mechanisms for knowledge transfer in the MNE network', *Journal of World Business*, **53**(4), 415–32.

Case D
Uninor: Beyond local responsiveness – multidomestic MNEs at the bottom of the pyramid*

Paul N. Gooderham, Svein Ulset and Frank Elter

D.1 Introduction

This case illustrates how moving into bottom-of-the-pyramid (BOP) settings affects MNEs and their business models. We focus specifically on Telenor's Indian subsidiary, Uninor. With 172 million subscribers in 13 markets and with 2010 revenue of 95 billion Norwegian krone (NOK), Telenor ranks seventh among the world's mobile operators. Telenor has its corporate headquarters in Oslo and significant operations in Scandinavia, Central and Eastern Europe and Asia. Although it is a decentralized MNE with considerable local autonomy at the business unit level, regional managers have provided a measure of regional coordination.

When Telenor entered India in 2009, it was far from a newcomer in Asian emerging economies. However, its India entry was different in important ways. In the case of Telenor's operation in Bangladesh, its entry in 1999 was that of a first-mover – there was little competition – and was undertaken as part of a joint venture with the high-profile Grameen Bank of Bangladesh. The joint venture, GrameenPhone, enabled Telenor to serve 'the wealthier people and the business community (profitably)' (Seelos and Mair, 2007, p. 56). As an addition to this top-of-the pyramid operation, GrameenPhone in close alliance with Grameen Bank undertook the organization of GrameenPhone's less commercial activities in rural, BOP, areas. In Pakistan, which Telenor entered in 2005, it was also an early entrant and similarly able to target and serve the local top-of-the-pyramid. Similar conditions applied to its entries into Thailand (DTAC) and Malaysia (Digi).

Thus, prior to its India entry, Telenor had had a ten-year history as a successful top-of-the-pyramid operator in Asia – with the exception of Malaysia, where it occupied the number 3 position in the market, Telenor had always been either number 1 or 2 in its Asian markets. Not only had it enjoyed substantial first-mover advantages but tariff regimes had been stable. These conditions enabled Telenor to pursue its standard strategy of adaptive business model replication. In India, none of this applied. Telenor was a late entrant that faced strong incumbents at the top-of-the-pyramid and a tariff regime in flux. In 2010, failing revenue streams meant that Uninor either had to accept complete defeat and withdraw from India, or abandon its top-of-the-pyramid strategy and develop a business model appropriate to the BOP market. It chose the latter.

D.2 The failure and the turnaround of Uninor

India is the second largest economy in the world, with 50 per cent of its population under 25 years of age. Since 2001, the Indian mobile market has been the fastest growing in the world – between 2001 and 2011, it expanded from 3–4 million to almost 900 million 'SIM' subscribers. However, lack of brand loyalty and, from 2009, a relatively large number of operators, means that it is also a highly competitive market – particularly below the top-of-the-pyramid, many subscribers have two or more SIM cards that they use according to whichever company at any one time is providing the best deal.

Despite this competitiveness and despite the presence of strong local incumbents, in late October 2008, after several years of probing the potential of the Indian market, Telenor formally announced its plans to enter the Indian mobile market. A window of opportunity had opened when in early 2008 the Indian telecom ministry decided to increase the number of licensed operators from seven to 15. Defying industry analysts who stressed the ultra-competitiveness of the Indian telecom market, Telenor entered India by paying $1.1 billion (61.35 billion Indian rupees – INR) for a 60 per cent stake in one of the new licensees, Unitech Wireless. Together they launched the Uninor brand.

To lead the local operation, Telenor corporate CEO Jon Fredrik Baksaas selected one of Telenor's most successful Norwegian subsidiary managing directors (MDs). Corporate headquarters held him in particular regard for his highly effective turnaround of one of Telenor's Central European operations. Rapidly installed at Uninor, he had to confront the size and diversity of the Indian telecom market – consisting of 1.2 billion people, 29 languages, 2000 ethnicities, huge distances, social inequalities, many rival companies, and uncertain regulations. Pre-entry, Telenor had neither the time nor the resources to develop comprehensive business cases covering each of the 'circles' (i.e., regions) it planned to enter. Instead, Telenor relied on the experience of its Norwegian expat MD fresh out of Central Europe and his European team of managers to adjust the company's well-established business model to yet another setting. Delegating the responsibility to the subsidiary MD for getting the Telenor business model into place and making any necessary local adaptations was standard practice at Telenor.

The notion was that Uninor was to focus on the top-of-the-pyramid and was to do so based on Telenor's 'premium service' business model: that is, a high level of customer service; choice of plans; comprehensive presence; and high-end value-added services (but not streaming). The Uninor MD set about constructing the Uninor brand around the ambition to target 'aspirational' India, using 'emotional messages' to stimulate growing consumption of premium services. In terms of Figure D.1, Uninor positioned its business model in the top left quadrant alongside the long-established Indian national champion, Bharti Airtel.

In this positioning, Uninor was aligning its operations with the recommendations it had received from the consultancy McKinsey, hired by Telenor to assist in Uninor's implementation phase. Two factors in particular underpinned the recommendations. First, there was an assumption that the high average revenue per user (ARPU) that Telenor required from Uninor was most readily achievable in the premium services, higher-income segment of the market. Second, although incumbent operators already occupied most of the premium service market, the assumption was that there was a sufficiently

Note: Within the quadrants with more than one company, there is minimal difference in the positioning of the companies.

Figure D.1 Uninor's initial market positioning

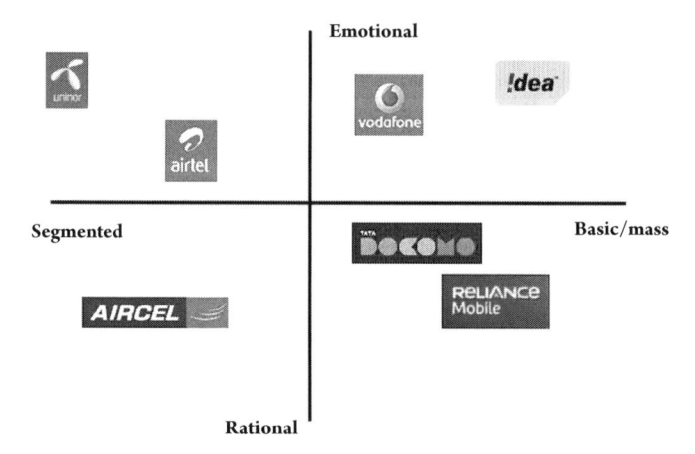

high level of churn to provide an opportunity to capture a viable share of the top-of-the-pyramid market.

To achieve the aggressive target of launching services in the Indian market within nine months after the entry decision, Uninor allied itself with Ericsson (Swedish MNE) as its equipment supplier and Indian Wipro as its IT partner. Further, Uninor decided that the pressure to launch its services and the availability of a local call-centre industry meant that unlike any other Telenor business unit it would *outsource its customer service*. In order to avoid lock-in it chose four competing firms to deliver customer service. Not only was this expedient for getting the launch underway, but Uninor calculated that it led to a much lower cost and greater flexibility than if it had had the opportunity to develop customer service in-house.

Following its launch in December 2009 in eight of India's 22 telecom circles, Uninor made a strong start. The company racked up 1.3 million subscribers in its first month of operation. As it launched services in five additional circles, giving it coverage of over 75 per cent of India's population, Uninor was capturing a higher share of new subscribers than the other newcomers. However, almost as soon as it started launching its services, it registered that most higher-income potential subscribers seemed more reluctant than had been assumed to move from incumbent operators to an unfamiliar late entrant. With a limited subscriber base, the giant incumbents like Bharti and Vodafone with subscriber bases of 75–100 million each and unrivalled network coverage across all of India's 22 telecom circles dwarfed Uninor. By early 2010, Uninor's distribution channels began to lose confidence in Uninor's services and retailers demanded additional commission to accommodate them. With a premium service offering and a business model that did not differ significantly from the established top-of-the-pyramid incumbents, the Uninor campaign rapidly lost momentum. As 2010 progressed, Uninor's results quickly deteriorated. Further, in a highly congested market, a price war broke out causing rapidly shrinking margins. When Telenor took its decision to enter India, the average tariff for a mobile phone call was 2.5 US cents a minute. By 2010, it was less than 1 US cent per minute (*Financial Times*, 2010).

By the end of June 2010, seven of the 15 operators accounted for 96 per cent of India's 636 million mobile subscribers, 'leaving the newcomers (such as Uninor) to battle it out for the scraps' (Total Telecom, 2010). Panic broke out at Telenor corporate headquarters.

The Uninor MD considered declining growth to be more of a normal downtime event following a massive service launching, and decided to stick with the Telenor business model. However, the Telenor Asia manager Sigve Brekke was of another opinion. As the more Asia-experienced of the two, Brekke read the signals from leading media, distributors, retailers, subscribers and competitors entirely differently. Following a series of unsuccessful attempts at revamping the Uninor launch, Telenor Corporate CEO Jon Fredrik Baksaas finally decided to intervene. After just 18 months in India, Uninor's first MD and his entire team returned to Norway. Telenor announced the instalment of an entirely new management team headed by Brekke.

One member of Brekke's new management team was the Indian-born, Canadian-educated COO, Yogesh Malik, who arrived at Uninor in November 2010. Malik had worked for Telenor at its corporate headquarters as well as having had roles in its operations in Ukraine and Bangladesh. Brekke and Malik were both committed to a radical turnaround initiative that would involve moving down the pyramid significantly beyond the 15 per cent of the population with incomes above $10 a day (*Open Magazine*, 2011).

In terms of Figure D.1, Uninor aimed to move from the top left quadrant to the bottom right. Serving BOP customers with their limited spending power meant taking their needs explicitly into account and then developing an entirely new business model that addresses these (Demil et al., 2015). In the view of Brekke and Malik, the only serviceable part of the Uninor operation was the outsourcing of customer service. Every other aspect of the operation needed to be drastically changed.

D.3 Perceived benefit and price

A feature of Uninor's top-of-the-pyramid business model was the segmented marketing of premium services with an overtly emotional, aspirational appeal. Uninor definitively abandoned this approach. It replaced it with mass marketing of basic local services with a purely utilitarian appeal: the essence of the message it repeatedly communicated was 'Uninor provides you with the best basic local services at the lowest price'. This new 'value for money' position was underscored by advertisements that were intended to be 'simple, clear and light-hearted' and where plain but functional product benefits would be readily evident to prospective BOP customers.

A critical part of the offering to highly price-sensitive BOP customers was a significant reduction in Uninor's tariffs particularly at 'excess capacity' times of the day. Uninor was the first mobile operator in India to introduce 'dynamic pricing', a concept that gave consumers substantial discounts based on current network traffic at an individual site. For BOP customers, the reward for placing their calls at times and places where there was excess network capacity was 'super-low' call charges.

D.4 Value delivery

A business model's value proposition is a function of the difference between customers' perceived benefit and the price they pay. Before directly analysing the outcome of changes to Uninor's value proposition, it is important to consider its value delivery. Without addressing this aspect of its business model, Uninor would have been unable to deliver a price suited to the BOP market. Failing to meet that condition would have meant no perceived benefit could emerge. Our analysis of Uninor indicates two significant changes to value delivery. The first of these involved cost cutting and the second the development of an innovative distribution system.

One very palpable aspect to basic cost cutting at Uninor involved making 600 of its total 2600 employees redundant. For those who remained they had to adapt to being involved in a very different operation to the one they had joined. Gone was any perception that they were working for a company serving aspirational India and in its place was the notion that from now on all activities aimed at delivering ultra-low-cost basic services. Uninor had already outsourced its customer service and this was to be further developed. However, Uninor's new, acute focus on getting rid of all unnecessary costs led to fundamental changes in its network operations, its mode of partnering with its IT vendor and its sales distribution.

To enhance utilization of its networks, Uninor developed a *cluster-based operating model*. The first step was to concentrate base stations in high traffic areas. Thereafter, Uninor's local Indian engineers developed a network utilization method that meant squeezing more network capacity out of its base stations than any of its competitors. Uninor then grouped neighbouring base stations to form clusters headed by managers whose task was to enable local dynamic pricing as a means to achieving the highest possible revenue streams.

Another novel initiative aimed at cost reduction concerned aligning its IT vendor, Wipro, with Uninor's goals. Uninor had already outsourced application development and management to Wipro. It now persuaded Wipro in lieu of direct payment to accept 'gain sharing'. As a result, the Uninor–Wipro relationship became so close that Wipro engineers literally moved into Uninor's headquarters in Gurgaon in Northern India on a permanent basis. Incentivized and integrated, Wipro IT engineers focused on significantly reducing the number of IT service personnel it employed at Uninor and in simplifying the IT architecture.

Both of these cost-cutting efforts represented significant contributions to enhancing value delivery suitable to a BOP market. However, equally important was developing *a cost-effective distribution system* geared to and embedded in the BOP market. One aspect to the new distribution system involved Uninor replacing its top-of-the-pyramid points of sale with an extensive network of lower-level retailers. These 'Mom and Pop stores' sold a vast array of products (combs, candy, comics, 'you-name-it-we've-got-it') aimed at the BOP market. Part of this extensive assortment of merchandise included the competing offerings of other mobile operators. Any one Mom and Pop store would be displaying the logos of four or five of Uninor's competitors, meaning that Uninor had to address how to confer some advantage on its particular offerings.

A second aspect to Uninor's overhaul of its distribution system involved abandoning distributors who offered competing products and services to retailers. Instead, it set about developing a network of Uninor exclusive but independent distributors, thereby avoiding divided loyalties. Most of these distributors were local entrepreneurs who had proved themselves in other, unrelated businesses. Attached to each distributor was a comprehensive network of field sales agents, known as 'retail sales executives' (RSEs). While the distributors supervised the RSEs, they did not employ them. Instead, RSEs were employees of employment agencies but trained and incentivized by Uninor to in turn coach and incentivize storeowners to voice the benefits of the Uninor offerings to customers. The outcome was that the Mom and Pop stores were supplied with Uninor products and services (SIM cards, subscriptions, recharges, special offers, etc.) by a dedicated sales arm that Uninor did not actually own. By the end of 2011, Uninor had 400 000 bottom-of-the-pyramid points of sale served by 7000 RSEs attached to 1700 distributors across 13 circles, serving 36 million subscribers.

One particular aspect of creating a cost-effective distribution system involved the status and the motivation of the RSEs. As employees of employment agencies such as Manpower and Adecco, they were guaranteed medical insurance and a certificate of employment, both of which are highly valued by BOP personnel. Although employed by agencies, Uninor not only selected all RSEs, it also provided them with training and an undertaking that success would lead to direct employment and a career within Uninor. In contrast, in other mobile operators, RSE equivalents were employees of the distributor who, in Uninor's view, generally engaged in recruiting substandard employees, avoided training them properly, frequently underpaid them and denied them medical insurance. That type of human resource policy could be sufficient for incumbents with well-regarded brands and sales performance driven by market pull, but Uninor saw it as entirely unsuitable for them as a newcomer. Uninor's very different approach to their RSEs reflected their belief that only by developing a push model could it achieve cost-efficient sales in the context of a BOP market.

Value proposition

At the close of 2011, Uninor's combination of 'no-frills' services and mass market '*sabse sasta*' or 'lowest-in-the-market' tariffs had resulted in significant increases to its customer market share relative to other operators. In perceiving benefit as exceeding price, BOP customers were responding to a value proposition that resonated with them. In the next years, an ever-increasing number of BOP customers bought in to the Uninor combination of basic services and 'lowest-in-the-market' tariffs. In May 2014, Uninor reported that in the first quarter of 2014 it had achieved a 20 per cent share of incremental customer market share in its circles of operation. In simple terms, every fifth new mobile subscription in these circles went to Uninor. Compared to the same quarter in 2013, it had expanded its customer base by 25 per cent. In other words, Uninor's value proposition was succeeding in the BOP market.

Value capture and value creation

In terms of value capture, which we operationalize as EBITDA (earnings before interest, tax, depreciation and amortization), for the first time since it entered India Uninor achieved break-even in December 2013. Concerning value creation, Uninor reported a year on improvement of gross revenue by 44 per cent and 13 per cent on its ARPU. At the core of Uninor's BOP business model is considerable attention to value delivery. Without reducing costs significantly, no BOP value proposition could have emerged. Likewise, value capture and value creation would have failed.

D.5 Global replication of BOP innovations

In 2011, Uninor's difficulties in India were not the only source of concern at Telenor corporate headquarters. Another concern was the lack of coordination across Telenor.

We have observed that Telenor had developed as an essentially multidomestic MNE, that is, a decentralized MNE with each business unit having extensive local autonomy to adapt services to the local market. In 2004, Telenor developed a knowledge management information system (KMIS) that generated systematic overviews of local best practices (Gooderham and Ulset, 2007). Further, corporate-wide teams drawing on a range of local senior executives employed the KMIS to select best practices for replication across business units. However, as a multidomestic MNE, Telenor business units retained a veto and would regularly reject any best practice initiative that they viewed as maladapted to their specific local needs. Thus, while Telenor corporate headquarters was not ignorant of developments at its various business units, local autonomy meant that it lacked the capabilities to convert its knowledge of local best practices to global best practices.

In 2011, Telenor concluded that this degree of local autonomy was preventing effective implementation of global best practices. While building on previous experiences, it decided to create a new central unit, 'Group Industrial Development' (GID), which was given responsibility for cross-unit learning, replication of best practices within marketing and technology and the governance of selected functions such as shared services and procurement (Elter, Gooderham and Ulset, 2014).

D.6 GID

In 2012, GID decided that procurement or sourcing was an obvious function with which to start – globally coordinated sourcing of equipment would reap scale advantages that would benefit all business units. GID established a sourcing organization that had as its aim to realize savings of NOK3 billion by the end of 2015. Already by the end of 2013, there was broad recognition of GID's success in delivering substantial savings across Telenor's business units.

GID's achievements with global sourcing was at least in part a political feat. Although it had a mandate from CEO Baksaas, GID nevertheless had to develop its operations in the context of a multidomestic MNE with a relatively autonomous business unit and MDs who have a focus on their own respective results. The governance outcome was certainly not a centralized autocracy but nor was it the voluntarism that had characterized Telenor until 2012. One aspect to GID was that from the outset it recognized that developing centralized solutions and delivering these as 'manuals' to the business units (BUs) would not work by themselves. Instead, GID recruited among managers who had had operational roles in the various BUs and who could therefore enter into a dialogue based on a mutual understanding of local BU needs with erstwhile BU colleagues about what 'blueprints' could work.

Thus, while GID had a clear mandate to centralize and coordinate sourcing, it did so based on a robust dialogue. Olav Sande, who was a manager in Uninor from 2009 to 2011 prior to joining GID, commented that he could only recall one occasion when dialogue did not work and when differences escalated into a head-on collision with a BU that was resolved top-down. Otherwise, instead of the use of fiat, GID would allow recalcitrant BUs to opt out of corporate purchasing solutions on the condition that they accepted full transparency and full accountability to verify that their local solutions had delivered superior results. However, these were exceptions and as GID delivered substantial, rigorously quantified and thoroughly communicated savings based on 'robust dialogue' and an understanding that it needed to prove its worth through demonstrable value delivery, its standing increased and BU exceptionalism decreased.

D.7 GID and transfer from BOP

In 2014, GID had become so well established that it could move beyond sourcing. Its decision to assess what could be replicated from Uninor's reinvented business model across other Telenor business units was partly a function of the recognition of Uninor's success but also partly because GID contained a number of former Uninor managers who had inside knowledge of how it had achieved a successful turnaround. GID identified four particular practices as fundamental to the Uninor BOP business model: the outsourcing of customer service; the cluster-based operating model; gain sharing with IT vendors; and the cost-effective distribution system geared to and embedded in the BOP context. One conclusion GID drew with Sigve Brekke, who by 2014 had relinquished his MD role at Uninor to exclusively concentrate on his role as Telenor Asia manager, was that all of these practices – indeed the whole of the Uninor model – were transferable to Telenor's new BOP operation in Myanmar.

Another conclusion drawn by GID and Brekke was that the outsourcing of customer service, the cluster-based operating model and gain sharing with IT vendors were all transferable to Telenor's other Asian business units. However, GID and Brekke viewed the Uninor distribution system inappropriate to the significantly more top-of-the-pyramid operations of these business units. There was simply no need to employ a combination of local entrepreneurs, Mom and Pop stores and an army of RSEs in these settings.

Finally, GID concluded that the Uninor distribution system was also equally unsuitable for Telenor's Scandinavian and European business units that operate in almost exclusively postpaid markets as opposed to Uninor's prepaid market. Based on the learning from Uninor, gain sharing with IT vendors was introduced particularly in the original market, Norway. Additionally, GID viewed the outsourcing of customer service as a practice with significant potential for all markets, including Scandinavian and European markets, where there is a functional call-centre industry. The prospect of outsourcing customer service was subject to a great deal of discussion. There were sceptics who regarded customer service as a core competence in their customer-centric top-of-the-pyramid positioning. However, GID recruited the head of this function at Uninor and gave him the opportunity to create a business case adapted to the specific requirements of the Scandinavian and European business units. In this, he and his team were effective and GID began to replicate modified versions of customer service outsourcing across all Scandinavian and European business units. The cluster-based operating model was viewed as having significant potential in all Asian markets.

London and Hart (2004) suggest that BOP business models can have relevance for top-of-the-pyramid business units. The evidence is that because of the formation of GID, which not only had a mandate to identify and transfer best practices across Telenor, but by 2014 also a high standing across Telenor, certain core practices developed by Uninor crossed into top-of-the-pyramid business units (BUs) not least in Asia but also in Scandinavia and Europe. However, we also observe that the replication of the entire Uninor business model was confined to Myanmar, another BOP market. We summarize our findings in Table D.1.

D.8 Conclusion

At least two resources were central for Uninor's ability to engage with business development at BOP – a 'deep pocket' and managerial capabilities. Thus, the turnaround at Uninor was partly dependent on Telenor having the resources or 'slack' to allow Uninor to survive its initial failure (Berrone et al., 2013). In addition, Telenor could draw on managers with well-developed BOP insight (ibid.). Headed by Sigve Brekke, Uninor's second management team brought to bear an entirely different repertoire of skills and insights that enabled it to innovate rather than to continue with local adaptation. The question as to why Telenor did not draw on these managers prior to the launch of Uninor would appear to be a product of an assumption that Uninor would be operating, as usual, at the top-of-the-pyramid and a degree of 'overconfidence' that competition could be overcome (Cain, Moore and Haran, 2015). Thus, its initial choice fell on managers who had been successful and, because they were in geographically proximate areas to Telenor corporate headquarters, were relatively frequent visitors to corporate headquarters.

Table D.1 Transfer of practices from BOP in India to other business units (BUs) in Telenor

Practice Developed in Uninor	Transferred to Other Asian Markets	Transferred to European Top-of-the pyramid Markets
Outsourcing of customer service Outsourcing practice established in Uninor. Generic blueprints developed by GID based on Uninor experiences and some early outsourcing attempts in other markets	Blueprints deployed in two additional BUs	Blueprints deployed in five business units in Europe. Local adaptations influenced by maturity of local call-centre industry
Cluster-based operating model (CBOM)	All Asian BUs	Modified versions in all European BUs
Gain sharing with IT vendor New partner model for IT services co-developed with Wipro (IT development and maintenance)	Agreement between Uninor and Wipro was extended to most other Asia operations	Gain-sharing model with vendor applied in Scandinavia, but with other vendors
Cost-effective distribution systems Systems developed in Uninor together with Wipro (distribution, intelligence, commission management towards retailers)	Modified version in all Asia BUs	
Replication of the whole Uninor operating model	When establishing a new operation in Myanmar the whole operating model used in Uninor was replicated with some adaptations to Myanmar, a pure BOP market	

Eventually, necessity triggered the need for Telenor to look for managerial resources outside its immediate circle. Sigve Brekke, who for many years had been located in Asia but who had been preoccupied with fine-tuning these operations during the Uninor launch, was persuaded to double up as Telenor Asia manager and MD of Uninor for an interim period and to recruit managers who were locally adapted.

The transfer of BOP practices was only possible because GID had achieved a standing across Telenor that gave it the credibility to engage in the facilitation and coordination of their transfer. Part of this standing derived from its ability to deliver substantial savings from sourcing that benefitted the BUs. However, a second part derived from its style of interacting with BUs. Instead of top-down, centralized autocracy, because GID contained many managers with extensive BU experience, GID was able to develop a relationship with the BUs based on 'robust dialogue'. Finally, GID's understanding of its authority was based on having to 'prove its worth' to the BUs rather than being able to deploy sanctions.

We would go beyond arguing that the transfer of BOP practices was contingent on the existence of GID. The particular character of GID was critical. Had the BUs perceived GID as too domineering, there may have been resistance to transfer from BOP. Equally, had a domineering GID existed at the point in time at which Uninor engaged in business model reinvention, this could have blocked BOP innovation. After all, one critical advantage of Telenor's multidomestic heritage was that Brekke and his team had considerable autonomy to engage with the turnaround at Uninor and thus significant latitude to innovate. A more globally integrated MNE would likely have insisted that corporate blueprints be given yet another opportunity. It appears that in the context of multidomestic MNEs, the ability for capabilities developed in BOP business environments to travel up the pyramid is conditional on the emergence of a global integrative function regarded by BUs as credible, capable and non-threatening (Bartlett and Ghoshal, 1995).

CASE DISCUSSION

1. What were the main challenges that the managers of Uninor faced when entering the Indian market?
2. Compare the way in which Uninor wanted to compete at the top-of-the-pyramid with the way they competed in the bottom of the pyramid and discuss if the change in strategy helped Uninor overcome liability of foreignness in India.
3. Discuss whether Uninor built its competitive position in the market on FSAs (here Telenor's specific advantages) when it tried to compete in the top-of-the-pyramid and when it succeeded in establishing a market position in the bottom of the pyramid.
4. Discuss whether other firms can learn from the Telenor experience.

NOTE

* Originally published as: Gooderham, P.N., S. Ulset and F. Elter (2016), 'Beyond local responsiveness – multi-domestic multinationals at the bottom-of-the-pyramid', in T. Ambos, B. Ambos and J. Birkinshaw (eds), *Perspectives on Headquarters–Subsidiary Relationships in the Contemporary MNC* (pp. 3–26), Bingley, UK: Emerald Group Publishing Limited.

REFERENCES

Bartlett, C.A. and S. Ghoshal (1995), *Transnational Management: Text, Cases and Readings in Cross-Border Management*, 2nd edition, Chicago, IL: Irwin.

Berrone, P., A. Fosfuri, L. Gelabert and L. Gomez-Mejía (2013), 'Necessity as the mother of green inventions: Institutional pressures and environmental innovations', *Strategic Management Journal*, **34**(8), 891–909.

Cain, D.M., D.A. Moore and U. Haran (2015), 'Making sense of overconfidence in market entry', *Strategic Management Journal*, **36**(1), 1–18.

Demil, B., X. Lecocq, J.E. Ricart and C. Zott (2015), 'Introduction to the SEJ Special Issue on business models: Business models within the domain of strategic entrepreneurship', *Strategic Entrepreneurship Journal*, **9**(1), 1–11.

Elter, F., P.N. Gooderham and S. Ulset (2014), 'Functional-level transformation in multi-domestic MNCs: Transforming local purchasing into globally integrated purchasing', in T. Pedersen, L. Tihanyi, T.M. Devinney and M. Venzin (eds), *Orchestration of the Global Network Organization: Advances in International Management* (pp. 99–120), Bingley, UK: Emerald Group Publishing Limited.

Financial Times (2010), 'Telecommunications: A tough call', 24 May 2010.

Gooderham, P.N. and S. Ulset (2007), 'Telenor's "third way"', *EBF – European Business Forum*, **31**, 46–9.

London, T. and S.L. Hart (2004), 'Reinventing strategies for emerging markets: Beyond the transnational model', *Journal of International Business Studies*, **35**(5), 350–70.

Open Magazine (2011), 'The wealth report', 12 March 2011, accessed 22 January 2019 at http://www.openthemagazine.com/article/business/the-wealth-report.

Prahalad, C.K. and L. Lieberthal (2003), 'The end of corporate imperialism', *Harvard Business Review*, **81**(8), 109–17.

Seelos, C. and J. Mair (2007), 'Profitable business models and market creation in the context of deep poverty: A strategic view', *The Academy of Management Perspectives*, **21**(4), 49–63.

Total Telecom (2010), 'Mobile services in India: Too many cooks', *Total Telecom Plus*, September, 2010, accessed on 18 April 2019 at https://www.totaltele.com/view.aspx?C=0&ID=458382.

Zott, C., R. Amit and L. Massa (2011), 'The business model: Recent developments and future research', *Journal of Management*, **37**(4), 1019–42.

4
Strategic decisions: Operating modes

4.1 Introduction

As we discussed in Chapter 2, once a firm decides to internationalize, it must also choose how to internationalize. There are multiple operating modes that firms can utilize, each with distinct benefits and costs. Several theoretical perspectives are used to understand the choice of operating mode (see, e.g., Forsgren, 2017 and Welch, Benito and Petersen, 2018, for comprehensive overviews). However, different theories tend to emphasize different decision criteria. The purpose of this chapter is to briefly describe the most common operating modes and discuss the theoretical rationales behind these choices.

4.2 Foreign operating modes

Once a firm has decided to enter the international arena a firm can choose from a range of operating modes that require different levels of commitment in the foreign markets. Operating modes are sometimes referred to as entry modes, reflecting that the operating mode was decided upon entry to a foreign market. Operating modes selected upon entry to a foreign market often evolve or change over time (Benito, Petersen and Welch, 2009; Welch et al., 2018). We will therefore use the terminology 'operating mode' rather than 'entry mode' in this book to reflect ongoing dynamics and the flexibility to change operating modes over time. An MNE's choice of operating mode reflects a fundamental decision to carry out its activities in foreign countries using market contracts or setting up a firm. Internalization theory (Buckley and Casson, 1976) explains the choice between markets or firm modes of operation as one that depends on the relative costs and benefits of these two different ways of carrying out activities.

Many scholars have contributed to our understanding of what factors shape the costs and benefits of carrying out activities across markets or within firms (Coase, 1937, 1988; Hart, 1995; Masten, 1993; Williamson, 1975,

1985). This literature points to two important differences between activities carried out in the firm and across markets. The first difference stems from the definition of the firm as a legal entity that owns resources. Ownership over resources provides a firm with legal rights to decide on how to use these resources. Thus, a firm that chooses to produce and distribute goods by setting up a subsidiary in a foreign market has the power to decide on how its assets are to be used in that subsidiary. If the firm instead makes the choice to sell its production knowledge to another firm using a licensing contract (market contracting) it does not have the same decision rights. For example, its contracting partner could decide to break the contract and leave the relationship. The transaction cost theory (Williamson, 1975, 1985) and the property rights theory of the firm (Hart, 1995) argue that the possibility of hold-up from suppliers determines whether a firm should own those resources that are most important to the value-creating activities it conducts. Hold-up occurs if a supplier (or buyer) breaks a market contract and renegotiates contractual terms to its favour and to the harm of the focal firm's investment in activities and resources that it cannot use outside the contract.

In international business, entry modes are often classified as equity and non-equity modes of entry (Santangelo and Meyer, 2017, p. 1117; see also Table 4.1). If a firm chooses to conduct its foreign activities using an equity mode of entry, it has made the choice to fully or partially own (or control through ownership of shares) the assets that are needed. The equity entry modes are full or controlling ownership of a subsidiary or joint venture or engaging in a strategic alliance supported by mutual ownership (swapping of shares). One downside for an MNE that chooses equity modes of entry is the risk it faces of losing its assets if the country it operates in expropriates its assets. Another related risk arises if the subsidiary or joint venture fails in the foreign market. An MNE that invests in setting up a firm often faces high sunk costs that make it difficult to simply 'swap' to a different producer if the

Table 4.1 An overview of common operating modes

Non-equity (Contractual) Modes	Equity Modes
Exporting (indirectly or through third party distributor)	Exporting with MNE-owned sales subsidiaries
Licensing	International joint ventures (equity-based alliances)
Franchising	Wholly-owned subsidiaries
Contract manufacturing and service provision	
Non-equity alliances	

subsidiary or joint venture is not competitive. If the MNE instead chooses to enter using a market contract it would usually have terms that allow it to terminate the relationship with significantly fewer losses.

The second difference between conducting an activity within a firm and using a market contract pertains to the definition of the firm as a governance structure that is supported by different legal principles compared to market contracts. This difference implies that within the boundary of a firm, managers use administrative control as a means to adapt value-creating activities to unforeseen changes. When an MNE decides to set up a subsidiary with employees in a foreign country, the managers in that subsidiary have authority to make decisions and to solve conflicts (within the mandate they have from HQ). In fact, most often courts will not listen to cases that involve firm-internal conflicts, thus allowing managers to be the judges of firm-internal matters (Williamson, 1985). If instead the MNE decides to carry out its activities using a market contract such as, for example, a franchise contract, the parties would need to renegotiate their contract when major unanticipated changes in the market made adaptation necessary. Moreover, the MNE could not without consent from the franchisee monitor its employees. Higher agency cost within firms can outweigh the benefits from flexibility and easy control.

Within firms, agency costs arise because of the difficulty in creating incentives that compel employees to deliver efficient effort. Employees may work on input that cannot be measured or they may undertake a variety of activities individually or in teams, all of which makes it difficult to create rewards that ensure maximum effort. Low agency costs represent one of the benefits to MNEs when they use market contracts as entry modes. In part, this is so because firms only use contracts when they can specify the input or output they need and determine a way of sharing the value that is created in the contracting relationship. For example, in a franchise contract, the parties specify each of the parties' rights and duties as well as how the value created (either the profit or the revenue) will be shared in ways that provide the parties with the best incentives to deliver effort. Another but distinct consideration is the issue of how the MNE should best deploy the advantages it has from the knowledge it has accumulated. The knowledge a firm has developed is difficult to price ('buyer uncertainty') and difficult to protect from imitation. This situation is often referred to as 'market failure'. Firms have to decide what activities should be internalized and which can be organized using market-based contracts.

In sum, the operating modes we now discuss vary in terms of the risk they involve; they require diverse organizational, management and resource demands; and they differ in the amount of control that can be exercised over foreign operations. The operating modes that require a high level of equity commitment also involve a high risk of losing the investment while low-equity entry modes can entail a high risk of hold up. The equity modes of entry often have higher agency costs, but they also allow for more flexibility. Finally, the equity modes allow for direct control of employees and activities, whereas the non-equity modes typically require contractual consent. The operating modes are not mutually exclusive as MNEs often combine or 'package' different operating modes (Welch et al., 2018). In other words, although we introduce operating modes and ownership structures separately, many MNEs combine multiple operating modes and bundles of ownership structures evolve over time.

We will now briefly describe the most common operating modes.

4.3 Exporting

Exporting can be a good starting point and relatively low-risk entry strategy as it involves little capital investment and lower exit barriers. As such, it is an obvious alternative for firms lacking in capital resources. However, the umbrella term 'exporting' includes a variety of activities, some of which can be complex as well as risky. Tariffs, quotas or various conditions of trade agreements make exporting less attractive. Geographical distances can also generate higher transportation costs and reduce the feasibility of sending end products to a foreign market.

There are different forms of export. Firms can choose to export indirectly (e.g., through other firms that are present in the domestic market), through third party distributors in the foreign market or by establishing foreign sales subsidiaries (Welch et al., 2018). Each alternative has both advantages and disadvantages. Exporting indirectly through a trading company can speed up the process and eliminate barriers associated with a lack of knowledge about the foreign markets. In the long term, however, such indirect relationships with markets may stunt growth opportunities and reduce the MNE's ability to respond to specific market needs. Exporting through third party distributors in foreign markets brings the MNE closer to the foreign market while tapping into existing local expertise. Foreign distributors often have well-established distribution channels and thus complement the MNE's transferrable FSAs with location-specific advantages. However, in order to succeed with this operating mode, the MNE needs to ensure alignment between local marketing and sales activities and the MNE's strategy. To achieve this the MNE often needs to be involved in a cooperative relationship with the local distributor. In his study of distributor agreements, Arnold (2000) found that relationships with third party distributors often fail because firms overestimate the abilities of local partners to identify and meet needs in terms of growth and market development.

Some firms instead choose to set up a wholly-owned sales subsidiary. This option relies on the firm's ability to establish or tap into local distribution channels, which may be both costly and time consuming.

4.4 Licensing

Licensing is another operating mode often perceived as low commitment and low financial risk. It is particularly useful in countries where regulations limit market entry or where tariffs and quotas make exporting a non-viable strategy. It is also often preferred when the target country is culturally distant from the home country or there is little prior experience of the host country. A licensing agreement gives a firm in a host country the right to produce and sell a product for a specified period in return for a fee. A licence requires that the contracting parties make explicit what needs to be transferred. It also presumes that contracts can be enforced in ways that protect the transferred knowledge from imitation by third party. As we have already noted above, this is not necessarily the case. Indeed, the main weakness with licensing is the licensor's lack of control over the licensee. This applies to quality standards that, if disregarded, can be detrimental to the brand's image. It also applies to the monitoring of sales that form the basis for royalty payments. That is why licensing is primarily suitable for the mature phase of a product's life cycle in which the technology that is transferred to the licensee is older and standardized. In other phases of a product's life cycle, direct ownership is more viable to avoid the risk that the licensee appropriates the competence underlying the product, thereby becoming a direct competitor. Countries with weak institutions (e.g., legal systems to protect patents and settle contractual disputes) are therefore less attractive for licensing as it increases the risk for unwanted knowledge dissemination (Hennart, 2009).

4.5 Franchising

Franchising is similar to licensing but more comprehensive. For a fee and royalty payments the franchisee receives a complete package comprising the franchiser's trademark, products and services, and a complete set of operating principles, thereby creating the illusion of a worldwide company. The franchising agreement thus typically details the business concept and restrains the franchisee to specific marketing strategies and promotions

(Welch et al., 2018). Over 90 per cent of McDonald's 36 000 outlets in more than 100 countries are franchised (McDonald's, 2018). McDonald's, like many other franchisers, places great emphasis on ensuring consistent quality. Notwithstanding the detailed contractual agreements, which in McDonald's case even includes a strict training program, McDonald's allows local markets significant latitude to evaluate the need for local adaptation of menu items, marketing, community involvement and how the local businesses are managed (ibid.).

4.6 Contract manufacturing and service provision

Nike distinguishes between design, product development and marketing on the one hand and shoe and clothing manufacturing on the other. Nike does not carry out the latter activities as they have outsourced these to independent plants in developing economies such as China, Indonesia, Thailand and Vietnam, primarily for cost reasons. The main benefits to Nike are that it has none of the problems of local ownership, nor does it invest its own capital in manufacturing. Nonetheless, various pressure groups have ensured that Nike at various times has been the focus for international scrutiny because of allegations of sexual harassment and physical and verbal abuse of workers at its contract factories. Increasingly, Nike has recognized that it cannot relinquish moral responsibility for conditions at contractor manufacturers. It has even commissioned outside groups such as the Global Alliance for Workers and Communities to examine conditions in its contractor plants as a means to improve those conditions (see Chapter 5).

Mobile phone vendors, including Sony Ericsson, Apple and Motorola, have applied the same model to handset manufacturing. They outsource the production of handsets to Asian companies, such as the Singapore-based Flextronics, on a contractual basis while retaining control of research, design, branding and marketing. The key advantage to mobile phone vendors in not owning their own factories is that they have the flexibility to ramp production up or down in accordance with extreme fluctuations in demand without long-term capital investments or an increase in their labour forces. The disadvantage lies in that they are handing over control of a vital part of their supply chain. Not only is quality control more problematic, there is also a dependency on the contract equipment manufacturer (CEM) possessing or having access to the necessary parts.

Contract arrangements are by no means confined to manufacturing. Nearly half of the 500 largest MNEs regularly use Indian IT service providers on a contractual basis, attracted by the combination of low costs and advanced processing skills. The contracts involve a spread of IT services from low-value work, such as systems maintenance, to the more lucrative development of new applications such as internet-based portals. Distribution may also be outsourced. When MNEs use contracts this extensively, the MNE becomes a nexus of contractually determined obligations that together constitute a complete supply chain. This emerging organizational form makes for a new set of managerial challenges – the management of contracts and relationships across borders.

4.7 Foreign direct investments (FDI)

Firms can make different kinds of FDI. Some firms prefer to build wholly-owned subsidiaries 'from scratch', that is, engage in greenfield investment. Others choose to acquire an existing local firm to benefit from its advantages. Another FDI choice is to form an international joint venture (IJV) where equity levels can vary (next section). Finally, firms can enter into strategic alliance with suppliers or even competitors where the partners acquire minor shareholdings in the strategic partner. Firms are more likely to seek equity-based strategic alliances with local partners when diversifying into a less related sector, or when the scale of foreign operations is large compared to the size of the firm (Grøgaard and Verbeke, 2012). Collaboration with a local partner allows the firm to extend its competitive advantages into more locations faster and with reduced cost and market uncertainty. This enables it to focus its resources on further developing its core competencies. Another advantage is that a local partner can provide necessary complementary assets such as knowledge of the local economy or product-specific knowledge.

One view is that a wholly-owned subsidiary may be preferred whenever the MNE needs control over its intangible assets, whether they be technology or brand loyalty (Anderson and Gatignon, 1986; Gatignon and Anderson, 1988; Shrader, 2001). Further, full ownership of subsidiaries is preferable if prospective partners are located in countries with low levels of transparency. By low transparency we are referring to untrustworthy and badly functioning public institutions like the police and judiciary that make contracts difficult to enforce. The annual Corruption Perceptions Index published by Transparency International broadly captures these risks. Table 4.2 includes a sample of the more than 170 countries included in the index for 2016.

However, Brouthers (2002) has argued that it is precisely in settings with low levels of transparency that local partners may actually be preferred to full ownership because of their ability to supply significant local institutional and cultural knowledge. Indeed, this may explain why MNEs often choose

Table 4.2 The Corruption Perceptions Index 2016 (0 = very corrupt to 100 = very 'clean')

Country	Score
Denmark	90
Sweden	88
Norway	85
Netherlands	83
Germany	81
United Kingdom	81
USA	74
Japan	72
France	69
Spain	58
Italy	47
China	40
India	40
Mexico	30
Russia	29
Bangladesh	26

Source: Transparency International (2016), 'Corruption Perceptions Index 2016', accessed 11 February 2019 at https://www.transparency.org/news/feature/corruption_perceptions_index_2016.

joint ventures in settings that they regard as foreign and high risk (Brouthers, 2002; Gatignon and Anderson, 1988). In other words, when firms take the chance of entering high-risk countries, some form of IJV is often preferable to full ownership despite the difficulty in enforcing contracts.

4.8 International joint ventures (IJVs)

The establishment of international joint ventures (IJVs) has been an increasing trend since the 1970s. IJVs are defined by Chen, Park and Newburry (2009, p. 1133) as 'legally independent entities formed by two or more parent firms from different countries that share equity investments and consequent returns'. The basis of most IJV structures involves an MNE and a local partner pooling their respective competitive advantages to produce a product or service together.

Until recently, an IJV was the only means of entry into India because local participation was mandatory. Although China has eased its restrictions on full foreign ownership, some industries are still considered 'restricted areas'. However, even when local participation is not obligatory, an IJV may be appropriate because a local partner can provide intermediate inputs such as local market knowledge, access to distribution networks and natural resources, as well as making the MNE an insider in the host country. In the case of emerging markets such as China, the MNE typically contributes product and process technology, brand name/trademark, and international marketing support; while the local partner contributes local knowledge-related expertise such as local marketing, local personnel management, and management of local government relations (Hitt et al., 2000; Inkpen and Beamish, 1997).

Generally, an IJV consists of an MNE and a local partner each holding equity in the IJV. Equity proportions vary but usually relative ownership approximates to 50–50, although there are many variations including IJVs with more than two partners including relatively passive partners with minority holdings. Control of the five to ten management positions that typically constitute the top management group of an IJV is a central issue in IJV negotiations, particularly concerning the top position of general manager. This position usually goes to the partner that has the dominant equity position or some other basis of power such as critical technology. The partner that does not win the top position will argue strongly for other slots that guarantee the desired level of representation. Typically, members of the management group of IJVs have two agendas: on the one hand, they are expected to commit themselves to the success of the IJV, on the other they are 'delegates' of their respective parents. As legal entities, IJVs have boards of directors who set strategic priorities and make decisions regarding the use of profits and investment policy (Hambrick et al., 2001).

The benefits of IJVs are that they provide a combination of rapid entry into new markets, risk-sharing and increased economies of scale. The problem they face relates to diverging expectations and objectives. Rarely is there an equal match between the two partners since the MNE is usually the stronger partner in terms of technology and management skills. The result is that the local partner may come to view the MNE as overzealous in protecting its core technology and in imposing its control on the joint venture, while the MNE finds it difficult to trust its local partner. The friction that this generates is a major explanation of why many IJVs result in partner dissatisfaction or outright failure. Indeed, some surveys have suggested such outcomes for about half of MNEs with IJVs (Bamford, Ernst and Gubini, 2004), and there is evidence of particular difficulties for IJVs involving Chinese partners (Child and Yan, 2003).

The IJV literature strongly suggests that it is uncommon to find congruent underlying motivations for forming the IJV (see, e.g., Parkhe, 1991). In countries such as China neither parent is likely to be primarily committed to the long-term overall success of the IJV. Thus, it may be the case that a Western partner is seeking market experience whereas the Chinese partner's primary motive is technology acquisition (Luo, Shenkar and Nyaw, 2001), with the Western partner being concerned that its know-how will be appropriated by its Chinese partner. Thus, Chen et al. (2009, p. 1142) characterize the IJV 'as a mixed motive game between parents who cooperate and compete at the same time'.

Because of its multiparty nature – foreign partner, local partner and management – the IJV control system can be 'particularly troublesome' (ibid., p. 1151). While the literature on IJVs acknowledges the importance of legally enforceable contracts in resolving opportunism (e.g., Chen, 2010), it also stresses that the effectiveness of contractually based control is questionable in emerging economies such as China. The reason is that there is a relatively lower legislative quality and effectiveness in law enforcement (Pistor and Xu, 2005). This institutional deficiency in emerging economies accentuates the distinction between control through ownership control and operational management control. Some argue that it is particularly the latter that is critical for exercising influence over IJV operations in the context of emerging economies such as China (cf. Steensma and Lyles, 2000).

Choi and Beamish (2004) outline four broad management options available to MNEs and their local partners:

- Each partner controls its own firm-specific advantages (split control management).
- Both partners share control over all firm-specific advantages (shared management or shared control).
- The MNE partner assumes a dominant control over all firm-specific advantages (MNE partner–dominant management).
- The local emerging market partner assumes a dominant control over all firm-specific advantages (local partner–dominant management).

Choi and Beamish's review of previous research indicates an exclusive focus on the latter three options and, in regard to these three options, no consensus about their effect on IJV performance. Their own research includes all four options and suggests that split control management can have a positive effect on IJV performance in contrast to the other three alternatives that did not show any significant performance effects.

In his seminal research on IJVs, Madhok (1995a) was interested in why alliances such as IJVs between firms are so popular when the available evidence suggests that the majority end in dissatisfaction or outright failure. He argued that in understanding why some IJVs are successful it is necessary to go beyond just the issues of ownership and control and to include the relationship between the partners. In particular, including the concept of trust between partners enriches the insights of purely ownership-centred explanations. Further, Madhok acknowledged that trust functions differently in different institutional contexts and different countries/cultures manifest different propensities to trust. 'In fact, in some cultures, giving your word is tighter than putting something in the contract' (Madhok, 2006a, p. 6). Understanding what makes for the successful management of IJVs involves an analysis of cultural and institutional contexts.

Madhok distinguishes between two types of trust – structural and social trust – both of which are necessary for the sustenance of an IJV relationship. Neither is sufficient in and of itself. The structural aspect of trust refers 'to the complementarity of the resources contributed' (Madhok, 1995b, p. 59) and is the economic basis for the IJV. The social aspect refers to the intrinsic quality of the relationship itself.

Madhok distinguishes two reasons why the structural dimension is insufficient by itself:

> Firstly, a weak social foundation undermines the potential value of the synergy that can be gained by two firms pooling their assets together, since contributions become much more tentative... Furthermore, the cost of the operation increases since the greater expectation of opportunism by a partner causes the other to bear higher costs of installing safeguards against opportunism. (Madhok, 2006b, p. 121)

Second, because contributions to the IJV cannot be continuously evenly matched, the social dimension 'provides the tolerance through the social "glue"' (ibid.) to preserve the relationship during periods of disequilibrium and inequity. In other words, deeply embedded social relations mitigate the breakdown of the relationship in periods of flux and inequity. However, social trust is not 'superglue': if 'complementary assets' disappear for an extended period then no amount of social trust can save the IJV.

4.9 Wholly-owned subsidiaries

Disregarding any local ownership restrictions imposed by host country governments, MNEs prefer wholly-owned subsidiaries to IJVs when this is considered more efficient in terms of governance costs and access to intermediate inputs. Similarly, knowledge that is tacit or poorly codified is difficult and costly to transfer across organizational boundaries may be a factor that leads to full ownership. This calculation may well stem from problems in locating a reliable or knowledge-rich partner but it is also to some extent influenced by the MNE's national culture. It has, for example, been shown that all things being equal the propensity for US firms investing in Japan to choose joint ventures over wholly-owned subsidiaries is substantially higher than for Japanese firms investing in the USA (Makino and Neupert, 2001).

Wholly-owned subsidiaries can be established through mergers and acquisitions (M&As) on the one hand and start-ups (e.g., greenfield investments) on the other. Although it is often difficult to distinguish between mergers and acquisitions in precise terms, mergers are usually the result of a friendly arrangement between companies of roughly equal size, whereas acquisitions are unequal partnerships that can also be the product of a hard-fought battle between acquiring and target companies. Since the beginning of the 1990s, more firms have engaged in M&As for an FDI. By the end of the 1990s, most new FDI was in the form of M&As and the preference for M&As over greenfield investments has continued over the past decades (UNCTAD, 2018). The preference for M&As has partly been attributed to asymmetric information, where 'financial markets usually provide efficient mechanisms to set the value of M&A targets, while there is no such mechanism to assess the value of greenfield investments' (UNCTAD, 2010, p. 9). This also makes M&As more vulnerable to economic downturns as access to capital shrinks and the market evaluation mechanisms are more volatile.

M&As have the advantage of providing rapid entry into a market and therefore economies of scale. Established product lines, distribution channels and insider status are all obtained. They can also be of great value as a means of capturing new expertise. On the other hand, the difficulties encountered in integrating the acquisition into the culture and overall strategy of the MNE should not be underestimated, particularly in the case of acquisitions where there may be deep resentment amongst employees in the acquired unit. Frequently, despite due diligence, the acquirer also lacks a proper understanding of what has been acquired. A new identity for the acquired firm has to be developed and as acquired businesses often involve a seat on the parent board there may be board-level disagreement as to precisely what that identity is. The difficulties are such that as many as 50 per cent of M&As fail (Child, Faulkner and Pitkethly, 2001).

Michael Porter counsels:

> [B]e especially careful when making and integrating acquisitions. You buy a Spanish company and all you're going to hear from them is how things are done

in Spain. Economists have been studying mergers for twenty years and they find that the seller gets most of the value, not the buyer. Foreign acquisitions must be forcefully repositioned around your strategy, not allowed to continue theirs (unless, of course, theirs is better!). (Porter in Magretta, 2012, p. 195)

Greenfield investments do not involve having to grapple with the problem of integrating existing organizational cultures and creating a unified purpose. Such foreign investments can thus develop in a more gradual and controlled way. Nevertheless, as an operating mode when entering a foreign market, it generally carries the highest risk particularly in countries with nationalistic attitudes toward foreign ownership. Greenfield investments also require the longest time to establish, the greatest contribution of know-how, and the ability of the MNE to overcome elements of distance by developing necessary location-bound FSAs.

The choice of greenfield versus acquisition tends to be affected by the industry the MNE is operating in. MNEs operating in industries that are driven by unique or superior technical expertise are characterized by a preference for greenfield investments since they can build their operations in a way that minimizes the costs in transferring their knowledge. This is particularly attractive when necessary complementary assets are easily transacted in the foreign market. An acquisition will often involve dealing with incompatible methods for absorbing and processing knowledge and even a low motivation for new knowledge. Harzing (2002) has shown that differences in firms' international strategies also have an influence on the choice of entry mode. MNEs that are particularly focused on adapting their products and policies to the local market tend to prefer acquisitions because the acquired subsidiary will at the outset be aligned with host country conditions, while MNEs that regard their subsidiaries as pipelines for standardized, cost-efficient products will prefer greenfields where higher levels of control and coordination can be achieved. Finally, there is the impact of prior experience. MNEs that have successfully employed acquisitions will be more likely to choose acquisitions in subsequent entries (Chang and Rosenzweig, 2001).

4.10 Summary

Choosing the appropriate operating mode is a complex task that requires continuous flexibility. Despite decades of research within this area, the factors that influence these strategic choices and subsequent performance outcomes are still unclear (Dikova and Brouthers, 2016). Even though we present each choice of operating mode as distinct, there is no end-state and within one and the same MNE there may be a mix of operating modes.

Recent research within this field reflects this complexity, with an increased attention to operating mode flexibility and mode combinations (Welch et al., 2018). The case study following this chapter addresses the challenges of IJVs. BKT, a Swedish MNE, has experienced rapid international growth through a mix of operating modes. In China, it has set up two ostensibly identical joint ventures. However, they perform very differently. The case study provides an opportunity to explore why BKT experienced these performance differences and how it chose to address these.

REFERENCES

Anderson, E. and H. Gatignon (1986), 'Modes of foreign entry: A transaction cost analysis and proposition', *Journal of International Business Studies*, **17**, 1–16.

Arnold, D. (2000), 'Seven rules of international distribution', *Harvard Business Review*, **78**(6), 131–7.

Bamford, J., D. Ernst and D.G. Gubini (2004), 'Launching a world-class joint venture', *Harvard Business Review*, **82**(2), 91–100.

Benito, G., B. Petersen and L. Welch (2009), 'Towards more realistic conceptualisations of foreign operation modes', *Journal of International Business Studies*, **40**(9), 1455–70.

Brouthers, K.D. (2002), 'Institutional, cultural and transaction cost influences on entry mode choice and performance', *Journal of International Business Studies*, **33**(2), 203–21.

Buckley, P.J. and M.C. Casson (1976), *The Future of the Multinational Enterprise*, London: Macmillan.

Chang, S.J. and P.M. Rosenzweig (2001), 'The choice of entry mode in sequential foreign direct investment', *Strategic Management Journal*, **22**(8), 747–76.

Chen, D., S.H. Park and W. Newburry (2009), 'Parent contribution and organizational control in international joint ventures', *Strategic Management Journal*, **30**(11), 1133–56.

Chen, S.F.S. (2010), 'A general TCE model of international business institutions: Market failure and reciprocity', *Journal of International Business Studies*, **41**(6), 935–59.

Child, J. and Y. Yan (2003), 'Predicting the performance of international joint ventures: An investigation in China', *Journal of Management Studies*, **40**(2), 283–320.

Child, J., D. Faulkner and R. Pitkethly (2001), *The Management of International Acquisitions*, Oxford: Oxford University Press.

Choi, C.B. and P.W. Beamish (2004), 'Split management control and international joint venture performance', *Journal of International Business Studies*, **35**(3), 201–15.

Coase, R. (1937), 'The nature of the firm', *Economica*, **4**, 386–405.

Coase, R. (1988), 'The nature of the firm: Influence', *The Journal of Law and Economics*, **4**(1), 33–47.

Dikova, D. and K. Brouthers (2016), 'International establishment mode choice: Past, present and future', *Management International Review*, **56**(4), 489–530.

Forsgren, M. (2017), *Theories of the Multinational Firm: A Multidimensional Creature in the Global Economy*, Cheltenham, UK and Northampton, MA, USA: Edward Elgar Publishing.

Gatignon, E. and E. Anderson (1988), 'The multinational corporation's degree of control over foreign subsidiaries', *Journal of Law, Economics and Organization*, **4**, 304–36.

Grøgaard, B. and A. Verbeke (2012), 'Twenty key hypotheses that make internalization theory the general theory of international strategic management', in A. Verbeke and H. Merchant (eds), *Handbook of Research on International Strategic Management*, Cheltenham, UK and Northampton, MA, USA: Edward Elgar Publishing.

Hambrick, D.C., J. Li, K. Xin and A.S. Tsui (2001), 'Compositional gaps and downward spirals in international joint venture management groups', *Strategic Management Journal*, **22**(11), 1033–63.

Hart, O. (1995), *Firms, Contracts and Financial Structure*, Oxford: Clarendon Press.

Harzing, A.W. (2002), 'Acquisitions versus greenfield investments: International strategy and management of entry modes', *Strategic Management Journal*, **23**(3), 211–27.

Hennart, J.F. (2009), 'Down with MNE-centric theories! Market entry and expansion as the bundling of MNE and local assets', *Journal of International Business Studies*, **40**(9), 1432–54.

Hitt, M.A., M.T. Dacin and E. Levitas et al. (2000), 'Partner selection in emerging and developed market contexts: Resource-based and organizational learning perspectives', *Academy of Management Journal*, **43**(3), 449–67.

Inkpen, A.C. and P.W. Beamish (1997), 'Knowledge, bargaining power, and the instability of international joint ventures', *Academy of Management Review*, **22**(1), 177–202.

Luo, Y., O. Shenkar and M. Nyaw (2001), 'A dual parent perspective on control and performance in international joint ventures: Lessons from a developing economy', *Journal of International Business Studies*, **32**(1), 41–55.

Madhok, A. (1995a), 'Revisiting multinational firms' tolerance for joint ventures: A trust-based approach', *Journal of International Business Studies*, **26**(1), 117–38.

Madhok, A. (1995b), 'Opportunism and trust in joint venture relationships: An exploratory study and a model', *Scandinavian Journal of Management*, **11**(1), 57–74.

Madhok, A. (2006a), 'How much does ownership really matter? Equity and trust relations in joint venture relationships', *Journal of International Business Studies*, **37**(1), 4–11.

Madhok, A. (2006b), 'Revisiting multinational firms' tolerance for joint ventures: A trust-based approach', *Journal of International Business Studies*, **26**(1), 117–37.

Magretta, J. (2012), 'FAQs: An interview with Michael Porter', in *Understanding Michael Porter: The Essential Guide to Competition and Strategy*, Boston, MA: Harvard Business School Publishing.

Makino, J. and K.E. Neupert (2001), 'National culture, transaction costs, and the choice between joint venture and wholly owned subsidiary', *Journal of International Business Studies*, **31**(4), 705–13.

Masten, S.E. (1993), 'A legal basis for the firm', in O.E. Williamson and S.G. Winter (eds), *The Nature of the Firm: Origins, Evolution and Development*, Oxford: Oxford University Press.

McDonald's (2018), 'Our business model', accessed 23 January 2019 at https://corporate.mcdonalds.com/corpmcd/about-us/our-business-model.html.

Parkhe, A. (1991), 'Interfirm diversity, organizational learning, and longevity in global strategic alliances', *Journal of International Business Studies*, **22**(4), 579–601.

Pistor, K. and C. Xu (2005), 'Governing stock markets in transition economies: Lessons from China', *American Review of Law and Economics*, **7**(1), 184–210.

Santangelo, G. and K. Meyer (2017), 'Internationalization as an evolutionary process', *Journal of International Business Studies*, **48**(9), 1114–30.

Shrader, R.G. (2001), 'Collaboration and performance in foreign markets: The case of young high-technology manufacturing firms', *Academy of Management Journal*, **44**(1), 45–60.

Steensma, H.K. and M.A. Lyles (2000), 'Explaining IJV survival in a transitional economy through social exchange and knowledge-based perspectives', *Strategic Management Journal*, **21**(8), 831–51.

UNCTAD (2010), *World Investment Report, 2010: Investing in a Low-carbon Economy*, New York and Geneva: UNCTAD.

UNCTAD (2018), *World Investment Report, 2018: Investment and New Industrial Policies*, New York and Geneva: UNCTAD.

Welch, L.S., G.R.G. Benito and B. Petersen (2018), *Foreign Operating Methods: Theory, Analysis, Strategy*, 2nd edition, Cheltenham, UK and Northampton, MA, USA: Edward Elgar Publishing.

Williamson, O.E. (1975), *Markets and Hierarchies: Analysis and Antitrust Implications*, New York: Macmillan.

Williamson, O.E. (1985), *The Economic Institutions of Capitalism*, New York: Free Press.

Case E
BKT – IJVs and the role of effective boundary-spanning activities*

Paul N. Gooderham, Michael Zhang, Atle Jordahl and Kirsten Foss

E.1 Introduction

This case explores the relationship between the formal governance structure of international joint ventures (IJVs) and the informal interpersonal relations among the main boundary spanners in relation to maintaining social trust in the IJV. *International joint ventures* (IJVs) are defined as legally independent entities formed by two or more parent firms from different countries that share equity investments and consequent returns. Silva, Bradley and Sousa (2012) observe that the success of IJVs is less related to ownership structure and more to the presence of trust between the IJV partners.

In the context of an IJV, *boundary spanners* are the individual managers who are the leading representatives of the IJV organizational constituencies and who operate at its various organization–organization interfaces (Luo, 2009; Zaheer, McEvily and Perrone, 1998). Their role is to create the linkages across the organizational boundaries of the IJV and in so doing they have a critical role in the creation of shared meaning and trust (Dyer and Chu, 2000; Li, Poppo and Zhou, 2010; Parkhe, 1991; Zaheer and Kamal, 2011).

Trust is a construct with different meanings. In the context of this case, trust refers to social trust (Madhok, 1995), which denotes the quality of the relationship between IJV partners that is developed after the creation of the IJV. We view the social dimension of trust as being embedded in relational actions and interactions involving social and cognitive processes (Salk and Shenkar, 2001). It is very different from structural trust, which refers to the resource complementarity that constituted the ex-ante or original inducement for both partners to enter the relationship. Structural trust depends on the value added for both partners stemming from the complementarity of the resources contributed by the IJV partners (Madhok, 2006).

IJV partners consistently seek to have 'due representation' in the management of IJVs (Hambrick et al., 2001). The management of IJVs varies but if an appointee of the local partner is the managing director, typically the Western MNE will seek to have an expatriate representative located at the IJV to ensure direct interaction between it and the IJV. The manager of the MNE business unit delegated with the responsibility for interacting with the IJV will effectively also be part of the management group. Each of the individuals occupying these positions is interacting with individuals who are located in different organizational systems and each is therefore engaged in boundary-spanning roles (Johnson and Duxbury, 2010). Boundary-spanning roles involve sharing information with other boundary spanners and acting as a 'relationships lubricant' for effective cooperation and problem solving with the IJV exchange partners (Huang et al., 2016, p. 1558). The interaction between boundary spanners is not only complex because of having to operate across diverse business environments but also because of the competing interests of the IJV partners they represent (Gong et al., 2005; Mohr and Puck, 2013).

Schotter and Beamish (2011) propose that boundary-spanning ability is a function of individual personality, organizational ambidexterity and high levels of knowledge concerning products and/or services. This indicates a mixed bundle of capabilities consisting of industry experience at national and international levels, IJV experience, and cultural intelligence (CQ).

The concept of CQ aims at capturing variations in individuals' ability to operate across culturally diverse settings. Earley and Ang (2003) distinguish three facets of CQ: (1) *cognitive* CQ is the knowledge of the norms, practices, and conventions in different cultures and draws on metacognitive abilities such as strategies that individuals employ to acquire and understand cultural knowledge; (2) *motivational* CQ is the propensity to act on the cognitive facet and to persevere in acquiring knowledge and to overcome stumbling blocks and failure; and (3) *behavioural* CQ is the capability of a person to enact his or her desired and intended actions in a given cultural situation. Some researchers argue that the concept of CQ clearly has relevance for any analysis of the capabilities of IJV boundary spanners (Ng, Van Dyne and Ang, 2009; Ramalu et al., 2010).

The case study covers two IJVs involving Western and Chinese partners and with boundary spanners who engage cross-border boundary interactions covering four countries. While both IJVs were facing downturns, the responses were markedly different. The one IJV, located in Dalian, is experiencing a breakdown in trust, which is further inhibiting its performance. However, the other IJV, located in Shanghai, is continuing to operate in a manner characterized by optimism and trust. The question we explore is what differentiates these two apparently similar IJVs.

E.2   Background

The case setting

Our case context comprises a Swedish MNE, BKT, two of its wholly-owned subsidiaries (WOSs) in Germany and two of its joint ventures in China. Founded in 1962, BKT of Sweden remained a domestic company until 2001 when it rapidly expanded its foreign activities in Western Europe, Canada and in the Far East through a mix of entry strategies that included acquisitions, greenfields and joint ventures (see the Appendix at the end of the chapter). In 2009, BKT directly employed 1550 personnel worldwide, of whom 450 were located in Sweden and 640 in China. Only eight persons were employed at corporate headquarters in Sweden. In all, BKT comprised 27 business units in 14 countries, meaning that in a number of the countries in which it operated it had multiple business units. This was not least the case in China, where BKT had both IJVs and WOSs in Dalian and Shanghai.

The formal governance structure of IJVs in China

An incorporated joint venture is a business arrangement where two parties create a new business entity. The creation often entails sharing investments as well as profits created by the joint venture. The capital contributed by the partners to the joint venture can be cash, patented and unpatented technology, material and equipment and other property rights such as trademarks. Often, the Chinese partner contributes cash, land development or clearance fee and land use rights, while the foreign partner contributes cash, construction materials, technology, equipment and machinery (InterChinaConsulting.com, 2011). The formal governance structure of an incorporated joint equity IJV in China is based on a joint venture agreement and the Articles of Association. The joint venture agreement is a document that typically mentions the purpose of the joint venture, the parties, the business of the joint venture and how the joint venture is to be managed, including deciding on what issues require unanimous board approval. The Articles of Association document regulates the interaction between shareholders and directors. It is a document that specifies the rules of operations of the joint venture (e.g., division of the share of capital, appointment and removal of directors, procedures of board meetings etc.). These documents are underpinned by the Law of the People's Republic of China on Equity Joint Ventures Using Chinese and Foreign Investment. In addition, there are also the ancillary documents (termed 'offsets' in the US) covering know-how and trademarks and supply-of-equipment agreements. An incorporated joint venture is an independent legal entity and can enter contracts in its own name, acquire rights (such as the right to buy new companies), and it has a separate liability from that of its founders, except for invested capital. It can sue (and be sued) in courts in defence or its pursuance of its objectives.

The formal governance structure of the two BKT joint ventures

In the BKT case, each incorporated IJV involves a partnership between Chinese state-owned enterprises (SOEs) and one of BKT's two German operations: the Dalian SOE partner is BKT-Lübeck (hereafter 'Lübeck') and the Shanghai SOE partner is BKT-Bremen (hereafter 'Bremen').

The two BKT joint ventures in China are engaged in the same industry, and their mandates are to produce and deliver parts to European vehicle manufacturers operating in their respective regions of China. They employ the same formal control and ownership mechanisms with balanced ownership structures (50–50). The structure of the board and the management group is also identical. Each contained an SOE-nominated and -appointed Chinese managing director (MD), a German contact manager located in Germany and a Scandinavian expatriate chairman appointed by BKT. The boards of each of the joint ventures contained an equal number of representatives of BKT and their respective SOE. Together with the chairman it is the duty of the MD to provide the board with financial information. The board could remove the MD but the replacement would be appointed by the SOE.

Each joint venture operated using the internationally recognized BKT brand name. Further, the formal agreement stipulated that they had access to BKT intellectual property and that when necessary Lübeck and Bremen would contribute training of the joint venture personnel. In practice, the quality of knowledge sharing would involve the willingness of Lübeck and Bremen as well as the receptivity of their joint venture partners. In addition to the joint venture agreement, the two BKT joint ventures have contractual arrangements with their parent companies for inputs and services. However, the MDs have latitude to make local purchases providing these do not impair the quality associated with BKT. Although entirely independent of each other and serving different regions in China, the notion is that the two joint ventures should regard themselves as 'part of the BKT family'.

Boundary spanners in the two BKT joint ventures

Apart from the chairmen of their boards, neither the Shanghai-JV nor the Dalian-JV employs any BKT expatriates. BKT employees from the European operations are only at these operations when there are well-defined tasks to carry out. Table E.1 contains their identities and positions.

Data were collected through semi-structured interviews. It was made clear to the participants that their answers would be treated in confidence and that their anonymity would be safeguarded. To corroborate the collected data we conducted six additional semi-structured interviews including two senior managers at BKT corporate headquarters, two senior managers at BKT's wholly-owned Norwegian subsidiary and a senior manager at Bremen. Table E.2 contains the identities of the six supplementary informants. Of these six informants, we came to recognize that Mr Larsen plays a particularly significant role in the case.

Table E.1 The boundary spanners of BKT's Chinese IJVs

Boundary Spanner Role	IJV	
	Dalian-JV	Shanghai-JV
SOE-appointed Chinese MD	Mr Wang	Madam Tan
German contact manager located in Germany	Ms Neuhaus (Lübeck)	Mr Schmidt (Bremen)
Scandinavian expatriate IJV chairman	*Current* Mr Hansen *Former* Mr Ericsson	Mr Ericsson

Table E.2 The locations, identities and positions of the supplementary informants

Business Unit	Location	Informant	Position
BKT HQ	Sweden	Ms Dale	After-sales manager
BKT HQ	Sweden	Mr Nordhaug	Deputy CEO
Stavanger	Stavanger, Norway	Mr Selart	MD
Stavanger	Stavanger, Norway	Mr Lindberg	Chief FO
Bremen	Bremen, Germany	Mr Meyer	Operations manager
BKT-Auto Shanghai	Shanghai, China	Mr Larsen	MD

E.3 The Dalian-JV

The Dalian-JV was established at a new industrial site on the outskirts of Dalian in 2005. BKT's decision to enter into this 50–50 joint venture was a product of its generally positive experience with the Shanghai-JV. Indeed, the legal document that formed the contractual basis of the Shanghai-JV was used in establishing the Dalian-JV as an authorized entity. Its MD is a local Chinese national, Mr Wang.

In its first fully operational year of 2007, the Dalian-JV posted substantial profits. It appeared that the assessment that the newly established JV would generate successful performance was confirmed. However, during 2008 the market contracted, resulting in a considerably significant reduction of profits. While the relationship between Ms Neuhaus of Lübeck and Mr Ericsson, the Norwegian chairman, remained cordial, the relationship between the latter and Mr Wang rapidly became acrimonious. As a result, it was decided to appoint a new chairman, Mr Hansen, a Swede. Unlike Mr Ericsson who had spent 30 years in China and who spoke rudimentary Chinese, Mr Hansen spoke no Chinese. Mr Hansen's career had been spent in various managerial roles in the Scandinavian aquaculture industry. With his career coming to an end he revealed that he had no intention of learning any Chinese.

The relationship between Mr Hansen and Mr Wang was little better than that between the latter and Mr Ericsson. In meetings, Mr Wang refused to consent for Mr Hansen to operate with his own interpreter, insisting that he rely on Mr Wang's. Mr Hansen informed us that after a stand-off with Mr Wang he had reluctantly decided that if outright conflict was to be avoided it was better to concede the right to act as chair at the Dalian-JV board meetings. Another issue was that Mr Hansen regarded Mr Wang's interpretation of the contractual arrangements as limiting his insight into significant aspects of the workings of the JV. The financial accounts were prepared by appointees of Mr Wang and it was Mr Wang who single-handedly negotiated with the subcontractors, all of whom belonged to his own personal network.

The one area of agreement between Mr Hansen and Mr Wang was that they both viewed their respective relationships with Lübeck's Ms Neuhaus as highly problematic. Ms Neuhaus was highly critical of the quality of workmanship carried out by Mr Wang's network of local Chinese subcontractors. Some of these deviations, according to Mr Hansen, were no more than cosmetic, so he considered Ms Neuhaus and her colleagues at Lübeck as indiscriminately 'overly sensitive' in their approach to quality issues. However, he also regarded Mr Wang as being unreasonable in refusing to accept requests from Ms Neuhaus that Lübeck's inspectors should be allowed to carry out quality checks at the subcontractors to pre-empt problems.

Mr Wang's primary disquiet with Ms Neuhaus was that she refused to undertake the unblocking of core technical parameters, meaning that the components Lübeck delivered to the Dalian-JV could not be replicated locally. He remarked that if this issue could not be resolved 'there will be a big problem'. Rather than trying to develop common cause with Mr Hansen, Mr Wang bypassed him and communicated his concerns directly to BKT corporate HQ. Subsequently, a relationship of distrust emerged amongst the key boundary spanners.

From the perspective of Ms Neuhaus, the explanation for distrust was very different. She reported that she found dealing with the Dalian-JV 'exasperating not least because of the Dalian-JV's continual reinterpretation of the joint venture contract' and the 'tremendous quality problem' in regard to its output. Ms Neuhaus stated that the poor quality of workmanship at the Dalian-JV 'hurts' Lübeck employees who have 'an obsession with quality'. She complained about the high production staff turnover at the Dalian-JV that resulted in a constant stream of new production employees who had to be trained. She further objected to Mr Wang's decision to locally purchase steel structures of 'a cheaper and inferior quality than stipulated'. She attributed Mr Wang's decision to purchase locally as an abuse of the contract. However, 'joint ventures cannot be taken to court'. So 'the challenge is to find the right tone'. To date, Ms Neuhaus felt that this was unattainable because in regard to quality and prices 'the Chinese do whatever they want' and they also win all of the arguments not least because 'when they do not get their way they threaten to stop production'.

Ms Neuhaus was conscious that immediately prior to its acquisition by BKT in 2004 the Lübeck operation was bankrupt and that the relationship with the Dalian-JV had brought in 95 per cent of Lübeck's orders. She further accepted that the Dalian-JV, under the 'well-connected Mr Wang has opened up a lot of doors for us in China'. Nevertheless, Ms Neuhaus stressed that the basic attitude at Lübeck is that 'they [the Chinese] will take all our knowledge' accompanied by bitterness that 'Dalian-JV will have acquired everything in the space of a few years that has taken us 60 years of consistent effort to develop'.

Around BKT we observed an acute awareness of the distrust between the three formal boundary spanners involved with the Dalian-JV and pronounced views on them. While all of these views obviously reflect the interests and the biases of our informants, overall there were many common perceptions of these three managers.

Mr Ericsson, the former chairman of the Dalian-JV, was critical of Mr Wang due to a lack of transparency at the Dalian-JV. Madam Tan, the MD of the Shanghai-JV, regarded Mr Wang as no more than, a 'metal-bashing production boss' with 'no feel for marketing'. In other words, in her view, Mr Wang lacked relevant industry experience. Mr Schmidt of Bremen had a similar view, claiming that Mr Wang is just a 'production guy' with no marketing skills. Furthermore, he viewed Mr Wang as 'having a power focus rather than a business orientation'. Mr Selart, the MD of BKT-Stavanger (hereafter 'Stavanger'), was also scathing, claiming that 'Mr Wang has been a problem from day one'. At BKT's corporate headquarters, Mr Nordhaug viewed Mr Wang as a source of conflict and Ms Dale, from BKT's After-Sales Services, characterized him as insufficiently commercial in his outlook and was concerned about the long-term implications of the quality problem at the Dalian-JV.

Both Mr Ericsson and Mr Selart pointed to Mr Hansen's lack of both national and international industry experience, which meant that he was easily deceived and isolated. Mr Schmidt was unimpressed with his compatriot Ms Neuhaus. He regarded her as being locked into an inflexible and 'typically German' mindset. More significantly for him was her dread of giving away knowledge to the Chinese and her fear that it would cost Lübeck jobs. The chief financial officer at Stavanger, Mr Lindberg, also viewed Ms Neuhaus as blinkered in her relationship with the Dalian-JV. In his view, Ms Neuhaus and her colleagues were failing to explore future possibilities such as developing new products for the Korean market.

E.4 The Shanghai-JV

The Shanghai-JV is a 50–50 joint venture located in Shanghai. Until some months before we conducted our research it had been a consistently profitable operation. However, it then experienced a severe contraction in its market that its MD, Madam Tan, believed would last for at least three years. However, we observed that despite the downturn for the Shanghai-JV and its bleak immediate prospects the relationships between its three boundary spanners, Madam Tan, Mr Ericsson and Mr Schmidt were characterized by mutual trust.

Madam Tan joined the Shanghai SOE in 1992 and since 1998 had been directly involved with Stavanger. Approaching retirement, she had succeeded in learning sufficient English since 1998, when she spoke little English, to be able to communicate effectively without the aid of an interpreter.

Madam Tan regarded the cooperation with Bremen, as well as with Stavanger, as having been very positive. Furthermore, she had every confidence in BKT's capability in regard to technology development. She planned to use the downturn to train and develop her employees in order to be able to grow when the market revives.

Madam Tan's positive outlook on the IJV was not confined to the capabilities Bremen was contributing. She explained that the relationship that had evolved between the partners had meant that there was increasingly less need for formal meetings. In 2001 there were eight board meetings a year. By 2009 this had been reduced to two.

Mr Ericsson was appointed chairman of the Shanghai-JV board in 2005. He was engaged on the strength of more than 30 years of industry experience in China and other Asian countries. As we noted above, despite his many years in China, Mr Ericsson's Chinese language skills had never progressed beyond the rudimentary. Mr Ericsson shared Madam Tan's generally positive analysis of the JV. As chairman, he was tasked with leading board meetings and writing the minutes. He felt that he not only had a good insight into the finances, but he was also able to request reports on all dealings with suppliers. Mr Ericsson had a casting vote.

Mr Schmidt, the MD of Bremen and its boundary spanner, recounted that at the beginning there were problems relating to quality and 'a lot of fights' with Madam Tan as 'you have to be strong in China'. He reflected that 'in Germany you are used to perfect workshops containing employees who are so technically proficient that they are able to independently correct design problems. In China, because of the lack of experience this is not the case'. The lesson he drew from this insight was that every aspect of a design has to be entirely correct and explicitly communicated. Once this approach had been established Mr Schmidt concluded that his partnership with Madam Tan and Mr Ericsson had worked well.

Mr Meyer, a management colleague of Mr Schmidt, viewed the Shanghai-JV as being an 'excellent' partner and BKT as having been fortunate to enter an IJV with it. These views were echoed at BKT's corporate headquarters.

E.5 The virtual boundary spanner

In response to the deteriorating performance and trust relationship amongst the management at the Dalian-JV, the BKT board regularly called on Mr Larsen, the MD of its WOS, BKT-Auto Shanghai, to parley between the formal boundary spanners involved in the Dalian-JV. Mr Larsen, a Swede, was locally married with two children and had seven years of experience in China, during which he had forged good relationships with both Madam Tan and Mr Wang. While both Mr Ericsson and Mr Hansen lived in apartments in international hotels, Mr Larsen lived in a suburb with Chinese neighbours. Further, while Mr Larsen used English as his main working language, his Chinese language skills were such that he could converse with some fluency with those Chinese employees who could not speak English.

Mr Larsen's relationship with Mr Wang predated the Dalian-JV. Mr Larsen commented that Mr Wang was uniquely prepared to speak in English to him on the phone. Although there was no intention on the part of BKT that Mr Larsen should actually displace Mr Hansen, he was significantly supplementing what was meant to be a key part of the task portfolio of the IJV chairman. In calming Mr Wang by assuring him of BKT's 'good intentions' he functioned as a critical 'virtual' boundary spanner. He was also a calming influence on Ms Neuhaus.

Despite his ability to forge social trust with both Mr Wang and Ms Neuhaus, Mr Larsen was not uncritical of them. He remarked that Mr Wang had 'an extremely hierarchical style of management' that contrasted with what he regarded as his own 'non-authoritarian Scandinavian style of management'. Equally, Mr Larsen was critical of Ms Neuhaus and other Lübeck managers, describing them as 'shrill and heavy-handed'.

E.6 Summary

Despite a broad range of contextual commonalities including ownership, industry, contractual arrangements, governance structures, and national cultures, the common challenging market conditions have led the boundary spanners of the two IJVs to very different responses. In Tables E.3 and E.4 we summarize the mixed bundles of capabilities each set of boundary spanners brought to their respective IJVs (detailed measurements and analysis are omitted due to the length limit).

The first three columns of Table E.3 contain the current formal boundary spanners involved in the Dalian-JV. None has international industry

Table E.3 Mixed bundles of capabilities of boundary spanners involved in Dalian-JV

Bundles of Capabilities	Mr Hansen	Mr Wang	Ms Neuhaus	Mr Ericsson	Mr Larsen
Industry experience					
National	None	Moderate	Substantial	Substantial	Substantial
International	None	None	None	Substantial	Substantial
IJV experience	None	None	None	Substantial	None
Degree of CQ	Low	Low	Low	Moderate	Substantial

Table E.4 Mixed bundles of capabilities of boundary spanners involved in Shanghai-JV

Bundles of Capabilities	Mr Ericsson	Madam Tan	Mr Schmidt
Industry experience			
National	Substantial	Substantial	Substantial
International	Substantial	Substantial	Substantial
IJV experience	Substantial	Substantial	Substantial
Degree of CQ	Moderate	Substantial	Moderate

experience, IJV experience or moderate or high levels of CQ. As the former chairman of the Dalian-JV and the current chairman of the Shanghai-JV, Mr Ericsson features in both Tables E.3 and E.4. While social trust is characteristic of his relationships within the Shanghai-JV, at the Dalian-JV Mr Ericsson's relationship with Mr Wang became so abrasive that the former had to leave. It would appear that his substantial levels of national and international industry experience and IJV experience did not compensate for only a moderate degree of CQ when engaging across significant cultural distance with a boundary spanner such as Mr Wang, who as Table E.3 indicates, is lacking international industry experience, IJV experience and CQ. The role of the virtual chairman at the Dalian-JV, Mr Larsen, is critical in maintaining the survival of the Dalian-JV. As the last column in Table E.3 indicates, although Mr Larsen is lacking in IJV experience, he does have substantial national and international industry experience and substantial CQ. When we compare Mr Larsen with Mr Ericsson, it would appear this latter factor is a critical component in his bundle of boundary-spanning capabilities.

Table E.4 shows that all three boundary spanners involved in the Shanghai-JV – Madam Tan, Mr Ericsson and Mr Schmidt – had substantial levels of international industry and IJV experience and either moderate or, in the case of Madam Tan, substantial levels of CQ. In all, the bundles of boundary-spanning capabilities in the Shanghai-JV are significantly superior to those in the

Dalian-JV. In assessing Madam Tan's CQ, we note her willingness to develop her English-language skills in order to be able to interact directly with her foreign partners and that she has developed 'the ability to initiate interaction, to carry on meaningful dialogues and to clear up misunderstandings' (Eschbach, Parker and Stoeberl, 2001, p. 281). In turn this has created a common cognitive schema between her and both of her Western partners that is at the basis of a positive sensemaking of the new uncertainty faced by the Shanghai-JV. Given the degree of cultural distance between Western Europe and China it seems possible that Madam Tan's substantial degree of CQ has been a critical factor in regard to maintaining social trust between the other boundary spanners involved in the Shanghai-JV during the performance downturn.

E.7 Conclusion

IJVs are characterized by persistent institutional, cultural and organizational diversity, and this is especially so in the case of China given its distinct institutional (transitional economy), cultural (Confucianism embedded in China's long history), and organizational (dominant SOEs) settings. Madhok (1995) argues that the structural dimension of trust is largely sufficient for satisfactory IJV performance until disequilibrium and inequity arise. It is at that point that the social dimension of trust becomes critical in that it mitigates the threat of breakdown. Dulac et al.'s (2008, p. 1084) statement that, 'Once a (social exchange) relationship is perceived as being of high quality, future transactions in the relationship may be more likely to be viewed as fair, regardless of actuality', is clearly pertinent to Madam Tan's interpretation of the quality of the trust relationship with her partner boundary spanners.

Without the bundles of capabilities of its boundary spanners, the performance downturn the Shanghai-JV was undergoing would have severely undermined social trust. In contrast, in the case of the Dalian-JV, as the performance of the JV declined the perception of complementary resources eroded and was replaced by a stand-off in regard to the transfer of knowledge. The relationship between the Dalian-JV boundary spanners rapidly became distrustful. The role of the virtual boundary spanner at the Dalian-JV, Mr Larsen, is critical in maintaining its survival. Like Madam Tan, he too has a significant degree of CQ.

CASE DISCUSSION

1. Did BKT choose the right entry mode in China?
2. What kind of problems arose due to the entry mode?
3. What kind of issues arose due to cultural or personal issues?
4. Could problems be solved simply by changing the formal contracts in the Dalian-JV?

> **NOTE**
>
> * Acknowledgement: this is an adapted version of an article originally published as Gooderham, P.N., M. Zhang and A. Jordahl (2015), 'Effective boundary spanners in IJVs experiencing performance down-turn', in A.A. Camillo (ed.), *Global Enterprise Management, Volume II, New Perspectives on Challenges and Future Developments* (pp. 91–106), Basingstoke: Palgrave Macmillan.

> **REFERENCES**
>
> Dulac, T., J.A.-M. Coyle-Shapiro, D.J. Henderson and S.J. Wayne (2008), 'Not all responses to breach are the same: A longitudinal study examining the interconnection of social exchange and psychological contract processes in organizations', *Academy of Management Journal*, **51**(6), 1079–98.
> Dyer, J. and W. Chu (2000), 'The determinants of trust in supplier–automaker relationships in the U.S., Japan and Korea', *Journal of International Business Studies*, **31**(2), 259–85.
> Earley, P.C. and S. Ang (2003), *Cultural Intelligence: Individual Interactions Across Cultures*, Stanford, CA: Stanford University Press.
> Eschbach, D.M., G.E. Parker and P.A. Stoeberl (2001), 'American repatriate employees' retrospective assessments of the effects of cross-cultural training on their adaptation to international assignments', *The International Journal of Human Resource Management*, **12**(2), 270–87.
> Gong, Y., O. Shenkar, Y. Luo and M.K. Nyaw (2005), 'Human resources and international joint venture performance: A system perspective', *Journal of International Business Studies*, **36**(5), 505–18.
> Hambrick, D.C., J. Li, K. Xin and A. Tsui (2001), 'Compositional gaps and downward spirals in international joint venture management groups', *Strategic Management Journal*, **22**(11), 1033–53.
> Huang, Y., L. Luo, Y. Liu and Q. Yang (2016), 'An investigation of interpersonal ties in interorganizational exchanges in emerging markets', *Journal of Management*, **42**(6), 1557–87.
> InterChinaConsulting.com (2011), 'Establishment of a joint venture (JV) in China', June 2011, accessed 12 September 2018 at https://www.caixabank.es/deployedfiles/particulars/Estaticos/PDFs/InfolineaAbierta/JVinChina.pdf.
> Johnson, K.L. and L. Duxbury (2010), 'The view from the field: A case study of the expatriate boundary-spanning role', *Journal of World Business*, **45**(1), 29–40.
> Li, J., L. Poppo and K. Zhou (2010), 'Relational mechanisms, formal contracts, and local knowledge acquisition by international subsidiaries', *Strategic Management Journal*, **31**(4), 349–70.
> Luo, Y. (2009), 'From gain-sharing to gain-generation: The quest for distributive justice in international joint ventures', *Journal of International Management*, **15**(4), 343–56.
> Madhok, A. (1995), 'Revisiting multinational firms' tolerance for joint ventures: A trust-based approach', *Journal of International Business Studies*, **26**, 117–37.
> Madhok, A. (2006), 'How much does ownership really matter? Equity and trust relations in joint venture relationships', *Journal of International Business Studies*, **37**(1), 4–11.
> Mohr, A. and J. Puck (2013), 'Revisiting the trust–performance link in strategic alliances', *Management International Review*, **53**(2), 269–89.
> Ng, K., L. van Dyne and S. Ang (2009), 'From experience to experiential learning: Cultural intelligence as a learning capability for global leader development', *Academy of Management Learning and Education*, **8**(4), 511–26.
> Parkhe, A. (1991), 'Interfirm diversity, organizational learning, and longevity in global strategic alliances', *Journal of International Business Studies*, **22**(4), 579–601.
> Ramalu, S., R. Rose, N. Kumar and J. Uli (2010), 'Doing business in global arena: An examination of the relationship between cultural intelligence and cross-cultural adjustment', *Asian Academy of Management Journal*, **15**(1), 79–97.

Salk, J.E. and O. Shenkar (2001), 'Social identities in an international joint venture: An exploratory case study', *Organization Science*, **12**(2), 161–78.

Schotter, A. and P.W. Beamish (2011), 'Performance effects of MNC headquarters–subsidiary conflict and the role of boundary spanners: The case of headquarter initiative rejection', *Journal of International Management*, **17**, 243–59.

Silva, S., F. Bradley and C.M.P. Sousa (2012), 'Empirical test of the trust–performance link in an international alliances context', *International Business Review*, **21**(2), 293–306.

Zaheer, A. and D. Kamal (2011), 'Creating trust in piranha-infested waters: The confluence of buyer, supplier and host country contexts', *Journal of International Business Studies*, **42**, 48–55.

Zaheer, A., B. McEvily and V. Perrone (1998), 'Does trust matter? Exploring the effects of interorganizational and interpersonal trust on performance', *Organization Science*, **9**(2), 141–59.

Appendix

Table EA.1 Overview of BKT's global operations beyond its headquarters in Sweden

Operation	Europe			Far East		
	Norway	Germany		China		
Main business units	Stavanger	Bremen	Lübeck	Shanghai-JV	Dalian-JV	Auto Shanghai Axles	Auto Dalian Alternators
Product/technology	Electrical components	Fenders	Wheels	Design and marketing of fenders	Manufacturing and marketing of wheels		
Year of entry	1983	2001	2004	2001	2005	2004	2008
Entry mode	Acquisition	Acquisition	Acquisition	JV	JV	Turn JV to WOS	Greenfield
Ownership	100% WOS	100% WOS	100% WOS	50–50	50–50	100% WOS	100% WOS
Governance/partnership				Stavanger as formal and Bremen as de facto partner: Shanghai SOE	Lübeck: Dalian SOE		
Management/control	Local MD	Local MD	Local MD	BKT-appointed foreign expatriate as chairman Chinese SOE-appointed local manager as MD	BKT-appointed foreign expatriate as chairman Chinese SOE-appointed local manager as MD	Expat MD	Expat MD
No. of personnel	80	110	60	80	80	120	40

Part II

The external context

5
Managing external stakeholders in MNEs

5.1 Introduction

The actions of managers have consequences beyond their firms. Stakeholder theory or stakeholder thinking is a framework that can assist managers in MNEs to manage their relationships with significant external groups. In this chapter, we present stakeholder theory as well as frameworks that can help managers identify and manage their relationships to key stakeholders. Stakeholder theory is used in a broad array of disciplines such as business ethics, corporate strategy, finance, accounting, management and marketing (Parmar et al., 2010). This chapter discusses MNEs' management of stakeholder relations through cooperating with non-governmental organizations (NGOs) and global union federations (GUFs). Partnerships with NGOs and GUFs are an important means through which MNEs access resources and knowledge that can help them overcome liabilities of foreignness (Oetzel and Doh, 2009). Further, these relationships can enable MNEs to acquire social legitimacy across their global operations (Marano and Tashman, 2012; Oetzel and Doh, 2009).

5.2 Stakeholder theory

The concept of 'stakeholders' appeared as early as in 1963 in a memorandum from the Stanford Research Institute and was meant to challenge the notion that a manager's exclusive responsibility was to shareholders. The stakeholder concept was reintroduced into management by Freeman (1984), who suggested that managers should develop a vocabulary suited to responding to the problems they encounter with external groups in volatile environments.

Freeman and other scholars applied the concept of stakeholders to address three interconnected problems relating to international business:

- The problem of value creation and trade: how does value creation and trade take place in a rapidly changing global business context?
- The problem of the ethics of capitalism: what are the connections between capitalism and ethics?
- The problem of managerial mindset: how should managers think about management in order to create value while at the same time explicitly connecting business and ethics? (Parmar et al., 2010)

From a stakeholder perspective, MNEs like all firms comprise a set of relationships among groups (and individuals) who have a stake in their activities (Freeman, 1984; Jones, 1995; Walsh, 2005). The way businesses trade and create value is influenced by the relationships among stakeholders. According to Freeman, managers must create as much value as possible and manage the distribution of that value. When there is a conflict of interest among stakeholders, managers need to rethink by taking into consideration the needs of a broad group of stakeholders (Harrison, Bosse and Phillips, 2010). If trade-offs need to be made, managers must work on making these trade-offs as successful as possible for all parties (Freeman, Harrison and Wicks, 2007).

Managers' decisions on how to handle trade-offs that involve different stakeholder group interest are not straightforward. The approach stakeholder theory takes to resolving conflicts of interest has a moral underpinning that incorporates values and considerations of potential harm and benefits for large groups and individuals (Phillips, 2003a). Stakeholder theory has often been criticized for being primarily concerned with the distribution of financial output (Marcoux, 2000). However, its moral underpinning is not just concerned with the fairness attached to how the financial output is distributed among stakeholders but also with the fairness attached to the procedures through which such decisions are made. For example, Phillips, Freeman and Wicks (2003) argue that stakeholders deserve a say in how resources are allocated, and that such involvement affects how they view and accept the distribution of resources. Moreover, stakeholder involvement can also help managers rethink their approach to problem solving in ways that create more value.

Stakeholder theory directs attention to the idea that doing business is dependent on, and has consequences for, many different groups of individuals. Thus, the specific application of stakeholder theory depends on the kind of problem to which it is applied. Some researchers view stakeholder theory as a moral theory that is superior to management theories that mainly address shareholder interest (Boatright, 1994; Donaldson and Preston, 1995).

However, looking at the broad application of stakeholder theory across many fields, it is not in itself a cohesive, consistent moral doctrine. Within the broad framework of stakeholder theory, there are a variety of perspectives on the use and application of moral and ethical positions.

5.3 Who are the MNEs' relevant stakeholders?

As 'global corporate citizens' MNEs may be held accountable for their impact on the economic and political development of the local communities in which they operate. Given the intense, negative attention that MNEs, such as Nike and Royal Dutch Shell, received from NGOs for perceived ethical violations in the 1990s, most MNEs have come to recognize the importance of engaging with a wider range of stakeholders.

The primary criticism of stakeholder theory is that it suggests that managers should focus on satisfying the needs of various stakeholder groups, but fails to provide a definition of stakeholders and recommendations as to which stakeholder groups are most important. In a review of stakeholder definitions, Miles (2017) identified 885 definitions of stakeholders. Although there is an agreement on the essence of the concept as one that involves the relationships between an organization and its stakeholders, there are wide differences in who is considered a stakeholder (ibid.). From one perspective, 'any occurring entity' including the environment is a stakeholder (Starik, 1995). From a business ethics perspective, stakeholders are restricted to 'those to whom the organization has a moral obligation' (Phillips, 2003a, p. 30), and from a strategic stakeholder management perspective the focus is mainly on 'those groups without whose support the organization would cease to exist' (Stanford Research Institute, 1963). The way in which the nature of the relationship between the business and the stakeholder is described also differs. Some definitions look at contractual relations, others at moral relations and yet others at claims or implicit interests.

Miles (2017) identified four types of stakeholder definitions: (1) influencers, (2) claimants, (3) collaborators and (4) recipients. The classification is based on a distinction between being subject to influence and being able to influence and on whether the stakeholder is active or passive in pressing claims and seeking power. Miles also made a distinction between stakeholder definitions that emphasize stakeholder power as underpinned by a legal framework or other sources of coercive power or by moral obligations and social pressure. The latter distinctions are often important to managers because as Miles (2017, p. 445) points out, 'contractual claims have a mandatory right to have their claims addressed, whereas moral claimants rely on moral obligations/

philanthropy'. The classification of definitions takes into account the essence of stakeholder theory: that there must be a relationship between the organization and the stakeholder. This is important, as many groups can potentially be stakeholders such as terrorist groups who have the capacity to influence a business's strategy or goal achievement. However, according to Miles (2017), these are not stakeholders as they do not have a relationship with the organization, whereas activist groups may have a relationship based on social pressures that create moral obligations for organizations to consider.

Influencer stakeholders emphasize the ability to exert influence on businesses. For managers in MNEs, stakeholders that fall into the category of influencers are important because they are likely to have critical, urgent and explicit claims that warrant management attention. MNEs often have an obligation to these stakeholders based on legally supported claims or principal–agent relations that provide the stakeholder with a high degree of power to have claims recognized. Not all stakeholders that meet the influencer definition have power underpinned by law, but they may have coercive power or power due to the resources they control or can mobilize (Mitchell, Agle and Wood, 1997). In general, the more dependent an MNE is on the resource that a stakeholder can mobilize the greater the stakeholder's power to have claims recognized. For example, activist groups can be influencers if they have an active influencing strategy and mobilize the actions of others (Frooman, 1999). Influencer definitions of stakeholders often describe the relationship between the MNE and stakeholder as either cooperation or as one that inflicts harm on the MNE. Among the most common type of stakeholders that meet the definition of influencers are shareholders, purchasers, suppliers, partners, competitors and NGOs.

Claimant stakeholders have claims that are derived from moral or social rights rather than legal rights. The nature of these stakeholder relationships is often based on informal and not legally supported claims on management that stem from a general acknowledgement of moral responsibility or duty of care. The main focus is on how an organization's actions influence the stakeholder. Managers who attend to the needs of pure claimant-type stakeholders do so because they have adopted a strategic focus on a broad set of stakeholders. Typically, businesses are not dependent on these stakeholder groups for key resources or survival. An example of a stakeholder group that fits the claimant definition is that of employees who are negatively affected by an MNE's work practices but who are employed in countries lacking in effective institutions ('institutional voids'). In these situations, moral or ethical norms underpin stakeholder claims, and not regulations or legally grounded collective actions.

Collaborator stakeholders are willing to cooperate with the MNE. They indirectly influence an MNE if their collaboration is necessary in order for the MNE to achieve its goals but their power is often relatively weak. As such, the claims of collaborator stakeholders do not warrant any particular urgency of attention. Examples of this type of stakeholder are universities collaborating with MNEs on research activities, standard-setting bodies such as the International Organization for Standardization (ISO) and consumers.

Recipient stakeholders are passive recipients of the impact of MNE activities. Within this category, stakeholders are those 'who are affected significantly by the company's actions' (Carson, 1993, p. 172) or '[d]irectly affected by the operation of the firm' (Lea, 2004, p. 207). These definitions describe stakeholders who have a latent claim on an MNE. An example of recipient stakeholders are communities that have an MNE subsidiary in their vicinity that is polluting the local environment without their having any knowledge of this and how it is affecting their lives. Further, they do not have the resources to become informed. Because of their lack of power, managers may choose to ignore recipient stakeholders. However, if recipient stakeholders do become aware of what is being inflicted on them, latent claims may become explicit claims. In such cases, if they develop an active strategy and mobilize to have their claims recognized, recipient stakeholder groups can swiftly evolve into influencer stakeholder groups.

Although many stakeholder definitions are a combination of the four above-mentioned 'pure' definitions, operating with the four-fold classification of stakeholders helps managers to consider variations in stakeholder impact on their operations. Specifically, it can help them to respond to three key management questions raised by Frooman (1999): 'Who are the stakeholders?', 'What do they want?', and 'How are they going to try to get it?' For MNEs, a stakeholder that is identified as being an influencer in one context may be a claimant or recipient in another. For example, labour groups are often influencer stakeholders in Western countries where unions and legislation support many of their stakeholder claims. In other contexts, where these institutions are weak and with no independent media that can be relied on to exercise influence, the same labour groups are claimants and recipients.

Ackermann and Eden (2011) are, however, sceptical as to the value of relying on such a typology of stakeholders. Managers should simply focus on the most important stakeholders. One approach is to apply Mitchell et al.'s (1997) framework that ranks stakeholders on their power, legitimacy and urgency. Power refers to their ability to exercise force, violence or restraint (coercive power) as well as their control over material or financial resources.

Power can also stem from legal rights, control over resources, or be grounded in moral obligations and ethical concerns. Legitimacy is 'a generalized perception or assumption that actions of an entity are desirable, proper or appropriate within some socially constructed system of norms, values, beliefs and definitions' (Suchman, 1995, p. 574). Urgency has two attributes: time sensitivity that denotes the degree to which managerial delays in attending to the claim or relationship is unacceptable, and criticality, which refers to the importance of the claim or relationship (Mitchell et al., 1997). Although the four-fold stakeholder typology does focus on these three factors, it is reasonable to suppose that influencers, and to some extent claimants, possess power, legitimacy and urgency.

In addition to applying these three factors in a stakeholder analysis, managers need to identify the interconnections between stakeholders. To that end, managers can apply social network analysis. This technique focuses attention on the structure of interaction among stakeholders (Rowley, 1997). Managers should identify the formal as well as the informal ties among stakeholders. Stakeholders that might appear to have little power may have formal or informal connections with powerful interest groups such as NGOs or GUFs.

5.4 Unique stakeholder relations

In the next two sections, we present NGOs and GUFs, two types of stakeholder that are often considered as having interests opposed to those of MNEs.

MNE stakeholder relationships to NGOs

There is no doubt that MNEs such as Nike, Gap and Royal Dutch Shell have in the past viewed NGOs as adversaries. However, partnerships between these former opponents are becoming increasingly common, particularly when MNEs develop corporate social responsibility (CSR) strategies (Marano and Tashman, 2012; Peloza and Falkenberg, 2009; Yaziji and Doh, 2009). When MNEs and NGOs work together they can utilize each other's core competencies, and may even develop new core competencies that would be costly, inefficient and time consuming for either MNEs or NGOs to develop on their own.

Yaziji (2004) suggests that NGOs have four key strengths that make them viable partners for MNEs. First, NGOs have a concern with legitimacy, which is to say that they legitimately care about social issues and are committed to societal improvement. By collaborating with an NGO, an MNE can show that it too cares about the same social issues. Second, NGOs have a keen awareness of social forces. By collaborating with an NGO, an MNE may gain increased insight into social and environmental shifts in consumer preference and demand, resulting in a competitive advantage. Third, NGOs have distinct networks that are different from the networks of MNEs. Not only do NGOs have access to regulators, lobbyists, other NGOs, and legislators, they are also very efficient at gathering and disseminating information throughout these networks. Collaborating with an NGO will provide an MNE with access to these alternative networks. Finally, and perhaps most importantly, NGOs have their own specialized areas of expertise in the form of lawyers, scientists, technical experts and policy analysts. Collaborating with NGOs means that MNEs can tap into these sources of expertise that can enhance their ability to improve society across different national contexts.

MNE partnerships with NGOs have resulted in numerous voluntary codes of corporate behaviour (Marano and Tashman, 2012). A partnership with an NGO with strong international credentials may help the MNE develop policies and strategies that confer global legitimacy. Moreover, NGO partnerships often help firms engage in non-market global initiatives that can help the MNE overcome negative legitimacy spillovers.

Strategic partnerships between two MNEs are complex to manage, even though both partners have the same goal – to make a profit. In terms of partnerships between MNEs and NGOs, the level of complexity is significantly greater, as one partner is seeking to increase value for the firm, while the other partner is seeking to add value to society. MNEs bring technical expertise as well as human and financial capital to the partnership, while NGOs bring human capital as well as social and technical expertise. The potentially adversarial nature of these partnerships makes for strange bedfellows. NGOs, much like MNEs, have valuable brands, and both brands may become damaged if either partner reneges on its promises. Berger, Cunningham and Drumwright (2004) suggest that selecting the right NGO to collaborate with is essential to the survival and productivity of the partnership. Much like an alliance between MNEs, both the NGO and MNE must look at the strategic fit of the partner with regard to mission, resources, management, workforce, objective, product or cause, corporate culture, time lines, and definition of project success.

MNE and GUF stakeholder relations

GUFs are dominated by the large, powerful unions, predominantly from the developed world, that make relatively large inputs to their resources. The

GUFs' daily work is in supporting their affiliates and in taking initiatives that assist their affiliates in their dealings with MNEs. The GUFs conduct campaigns in particular MNEs where fundamental principles are concerned and their general secretaries are very often in regular contact with CEOs. This often happens even when the MNEs are only weakly unionized because the MNEs are aware of the GUFs as important players in the labour relations and CSR areas and sometimes want to 'sound out' the general secretaries on various issues.

MNEs that operate global value chains that involve outsourcing and contract labour in the context of countries that are characterized by institutional voids are particularly exposed to the risk of being involved in labour practices that are unacceptable in their countries of origin (Greven, 2006). Against this background, many MNEs have engaged in dialogues with GUFs. GUFs provide expertise on international labour issues. Further, they are unlikely to be accused of being biased in favour of MNEs. Unlike NGOs, GUFs are also more directly concerned with the fate of MNE employees than NGOs and therefore less likely to jeopardize jobs by being overtly critical. Thus, GUFs have generally not adopted the radical tactics of 'anti-corporate campaigning' used by some NGOs (ibid.). Although not uncritical of MNEs, the future of GUFs is linked to the future of MNEs. The GUF general secretaries and senior MNE managers often know one another from global industrial conferences such as the World Economic Forum. GUFs are stakeholders in a larger setting of formal and informal stakeholder relationships.

Individual trade unions at the national level may choose to affiliate to GUFs; this is a matter of free choice on both sides and some are not affiliated. GUFs must offer tangible benefits to their affiliates to secure and maintain affiliations. Trade unions represent the voice of organized labour and in some countries they are considered the legitimate voice of working people. Only free and independent trade unions can be members of GUFs. In some countries (e.g., China and Belarus), trade unions have been subordinated to political parties or the interests of the state and cannot be considered 'free' or 'independent' trade unions by any reasonable judgement (Croucher and Cotton, 2011).

The GUFs' major task is to reconcile different unions together in one global body, support affiliates in dealing with MNEs and defend rights of unions by pressurizing international organizations and national governments. The rights of unions to operate freely is something that all unions can agree on even if they operate in very different national contexts and in very different ways.

> **BOX 5.1**
>
> ## KEY INSTRUMENTS FOR REGULATING THE EMPLOYMENT RELATIONSHIP
>
> | | |
> |---|---|
> | Global level | ILO conventions |
> | | OECD guidelines |
> | Regional level | European Union law |
> | | Treaty law (e.g., North American Free Trade Area) |
> | National government | Statutes |
> | Private regulation | NGO monitoring and reporting |
> | | Agreements with GUFs |
> | Self-regulation | Company codes of conduct |
>
> Source: Croucher, R. (2013), 'Global industrial relations', in P.N. Gooderham, B. Grøgaard and O. Nordhaug (eds), *International Management, Theory and Practice*, Cheltenham, UK and Northampton, MA, USA: Edward Elgar Publishing.

GUFs' intimate knowledge of labour issues as well as of national unions and governments and international organizations are significant reasons for trade unions to join them. They are also important reasons for MNEs to enter into dialogue with them, as a single and authoritative source of information on a subject they may feel weakly informed about.

The global regulatory system provides only weak constraints and elementary guidance for MNEs on labour issues. Box 5.1 shows the key instruments that play a role in regulating labour issues in a schematic way.

At the lowest level of compulsion, we find company self-regulation (Kolben, 2011) such as company codes of conduct, and 'private regulation' through reporting procedures and external monitors. The 'private' regulations are labour regulations that are carried out through voluntary associations such as Social Accountability International, the Fair Labor Association, the Global Compact or the Global Reporting Initiative. At the top level of the regulatory hierarchy are 'public' forms of regulation that are strictly external to companies such as the International Labour Organization (ILO). The ILO sets labour standards that constitute a 'floor' of basic rights, which are part of its wider 'decent work' agenda (Sengenberger, 2001) and MNEs sometimes use these as benchmarks for their labour practices.

A second important global body providing public regulation and guidance is the Organisation for Economic Co-operation and Development (OECD). The OECD has an expert committee, the Trade Union Advisory Committee (TUAC). The *OECD Guidelines for Multinational Corporations* constitute a significant part of the global system of regulation on labour matters. Complaints that the guidelines have not been followed may be made to the OECD's National Contact Points, who are expert individuals nominated by governments to investigate such complaints.

GUF campaigning combined with use of the global regulatory system can pressure MNEs to change their practices. However, some MNEs, aware of this possibility and sensitive to their own reputations, have sought to pre-empt this type of pressure. They have taken a proactive stance, and have sought advice and entered into dialogue with GUFs rather than being forced to react after the event. For example, many MNEs have signed global labour agreements ('international framework agreements' sometimes called 'global framework agreements') with GUFs. They are generally simple statements of the company's agreement to observe ILO conventions on fundamental issues such as the right of unions to organize and bargain collectively and the company's avoidance of child labour. These agreements are a means to an end: to establish effective unions in MNEs' developing world operations where workers are normally in a very weak position with regard to employers. Yet these agreements co-exist with, and are not a substitute for, dialogue between GUFs and MNEs. These agreements may provide central MNE managers with a way of extending existing cooperative arrangements with employee representatives across their international operations (Schömann et al., 2008).

5.5 Summary

In this chapter, we have introduced stakeholder theory and discussed how managers can use the stakeholder framework to identify important groups that have a strategic influence on MNE operations. MNEs operate in a varied and dynamic global environment with differing laws, regulations, forms of government and cultural norms. MNEs are also faced with different views of what constitutes legitimate actions. Partnerships with NGOs and GUFs can help MNEs overcome legitimacy deficits in local environments, as such actors can help managers make sense of the norms and use their standing in civil society to confer social legitimacy to the MNE.

REFERENCES

Ackermann, F. and C. Eden (2011), 'Strategic management of stakeholders: Theory and practice', *Long Range Planning*, **44**(3), 179–96.

Berger, I., P. Cunningham and M. Drumwright (2004), 'Social alliances: Company/nonprofit collaboration', *California Management Review*, **47**(1), 58–90.

Boatright, J.R. (1994), 'Fiduciary duties and the shareholder–management relations: Or, what's so special about shareholders?', *Business Ethics Quarterly*, **4**(4), 393–407.

Carson, T.L. (1993), 'Does the stakeholder theory constitute a new kind of theory of social responsibility', *Business Ethics Quarterly*, **3**(2), 171–6.

Croucher, R. (2013), 'Global industrial relations', in P.N. Gooderham, B. Grøgaard and O. Nordhaug (eds), *International Management, Theory and Practice*, Cheltenham, UK and Northampton, MA: Edward Elgar Publishing.

Croucher, R. and E. Cotton (2011), *Global Unions, Global Business: Global Union Federations and International Business*, 2nd edition, Faringdon, UK: Libri Publishing.

Donaldson, T. and L.E. Preston (1995), 'The stakeholder theory of the corporation: Concepts, evidence, and implications', *Academy of Management Review*, **20**, 65–91.

Freeman, R.E. (1984), *Strategic Management: A Stakeholder Approach*, Boston, MA: Pitman Publishing.

Freeman, R.E., J. Harrison and A. Wicks (2007), *Managing for Stakeholders: Business in the 21st Century*, New Haven, CT: Yale University Press.

Frooman, J. (1999), 'Stakeholder influence strategies', *Academy of Management Review*, **24**, 191–205.

Gibson, K. (2000), 'The moral basis of stakeholder theory', *Journal of Business Ethics*, **26**(3), 245–57.

Greven, T. (2006), 'US strategic campaigns against transnational enterprises in Germany', *Industrielle Beziehungen*, **1**(3), 1–17.

Harrison, J.S., D.A. Bosse and R.A. Phillips (2010), 'Managing for stakeholders, stakeholder utility functions and competitive advantage', *Strategic Management Journal*, **31**(1), 58–74.

Jones, T.M. (1995), 'Instrumental stakeholder theory: A synthesis of ethics and economics', *Academy of Management Review*, **20**, 404–37.

Kolben, K. (2011), 'Transnational labor regulation and the limits of governance', *Theoretical Inquiries in Law*, **12**(2), accessed 11 February 2019 at https://doi.org/10.2202/1565-3404.1274.

Lea, D. (2004), 'The imperfect nature of corporate responsibility to stakeholders', *Business Ethics Quarterly*, **14**, 201–17.

Marano, V. and P. Tashman (2012), 'Partnerships and the legitimacy of the firm', *International Business Review*, **21**(6), 1122–30.

Marcoux, A.M. (2000), 'Balancing act', in J.R. DesJardines and J.J. McCall (eds), *Contemporary Issues in Business Ethics*, 4th edition (pp. 92–100), Belmont, CA: Wadsworth.

Miles, S. (2017), 'Stakeholder theory classification: A theoretical and empirical evaluation of definitions', *Journal of Business Ethics*, **142**(3), 437–59.

Mitchell, R.K., B.R. Agle and D.J. Wood (1997), 'Towards a theory of stakeholder identifications and salience: Defining the principle of who and what really counts', *Academy of Management Review*, **22**, 853–86.

Oetzel, J. and J.P. Doh (2009), 'MNEs and development: A review and reconceptualization', *Journal of World Business*, **44**(2), 108–20.

Parmar, B.L., R.E. Freeman and J.S. Harrison et al. (2010), 'Stakeholder theory: The state of the art', *The Academy of Management Annals*, **4**(1), 403–45.

Peloza, J. and L. Falkenberg (2009), 'The role of collaboration in achieving corporate social responsibility objectives', *California Management Review*, **51**(3), 3–113.

Phillips, R.A. (2003a), 'Stakeholder legitimacy', *Business Ethics Quarterly*, **13**, 25–41.

Phillips, R.A. (2003b), *Stakeholder Theory and Organizational Ethics*, San Francisco, CA: Berrett-Koehler.

Phillips, R.A., R.W. Freeman and A.C. Wicks (2003), 'What stakeholder theory is not', *Business Ethics Quarterly*, **14**(4), 479–502.

Rowley, T.J. (1997), 'Moving beyond dyadic ties: A network theory of stakeholder influence', *Academy of Management Review*, **22**, 887–910.

Schömann, I., A. Sobazk, E. Voss and P. Wilke (2008), *Codes of Conduct and International Framework Agreements: New Forms of Governance at Company Level*, Dublin: European Foundation for the Improvements of Living and Working Conditions.

Sengenberger, W. (2001), 'Decent work: The international labor organization agenda', *Dialogue and Cooperation*, **2**, 39–55.

Stanford Research Institute (1963), 'Internal memo' (unpublished), Stanford, CA: Stanford Research Institute.

Starik, M. (1995), 'Should trees have managerial standing? Towards stakeholder status for nonhuman nature', *Journal of Business Ethics*, **14**, 207–17.

Suchman, M.C. (1995), 'Managing legitimacy: Strategic and institutional approaches', *Academy of Management Review*, **20**(3), 571–610.

Walsh, J.P. (2005), 'Taking stock of management', *Academy of Management Review*, **30**(2), 426–38.

Yaziji, M. (2004), 'Turning gadflies into allies', *Harvard Business Review*, February, 110–15.

Yaziji, M. and J.P. Doh (2009), *NGOs and Corporations: Conflict and Collaboration*, Cambridge, UK: Cambridge University Press.

Case F

The regulation of contract workers: A case study of LafargeHolcim and a GUF's attempt to defend workers' rights in India

Aranya Pakapath and Elizabeth Cotton

> The unwavering support of IndustriALL to exert pressure on LafargeHolcim at the international level immensely helped in bringing management to the negotiating table. We will continue our efforts towards constructive social dialogue to protect workers' rights. PCSS will also focus on young workers in order to improve their working conditions now and in the future.
> (Lakhan Sahu, PCSS Organizing Secretary)

F.1 Understanding the context

Over the last 30 years, multinational firms have increasingly used labour from outside of a corporation's boundaries. For example, multinational firms have outsourced much of their production and other activities. Moreover, many multinationals increasingly use contract labour in subsidiaries, signalling a change in the employment relationship. Contract labour is often obtained from a third party – a contractor or a private employment agency (ILO, 2009a). Although data continues to be imprecise about the scale and nature of changes in the employment relationship, over the last 30 years externalized labour has expanded dramatically in regions such as Asia, Latin America and Central Europe (ICEM, 2004; IMF, 2007; ITUC, 2014; Theron, 2005). Multinational firms use contract labour in part to obtain more flexibility in production so that they can easily adapt their supply of work services to market conditions. The growth in the use of contract work and other indirect employment leads to an absence of labour protection (Aviles, 2009) such as legislation against unfair dismissal. It also impacts on core labour rights such as freedom of association and collective bargaining. This means that the growth in flexible labour is linked to a growth in workplace precarity and insecurity (Doogan, 2009).

In developing countries, MNEs, labour and unions face three deficits relating to the institutional environment. First, there is a lack of enforced employment legislation in these countries (Cotton, 2014); second, MNEs have found it difficult to manage their global supply chains in developing and transition economies; third, multilateral organizations such as the International Labour Organization (ILO) and Organisation for Economic Co-operation and Development (OECD) do not have the capacity to implement and monitor international standards in developing and transition economies. These deficits have triggered a growth of global governance mechanisms and regulatory initiatives from international non-state and private sectors (Ruggie, 2008), including trade unions and their international organizations – the global union federations (GUFs).

In the main, trade unions regard the growth of externalized labour as directly responsible for the erosion of permanent jobs and decent work (Fashoyin, 2010). Thus, MNEs' increased use of externalized labour is regarded as undermining the power that unions have in both recruiting and representing their members. Since the use of contract and agency labour is widespread across most sectors and regions, many unions now prioritize organizing temporary agency workers as a matter of organizational survival (Cotton, 2013; ICEM, 2004).

The GUFs have supported local trade unions' ambitions in this regard. The work of the GUFs utilizes a broad range of strategies, including the use of transnational private labour regulation (TPLR) mechanisms such as international framework agreements (IFAs) and industry standards (Müller and Rüb, 2005) to secure international agreement with MNEs.

However, unions experience that a regulatory approach to externalized labour has inherent weaknesses (Aviles, 2009). In many national contexts, externalized labour is set up precisely to avoid labour protection (McCann, 2008) by placing the employment relationship outside the scope of existing labour law, leaving temporary agency workers vulnerable to exploitation (ILO, 2009b).

The United Nation's prioritization of enforcement of the governance principles outlined in *Promotion and Protection of All Human Rights, Civil, Political, Economic, Social and Cultural Rights, Including the Right to Development*

(Ruggie, 2008) aims to promote 'due diligence' in global supply chains. It is on the basis of this human rights framework that GUFs' leverage with MNEs exists and how international agreements can be negotiated and secured (Cotton and Gumbrell-McCormick, 2012).

Industrial GUFs have used IFAs as a strategic tool (Croucher and Cotton, 2011) to secure the rights of contract workers. Within some IFAs there is express agreement that the use of permanent direct employment is preferred. This is, for example, the case for agreements with Norske Skog, Aker, Vallourec, GDF Suez and GEA AG. The implementation of these agreements varies greatly and the evidence in developing countries is not strong. However, where the GUFs invest in solidarity and education activities to build the capacity of affiliates in developing countries we see higher levels of implementation (ibid.).

This case study focuses on the long-running industrial dispute in India with the cement multinational company LafargeHolcim. The case study explores the relationships between a GUF, IndustriALL, representing trade union members in the chemicals, energy and mining sectors, and their Indian affiliate Pragatisheel Cement Shramik Sangh (PCSS) and their international affiliates organizing workers in LafargeHolcim. This case study is a longitudinal study of a series of disputes and industrial relations problems for contract and agency workers in the Indian cement sector and the relationships between the international and national parties involved. Both authors have been engaged in these ongoing disputes as part of their previous work for IndustriALL (previously the ICEM prior to merger in 2012).

F.2   LafargeHolcim

LafargeHolcim is the largest producer of building materials, created out of a merger in 2015 between the Swiss multinational Holcim and the French multinational Lafarge. This merger thus brought together two of the four MNEs that control the cement sector, including Cemex and HeidelbergCement. During the merger much was made about the cultural barriers to merger between the two companies, focusing on the different 'egos' of the senior leadership team, including the flamboyant Lafarge CEO Bruno Lafont and the German industrialist Wolfgang Reitzle, who came from the German chemicals company Linde and was known for his careful and measured approach. LafargeHolcim is headquartered in Switzerland but retains key functions in France, and owns operations in 80 countries, with a directly employed workforce of 81 000. Although data is not available, LafargeHolcim makes extensive use of contract workers in its local operations and this case study focuses on the treatment of 1500 contract workers in its Indian operations.

F.3 LafargeHolcim in India

In 2016, LafargeHolcim and its Indian subsidiaries (ACC Jamul Cement Workers) and an active trade union Pragatisheel Cement Shramik Sangh (PCSS) representing 1500 cement workers reached an agreement after many years of industrial dispute, particularly in relation to the rights of contract and agency workers. Since the early 2000s, ACC had been violating the industry-wide Cement Wage Board Agreement[1] and refused to implement a 2006 legal ruling for regularization of hundreds of contract workers.

During 2012, LafargeHolcim started to build a new production plant in Jamul, with the intention of closing the ACC plant and replacing the existing 1200 workers with just 90 contract workers. The same year, PCSS in cooperation with IndustriALL initiated an international campaign to secure rights for contract workers in LafargeHolcim. The campaign included solidarity action from Unia, the Swiss trade union, and filing a complaint against LafargeHolcim to the Swiss National Contact Point (NCP) of the OECD. The complaint submitted that LafargeHolcim was breaking the OECD's *Guidelines for Multinational Enterprises* by violating Indian labour standards and court orders, by refusing to implement legal rulings over regularizing contract workers and paying industry standard wages and collective bargaining in good faith with PCSS.

In 2014, a settlement was agreed between PCSS and LafargeHolcim management by the OECD NCP. The settlement secured jobs of 536 of the 932 contract workers involved in the dispute. A payment plan was agreed to increase over time wages to reach the Cement Wage Board rates (approximately four times the national minimum wage). A redundancy package was agreed for those workers who would not be transferred to the new Jamul plant.

For both PCSS and the GUFs involved in this long-running campaign, this agreement gave rise to a renewed period of campaigning and organizing within the company to ensure implementation of the OECD settlement. LafargeHolcim had a poor record with respect to working conditions, with 86 workers, mainly casual contracts, losing their lives in 2016.

In June 2017, a memorandum of agreement was signed between the Swiss cement manufacturer LafargeHolcim and two GUFs, IndustriALL and

Building Workers International (BWI), to sign an IFA that would secure trade union and basic workers' rights, including health, safety and environmental (HSE) standards. This memorandum represented an important gain for LafargeHolcim workers internationally, securing a protected and recognized space for local negotiations and collective bargaining to take place.

However, in January 2018, the company returned to a position of non-engagement with the GUFs and their affiliates and had withdrawn their agreement to negotiate an IFA. An international campaign 'LafargeHolcim: Keep Your Word, Respect Workers' Lives!' was launched supported by 74 union leaders from 40 countries, part of the LafargeHolcim Global Union Network, demanding meaningful negotiations at international level.

F.4   Chronology of the LafargeHolcim dispute

The ACC Jamul plant, bought by Holcim in 2005, has a long history of using contract workers and with it a series of long-running disputes about working conditions and pay. Since the 1990s, the Indian union PCSS has organized contract workers in the cement industry in the Chhattisgarh state of India and has attempted to secure dialogue with ACC Jamul plant management over the issue of regularization of contract workers and improvement of working conditions.

The Indian legal frame that regulates the relationship between contract workers and employers in the cement industry is the industry-wide Cement Wage Board Agreement that prohibits contract labour in the process work of the cement industry, allowing contract labour only in the loading/unloading work in the plant.

One important incident in the relationship between Holcim and the Indian unions representing contract workers was a court case in the 1990s involving 573 contract workers working for two main contractors. The court case was the culmination of a long-running industrial dispute between ACC and Indian unions. Many of the contract workers had worked for ACC for 25 years. The claim related to the right to collective bargaining and direct contracts of employment. Part of the claim related to ACC's classification of contract workers as 'process' and 'non-process' workers, despite their long-term continuous service in all areas of the production process. This categorization of workers allowed ACC to evade the national wage agreement and thus pay the workers the minimum wage only.

The case proceeded to the Industrial Court in 2000, and in 2006 the court ruled in support of the workers' claims for collective bargaining and regularization of the 573 contract workers. ACC/Holcim appealed to the High Court against the Industrial Court's verdict on regularization of contract workers. The High Court issued its ruling in 2011, partially upholding the Industrial Court's ruling of 2006.

In the process leading up to the court case IndustriALL played an important role. Already from 2007 IndustriALL initiated solidaristic work on behalf of the ACC workers. IndustriALL already had long-term experience of organizing within the Indian context as they had carried out several decades of educational and campaigning work with affiliates in India.

The process started with the initiation of a fact-finding mission involving Aranya Pakapath representing IndustriALL and Mr B.K. Das, retired general secretary of the Indian National Mineworkers' Federation (INMF) and executive member of IndustriALL. Following this mission, IndustriALL initiated the production of a documentary film to highlight the situation of contract workers in the cement industry in Chhattisgarh. The documentary was disseminated widely internationally through IndustriALL, its affiliates and international labour networks and awarded the second best film at the International Labour Film festival in Geneva, 2009.

In 2010, the Indian union PCSS became affiliated to the IndustriALL. Their affiliation led to an expansion of IndustriALL's campaigning and educational support to PCSS members. For example, PCSS became involved in IndustriALL's long-running 'Stop Precarious Work Now!' campaign, which was coordinated internationally and regionally to support local unions carrying out campaigns for precarious workers.

A key part of this campaign was to raise awareness of the situation of the ACC workers internationally. In 2011, IndustriALL addressed the International Labour Conference on behalf of the workers and in 2012, PCSS conducted a two-week tour of Switzerland, meeting trade unions and solidarity organizations, including NGOs MultiWatch and Solifonds, to raise international support for the campaign. This included a protest at the annual general meeting of Holcim in Zurich.

In 2012, PCSS with the support of IndustriALL, Unia and Solifonds, filed a complaint against Holcim before the Swiss National Contact Point of the OECD in Berne, Switzerland, alleging that Holcim was disobeying the guidelines for multinational enterprises by violating Indian labour standards and court orders, by refusing collective bargaining in good faith. Further violations are outlined in the complaint with respect to the surrounding communities around the LafargeHolcim plants. The company acquired land from local farmers and went on to reduce living conditions in local communities.

During this sustained period of national and international campaigning, ACC management adopted an aggressive attitude towards the PCSS. In 2011, PCSS leadership and activists were wrongfully accused by ACC management of theft. In January 2014, seven PCSS leaders were imprisoned on the basis of these charges but shortly afterwards released following the intervention of IndustriALL. In the absence of any evidence for the accusations the court ruled against ACC.

The OECD's *Guidelines for Multinational Enterprises* is an important tool for trade union campaigns and the submission of complaints to the OECD National Contact Points was an established strategy of the GUFs. Following a directive from the Swiss OECD NCP, PCSS with the support of IndustriALL entered into negotiations with local management in 2014. In January 2016, a settlement for over 1000 LafargeHolcim workers was reached such that jobs were secured for 536 contract workers in the two ACC plants. The settlement also provides for the progressive readjustment of the salaries of the contract workers to reach the national wage agreement for the cement industry. The remaining 458 workers that lost their jobs secured a severance package. In the course of the negotiation, the union and its membership was posed with a difficult choice between benefits of regularization and arrears to a small group of workers as directed by the High Court or minimizing the retrenchment that the company was proposing. The workers who had the High Court order pushed for maximum absorption of existing workers in the new and the old plant with better working conditions and the maximum compensation package with alternative livelihood support to those who were to lose jobs. For PCSS this marks the start of the next phase of its struggle to ensure the full implementation of the agreement and to take forward the lessons from this case study.

F.5 Conclusion

Although only a small percentage of people work directly for MNEs, they influence the employment relationship indirectly through their control of global supply chains and as main users of contractors and private employment agencies. They also have financial and political influence on national institutions and labour regulation. As a result, MNEs continue to be a major focus of interest to trade unions and the GUFs, which is reflected in the priority given by them to their international regulatory and solidaristic work. Currently, the GUFs carry out their regulatory work in a number of ways, including their participation in international dialogue, significantly through the ILO and the OECD, and negotiating international agreements with employers that enshrine these international standards such as IFAs.

GUFs are multilateral organizations and therefore able to coordinate relations between three or more states and mobilize affiliated national trade unions to engage meaningfully on human rights and international standards. The GUFs are the vehicles through which trade unions are recognized as legitimate social partners by the United Nations and international bodies such as the ILO, OECD and the Global Compact. MNEs also recognize the value of GUFs multilateral structures in their corporate social responsibility and governance agendas. This function has high currency with some developing country trade unions where leverage with multinational employers at national level is weak.

MNEs have not committed the resources to build local capacity to implement international agreements. Instead, they have distributed agreements internationally and funded communication and review activities. The capacity of the GUFs to monitor and implement the agreements at an international level is also limited, mainly because of financial restrictions. Despite the large-scale, coordinated campaigning and educational work of the GUFs directed at contract and agency labour, and precarious work more broadly, there continues to be reluctance on the part of MNEs to take responsibility for the governance of global supply chains.

This case study shows that where local unions are able to organize precarious workers around key demands, they can engage with the GUFs' international networks organized around those same demands.

CASE DISCUSSION

1 Identify the relevant stakeholders in the LafargeHolcim controversy.
2 Discuss how the institutional factors influenced stakeholder relations between LafargeHolcim and a global union federation (GUF).
3 Discuss the ways in which the trade union in the case study mobilized solidaristic support locally and internationally.
4 Discuss the possible actions that LafargeHolcim and MNEs in general can take as a means of managing their relations with trade unions.

NOTE

1 Cement Wage Board Agreement: industry-wide agreement negotiated and signed between Cement Manufacturers' Association (CMA), which represents the employers of the cement industry, and the national federations of cement workers (INTUC, BMS, AITUC, HMS, CITU and LPF). The existence of mandatory Cement Wage Board Agreement since 1978 is well recognized by all parties involved. This industry agreement is negotiated every five years.

REFERENCES

Aviles, A.O. (2009), 'The "externalization" of labour law', *International Labour Review*, **148**(1–2), 47–67.

Cotton, E. (2013), 'Regulating precarious work: The hidden role of the global union federations', in M. Sergeant and M. Ori (eds), *Vulnerable Workers and Precarious Working* (pp. 71–91), Newcastle-upon-Tyne, UK: Cambridge Scholars Publishing.

Cotton, E. (2014), 'Transnational regulation of temporary agency work: Compromised partnership between private employment agencies and global union federations', *Work, Employment and Society*, **29**(1), 137–53.

Cotton, E. and R. Gumbrell-McCormick (2012), 'Global unions as imperfect multilateral organisations: An international relations perspective', *Economic and Industrial Democracy*, **33**(4), 707–28.

Croucher, R. and E. Cotton (2011), *Global Unions, Global Business: Global Union Federations and International Business*, 2nd edition, Faringdon, UK: Libri Publishing.

Doogan, K. (2009), *New Capitalism? The Transformation of Work*, Cambridge, UK: Polity Press.

Fashoyin, T. (2010), 'Trends and developments in employment relations and the world of work in developing countries', *The International Journal of Comparative Labour Law and Industrial Relations*, **26**(2), 119–39.

ICEM (2004), *Contract/Agency Labour: A Threat to Our Social Standards*, Brussels: ICEM.

ILO (2009a), *Global Employment Trends – Update May 2009*, Geneva: ILO.

ILO (2009b), *Celebration of the 60th anniversary of Convention No. 98: The Right to Organize and Collective Bargaining in the Twenty-First Century*, Geneva: ILO.

IMF (2007), *Survey on Changing Employment Practices and Precarious Work*, Geneva: IMF.

ITUC (2014), *Precarious Work in the Asia Pacific Region*, Brussels: ITUC.

McCann, D. (2008), *Regulating Flexible Work*, Oxford: Oxford University Press.

Müller, T. and S. Rüb (2005), *Towards Internationalisation of Labour Relations?*, Bonn: Friedrich Ebert Stiftung.

Ruggie, J.G. (2008), *Promotion and Protection of All Human Rights, Civil, Political, Economic, Social and Cultural Rights, Including the Right to Development*, Geneva: ILO.

Theron, J. (2005), 'Employment is not what it used to be: The nature and impact of work restructuring in South Africa', in E. Webster and K. von Holdt (eds), *Beyond the Apartheid Workplace: Studies in Transition* (pp. 293–4), Pietermaritzburg: University of KwaZulu-Natal Press.

6
Corporate social responsibility

6.1 Introduction

The rapid growth in the number of MNEs, together with their increased economic and political power, has strongly accentuated the issue of their ethical, social and environmental responsibilities. This chapter will discuss why MNEs should focus on ethical, social and environmental responsibilities in response to stakeholder expectations as a means to create long-term competitive advantage. We will highlight core challenges that MNEs face when striving to act ethically and responsibly. Corporate social responsibility (CSR) is first defined and placed in the historical context of globalization. We then elaborate on why an MNE would want to consider its ethical, social and environmental responsibilities to various stakeholder groups and address the key question of whether or not an MNE can 'do well by doing good'.

6.2 Defining CSR

More than 60 years ago, Bowen (1953, p.44) defined CSR as the 'obligations of businessmen to pursue those policies, to make those decisions, or to follow those lines of action which are desirable in terms of the objectives and values of society'. The implication was that managers should consider their responsibilities toward a broad set of stakeholders encompassing many interests including social and environmental issues (Russo and Perrini, 2010). Dahlsrud (2008) examined the most commonly used definitions of CSR as found in journal articles and on corporate websites. Of the 37 identified definitions, the most frequent dimensions of CSR include: (1) stakeholders; (2) social responsibility; (3) economic factors; (4) the voluntary nature of CSR-related activities; and (5) the environment. Over half the definitions of CSR contained four or more of the identified dimensions, suggesting that although the exact wording of a universal definition of CSR has yet to be agreed upon, a central focus in most definitions is on the symbiotic and long-term relationship between business and society (Looser and Wehrmeyer, 2015).

One way for companies to address CSR issues is to use global standards and guidelines, including the Global Reporting Initiative (GRI) *G3 Sustainability Reporting Guidelines* (2006), and the International Organization for Standardization (ISO) *26000 Guidance on Social Responsibility* (2010). The GRI and the ISO 26000 are voluntary guidelines that can be adopted by an organization to assist with the reporting of social and environmental issues to various stakeholders. Both the GRI and the ISO 26000 adopt the definition of sustainable development put forth by the United Nations World Commission on Environment and Development (WCED) in 1987, which holds that '[s]ustainable development is development that meets the needs of the present without compromising the ability of future generations to meet their own needs' (WCED, 1987). The ISO 26000 goes one step further, and links sustainable development with social responsibility by stating that social responsibility reflects the organization's responsibility to the environment and society, while sustainable development sums up the broader expectations of society. As such, 'an organization's social responsibility should be to contribute to sustainable development' (ISO 26000, 2010).

Although the GRI *G3 Sustainability Reporting Guidelines* do not explicitly define CSR, the ISO 26000 has made a significant contribution to the field through its extensive definition of social responsibility as:

> The responsibility of an organization for the impacts of its decisions and activities on society and the environment through transparent and ethical behaviour that:
>
> - Contributes to sustainable development, including health and the welfare of society
> - Takes into account the expectations of stakeholders
> - Is in compliance with acceptable laws and consistent with international norms of behavior
> - Is integrated throughout the organization and is practices in its relationship.
> (ISO 26000, 2010)

The ISO 26000 expounds on six core subjects of social responsibility including: human rights, labour practices, the environment, fair operating practices, consumer issues, and community involvement and development (Box 6.1).

In this chapter, we use CSR as an umbrella concept, but also emphasize that MNEs must determine which CSR activities are strategically important to create value for both the firm and society.

> **BOX 6.1**
>
> ## ISO 26000 CORE SUBJECTS AND ISSUES OF SOCIAL RESPONSIBILITY
>
> **Core subject: Human rights**
> Issues: Due diligence, human rights risk situations, avoidance of complicity, resolving grievances, discrimination and vulnerable groups, civil and political rights, fundamental principles and rights at work.
>
> **Core subject: Labour practices**
> Issues: Employment and employment relationships, conditions of work and social protection, social dialogue, health and safety at work, human development and training in the workplace.
>
> **Core subject: The environment**
> Issues: Prevention of pollution, sustainable resource use, climate change mitigation and adaption, protection of the environment, biodiversity and restoration of natural habitats.
>
> **Core subject: Fair operating practices**
> Issues: Anti-corruption, responsible political involvement, fair competition, promoting social responsibility in the value chain, respect for property rights.
>
> **Core subject: Consumer issues**
> Issues: Fair marketing, factual and unbiased information and fair contractual practices, protecting consumers' health and safety, sustainable consumption, consumer service, support, and complaint and dispute resolution, consumer data protection and privacy, access to essential services, education and awareness.
>
> **Core subject: Community involvement and development**
> Issues: Community involvement, education and culture, employment creation and skills development, technology development and access, wealth and income creation, health, social investment.
>
> Source: ISO 26000 (2010).

6.3 Stakeholder theory applied to CSR

In the early years of globalization, MNEs had to confront entirely new ethical dilemmas on a global scale. Improved communication technologies meant that these ethical dilemmas often played out in the court of public opinion. MNEs such as Shell, Nestlé, Gap and Nike faced international criticism in the early 1990s as companies that exploited those in developing countries. This changed the way in which MNEs view their role in society and how they engaged in CSR-related practices. As discussed in Chapter 5, R. Edward Freeman (1984) developed stakeholder theory during this era. Stakeholder

Figure 6.1 Corporate responsibility: A tension between extremes – and a middle way

```
                    Substantial
                   responsibility
       ◄─────────────────────────────────►
       Limited                      Extended
    responsibility              responsibility
```

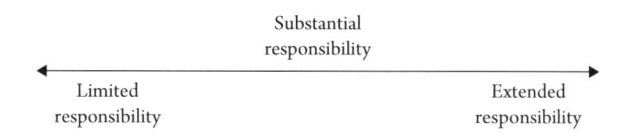

theory was an important development in the social responsibility of an MNE as it shifted the focus from profit maximization to gaining a social licence to operate through engaging with various stakeholder groups. The basic argument is that an MNE will not be able to make a profit if society does not grant it a social licence to operate. Managers have increasingly become aware of both the financial and reputational values of their firms and in 1997, Elkington introduced the 'triple bottom line' (economic, social and environmental factors) that made more explicit the costs to MNEs of failing to behave in a socially responsible manner. The triple bottom line as a CSR tool also illustrates that CSR is about balancing economic values, social values and environmental values supported by different stakeholders (Elkington, 1997).

The legitimate demands placed on MNEs by various stakeholders raise an interesting and fundamental question: what are the economic, legal, ethical and social responsibilities of an MNE? Figure 6.1 illustrates three main positions: (1) Friedman's (1970) focus on limited responsibility where executives' responsibility to society is to increase a firm's profits; (2) the idea of extended (and unequivocal) responsibility to conduct its business in a manner that is consistent with sustainable social and ecological systems (see, e.g., Ingebrigtsen and Jakobsen, 2007; Zsolnai and Ims, 2006); and (3) the central position of substantial responsibility for addressing all legitimate stakeholders who are substantially affected by the organization's activities (Freeman, 1984).

The location of managers on the spectrum in Figure 6.1 indicates the level of social responsibility they seek to implement in the MNE. Managers can use the following three questions from Jørgensen and Pedersen (2013) as an analytical tool to identify the level of CSR to implement as well as to better understand stakeholder reactions to MNE activities:

- To whom is the MNE responsible?
- What are the MNE's responsibilities to society?
- What are the limits of the MNE's responsibility?

The first question corresponds to the identification of the MNE's stakeholders. Who the relevant stakeholders are depends on the stakeholder

Figure 6.2 Carroll's pyramid of corporate social responsibility

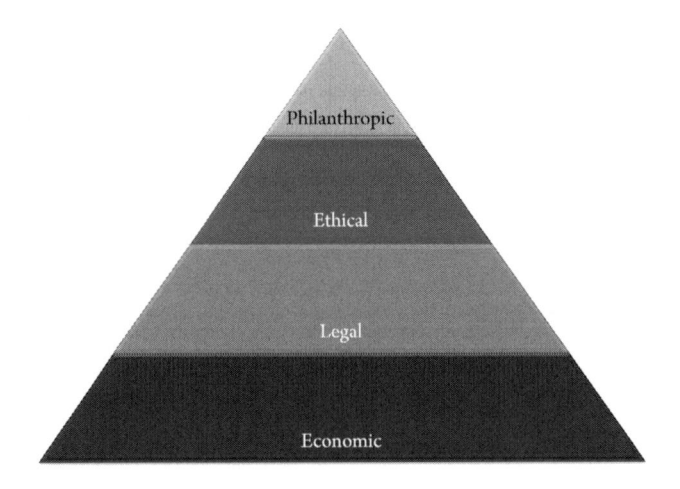

Source: Carroll (1991).

definition the MNE is using and on its view on what the core social responsibility issues are. One way for MNEs to determine which issues are core is to apply the ISO 26000 standard, as discussed in Section 6.2 of this chapter. The second question deals with what ways and to what extent the MNE is accountable to its stakeholders. In answering this question, managers can find guidelines in Carroll's (1991) pyramid, which we discuss below. The third question – and perhaps the most difficult one – is about considering the *limits of responsibility* of the MNE, and involves an assessment of what might be reasonably expected of it.

Archie B. Carroll (1991) attempted to address the question of what are MNEs' responsibilities to society by proposing his widely cited 'pyramid of corporate social responsibility' (Figure 6.2). For Carroll, CSR consists of four hierarchical responsibilities: economic, legal, ethical and philanthropic. The foundation of any business is its economic responsibility to society, which includes being profitable, providing employment opportunities, and generating taxes.

As an MNE strives to meet its primary goal of making a profit, it must also meet or exceed the minimum legal responsibilities set by various local and federal governments. The third level of Carroll's pyramid of corporate social responsibility is a company's ethical responsibilities to society. Although Carroll suggests that managers should abide by ethical standards that are consistent with the morals and standards of society, he does not explicitly state the extent of these obligations.

Margolis and Walsh (2003) help to clarify this issue by looking at a company's moral duty to aid and respond. The first moral duty occurs when a firm directly contributes to or causes a certain condition. This duty suggests that an MNE has the duty to respond if it is causing harm (e.g., environmental pollution), or has the potential to do harm (e.g., hazardous working conditions). Often, MNEs run into trouble when they shirk this basic duty, and become the target of various stakeholder and NGO actions. The second duty to respond occurs when the MNE benefits from an unjust condition that it has not created. An example of this type of duty would be paying a living wage to employees in developing countries. MNEs do not set the standards for minimum wages, yet they may benefit from paying extremely low wages to employees. Another example is a firm selling a product in one country that is banned in another country with higher safety regulations.

Yet another dimension in clarifying the ethical responsibilities of MNEs was suggested by Eells and Walton (1974) who put forward the principle of 'good neighbourliness' involving two distinct processes: (1) not doing things to spoil the neighbourhood; and (2) volunteering to help solve neighbourhood problems. There are commonalities between the above-mentioned moral duties 'to respond when a firm benefits from an unjust condition to which it did not contribute' and the duties to 'not do things to spoil the neighbourhood'. The idea that an MNE has an ethical or moral responsibility to solve neighbourhood problems remains controversial, and reflects a third ethical duty to respond out of benevolence.

Acting in a benevolent manner reflects the philanthropic responsibilities of Carroll's (1991) pyramid of corporate social responsibility, which suggests that firms should be good corporate citizens and contribute resources to provide social benefits for the community. MNEs who decide to extend their CSR to the ethical level implicitly acknowledge that stakeholders should be defined in a broad sense using, for example, claimant- and recipient-type definitions, as discussed in Chapter 5.

The final and most difficult question is that of the limits of an MNE's responsibility to society. Different positions exist on what constitutes the limits to business responsibility. One possible answer is that it depends on what the most powerful stakeholders consider to be the limits to an MNE's responsibility. This requires that MNEs distinguish between primary and secondary stakeholders, with the latter having no formal claims on the MNE but with the MNE possibly having a moral obligation to consider claims (e.g., Carroll and Bucholtz, 1993; Gibson, 2000). A different approach is to distinguish issues over which MNEs have no immediate influence from those that it *can* influence (see, e.g., Messner, 2009). For example, MNEs may face ethical issues that stem from poor work practices in independent second-tier suppliers in geographically distant locations. However, one can ask if that constitutes an adequate defence particularly once the MNE becomes aware of these conditions. Perhaps the best answer is that it requires good business judgement from managers.

6.4 The short- and long-term benefits of CSR investments

The question of company performance may seem irrelevant in the context of responsibility. However, broadly speaking, the overarching question of business is: how can companies achieve durable high performance? In addition, we can add the strategically oriented question: why do some companies achieve higher performance than others? In traditional economic theory, these questions are entirely oriented towards economic performance. Several scholars, most notably Michael Porter and Mark Kramer (2002, 2006, 2011), argue that it is possible for MNEs to 'do well by doing good'.

Meta-analyses by Margolis and Walsh (2003) and Orlitzky, Schmidt and Rynes (2003) provide some support for a link between social responsibility and financial performance. However, evidence of the link between financial performance and social responsibility is far from conclusive, perhaps due to the varying definitions of CSR utilized across studies as well as different metrics for capturing financial data.

Hillman and Keim (2001) found a positive correlation between CSR that addresses stakeholder needs and financial performance, whereas CSR consisting of philanthropic donations did not have the same correlation. McWilliams and Siegel (2001) suggested that consumers are willing to pay a premium for socially responsible goods, and that an optimum level of CSR can be identified that maximizes profits while at the same time meets stakeholders' demands. Indeed, companies such as TOMS Shoes have built their brands on a foundation of socially responsible behaviour. In 2006, Blake Mycoskie founded TOMS Shoes based on a shoe design worn by Argentinean farmers, with the intention of donating one pair of shoes to a child in need for every pair of shoes that were sold. Through 'Friends of TOMS', a non-profit affiliate of TOMS Shoes, more than 2 000 000 pairs of shoes have been donated to children in more than 44 countries around the world. Most recently, TOMS has expanded its product line to include eyewear and has maintained its 'One for One' philosophy of social responsibility. Mycoskie, realizing that sight-related disabilities are in most cases solvable, has pledged a pair of glasses or a sight-saving surgery for every pair of TOMS eyewear that are sold. TOMS Shoes, the Body Shop and Ben &

Jerry's have utilized socially responsible business practices to build strong brands. Although these companies are fairly exceptional they do indicate that strategically focused investments in CSR need not be a burden to the financial performance of the MNE.

6.5 Creating 'win–win' possibilities through strategic CSR investments

While early discussions of CSR in the business literature focused on CSR as a moral activity, the essence of recent debates on CSR is increasingly on 'doing good to do well' (McWilliams, Siegel and Wright, 2006; Zadek, 2000). According to Porter and Kramer (2002), doing good to do well requires that MNEs discover the overlap between social value to society and economic value to the firm. MNEs can identify such overlaps through a focus on location advantages across borders, categorized by Porter (1990) as a diamond model of national competitiveness (for an in-depth discussion of the diamond model in the context of MNEs, see Verbeke, 2009; see also Figure 6.3).

For example, an MNE can improve factor conditions through efforts such as employee training programmes and investment in physical infrastructure within developing countries. Second, an MNE may introduce programmes

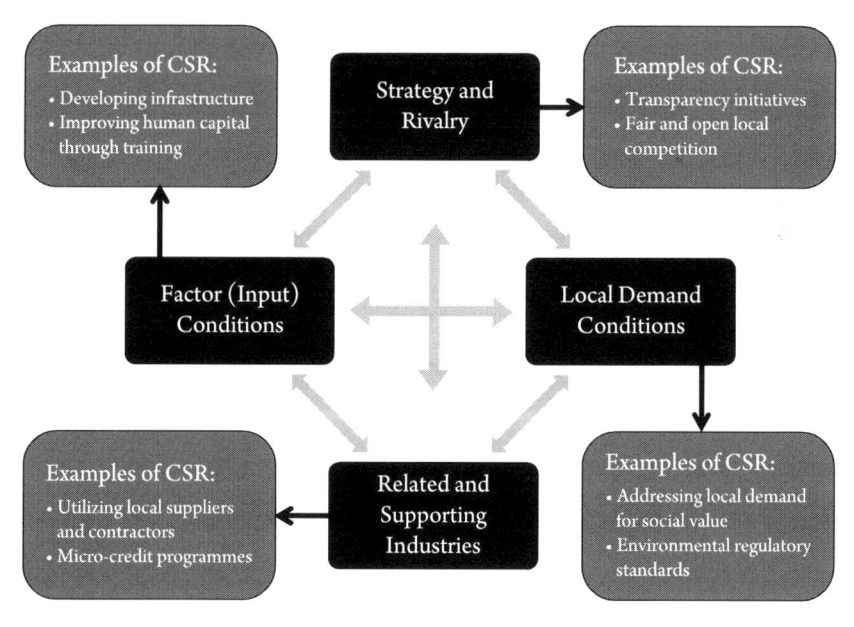

Source: Adapted from Porter and Kramer (2006).

Figure 6.3 Porter's (1990) diamond model and corporate social responsibility

that increase demand conditions through efforts to expand the size and quality of local markets. An example addressing demand conditions could include something as simple as providing free Wi-Fi service (a social value) in an effort to attract more customers (value to the firm). Third, it is possible to enhance the context for strategy and rivalry through efforts to increase transparency and reduce corruption. For example, the extractive industry has implemented the Extractive Industries Transparency Initiative (EITI) to ensure that payments to governments and government-linked entities are fully transparent. The EITI helps to ensure that host governments distribute taxes and revenue generated by mining and oil companies in a way that benefits those in the local community, while at the same time enhancing the image and reputation of the industry. Finally, MNEs can strategically implement CSR by promoting related and supported industries. Addressing related and supporting industries is often accomplished through working with local contractors in developing countries. Microfinance programmes, which involve providing low-interest loans to entrepreneurs in developing countries that would otherwise not qualify, are also an effective form of CSR that addresses related and supporting industries.

Porter and Kramer (2006) further expand on the idea of strategically implemented CSR by suggesting that each aspect of a firm's value chain can be infused with socially responsible practices that can add value to both the firm and society. Figure 6.4 shows how firms can be more socially responsible through the primary activities of inbound logistics, operations, outbound logistics, marketing and sales, and after-sales service, as well as through support activities including firm infrastructure, human resource management, technology development, and procurement.

Infusing the value chain with CSR-related activities leads to improvements within the MNE, while concentrating on infusing the four factors of the diamond model with CSR will lead to improvements outside the firm. In either case, the main point of strategically implemented CSR activities is that both the firm and society gain value. In their latest work on strategically implemented CSR, Porter and Kramer (2011, p. 66) introduce the concept of shared value, which they define as 'policies and operating practices that enhance the competitiveness of a company while simultaneously advancing the economic and social conditions in the communities in which it operates'. Porter and Kramer argue that the short-term economic approach to value creation held by most MNEs is outdated and comes at the expense of addressing the long-term needs and challenges faced by society. The authors suggest that the purpose of the corporation should be redefined as to create

Figure 6.4 — The social impact of the value chain

Support Activities

- **Firm Infrastructure** — Example of CSR: Social responsibility reporting
- **Human Resource Management** — Example of CSR: Safe working conditions, health care benefits
- **Technology Development** — Example of CSR: Product safety, supporting university research
- **Procurement** — Example of CSR: Enforce supply chain practices (e.g., child labour, bribery)

Primary Activities

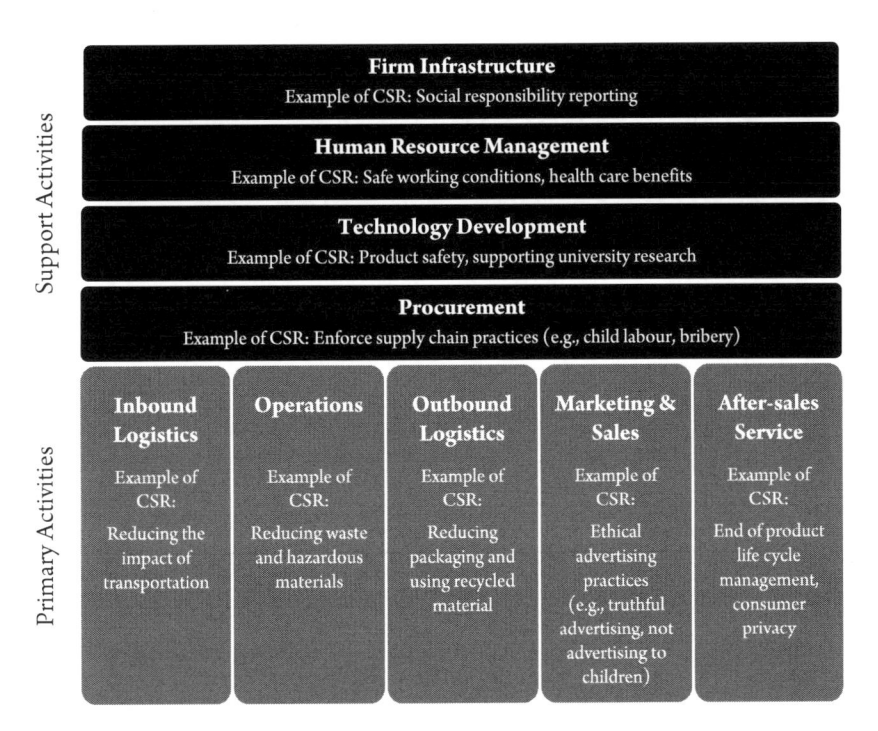

Inbound Logistics	Operations	Outbound Logistics	Marketing & Sales	After-sales Service
Example of CSR: Reducing the impact of transportation	Example of CSR: Reducing waste and hazardous materials	Example of CSR: Reducing packaging and using recycled material	Example of CSR: Ethical advertising practices (e.g., truthful advertising, not advertising to children)	Example of CSR: End of product life cycle management, consumer privacy

Source: Adapted from Porter and Kramer (2006).

Figure 6.4 The social impact of the value chain

shared value, as this will bring long-term benefit to both the MNEs and to society.

6.6 Internationalization strategies and the implementation of CSR in MNEs

Some researchers argue that MNEs' international strategies have CSR implications in their host countries. Christmann (2004) finds that MNEs following a global strategy also implement globally standardized environmental policies, and that standardization of environmental performance standards, environmental policies, and environmental communications results from pressures from different groups in the institutional environment. However, Strike, Gao and Bansal (2006) make a counter-claim that MNE activities have a downside when, for example, they outsource 'dirty' operations, source labour below subsistence pay and take advantage of lax regulations and lower standards. Husted and Allen (2006) make the distinction between 'local CSR', which meets the needs of the local community, and 'global CSR', which focuses more on macro issues with a global impact. Through their study of

MNE subsidiaries in Mexico, Husted and Allen find that most MNEs place importance on global issues such as the environment and human rights, but firms that have a high degree of local responsiveness in their product market activities also focus more on local CSR issues.

Muller (2006) points out that a global strategy may lead to an efficient transmission of CSR practices, but that implementation at the local level may lack ownership and legitimacy within the local community. CSR developed at the local level may better meet the needs of the local community while at the same time bring the organization more legitimacy within the local environment; however, these practices may be fragmented and reactive. In a study of subsidiaries in the automotive industry in Mexico, Muller finds that the most proactive subsidiaries with regard to CSR are given the most autonomy by headquarters, yet still closely follow the CSR strategy set by headquarters. MNEs with highly centralized control over their subsidiaries have the lowest CSR performance. Jamali (2010) finds that managers in a sample of subsidiaries in Lebanon have considerable autonomy to implement CSR practices based on the global guidelines set by headquarters. However, these guidelines are often detached from the needs of the local community, thus diluting the potential value of most CSR initiatives.

In a study of 52 subsidiaries in 14 MNEs, Crilly (2011) investigated the extent to which subsidiaries follow narrow shareholder interests or pursue broader stakeholder interests. His study builds on resource dependency and institutional theory. Resource dependency theory predicts that organizations attend to demands of those stakeholders who control important inputs while institutional theory explains stakeholder interaction on the basis of legal, normative and take-for-granted standards of conduct. Crilly found that it was often the case that country managers expressed stakeholder orientations that were at odds with those expressed at headquarters and that subsidiary managers were not aware of the practices implemented at headquarters. Moreover, many subsidiary managers emphasized the need to adapt to local stakeholder requirements.

Crilly also found that differences in stakeholder orientation reflected differences in the strategic objectives of subsidiaries. In subsidiaries that were engaged in R&D activities, the stakeholder orientation was broad and emphasis was on value creation for local partners. He also found that managers in asset-exploiting subsidiaries (Dunning, 1993) had less regard for non-shareholder stakeholders. Although subsidiaries needed to secure access to natural resources from governments and communities, in the absence of any sanctioning mechanisms the responses of these subsidiaries to local stakeholders were largely symbolic. The level of the independence of the subsidiary also matters for subsidiary stakeholder orientation, with subsidiaries with little independence conforming to CSR policies developed at headquarters. Some subsidiary managers mentioned the tension between local and global legitimacy. Indeed, the pressure from globally active stakeholders from Western countries meant that subsidiaries chose not to overlook the interests of local stakeholders. Not all subsidiaries perceived equal pressure to comply with pressure for social engagement. One factor is the overall size of the MNE. Crilly observed that global stakeholders were better informed about the social activities and infringements of large MNEs.

Kim et al. (2018) raise the same issue as Crilly when they argue that MNE subsidiaries present a major challenge to CSR implementation, because they have to meet the demands of a variety of host country stakeholders and garner legitimacy in what may be challenging institutional settings. What headquarters wants and needs in terms of CSR may at the subsidiary level be more difficult to deliver than headquarters assumes. Instead subsidiaries may be more concerned with highly local CSR initiatives such as philanthropic contributions to local social and public requirements such as sports facilities and educational opportunities. Such practical CSR investments enable the subsidiary to develop legitimacy locally and to build relationships with local stakeholders. Kim et al. argue that subsidiaries' engagement in practical CSR such as philanthropic investments is more likely to involve stakeholders who the firm deals directly with including their local employees and customers. Finally, Kim et al. (2018) find that the influence that local stakeholders have on subsidiary CSR engagement is moderated by the degree of subsidiary autonomy and the institutional environment in which it operates. In emerging economies with institutional voids, local stakeholders tend to be passive on CSR issues (Kim et al., 2018; Zhao, Tan and Park, 2014).

6.7 Summary

In this chapter, we have presented an instrumental stakeholder theory as a tool that managers can use in order to identify some of the external factors that influence MNE value creation and value distribution. We also emphasized that MNEs must pay careful attention to their economic, legal, ethical and social obligations to stakeholders in all the countries in which they operate, and try to strike a balance between global policies and local adaptation. The economic case has been made that companies can 'do well by doing good', by strategically aligning the creation of economic value with the creation of social value, representing a win–win situation for society. The two cases accompanying this chapter illustrate how two successful MNEs have struggled with, and addressed, CSR challenges.

REFERENCES

Bowen, H.P. (1953), *Social Responsibility of the Business*, New York: Harper & Row.

Carroll, A.B. (1991), 'The pyramid of corporate social responsibility: Toward the moral management of organizational stakeholders', *Business Horizons*, **34**(4), 39–48.

Carroll, A.B. and A.K. Bucholtz (1993), *Business and Society: Ethics and Stakeholder Management*, Cincinnati, OH: Western.

Christmann, P. (2004), 'Multinational companies and the natural environment: Determinants of global environmental policy', *Academy of Management Journal*, **47**(5), 747–60.

Crilly, D. (2011), 'Predicting stakeholder orientation in the multinational enterprise: A mid-range theory', *Journal of International Business Studies*, **42**(5), 694–717.

Dahlsrud, A. (2008), 'How corporate social responsibility is defined: An analysis of 37 definitions', *Corporate Social Responsibility and Environmental Management*, **15**(1), 1–13.

Dunning, J.H. (1993), 'Re-evaluating the benefits of foreign direct investment', *Transnational Corporations*, **3**(1), 23–52.

Eells, R. and C. Walton (1974), *Conceptual Foundations of Business*, 3rd edition, Homewood, IL: Irwin.

Elkington, J. (1997), *Cannibals with Forks: The Triple Bottom Line of the 21st Century Business*, Gabriola Island, BC: New Society Publishers.

Freeman, R.E. (1984), *Strategic Management: A Stakeholder Approach*, Boston, MA: Pitman Publishing.

Friedman, M. (1970), 'The social responsibility of business is to increase profits', *New York Times Magazine*, 13 September, 122–3.

Gibson, K. (2000), 'The moral basis of stakeholder theory', *Journal of Business Ethics*, **26**(3), 245–57.

Global Reporting Initiative (GRI) (2006), *Sustainability Reporting Guidelines – Version 3.0*, accessed 11 February 2019 at http://www.globalreporting.org/Services/ResearchLiberary/GRIPublications/.

Hillman, A.J. and G.D. Keim (2001), 'Shareholder value, stakeholder management, and social issues: What's the bottom line?', *Strategic Management Journal*, **22**(2), 125–39.

Husted, B.W. and D.B. Allen (2006), 'Corporate social responsibility in the multinational enterprise: Strategic and institutional approaches', *Journal of International Business Studies*, **37**(6), 838–49.

Ingebrigtsen, S. and O. Jakobsen (2007), *Circulation Economics: Theory and Practice*, Bern: Peter Lang.

International Organization for Standardization (ISO) (2010), *ISO 26000 Guidance on Social Responsibility*, accessed 11 February 2019 at https://www.iso.org/iso-26000-social-responsibility.html.

Jamali, D. (2010), 'The CSR of MNC subsidiaries in developing countries: Global, local, substantive or diluted?', *Journal of Business Ethics*, **93**(2), 181–200.

Jørgensen, S. and L.J. Pedersen (2013), 'Cermaq: From activist target to sustainability leader', in P.N. Gooderham, B. Grøgaard and O. Nordhaug (eds), *International Management: Theory in Practice* (pp. 306–25), Cheltenham, UK and Northampton, MA, USA: Edward Elgar Publishing.

Kim, C., J. Kim, R. Marshall and H. Afzali (2018), 'Stakeholder influence, institutional duality, and CSR involvement of MNC subsidiaries', *Journal of Business Research*, **91**, 40–47.

Looser, S. and W. Wehrmeyer (2015), 'Stakeholder mapping of CSR in Switzerland', *Social Responsibility Journal*, **11**(4), 780–830.

Margolis, J.D. and J.P. Walsh (2003), 'Misery loves companies: Rethinking social initiatives by business', *Administrative Science Quarterly*, **48**(2), 268–305.

McWilliams, A. and D. Siegel (2001), 'Corporate social responsibility: A theory of the firm perspective', *Academy of Management Review*, **26**(1), 117–27.

McWilliams, A., D.S. Siegel and P.M. Wright (2006), 'Corporate social responsibility: Strategic implications', *Journal of Management Studies*, **43**(1), 1–18.

Messner, M. (2009), 'The limits of accountability', *Accounting, Organizations and Society*, **34**(8), 918–38.

Muller, A. (2006), 'Global versus local CSR strategies', *European Management Journal*, **24**(2–3), 189–98.

Orlitzky, M., F.L. Schmidt and S.L. Rynes (2003), 'Corporate social and financial performance: A meta-analysis', *Organization Studies*, **24**(3), 403–41.

Porter, M.E. (1990), *The Competitive Advantage of Nations*, New York: Free Press.

Porter, M.E. and M.R. Kramer (2002), 'The competitive advantage of corporate philanthropy', *Harvard Business Review*, **80**(12), 56–68.

Porter, M.E. and M.R. Kramer (2006), 'Strategy and society: The link between competitive advantage and corporate social responsibility', *Harvard Business Review*, **89**(1), 62–77.

Porter, M.E. and M.R. Kramer (2011), 'Creating shared value', *Harvard Business Review*, **89**(1–2), 62–77.

Russo, A. and F. Perrini (2010), 'Investigating stakeholder theory and social capital: CSR in large firms and SMEs', *Journal of Business Ethics*, **92**(2), 207–21.

Strike, V.M., J. Gao and P. Bansal (2006), 'Being good while being bad: Social responsibility and the international diversification of US firms', *Journal of International Business Studies*, **37**(6), 850–62.

Verbeke, A. (2009), *International Business Strategy: Rethinking the Foundation of Global Corporate Success*, Cambridge, UK: Cambridge University Press.

WCED (The Brundtland Commission) (1987), *Report of the World Commission on Environment and Development: Our Common Future*, Oxford: Oxford University Press.

Zadek, S. (2000), *Doing Good and Doing Well: Making the Business Case for Corporate Citizenship*, New York: The Corporate Board.

Zhao, M., J. Tan and S.H. Park (2014), 'From voids to sophistication: Institutional environment and MNC CSR crisis in emerging markets', *Journal of Business Ethics*, **122**(4), 655–74.

Zsolnai, L. and K.J. Ims (eds) (2006), *Business with Limits: Deep Ecology and Buddhist Economics*, Bern: Peter Lang AG.

Case G

Managing CSR in supplier networks: The case of Apple

Kirsten Foss

G.1 About Apple

The principal idea driving Apple is innovation. In 2007, when the iPhone was launched, it was called the 'invention of the year' by *Time* (Yoffie and Rossano, 2012). Thus, Apple has been a global iconic brand for more than a decade.

Apple's main products and services include the following: Mac computer, iPhone, iPad, iPod, Apple Watch, iTunes, iCloud and Apple Pay (Reuters, 2019). Apple's customers are highly loyal to the brand, which allows Apple to set premium prices on its products (Yoffie and Rossano, 2012). Besides actual consumer preference for the design and quality of Apple's products, customers also face high switching costs in getting to know how to use competitors' products.

G.2 The competitive situation and challenges with suppliers

Over the last decade, Apple has experienced a significant growth. Its revenue rose from 8.2 billion US dollars in 2004 up to 182.8 billion US dollars in the year 2014 and in 2017 it reached 233.72 billion (Statista, 2018).

Since Apple's inception, in order to cut production costs it has outsourced most of its production to contractors. Companies manufacturing Apple products include Foxconn, Pegatron Corporation, Primax Electronics and Wintek Corporation. The firm's financial success is inseparable from its globally dispersed network of efficient suppliers based mainly in Asia (Chan, Pun and Selden, 2013).

Apple's drive to keep costs down has often been controversial and it has faced several tough issues regarding labour and human rights (Yoffie and Rossano, 2012). It was subjected to particularly negative publicity after the news of several suicides among young workers in Foxconn factories started to spread in the media (Huvelle and Baskir, 2012). In February 2012, Apple reacted by announcing that it had asked the Fair Labor Association to conduct a study of labour conditions in assembly centres like Foxconn (Apple, 2012).

Foxconn is a multinational electronics contract-manufacturing firm headquartered in New Taipei, Taiwan. It is the largest company in the world in electronics manufacturing and the third largest IT firm by revenue. Notable products in its portfolio include BlackBerry, Kindle, PlayStation, Wii and Xbox. Foxconn is also the lead manufacturer for Apple's iPads and iPhones.

In 2014, BBC went undercover to observe the working conditions for employees in Chinese Apple factories and exposed some alarmingly poor treatment of local workers (Bilton, 2014). The BBC findings resulted in very negative headlines for Apple. The BBC investigation revealed that Chinese workers in the assembly line were pressured into working 12-hour shifts when Apple made last-minute changes to its products or launch schedules (BBC, 2013; Bilton, 2014). According to a Foxconn human resource manager, these practices were a consequence of pressure stemming from Apple on its value chain (Chan et al., 2013).

These violations were revealed after Apple's announcement to improve the labour and human rights in their factories. The scandals in Chinese factories shed an unflattering light on Apple. It became apparent that Apple still has major problems with regard to dealing with its corporate social responsibility in China despite its earlier commitment to enhancing working conditions in local assembly centres.

Foxconn and Apple in 2017 and 2018

Most of the components of Apple iPhones are still produced in China and the Taiwanese Hon Hai Precision Industry Co, Ltd, better known as Foxconn, is still producing the lion's share. Foxconn is the single largest employer in mainland China with 1.3 million people on its payroll (Merchant, 2017a).

Author of the book *The One Device: The Secret History of the iPhone*, Brian Merchant (2017b), was able to gain access to Foxconn and he reported that the 'epidemic caused a media sensation – suicides and sweatshop conditions in the House of iPhone'. Suicide notes and survivors told of immense stress, long work days and harsh managers who were prone to humiliate workers for mistakes, unfair fines and unkept promises of benefits.

The corporate response spurred further unease: Foxconn CEO, Terry Gou, had large nets installed outside many of the buildings to catch falling bodies. The company hired counsellors and workers were made to sign pledges stating they would not attempt to kill themselves.

Steve Jobs, for his part, declared:

> 'We're all over that' when asked about the spate of deaths and he pointed out that the rate of suicides at Foxconn was within the national average.

However, critics pounced on the comment as callous, though he wasn't technically wrong. Foxconn Longhua was so massive that it could be its own nation-state, and the suicide rate was comparable to its host country's. The difference is that Foxconn City is a nation-state governed entirely by a corporation and one that happened to be producing one of the most profitable products on the planet. (Merchant, 2017a)

Brian Merchant interviewed a former worker at Foxconn:

> 'It's not a good place for human beings', says one of the young men, who goes by the name Xu. He'd worked in Longhua [Foxconn] for about a year, until a couple of months ago, and he says the conditions inside are as bad as ever. 'There is no improvement since the media coverage,' Xu says. The work is very high pressure and he and his colleagues regularly logged 12-hour shifts. Management is both aggressive and duplicitous, publicly scolding workers for being too slow and making them promises they don't keep, he says. His friend, who worked at the factory for two years and chooses to stay anonymous, says he was promised double pay for overtime hours but got only regular pay. They paint a bleak picture of a high-pressure working environment where exploitation is routine and where depression and suicide have become normalised. (Extract reproduced in Merchant, 2017a)

In 2018, the iPhone is made at a number of different factories around China, and this is in part Apple's response to the Foxconn scandal. Apple also conducted some damage control after the string of suicides by Foxconn employees in China. Tim Cook (now CEO of Apple), who was a lead operations manager in June 2010, met with Foxconn Chairman Terry Gou in Shenzhen together with two risk-management experts (Kanematsu, 2017). According to Kanematsu from the *Nikkei Asian Review*, Apple conducted a month-long probe to get a handle on the situation, and Cook inspected Foxconn factories himself on another two occasions: in 2012, shortly after the death of Apple founder Steve Jobs, and again in 2014. Apple has also taken action to stave off criticism from environmentalists. It set policies on buying renewable energy and avoiding hazardous materials in manufacturing, and Foxconn has put them into practice.

Kanematsu reports on the business relationship between Apple and Foxconn: 'As close as the two companies have become, Apple is careful to set boundaries' and an employee who was interviewed by Kanematsu says: 'Apple completes prototypes near its head office [in Cupertino, California], and never lets this process outside California'. The inscription on Apple's products reflects its determination to stay atop the food chain: 'Designed by Apple in California. Assembled in China' (Kanematsu, 2017). Kanematsu speculates on the consequences that Apple's supply strategy has for Foxconn:

> Apple's expansion into India, meanwhile, has the potential to weaken its bonds with Foxconn. The U.S. giant is proceeding with local production in the South Asian country, to get around tariffs on imported products. Wistron, another Taiwanese contract manufacturer, will assemble the iPhone SE at a factory in Bangalore. If Wistron proves itself in India – which looks primed to become a huge market on a par with China – Foxconn might start to seem replaceable. (Kanematsu, 2017)

CASE DISCUSSION

1. Discuss the managerial challenges faced by top management in Apple with respect to managing labour conditions in the supply chain.
2. Discuss Apple's response to the scandal.
3. What is the current relationship between Apple and Foxconn?

REFERENCES

Apple Inc. (2012), 'Fair Labor Association begins inspections of Foxconn', press release, 13 February 2012, accessed 26 January 2019 at https://www.apple.com/pr/library/2012/02/13Fair-Labor-Association-Begins-Inspections-of-Foxconn.html.

BBC (2013), 'Foxconn admits labour violation at China factory', *BBC News*, 11 October 2013, accessed 26 January 2019 at http://www.bbc.com/news/business-24486684.

Bilton, R. (2014), 'Apple "failing to protect Chinese factory workers"', *BBC Panorama*, 18 December 2014, accessed 26 January 2019 at http://www.bbc.com/news/business-30532463.

Chan, J., N. Pun and M. Selden (2013), 'The politics of global production: Apple, Foxconn and China's new working class', *New Technology, Work and Employment*, **28**(2), 100–115.

Huvelle, J.G. and C.E. Baskir (2012), 'A fair labor future for Foxconn? The 2012 FLA audit of Apple's largest Chinese supplier', *Peking University Transnational Law Review*, **1**(2), 212.

Kanematsu, Y. (2017), 'Foxconn Apple and the partnership that changed the tech sector', *Nikkei*

Asian Review, 13 July 2017, accessed 26 January 2019 at https://asia.nikkei.com/Business/Foxconn-Apple-and-the-partnership-that-changed-the-tech-sector.

Merchant, B. (2017a), 'Life and death in Apple's forbidden city', *The Guardian*, 18 June 2017, accessed 26 January 2019 at https://www.theguardian.com/technology/2017/jun/18/foxconn-life-death-forbidden-city-longhua-suicide-apple-iphone-brian-merchant-one-device-extract.

Merchant, B. (2017b), *The One Device: The Secret History of the iPhone*, London: Transworld Digital.

Reuters (2019), 'Apple Inc.', accessed 26 January 2019 at https://www.reuters.com/finance/stocks/companyProfile/AAPL.O.

Statista (2018), 'Apple's revenue worldwide from 2004 to 2018 (in billion U.S. dollars)', accessed 26 January 2019 at http://www.statista.com/statistics/265125/total-net-sales-of-apple-since-2004/.

Yoffie, D. and P. Rossano (2012), 'Apple Inc. in 2012', Harvard Business School, May 2012.

Case H

Nestlé Waters and its involvement in two controversial cases regarding water extraction

Kirsten Foss

H.1 Introduction

Nestlé is an MNE headquartered in Switzerland and recognized for its efforts in becoming a leader in nutrition, health and wellness. Nestlé organizes its subsidiaries into global zones with the exception of the globally managed businesses to which Nestlé Waters belongs. The Nestlé Waters group encompasses 49 brands, operates 95 production sites and has 33 700 employees in different subsidiaries.

On its homepage, Nestlé emphasizes its commitment to social responsibility across its various business areas. Nestlé describes itself as a company driven by clear principles. The company regulates the way it operates based on the Nestlé 'Corporate Business Principles'. Nestlé has a clear and organized global governance structure. The company's 'Role in Society' and the implementation of these principles in the 'Creating Shared Value' business strategy is managed and supervised by the board of directors, the chairman, the CEO and the executive board. Internal management bodies and external advisory committees also have an important role in counselling on these matters.

H.2 Creating shared value

The global business strategy 'Creating Shared Value' describes the Nestlé corporate goals under the categories of 'Nutrition', 'Health and Wellness', 'Rural Development', 'Environmental Sustainability', 'Water' and 'Human Rights'. The Nestlé Corporation works in different ways to implement its business goals across the different business groups. For example, in 2016,

Nestlé headquarters supported the launch of the CEO Water Mandate Guidance for Companies on Respecting Human Rights to Water and Sanitation (UN Global Compact, n.d.), and pilot-tested these guidelines in selected locations.

The 'Creating Shared Value' goals for 'Water' consists of: reduction of waste in water use in production across subsidiaries and suppliers; raising awareness of water conservation; as well as implementing effective water policies and stewardship. More specifically in the Nestlé Waters division, one of the aims of the 'Creating Shared Value' business strategy is to minimize the impact that its operations have on scarce water resources in the communities it supports. With 38 per cent of Nestlé Waters' factories situated in water-stressed regions, responsible water stewardship is a critical issue for Nestlé, as illustrated next in two controversial cases that involved Nestlé Waters' subsidiaries and their extraction of water in water-stressed regions.

H.3   The Bhati Dilwan case

Nestlé Waters entered Pakistan in 1998 through a merger with Milkpak Ltd, forming Nestlé Milkpak Ltd. The firm produced and sold the branded product 'Pure Life', which is bottled groundwater with Nestlé's mixture of added minerals. Nestlé Waters launched the product as a brand sold in developing countries. The product proved a great success in water-scarce Pakistan and in the other 170 countries where it was later launched. The bottled water is a healthy and clean choice for many Pakistani consumers but not affordable by everyone.

In 2003, Nestlé Waters decided to expand its operation in Pakistan and leased a plot of land near Karachi from the Sindh government. The construction of the new bottling plant was delayed due to a dispute regarding Nestlé Waters' renewing of its licence to operate in the country but when settled, Nestlé Waters built and operated its Sheikhupura factory near to the Bhati Dilwan village.

Nestlé's licence to operate did not contain restrictions on its extraction of water in the area. In fact, the use of groundwater in Pakistan was mostly unregulated and unmonitored. The villagers in Bhati Dilwan relied on hand-pumped water from the village well. The local villagers claimed that after the Sheikhupura factory started its operations, the groundwater levels had significantly decreased, making it impossible for the villagers to reach the better-quality water deep below their village. According to the villagers, the contaminated water had caused sickness especially among their children.

In 2010, the villagers sent a petition to Nestlé Waters asking for access to clean water but they did not receive a reply. In 2008 and 2012 respectively, the documentaries *Blue Gold, World Water War* and *Bottled Life: Nestlé's Business With Water* were released. The documentaries presented different cases worldwide of Nestlé Waters' commercial use of water supply and its impact on local communities. After the release of the documentaries, public attention regarding Nestlé and the utilization of scares, water resources grew.

The majority of complaints came from anti-globalization activists from the developed countries. For example, the Social Policy and Development Centre (SPDC) based in Pakistan stated that '[b]eing poor in Pakistan means that there is nowhere and no one to turn to for support or justice'. It is difficult to estimate the damage the documentaries had on Nestlé Waters' image, but in response it installed three clean drinking water facilities, new classrooms, toilets and sanitation facilities in two schools in Bhati Dilwan (Nestlé Waters, n.d.).

H.4 The Ontario case

Nestlé entered Canada in 1992 with the acquisition of the Perrier Group. The group was incorporated under Nestlé Waters' Canada operation. In Canada, Nestlé's main water sources are located in Aberfoyle, Ontario and Hope, British Columbia. Through to the year 2000, on a daily basis Nestlé Waters extracted about 1 million litres of water from the aquifer in Ontario.

However, in 2000, the Ontario Ministry of Environment established a mandatory restriction on the renewed licence: Nestlé was to reduce its maximum allowable water extraction by 20 per cent during times of moderate drought (Lui, 2013). Nestlé did not accept this restriction and appealed to the Ministry. The company argued that the Ministry of Environment did not apply the restriction uniformly, and that it was not the proper institution to implement this kind of restriction – the company claimed that the conservation authorities should apply the restriction. According to John Challinor (Nestlé's then director of corporate affairs), 'It's a matter of principle. Why should Nestlé Waters Canada be held to a different standard than every other water taker?' Eventually, Nestlé and the Ministry reached an agreement and the Ministry removed the restrictions.

After that, the Council of Canadians and WWW (Wellington Water Watchers) took control of the situation. Eventually, in February 2013, WWW and the Council of Canadians questioned the agreement between Nestlé Waters and Ontario's Ministry of Environmental Review Tribunal.

Both groups argued that the permit set out by the Ministry was inconsistent with the Public Trust Doctrine. According to this principle, 'important common resources – such as water and air – are held by government on behalf of the public, and must be managed for the benefit of current and future generations' (Barlow, 2013). That is, the water that Nestlé Waters is withdrawing from the aquifer belongs to all Canadians and cannot be held and sold by a private company that does not act on behalf of the interests of all Canadians. 'Ontario must prioritize communities' right to water above a private company's thirst for profit', said Maude Barlow, National Chairperson for the Council of Canadians (ibid.). The courts decided in favour of the two non-governmental organizations. Nestlé removed its appeal and agreed to reduce the amount of water it withdraws from the Ontario's aquifer during drought times.

CASE DISCUSSION

1. In what ways did the two cases represent a managerial challenge to Nestlé headquarters?
2. Compare the relevant stakeholders and Nestlé's engagement in the two cases and discuss why Nestlé Waters responded differently to the local demands for changes in the Bhati Dilwan and the Ontario cases.

REFERENCES

Barlow, M. (2013), 'Letter: Why Wellington County is standing up to Nestlé', *Alternatives Journal: Canada's Environmental Voice*, July 2013, accessed 26 January 2019 at https://www.alternativesjournal.ca/energy-and-resources/letter-why-wellington-county-standing-nestl%C3%A9.

Lui, E. (2013), 'Challenging Nestlé's water takings in Ontario', *Great Lakes Commons*, 23 May 2013, accessed 26 January 2019 at https://www.greatlakescommons.org/our-blog-b/2013/05/challenging-nestles-water-takings-in-ontario.

Nestlé Waters (n.d.), 'The world's largest bottled water company', accessed 11 February 2019 at https://www.nestle-waters.com/get-to-know-us.

UN Global Compact (n.d.), *The CEO Water Mandate: Respecting Human Rights to Water and Sanitation*, accessed 26 January 2019 at https://ceowatermandate.org/humanrights/.

RECOMMENDED DOCUMENTARIES

Blue Gold, World Water War (2008), director and co-producer Sam Bozzo, producer Mark Achbar (PBS), Purple Turtle Films.

Bottled Life: Nestlé's Business With Water (2012), directed by Urs Schnell, production DokLab Gmbh (Switzerland) and co-production Eikon Südwest Gmbh Germany.

7
National culture

7.1 Introduction

The main purpose of this chapter is to foster an awareness of how national culture affects managers in MNEs. National cultures differ from each other and these differences are commonly referred to as cultural distances. In international business, an MNE has implicitly or explicitly been explained 'with reference to the challenges and opportunities it faces as a result of distance' (Nachum and Zaheer, 2005, p. 247). However, agreeing on how to measure cultural distance between national cultures has proved challenging. We present and discuss the cultural distance measures developed by Geert Hofstede because these measures are the most widely used in international business studies. However, before we examine how cultural distance is measured we address the issue of how cultural distance affects MNE performance. In international business, the cultural distance construct has been used in realms such as foreign direct investments, headquarter–subsidiary relations, and expatriate selection and adjustment (Shenkar, 2012). Our main focus is on the influence that cultural differences have on the organization of MNE activities and the management of MNE employees.

7.2 Cultural distance and MNE performance

MNEs are different from domestic firms because MNEs have headquarters and subsidiaries in different geographical locations. Not only does physical distance pose a challenge for effective communication, but MNEs also have to learn to cope with cultural distance – that is, the underlying differences in national cultures for managers between their geographically distributed organizational units.

Most studies on cultural distance have assumed that cultural distance is a liability for MNE performance (Stahl and Tung, 2015). For example, Hutzschenreuter and Voll (2008) and Earley and Mosakowski (2000) argue that cultural distance adds complexity in a number of ways. Individuals have to learn to deal with work team members, customers, suppliers, and others who act differently from themselves and who have different belief systems and values. This can lead to barriers and friction in interpersonal relationships, which interferes with knowledge sharing across the MNE. Other studies have indicated negative correlations between cultural distance and organizational learning across national borders (e.g., Barkema, Bell and Pennings, 1996), choice of foreign entry mode, and the perceived ability to manage foreign operations (e.g., Kogut and Singh, 1988), the longevity of global strategic alliances (e.g., Parkhe, 1991), and post-acquisition integration process dynamics and performance (e.g., Björkman, Stahl and Vaar, 2007).

Nevertheless, when Tihanyi, Griffith and Russell (2005) undertook an empirical synthesis of prior research on the relationship between cultural distance and MNE performance they found no evidence of a negative relationship. Indeed, they even found an indication that high cultural distance may provide performance benefits in those cases when MNEs are operating in other developed countries. They speculate that when markets and institutions are well developed, cultural distance may actually stimulate innovation and creativity, which in turn leads to enhanced MNE performance.

Hutzschenreuter and Voll (2008) argue that the problem with prior research is that it failed to distinguish among different steps of MNE expansion. They argue that if too much cultural distance is added over a short period of time, the MNE will be overwhelmed and performance will be negatively affected. This is because without sufficient time, individuals within the MNE are unable to adapt their behaviour, and structures, systems and processes will not be correctly implemented so that the new subsidiaries will not be adequately integrated. Using German MNE panel data, they find strong support for this prediction. MNEs are limited in their ability to handle the complexity that arises from entering culturally distant markets. In other words, MNEs must give themselves sufficient time to learn before they add yet more complexity. Indeed, given time, it is possible that, as Tihanyi et al. (2005) suggest, cultural distance may actually stimulate innovation.

Potential positive effects of cultural differences have also been identified in studies of creativity, adaptability and problem-solving quality (e.g., Adler, 1983) in organizational learning (e.g., Lane, Salk and Lyles, 2001). Some more recent studies indicate that cultural distance has both negative and positive consequences (Dikova and Sahib, 2013; Reus and Lamont, 2009; Vaara et al., 2012). Stahl and Tung (2015, p. 398), in a review of studies on the impact that cultural distance has on MNE performance, conclude that culture does not have a large influence on MNE performance, but they emphasize that 'whether cultural differences have a positive or negative effect is contingent on contextual influences and management-related factors'. For MNE managers, this conclusion is a reminder that although cultural distance is challenging, they can influence the impact that culture has on MNE performance. But what is national culture?

7.3 The concept of culture

National culture is a well-established concept, but its precise conceptualization and measurement is 'still hotly debated' (Caprar et al., 2015; Stephan and Uhlaner, 2010, p. 1348). In international business, Geert Hofstede's approach to conceptualization and measuring culture has dominated the field for decades (Caprar et al., 2015; Nakata, 2009).

Hofstede (1980a, 1991; Hofstede, Hofstede and Minkov, 2010) characterizes cultural differences as pertaining to symbols, rituals, heroes and values. Hofstede suggests that values represent the core of culture, while rituals (e.g., how we greet one another), heroes (persons that are highly praised), and symbols (words, pictures, etc. that carry a particular meaning) are more superficial manifestations of the values that characterize a culture. When Hofstede set out to capture variations in value orientation across national cultures, he was inspired by anthropologists Ruth Benedict (1887–1948) and Margaret Mead (1901–78), as well as the work of sociologist Axel Inkeles and psychologist Daniel Levinson. These works centred on the idea that there are commonalities across societies with respect to the kinds of problems people face and that the values of societies reflect these problems. The underlying assumption in Hofstede's work is that culture is a stable set of shared values that are reflected in the behaviour of individuals in a particular group (such as a nation). This assumption guided Hofstede's search for dimensions that characterize cultural distance between nations.

Between 1967 and 1973, Hofstede surveyed and analysed data from 116 000 IBM employees in 40 different countries using a questionnaire containing about 150 questions about their preferences in terms of management style and work environment (see Hofstede, 1980a, 1983). Based on this data, Hofstede identified 32 items that measured work-related values. Hofstede reduced those to four value dimensions: power distance, uncertainty avoidance, individualism–collectivism and masculinity–femininity. Later he added a fifth dimension, long-term–short-term orientation, which we do not cover in depth here. Long-term refers to values such as perseverance and thrift, while short-term values include respect for 'saving face', tradition and social obligations in the sense of reciprocation of greetings, favours and gifts. Asian societies have high long-term orientations, while Anglo-Saxon and Western European societies have low long-term orientations. However, Hofstede (1994) acknowledges that his research on the implications of differences along this dimension is as yet not sufficient to allow the composition of stable differences similar to those for the other four dimensions.

7.4 Hofstede's four dimensions

Hofstede's four dimensions of culture are relevant to managers in MNEs because they have implications for organizational life. According to Hofstede et al. (2010), the power distance and uncertainty avoidance are the two dimensions that indicate differences among countries with respect to what organizations look like (the design of organizations) while the individualist–collectivistic and the masculine–feminine dimensions indicate how employees see themselves in the organization. Organizational designs can be described in many ways (see, e.g., Mintzberg, 1983), but Hofstede and other scholars conducting research on cross-national culture have mainly focused on hierarchical versus flat organizations and on centralization versus decentralization of decision making. Likewise, how employees view themselves in the organization is a multidimensional construct, while cross-cultural studies have mainly focused on issues such as what motivates employees and how culture has an impact on job designs.

Power distance

The power distance index was created from the following items:

1. Answers by non-managerial employees to the question: 'How frequently, in your experience, does the following problem occur: employees being afraid to express disagreement with their managers?'
2. Subordinates' perception of the manager's actual decision-making style (percentage choosing the description as either an autocratic or paternalistic style out of four possible styles plus 'none of these').
3. Subordinates' preference for their boss's decision-making style (percentage preferring an autocratic or a paternalistic style, or on the contrary, a style based on majority vote, but not a consultative style).

Questions 1 and 2 indicate the way the respondents perceive their daily work environment, whereas question 3 indicates their preferences for work environments. Hofstede et al. (2010) argue that the fact that the three questions are in the same cluster indicates that there is a close relationship between what one perceives and the reality one desires. According to Hofstede, there is a preference for a consultative style of decision making in countries where employees are perceived (by other employees) as not being afraid of their managers and where employees do not perceive their managers as autocratic or paternalistic. When the emotional distance between a manager and subordinates is small, subordinates will more likely approach and contradict managers. In countries on the opposite end of the power distance spectrum, employees (in similar jobs) are likely to prefer autocratic or paternalistic managers. These are countries where most employees are perceived as avoiding disagreeing with their managers. Organizations in contexts of high power distance are more hierarchical and employees are more dependent on their managers with significant emotional distance between subordinates and managers.

Hofstede et al. (2010) state that managers of MNE subsidiaries will experience greater employee satisfaction if they use a decision-making style that 'fits' the national culture in terms of power distance. Hofstede does not inquire into the causal relationship between 'what is' and 'what is desired', nor does he present any studies that substantiate this assumption.

Hofstede's arguments on the impact of power distance on organizational design, decision making and management styles have been subject to empirical enquiries by other scholars. For example, Van Oudenhoven (2001) conducted a study that examined Hofstede's classification of national cultures with a specific focus on the relationship between 'culture as perceived' and 'culture as desired'. The study supports Hofstede's argument that perceived differences in power distances reflect systematic differences across countries with more hierarchical organizations in large power distance countries compared to countries with low power distance. Van Oudenhoven's (2001) study does not show whether managers use more consultative leadership styles in the less hierarchical organizations and more autocratic in the more hierarchical organizations.

Uncertainty avoidance

This refers to the degree to which the members of a culture feel threatened by ambiguous or unknown situations. The uncertainty avoidance index was created from the following items:

1. On a scale from 1 to 5, how often do you feel nervous or tense at work?
2. Agreement with the statement: 'Company rules should not be broken even when the employee thinks it is in the company's best interest'.
3. The percentage of employees expressing their intent to stay with the company for a long-term career.

The three items were not correlated for individuals, but the differences in means by country were correlated. Thus, at the country level, Hofstede et al. (2010) argue that the correlation reflects a particular level of anxiety and dislike of ambiguity. Note that uncertainty avoidance is not the same as risk avoidance. Thus, high uncertainty-avoiding cultures may not be risk-avoiding cultures but they are likely to be cultures where members seek to avoid ambiguity. Hofstede et al. (2010) state that in societies with high scores on the uncertainty index there is an emotional need for rules, written and unwritten. According to Hofstede et al. (2010), organizations in these societies will deploy more formal rules that control the rights and duties of workers as well as work processes. Rules or rule-oriented behaviour in organizations may even become purely ritual or even dysfunctional in high uncertainty-avoiding countries. If a country is high on both uncertainty avoidance and power distance, discretionary actions by superiors can replace rules.

For managers in MNEs from low uncertainty-avoiding countries, it may appear that the rules in high uncertainty-avoiding countries are 'ceremonially adopted' (see Chapter 10) to reduce organizational members' anxieties. Employees and managers in low uncertainty-avoiding countries may have an emotional dislike of rules where, according to Hofstede et al. (2010), ambiguity and chaos are sometimes considered beneficial for creativity. Thus, managers and employees in low uncertainty-avoiding countries may find it more difficult to accept rules compared to employees of subsidiaries in high uncertainty-avoiding countries. Finally, employees in societies with high uncertainty avoidance exhibit higher levels of anxiety that often result in a pronounced need to work hard.

Hofstede argues that both the power distance and uncertainty avoidance dimensions are of importance for structuring the organization in ways that work well. The power distance dimension indicates whether decisions in organizations tend to be centralized or decentralized and the uncertainty avoidance dimension indicates the degree of formalization of decision making. Hofstede (1980a) provides an illustrative example of how managers in MNEs may experience a managerial challenge when dealing with subsidiaries that have different organizational structures in terms of centralization and formalization. Hofstede states that in hierarchical organizations, subordinates expect higher-level managers to initiate decisions, whereas in decentralized organizations, decisions are initiated at lower levels. In MNEs that have subsidiaries in both high and low power distance countries, and accordingly different organizational structures, this may create confusion as subordinates may have different expectations regarding the initiation of decisions:

For example, one U.S.-based multinational corporation had a worldwide policy that salary-increase proposals should be initiated by the employee's direct superior. However, the French management of its French subsidiary interpreted this policy in such a way that the superior's superior's superior – three levels above – was the one to initiate the salary proposal. (Hofstede, 1980b, p. 60)

The way in which such an issue is solved depends on whether the subsidiaries are located in high uncertainty-avoiding countries where managers rely on formal rules to solve the issues, or in low uncertainty-avoiding countries where managers are more likely to rely on interpersonal communication between headquarters and subsidiary to solve the issue.

Individualism–collectivism

According to Hofstede et al. (2010), individualism relates to the extent to which people are expected to look after themselves and their immediate families. Collectivism, in contrast, reflects societies where people from birth onward are integrated into strong, cohesive in-groups, which continue to protect people in exchange for unquestioning loyalty.

The survey items employed by Hofstede that formed the individualistic pool of the dimension were the following characteristics of the ideal job:

1. Personal time: to have a job that leaves you sufficient time for your personal or family life.
2. Freedom: to have considerable freedom to adopt your own approach to the job.
3. Challenge: to have challenging work to do – work from which you can get a personal sense of accomplishment.

These items stress the employee's independence from the organization.

From the collectivistic pool of the dimension were the following characteristics:

1. Training: having training opportunities (to improve your skills and learn new skills).
2. Physical conditions: having good physical working conditions (good ventilation and lighting, adequate work space and so on).
3. Use of skills: fully using your skills and abilities on the job.

These items refer to things the organization does for the employee.

The individualistic–collectivistic dimension has, according to Hofstede et al. (2010), implications for hiring practices, management styles and design of rewards. In collectivistic societies, an employer not only hires an employee based on his or her individual characteristics but also based on the in-group to which the employee belongs. In collectivistic societies, hiring based on group belonging (e.g., family relations with employer or with other employees) is considered preferable as it reduces the risk associated with asymmetric information about the person to be hired. In individualistic countries, such practices are often considered as nepotism. For a manager in an MNE with subsidiaries in both individualistic and collectivistic countries, this difference in what is 'the taken-for-granted' practice may be a challenge.

The relationship that individuals have with the firm is also different in individualistic and collectivist societies (Hofstede et al., 2010). In individualistic societies, there will be a sharper distinction between work and personal life. The relationship between the employer and the employee is perceived as a business transaction, whereas in a collectivistic society the relationship is perceived as one that resembles a family relationship. According to Hofstede et al. (2010), this difference influences how employees expect to be treated by their employer if they do not perform adequately. In an individualistic society, firing is a legitimate action against employees who do not fulfil the transactional arrangement, whereas in a collectivistic society the expectation is that the employer takes care of the employee by allowing him or her to perform other tasks. However, there are many types of employer–employee relationships in both types of society.

For managers in MNEs there will often be a difference in their roles as managers in individualistic as opposed to collectivistic countries. In individualistic countries, they are managers of individuals, whereas in collectivistic countries they are managers of groups. Accordingly, a number of management techniques and training packages that are developed in individualistic societies may fail if applied in collectivistic societies. For example, appraisal interviews are based on an individualistic norm where an employer openly discusses/assesses the performance of individual workers. Also, in highly individualistic societies, work should be organized and rewards should be designed in a way that self-interest and employer interest become aligned.

The individualistic–collectivistic dimension is the one of the four dimensions identified by Hofstede that has received most empirical attention. Oyserman, Coon and Kemmelmeier (2002) provided a meta-analysis of the many empirical studies subsequent to Hofstede's (1980a) work. Their analysis focused on how much 'Americans' differ from citizens of other countries. It showed that in most of the studies there was only a small statistical influence, explaining a variance of 1.2 per cent for individualism and 4.4 per cent for collectivism. This indicates that individuals do not vary significantly more across countries than they do within countries along the collectivism–individualism dimension. This implies that MNE managers also need to consider within-country variation when they consider whether to adapt performance and training systems before these are implemented in local subsidiaries.

The individualist–collectivistic dimension has also been found to be influenced by the socio-economic state of the country. In a meta-study of data covering 35 years of research, Taras and Steel (2009) found a significantly persistent change toward higher individualism and achievement orientation worldwide. The changes were most profound in countries that had experienced a dramatic economic and political change such as China and the former USSR republics. In particular, the relationship between the level of individualism and the wealth of the country seems to be one where economic growth causes individualism and not vice versa (Taras and Steel, 2009). The implication for managers is that the level of individualism may not be as stable as Hofstede assumes. This has implications for whether rewards, appraisals, hiring practices and other important human resource decisions should automatically be adapted to countries that according to Hofstede have high levels of collectivism.

The methodology underlying Hofstede's identification of the individualism–collectivism dimension has been subject to particular criticism. Bond (2002) points out that this dimension was a product of a decision by Hofstede to subdivide a larger factor that emerged through the original three-factor solution. Hofstede labelled the other factor 'power distance'. Bond also questions the validity of the individualism–collectivism dimension, which comprises six work goals. Personal time, freedom and challenge were added together to constitute the individualism end of the dimension; while use of skills, physical conditions and training were added together to define the collectivism end of the dimension. As Bond (2002, p. 74) remarks: 'The first three work goals bear obvious relations to individualism... How the last three work goals described anything resembling collectivism was, however, a mystery to many'. Further, Bond argues, had Hofstede remained true to his original three-factor solution, his findings would have been very different. He concludes that it is unlikely that the US would have been located at an extreme, as it is in terms of the individualism–collectivism dimension.

Masculinity–femininity

Hofstede et al. (2010) define masculine societies as those 'where emotional gender roles are clearly distinct: men are supposed to be assertive, tough and focused on material success, whereas women are supposed to be more modest, tender, and concerned with the quality of life'; and feminine societies as those where 'emotional gender roles overlap: both men and women are supposed to be modest, tender, and concerned with the quality of life' (Hofstede et al., 2010, p. 140).

Hofstede derived this dimension from an analysis of 14 work goals in the IBM questionnaire where the employees were asked to think of factors that were important to them in an ideal job, disregarding the extent to which they were present in their current job. The survey items that characterize the masculinity–femininity dimension are assessed according to the following characteristics:

Masculine characteristics:

1. Earnings: to have an opportunity for high earnings.
2. Recognition: to get the recognition you deserve when you do a good job.
3. Advancement: to have an opportunity for advancement to higher-level jobs.
4. Challenge: to have challenging work to do – work from which you can get a personal sense of accomplishment.

Feminine characteristics:

1. Manage: to have a good working relationship with your direct superior.
2. Cooperation: to work with people who cooperate well with one another.
3. Living area: to live in an area desirable to you and your family.
4. Employment security: to have security that you will be able to work for your company as long as you want to.

While the work goal 'challenge' was also associated with high individualism, no other work goals correlated with the other three dimensions of culture. The masculinity–femininity dimension was the only one where women scored systematically differently from men, with the exception of countries with extreme feminine characteristics. The masculine–feminine dimension was created based on the countries' factor scores in a factor analysis of the work goals.

	Masculinity index	
5		95
3 Feminine/ Weak uncertainty avoidance Socially motivated	1 Masculine/ Weak uncertainty avoidance Achievement motivated	8 Uncertainty avoidance index
4 Feminine/ Strong uncertainty avoidance Socially motivated	2 Masculine/ Strong uncertainty avoidance Security and esteem motivated	112

Figure 7.1 Employee motivation in countries that differ along the masculine–feminine dimension and the uncertainty avoidance dimension

In Hofstede et al. (2010), the main implication of this dimension for organizational life seems to be whether or not it is acceptable to be assertive and bold about performance. According to Hofstede et al. (2010), there is a great deal of overlap between societies where employees mainly desire those items that measure masculinity and societies where there is also much assertiveness. Hofstede provides an example of how American job interviewers often mistake understatements that interviewees from feminine countries make about their qualifications.

When the masculine–feminine dimension is considered together with the uncertainty avoidance dimension (Figure 7.1), then, according to Hofstede, one is able to derive systematic implications for how employees are motivated in countries that differ along the two dimensions.

The two dimensions together suggest the following types of motivation:

- **Achievement motivation** The combination of low uncertainty avoidance with a high degree of masculinity is characteristic of US and other Anglo-Saxon cultures. The management literature in these countries often assumes that Maslow's (1954) hierarchy of needs is relevant to understanding how employee motivation develops – that is, that once employees have satisfied their lower-order needs such as security, they eventually progress to needing opportunities for self-actualization. The assumption is that organizations need systems that encourage employees to move up the needs hierarchy. Thus, Hofstede observes that US organizations have management systems that focus on individual rewards for personal achievement and job enrichment. While Hofstede (1980b) accepts the validity of these practices for US organizations, he views them as inappropriate for countries such as Germany and the Scandinavian countries that are not located in quadrant 1 in Figure 7.1.

- **Security and esteem motivation** Countries in the second quadrant are security and esteem motivated. These are countries that are masculine and score high on uncertainty avoidance, such as, for example, Austria and Germany. In such societies, Hofstede argues, the fundamental motivation is directed towards meeting security needs rather than self-actualization. Thus, jobs should be clearly described.
- **Social motivation** Countries in the third and fourth quadrants are feminine rather than masculine and they are all characterized by social motivation because quality of life is an important motivational factor for employees in firms. Countries that score particularly high on femininity are the Scandinavian countries. In these feminine societies, managers can foster intrinsic motivation through restructuring jobs into semi-autonomous teams where creating good work relationships is key to enhancing performance.

Table 7.1 contains a small selection of Hofstede's country index scores for each of the four dimensions. The first two rows indicate the range of the

Table 7.1 Selected country index scores

Range/Country	Power Distance	Individualism	Masculinity	Uncertainty Avoidance
Largest score	104	91	95	112
Smallest score	11	6	5	8
Great Britain	35	89	66	35
United States	38	91	62	46
France	68	71	43	86
Italy	50	76	70	75
Greece	60	35	57	112
Austria	11	55	79	70
Germany (F.R.)	35	67	66	65
Norway	31	69	8	50
Sweden	31	71	5	29
Brazil	69	38	49	76
Guatemala	95	6	37	101
India	77	48	56	40
Japan	54	46	95	92
Malaysia	104	26	50	36
Singapore	74	20	48	8

Source: Hofstede (1991).

scores for each of the four dimensions for all of the countries included in Hofstede's original research. Thus, for power distance, the largest score Hofstede recorded was 104 and the smallest score was 11, whereas for uncertainty avoidance it was 112 and 8 respectively (see also Figure 7.1).

Anne-Wil Harzing, a prominent international management scholar, provides an Excel spreadsheet that contains an expanded number of country scores for the Hofstede dimensions. Go to http://www.harzing.com and then click on 'Resources'.

Hofstede identified various country clusters, arguing that the scores enable us to draw some broad distinctions between the Nordic, Anglo, Latin and Asian countries. For example, while the Scandinavian and Anglo-Saxon countries are similar in terms of the uncertainty avoidance, power distance and individualism–collectivism dimensions, they are markedly different in relation to the masculinity–femininity dimension. Latin countries coalesce markedly in terms of uncertainty avoidance and power distance, whereas Asian countries such as India and Malaysia are distinguished by their combination of large power distance and weak uncertainty avoidance.

7.5 General critique of Hofstede

Although Hofstede's four dimensions are widely used by researchers and by management consultants, the work of Hofstede has been subject to a number of criticisms. We now review these.

IBM as a source of data

Hofstede's sampling is based on employees across a single MNE, IBM. According to Hofstede et al. (2010), this research design provided matched samples of individuals in equivalent occupations across countries so that the work value distance between, for example, an average IBM employee in Germany and one in the UK is equivalent to that between an average German adult and an average UK adult. However, one can still ask whether IBM employees are in any way representative of entire nations. While this may be less of an issue in Western countries, in less industrialized nations, well-educated and well-paid IBM employees may be very different from the population at large (Schwartz, 1994). Further, IBM has a powerful US-derived organizational culture, may have socialized its employees so that their values do not reflect aspects of local national cultures or, equally, that this socialization may vary from country to country (McSweeney, 2002). Hofstede's (1994, p. 10) response is to argue that work organizations are not 'total institutions' and 'that the values of employees cannot be changed by an employer because they were acquired when the employees were children'. However, even this has been questioned. McSweeney (2002) observes that similar occupations have very different entry requirements and social status from country to country.

The contingency perspective criticism

Scholars within the contingency theory of organizations dispute the idea that organizations vary systematically as a response to difference in national cultures (see e.g., Hickson et al., 1974). Here the main assumption is that the design of organizations reflects the contingencies that organizations face (such as the level of uncertainty, the size of the organization, the maturity of the organization). According to contingency theory we are likely to observe more hierarchical organization in stable environments independently of whether these are located in national cultures with high or low power distance. Another central hypothesis in contingency theory is that as organizations grow larger in terms of employee numbers, they become more specialized and formalized in their procedures but more decentralized in terms of control and decision making. Only if contingencies vary systematically across countries should we expect organization design to vary systematically across countries. Donnalson (1986) reviewed many of the empirical studies that were conducted in organizations in Western as well as non-Western countries in order to identify the relative importance of national cultures (power distance) and contingencies in shaping organizations and decision making in organizations. He found that contingencies explain differences in organizational structures (such as differences in the degree of hierarchy and centralization of decision making) in the Western countries but not so strongly in non-Western countries (see Smith, 1992). This indicates that contingencies as well as power distance play a role in shaping the design of organizations.

Tayeb (1988) conducted a cross-cultural study in order to understand the impact of both contingencies and culture on organizational design. Tayeb compared a matched set of British and Indian firms and found that the *formal* organizational structure could be explained by differences across firms with respect to contingency factors such as size and environmental uncertainty. However, in firms with similar formal structures she found that decision making was carried out in different ways in the two cultures. In the British firms the centralization of decision making was accompanied by consultation between the managers and subordinates, whereas this was not the case in Indian firms. She concludes that American (and more broadly Anglo-Saxon) management theories can be implemented if they are culturally compatible, otherwise there will be employee resistance. As we noted above, this is also the view of Hofstede (1980b).

In sum, managers should expect that firms that face similar contingencies exhibit similar formal structures but the way in which actual decision making takes place may differ depending on the cultural setting. Thus, culture impacts in subtle ways on the way in which firms implement processes in similar structures to ensure coordination and control. The relative location of a country on the power distance dimension may be an indicator of how decision making and control are actually carried out in organizations in a particular country. One implication is that managers in Western MNEs should expect that decision making in centralized firms may differ depending on the national culture. What appears on the organizational chart to be a similar type of organization may in reality actually work in a very different manner.

Validity and causality

Hofstede's approach to measuring cultural values is by asking respondents to report their values. This raises two issues regarding the validity of his findings. First, we do not know for certain whether members of different cultures attach the same meaning to the constructs that scholars use when they seek to capture differences with respect to values (Tayeb, 1994). Second, we do not know anything about the relationship between individuals' self-reported understanding of their values and their actual behaviour (Earley, 2009). Third, the assumption that what is 'preferred' by employees is implemented in organizations is also problematic and is not sufficiently supported by empirical studies. In fact, recent studies of national culture emphasize that we need a better understanding of when and how culture matters (e.g., Kirkman, Lowe and Gibson, 2006). Zellmer-Bruhn and Gibson (2014) propose that the influence of culture on work practices depends on the context in which the practices operates. For example, whether employees interact face-to-face or whether it is virtual.

The question that this critique raises is whether Hofstede's four dimensions are a useful tool for managers who want to know what kind of behaviour to expect from employees in nations with different cultural values.

Level of analysis and the generalizability of the results

Another key debate within cross-cultural studies centres on the level of analysis and the relationships between individuals' cultural values and national cultures (see, e.g., Devinney and Hohberger, 2017; Kirkman, Lowe and Gibson, 2017). Hofstede asked employees in IBM subsidiaries about their work-related values and used these individual-level answers to describe the culture of the nations where these subsidiaries were located. Several scholars have debated whether one can simply aggregate and calculate the mean value from individuals' cultural perceptions to capture a collective phenomenon such as a nation's culture. One problem is to identify what values are common to all or nearly all members of the culture. For example, as Hofstede et al. (2010) point out, the items that were used to construct the power distance dimension do not correlate at the individual level. Thus, in the group of individuals within a particular nation who rate one item high there is no systematic pattern on how they rate the other items that together form the power distance dimension. According to Hofstede, this does not matter at the national level because the mean values of how individuals score on the items are correlated at the national level. However, Hofstede does not explain how the mean values are a representative description of a national culture along a particular dimension.

Another issue relates to the extent to which correlations between individuals' values and their preferences or behaviours are also reflected at the national level. In a study of collectivism and job satisfaction, Kirkman and Shapiro (2001) found that the two were positively correlated at the individual level, but negatively correlated at the country level.

Finally, few studies have indicated that the influence that culture has on important organizational practices or outcomes shows that countries that score high on a value dimension may use different practices (see, e.g., Chen, Meindl and Hui, 1998; Gabrielidis et al., 1997). The implication for managers of subsidiaries in countries rated differently on, for instance, power distance, is that there may be greater differences among employees within a national subsidiary compared to across subsidiaries in different nations with respect to the type of organization they experience and how they see themselves in the organization.

Equal distance or the 'illusion of symmetry'

The cultural distance measures developed by Hofstede identify a cultural distance between two countries as their relative position along cultural dimensions. The implicit understanding is that the distance is the same, for example, for Dutch managers in Chinese subsidiaries as they are for Chinese managers in Dutch subsidiaries (Shenkar, 2012). However, there are no studies that show that such symmetry exists. This means that we cannot assume that it is equally arduous, for example, for a French manager to move to Norway as it is for a Norwegian manager to move to France. In fact, Hofstede (1980a) mentions that it is often easier for managers to adopt to high power distance cultures than the reverse.

The stability of culture

Hofstede describes cultural values as a form of mental programming. Values are shaped in early childhood and reinforced by institutions and environmental factors. The underlying assumption is that culture is stable. The stability of cultural values is based on an assumption that changes in socio-economic conditions do not impact on culture. The stability of culture as values has been questioned by scholars who suggest that cultures converge (typically toward Western values) as countries modernize (see, e.g., Inglehart and Baker, 2000; Taras and Steel, 2009). Various studies of cultural change have identified various factors that appear to cause cultural change. These range from more anticipated factors such as economic growth to more unpredictable factors such as the 9/11 terrorist attack in 2001 on the World Trade Center in New York. The implication for managers is that they should be aware that cultural values can change over shorter periods of time than Hofstede assumes.

Equating nations with cultures

Several scholars have pointed out that the concept of nations is not necessarily the best unit for understanding culture. One reason is that the construct of nation is generally more applicable to the Western world than elsewhere. According to Tayeb (1994, p. 432), 'elsewhere the nation state is a novelty, and corresponds even less to any sense of cultural homogeneity or identity'. In many parts of Sub-Saharan Africa, nations denote a shared legislative system but citizens do not necessarily have a common culture. Gerhart and Fang (2005) argue that nations only serve as a unit of analysis if the cultural differences between nations are greater than differences within nations. In a statistical test based on Hofstede's data, they found that this assumption is not generally valid.

A further complication to the concept of nations is that not only do nations often consist of many subgroups, but that immigration and therefore increased levels of multiculturalism also impact the homogeneity of national cultures.

7.6 Other dimensions of culture

Hofstede differs in his focus on value dimensions from other researchers who focus on culture as meaning systems (see, e.g., Earley, 2009). Some researchers such as, for example, Zhang et al. (2013) and Leung and Morris (2015), argue that culture influences behaviour through the schemas or cognitive lenses that people use to make sense of ambiguous information. Others have criticized Hofstede for ignoring the importance of habits such as established repertoires of practices and emotions (Nakata, 2009). Thus, values are only one contributor to the meaning a group of individuals might attribute to a given stimuli, such as, for example, a new managerial initiative (Earley, 2009).

Leung and Morris (2015) have developed a 'situated dynamics framework' for the study of the influence that different aspects of culture have on behaviour and organizational outcomes. They argue that we may need different conceptualizations of situations where culture is best viewed in terms of values, norms and habits or cognitive schema. For example, values may play a significant role in situations involving fundamental ethical dilemmas or issues dealing with individuals' personal identities. In situations that call for individuals to interpret the meaning or implication of events, schemas are likely to be most important because the situations involve sensemaking and drawing of inferences, which are cognitive processes. Finally, when a situation calls for individuals to make choices between specific behaviours, norms and habits may matter most because behavioural tasks involve the selection of what is commonly deemed to be appropriate social behaviour.

This situated dynamics framework offers a more comprehensive understanding of different aspects of cultures and their domain for influencing organizations and how employees behave, however, so far, it has not been empirically tested.

7.7 Summary

In this chapter we have discussed the notion of national culture and introduced Hofstede's dimensions of cultural distance. We have discussed the implication of cultural distance for the organization of MNE activities and the management of employees. We identified and assessed the managerial implications of empirical studies that have addressed the relationships between Hofstede's cultural dimensions, MNE structures, and their use of management and motivation practices. Finally, we have introduced a new comprehensive framework that Leung and Morris (2015) have developed that is suited to distinguishing the relative importance of different elements of culture across diverse settings. The case that follows this chapter illustrates how a Danish MNE addresses increasing cultural diversity at its headquarters.

REFERENCES

Adler, N.J. (1983), 'A typology of management studies involving culture', *Journal of International Business Studies*, **14**(2), 29–47.

Barkema, H.G., J.H.J. Bell and J.M. Pennings (1996), 'Foreign entry, cultural barriers, and learning', *Strategic Management Journal*, **17**(2), 151–66.

Björkman, I., G.K. Stahl and E. Vaar (2007), 'Cultural difference and capability transfer in cross-border acquisitions: The mediating roles of capability complementarity, absorptive capacity and social integration', *Journal of International Business Studies*, **38**, 658–72.

Bond, M.H. (2002), 'Reclaiming the individual from Hofstede's ecological analysis – a 20 year odyssey: Comment on Oyserman et al.', *Psychological Bulletin*, **128**, 73–7.

Caprar, D.V., T.M. Devinney, B.L. Kirkman and P. Caliguri (2015), 'Conceptualizing and measuring culture in international business and management: From challenges to solutions', *Journal of International Business Studies*, **46**(9), 1101–27.

Chen, C.C., J.R. Meindl and H. Hui (1998), 'Deciding on equity or parity: A test of situational, cultural, and individual factors', *Journal of Organizational Behavior*, **19**(2), 115–29.

Devinney, T.M. and J. Hohberger (2017), 'The past is prologue: Moving on from culture's consequences', *Journal of International Business Studies*, **48**, 48–62.

Dikova, D. and P.R. Sahib (2013), 'Is cultural distance a bane or a boon for cross-border acquisition performance?', *Journal of World Business*, **48**, 77–86.

Donnalson, L. (1986), 'Size and bureaucracy in East and West: A preliminary meta-analysis', in S.R. Clegg, D.C. Dunphy and S.G. Redding (eds), *The Enterprise and Management in East Asia*, Hong Kong: Centre for Asian Studies, University of Hong Kong.

Earley, C. (2009), 'So what kind of atheist are you? Exploring cultural universals and differences', in C. Nakata (ed.), *Beyond Hofstede, Cultural Frameworks for Global Marketing and Management*, Basingstoke, UK: Palgrave Macmillan.

Earley, C. and E. Mosakowski (2000), 'Creating hybrid team cultures: An empirical test of transnational teams' functioning', *Academy of Management Journal*, **43**(1), 26–49.

Gabrielidis, C., W.G. Stephan and O. Ybarra et al. (1997), 'Preferred styles of conflict resolution: Mexico and the US', *Journal of Cross-Cultural Psychology*, **28**(6), 661–7.

Gerhart, B. and M. Fang (2005), 'National culture and human resource management: Assumptions and evidence', *International Journal of Resource Management*, **16**(6), 971–86.

Hickson, D.J., C.R. Hinnings, C. McMillan and J.-P. Schwitter (1974), 'The culture-free context of organization structure', *Sociology*, **8**, 59–80.

Hofstede, G. (1980a), *Culture's Consequences: International Differences in Work-Related Values*, Beverly Hills, CA: Sage.

Hofstede, G. (1980b), 'Motivation, leadership, and organization: Do American theories apply abroad?', *Organizational Dynamics*, **9**(1), 42–63.

Hofstede, G. (1983), 'Culture's consequences: International differences in work-related values', *Administrative Science Quarterly*, **28**(4), 625–9.

Hofstede, G. (1991), *Cultures and Organizations: Software of the Mind*, 1st edition, New York: McGraw Hill.

Hofstede, G. (1994), 'The business of international business is culture', *International Business Review*, **3**(1), 1–14.

Hofstede, G., J.G. Hofstede and M. Minkov (2010), *Cultures and Organizations: Software of the Mind*, 3rd edition, Boston, MA: McGraw-Hill.

Hutzschenreuter, T. and J.V. Voll (2008), 'Performance effects of "added cultural distance" in the path of international expansion: The case of German multinational enterprises', *Journal of International Business Studies*, **39**(1), 53–70.

Inglehart, R. and W. Baker (2000), *Modernization, Cultural Change and Democracy: The Human Development Sequence*, New York: Cambridge University Press.

Kirkman, B.L. and D.L. Shapiro (2001), 'The impact of cultural values on job satisfaction and organizational commitment in self-managing work teams: The mediating role of employee resistance', *Academy of Management Journal*, **44**(3), 557–69.

Kirkman, B.L., K.B. Lowe and C.B. Gibson (2006), 'A quarter century of culture's consequences: A review of empirical research incorporating Hofstede's cultural value framework', *Journal of International Business Studies*, **37**(3), 285–320.

Kirkman, B.L., K.B. Lowe and C.B. Gibson (2017), 'A retrospective on culture's consequences: The 35-year journey', *Journal of International Business Studies*, **48**, 12–29.

Kogut, B. and H. Singh (1988), 'The effect of national culture on the choice of entry mode', *Journal of International Business Studies*, **19**(3), 411–32.

Lane, P.J., J.E. Salk and M.A. Lyles (2001), 'Absorptive capacity, learning and performance in international joint ventures', *Strategic Management Journal*, **22**, 1139–61.

Leung, K. and M.W. Morris (2015), 'Values, schemas, and norms in the culture–behavior nexus: A situated dynamics framework', *Journal of International Business Studies*, **46**(9), 1028–50.

Maslow, A. (1954), *Motivation and Personality*, New York: Harper & Row.

McSweeney, B. (2002), 'Hofstede's model of natural cultural differences and their consequences: A triumph of faith – a failure of analysis', *Human Relations*, **55**(1), 89–118.

Mintzberg, H. (1983), *Structure in Fives: Designing Effective Organizations*, Englewood Cliffs, NJ: Prentice-Hall.

Nachum, L. and S. Zaheer (2005), 'The persistence of distance? The impact of technology on MNE motivations for foreign investment', *Strategic Management Journal*, **26**(8), 747–67.

Nakata, C. (ed.) (2009), *Beyond Hofstede, Cultural Frameworks for Global Marketing and Management*, Basingstoke, UK: Palgrave Macmillan.

Oyserman, D., H.M. Coon and M. Kemmelmeier (2002), 'Rethinking individualism and collectivism: Evaluation of theoretical assumptions and meta-analyses', *Psychological Bulletin*, **128**(1), 3–72.

Parkhe, A. (1991), 'Interfirm diversity, organizational learning, and longevity in global strategic alliances', *Journal of International Business Studies*, **22**(4), 579–601.

Reus, T.H. and B.T. Lamont (2009), 'The double-edged sword of cultural distance in international acquisitions', *Journal of International Business Studies*, **40**(8), 1298–316.

Schwartz, S.H. (1994), 'Beyond individualism/collectivism: New cultural dimensions of values', in U. Kim, H.C. Triandis and Ç. Kâğitçibaşi et al. (eds), *Cross-cultural Research and Methodology Series, Vol. 18: Individualism and Collectivism: Theory, Method, and Applications* (pp. 85–119), Thousand Oaks, CA: Sage.

Shenkar, O. (2012), 'Cultural distance revisited: Towards a more rigorous conceptualization and measurement of cultural differences', *Journal of International Business Studies*, **43**(1), 1–11.

Smith, P.B. (1992), 'Organizational behaviour and national cultures', *British Journal of Management*, **3**, 39–51.

Stahl, G.K. and R.L. Tung (2015), 'Towards a more balanced treatment of culture in international business studies: The need for positive cross-cultural scholarship', *Journal of International Business Studies*, **46**(4), 391–414.

Stephan, U. and L. Uhlaner (2010), 'Performance-based vs. socially supportive culture: A cross-national study of descriptive norms and entrepreneurship', *Journal of International Business Studies*, **41**(8), 1347–64.

Taras, V. and P. Steel (2009), 'Beyond Hofstede: Challenging the ten commandments of cross-cultural research', in C. Nakata (ed.), *Beyond Hofstede, Cultural Frameworks for Global Marketing and Management* (pp. 40–60), Basingstoke, UK: Palgrave Macmillan.

Tayeb, M. (1988), *Organizations and National Culture: A Comparative Analysis*, London: Sage.

Tayeb, M. (1994), 'Organizations and national culture: Methodology considered', *Journal of Organization Studies*, **15**(3), 429–46.

Tihanyi, L., D. Griffith and C. Russell (2005), 'The effect of cultural distance on entry modes choice, international diversification, and MNE performance: A meta-analysis', *Journal of International Business Studies*, **36**(3), 270–83.

Vaara, E., R.M. Sarala, G.K. Stahl and I. Björkman (2012), 'The impact of organizational and national cultural differences on social conflict and knowledge transfer in international acquisitions', *Journal of Management Studies*, **49**(1), 1–27.

Van Oudenhoven, J.P. (2001), 'Do organizations reflect national cultures? A 10 nation study', *International Journal of Intercultural Relations*, **25**, 89–107.

Zellmer-Bruhn, M.E. and C.B. Gibson (2014), 'How does culture matter? A process view of cultural interaction in groups', in M. Yuki and M. Brewer (eds), *Frontiers of Culture and Psychology Series: Culture and Group Processes* (pp. 166–94), Oxford: Oxford University Press.

Zhang, S., M.W. Morris, C.Y. Cheng and A.J. Yap (2013), 'Heritage-culture images disrupt immigrants' second language processing through triggering first language interference', *Proceedings of the National Academy of Science*, **110**(28), 11272–7.

Case I
Danvita: Cultural diversity in a Danish MNE

Vasilisa Sayapina and Katya Christensen

I.1 Introduction

Workforce diversity is a complex phenomenon and a major challenge for human resources (HR) managers in MNEs. This case study presents a Danish MNE, Danvita (not its real name), that has committed to pursuing a diversity strategy. The essence of a diversity strategy is a commitment to providing equal opportunities for employees regardless of their gender, age, nationality, disability and political or sexual orientation. In this case study, our focus is on cultural diversity. Drawing on individual perceptions of Danvita employees we explore how they experience diversity.

Diversity as a strategic resource

Scholars have different opinions about how diversity impacts organizational performance. On one hand, it has been argued that MNEs that are able to draw on a diverse mix of employees can develop a strategic advantage (Richard, 2000). This is because workforce diversity establishes the potential for diverse perspectives that in turn facilitate creative thinking and effective problem solving (Cox, 1991). Understanding and valuing diversity can enable constructive conflict resolution, reduce miscommunication and lead to lower employee turnover and result in cost savings (Robinson and Dechant, 1997). A diverse workforce that can draw on a variety of cultural insights can also have a positive impact on international marketing and sales (Blake-Beard, Finley-Hervey and Harquail, 2008; Cox, 1991; Cox and Blake, 1991; Robinson and Dechant, 1997). On the other hand, workforce diversity can also have negative implications. Some researchers have observed that groups characterized by high degrees of cultural diversity have lower levels of employee satisfaction and worse performance than in more homogeneous groups (O'Reilly, Caldwell and Barnett, 1989; Richard et al., 2003; Watson, Kumar and Michelsen, 1993).

Diversity as perceived by organizational members

The focus of this case is on the issue of how Danvita employees experience cultural diversity encouraged by the company's diversity strategy. 'As with many things in life, perception is reality', claim Allen et al. (2008, p. 22). Individual perceptions influence the way individuals interact with their colleagues and participate in the life of the organization. Based on their perceptions, organizational members participate actively or passively in the implementation of the company's strategies as well as support or oppose organizational change. Knowledge of how organizational members perceive diversity opens up a possibility for improvement and dialogue.

The case data was obtained by means of 17 qualitative interviews with seven Danish and ten international employees. Their narratives, however, should not be understood separately from the environment where the stories and events took place. Thus, the narratives were supplemented with direct observations of diversity training sessions and with documents containing the new diversity strategy, managerial speeches and company annual reports. In this way, information was obtained about the social context in which the employees' perceptions of cultural diversity were constructed and reconstructed on an everyday basis.

I.2   Denmark and Danish

The context in which the diversity case is unfolding contains elements of both national and organizational culture. Although there is considerable overlap, it is important to distinguish them. Despite its commitment to diversity and inclusion of international employees, the head office of Danvita is still operating in a broader context of Denmark. In Denmark, historical and religious development of the society led to the formation of a very particular institutional environment in which the state plays a significant role. Denmark has a well-developed welfare state that redistributes wealth and that ensures inequalities are relatively limited (Andersen and Svarer, 2007). The role of the Danish language as a uniting and protecting mechanism in Danish society must be acknowledged. Historically, the Danish language is an indicator of membership of and belonging to Danish society. Its significance for inclusiveness means that it may also function as a mechanism of exclusion of non-Danish speakers. This factor co-exists with Denmark's membership of the European Union and its policy of welcoming well-qualified professionals to work in Denmark.

I.3 Danvita and the HR challenges it is facing

> The aim is to create a culture where all employees feel valued and have the opportunity to reach their full potential. (Diversity strategy, Danvita)

Briefly about Danvita

Danvita has been a leader in the industry in which it operates. Annual reports indicate increased profits for 2009–11. In March 2012, Danvita had more than 32 800 employees worldwide distributed across affiliates and offices located in 75 countries. Just over 40 per cent of its employees are located in Denmark. In order to function successfully as an MNE, Danvita believes that it has to attract, develop and retain competent people from any location in the world. In 2009, it started a diversity initiative. At the core of this initiative is the operational guideline for HR, which states that the company will provide:

> [...] equal opportunities to all present and future people, regardless of gender, age, race, religion, nationality, cultural and social origin, disability, political or sexual orientation and family status. (Danvita)

In 2009, when the diversity strategy was launched, about 700 of Danvita's employees in Denmark were foreigners. Although 68 nationalities were represented it should be noted that half the foreign employees were from a handful of countries – the UK, the US, Germany and Sweden.

The highest percentage of the international employees was among the professionals and specialists. It was necessary to make an effort to make these employees feel welcome and willing to stay. The turnover rate for international specialists was three times higher than that among the specialists from Denmark. These numbers are not necessarily alarming since employees change jobs and employers frequently and international employees return home after rotations and expatriation. Nevertheless, feeling welcome and happy with their working environment, international employees can contribute to higher retention rates in the organization, which claims to be in need of workforce. Thus, the diversity strategy was developed.

Guiding principles

The guiding principles of Danvita's diversity strategy attempt to lay the foundation for equal treatment of all the organizational members. These principles highlight the strategy's focus on providing equal opportunities and selecting the best-qualified candidates in order to attract and retain talent from all over the world.

Supporting initiatives

A number of supporting initiatives contribute to the creation of a culture of inclusion. There is an International Club that is run on a voluntary basis and that aims at creating a network for foreign employees. The idea is that foreign employees have the opportunity to meet in a non-work environment and to experience the traditions and leisure activities of the host country. It also provides an arena in which to talk through their frustrations with more experienced colleagues.

Corporate way of speaking about diversity

Drawing on company documents we now present three company discourses on diversity.

Business and business needs

One discourse emphasizes the business needs of the company. Diversity is a way of dealing with these needs. The discourse portrays the company as 'a global company', having an 'expanding presence in the world'. The key issue is: 'As we expand, where are we going to find the people [we need]?' A representative of the top management team emphasizes the current growth and success of the company, which is going to be 'even larger and more global' and articulates the need for attracting talent: 'We want to be among the most attractive companies so that we can continue to attract – and retain – the talent we need'. The business discourse constructs diversity as the necessary attribute for sustainable growth, with satisfying the needs of international recruits as the means to this end.

Equality

A second discourse emphasizes diversity as an expression of equality. This discourse views diversity as a product of emphasizing talent regardless of any other considerations:

> We need to make a greater and more systematic effort to identify women and non-Danes with leadership potential when we are filling a management position... The company will never use either negative or positive discrimination. We will always

choose the best individual for a vacant position. (Interview with top management team representative, employee magazine)

The discourse sees selection of the 'best' individuals for positions as the guiding principle, with the provision of equal opportunities to all as the means to this end.

Inclusion

The third discourse involves how the company talks about diversity as inclusion. This discourse presents inclusion as a precondition for achieving diversity: 'Inclusion is an integral element of the diversity strategy, as this is about how to value and utilize all the differences among our people' (Danvita diversity strategy). While emphasizing inclusion, this way of talking about diversity constructs diversity in terms of differences. In the annual report for 2008:

> [...]inclusion of men, women, locals and non-locals must be considered for the succession list for all key positions. Mentorship will be offered and supportive network initiatives including expatriate networks and a 'family-buddy' system are being set up. (Annual report, 2008)

These three main corporate ways of speaking about diversity co-exist in the organizational space of the company. Of the three, the business discourse is the most pronounced discourse and the inclusion discourse by far the least pronounced.

I.4   Cultural diversity as perceived by employees

Cultural diversity as a social construct

An overview of respondent data is presented in Box I.1.

The overall perception of cultural diversity among the respondents can be narrowed down to two groups of employees: Danes and non-Danes. It is seen from the examples below where two employees express their perceptions of cultural diversity in Danvita as consisting primarily of Danes and international people (Respondent 2) and as Danes and non-Danes who do not speak Danish language (Respondent 14's quote):

> Awareness will take time, definitely. Of the three diversity training sessions we have had, the majority who attended were international people, but there were Danes who were there as well. (Respondent 2)

> **BOX I.1**
>
> ## RESPONSE DATA
>
> **Gender**
> | | |
> |---|---|
> | Seven respondents | Male |
> | Ten respondents | Female |
>
> **Position**
> | | |
> |---|---|
> | Seven respondents | HR |
> | Seven respondents | Specialists |
> | Three respondents | Administrative positions |
>
> **Geographies**
> | | |
> |---|---|
> | Seven respondents | Denmark |
> | Four respondents | USA |
> | Two respondents | Germany |
> | One respondent | Brazil |
> | One respondent | Spain |
> | One respondent | India |
> | One respondent | Portugal |
>
> **Age**
> | | |
> |---|---|
> | Two respondents | Age 20–30 |
> | Eight respondents | Age 30–40 |
> | Five respondents | Age 40–50 |
> | One respondent | Age 50–60 |
> | One respondent | Age over 60 |

> We do not typically write in English. We say that the company language is English, but normally we would write in Danish. Recently we found out that we have some standard operational procedures in our department that are only in Danish and nobody thought of actually translating them into English. It's just that the mindset has been very Danish and suddenly we all of a sudden become aware: 'Oh, there are some people that are not Danes and do not speak Danish'. (Respondent 14)

It might sound quite natural to refer to different groups of organizational members as Danes and non-Danes or locals and international people. However, the perception of the workforce in terms of categories carries the inherited danger of reinforcing stereotypes (Litvin, 1997). These perceptions of organizational members as divided into categories reinforce constructs of being local and non-local as fixed entities with characteristics that are believed to accompany those categories. For instance, interviews suggest that Danish employees are sometimes perceived as being better colleagues and employees because they speak Danish and understand how social relations work in Denmark, also because they possess country-specific knowledge that international employees lack. On the other hand, international employees are frequently perceived as not speaking Danish and being rather formal in communication, which makes it complicated to socialize and interact, while social relations at work are perceived as highly important in Denmark. Being international and therefore lacking knowledge of Danish laws and regulation is perceived as a disadvantage. This perception of individuals as first of all belonging to one or the other group and possessing certain characteristics (speaking Danish, understanding the way social relations work, etc.) reinforces stereotypes (e.g., that Danish colleagues are better colleagues and employees) since attention is being paid to the category the individual is locked in.

However, the interviews from Danvita also reveal an appreciation among organizational members that the company is attempting to create space for multifaceted difference. The right to be a unique individual and not to be ascribed to one of the pre-defined categories is valued and acknowledged by many organizational members:

> I am a bit special myself, I am a Jehovah Witness. It is a bit of a special religion here in Denmark. People do not know it very well. In relation to this, I think it is nice that there are differences. I like that the company does not have prejudices, and I myself try not to judge others. (Respondent 4)

> I am gay and I am a foreigner and I did not speak Danish and I did have the qualifications that they were looking for. By them accepting all these things was very, very important to me as a person. Because not only that they welcomed me as a professional, a foreigner, but they welcomed me privately. . . They were willing to see me as an individual beyond my private life, beyond my culture, beyond anything else. (Respondent 6)

As shown in the citations above, some of the interviewed organizational members perceive themselves as unique individuals with characteristics crossing over a number of categories. These employees prefer to be seen and appreciated for the complexity of the characteristics and qualities they embody.

However, the company continues to run two introductory programmes for new employees: one in Danish and one in English. While the rationale is that new employees should choose the language programme they are most comfortable with, it does mean that nearly all the international employees will choose the English-language version. Thus, from the very outset of their

Danvita careers, employees are entering the organization as belonging to one of two groups – the Danes and the non-Danes.

Language as an exclusion mechanism

The use of the Danish language is often perceived as an exclusion mechanism:

> I can point to incidents like our CEO's speech at the annual event that was in Danish; often communication is in Danish because people have not thought of it. It is still a part of a shifting mindset. . . Even small things like forwarding an e-mail from one person to another and asking for comments. Since it has been sent in Danish some people might not see what is written. Small things like that. (Respondent 1)

Others say that they feel the use of Danish language makes them feel unwelcome:

> I am usually the one who says: 'Hello, can you speak English?' but sometimes you do not do that because people usually point at you saying: 'He is the one who always does this'. And you get tired that people always find you the annoying person that makes them change into English. (Respondent 3)

> Mostly my communication would be in Danish: with my boss, with my colleagues. . .even though there are foreigners as well. . . When our Indian colleagues join us at lunch sometimes people continue in Danish I am sorry to say that. (Respondent 9)

Employment interviews often set the expectations regarding the company's corporate language:

> [The interviewee is referring to his employment interview] I said: 'I am not Danish, I do not speak Danish, I do not look like a Danish person and I would be working mostly with Danes. Is that a problem?' He said: 'Not at all. You do not even need to learn Danish because the corporate language is English and we do not want you to become Danish. We want to have your different perspective, your different point of view'. I took it as a statement and that's what I am following. (Respondent 2)

On day one of starting at Danvita:

> [a] manager started speaking to me in Danish and then I said: 'Sorry, I do not speak Danish. Would you mind speaking in English?' 'Oh, but how long have you been

here?' I said: 'That does not matter. The company language is English... I was told that Danish is not a requirement for my position'... That annoyed me that a person would not make an effort to be more inclusive. (Respondent 2)

As illustrated in the quotes above, some international organizational members have a perception that organizational reality does not coincide with the message of English being a corporate language.

On the other hand, we observed that some international employees take it for granted that the corporate language is Danish. These employees willingly learn Danish and do not see any contradiction between what they were promised during the employment interview and the reality:

During the interview we agreed that the working language would actually be Danish and that I therefore would have to learn Danish. (Respondent 7)

Some Danish employees also perceive Danish as the corporate language, not because they have been told so but because they take it for granted.

Reverse discrimination?

In Danvita there is a general belief that most of the Danish employees speak good English and are as comfortable in working and socializing in English as they are in Danish. However, some of our interviews with Danish employees indicated that these perceptions are not always correct:

I do not really like to speak English but it will be ok. I will practice. (Respondent 4)

If you go to the product sites there are many Danes working there who do not know English or the English they have is very limited, basic. So they would feel intimidated if there was a person from another country coming and they were forced to speak English. They would feel a little bit annoyed that it would disturb their routine in the group. So it depends where you are. (Respondent 14)

I have experienced that, for instance, in IT they have employed a lot of people from other countries than Denmark. So when you have an IT problem it could be very difficult to communicate so we both understand what we are talking about... That can be quite challenging. (Respondent 11)

I hold back. Mostly because I get a little bit embarrassed – what if I say words wrong or what if the grammar is not right and it sounds ridiculous when I speak... something like that. Sometimes I choke on the words. (Respondent 15)

The quotes above suggest that some local employees feel awkward when they are forced to speak a foreign language in order to include international employees. These organizational members refer to the necessity of speaking English as 'challenging', 'annoying' and 'embarrassing'. They feel rather 'intimidated' when they have to do it. In other words, some of the Danish employees perceive themselves in a situation of reverse discrimination because they feel at a disadvantage when they have to communicate with the international employees.

However, speaking English on an everyday basis is not only a challenge for the local employees. For most of the international employees, English is also a foreign language and makes communication challenging to the same degree.

Preventing segregation

Mentoring and the creation of social networks are perceived by a number of organizational members as a way to welcome new employees from abroad and contribute to the creation of a positive and inclusive climate for cultural diversity. The initiatives are also perceived as a way of creating a meeting point for locals and non-locals – a bridge allowing people to get to know each other better and to find common points of interests. The International Club is an existing example of a social network run by employees, which is perceived as giving a helping hand to international employees:

> It can mean one hell of a lot to have colleagues that are open-minded and show that support and extend that hand to you as a foreigner when you come to the organization. So in a way if we start at the lowest level of the organization we could create that awareness and create it together. (Respondent 13)

However, the concern was also raised regarding the existing danger of segmenting people into categories and those people cultivating their own networks separate from other organizational members. International employees need to feel included and welcome, also with their families. This includes practical assistance to establish their life in a new environment:

> I would like to interact with all kinds of people despite their mindset, political thoughts, sexual orientation and so on. For me it is the person that counts. That is what I think is important. Personally, I do not want to put people into boxes. (Respondent 15)

> They [Danish colleagues] should be part of this [International Club] to make it successful. Otherwise they are doing exactly the same as Danvita in Denmark,

not integrating people. If the international people coming here are not integrated by Danish people into their activities it is just more of the same, isn't it? That's a dilemma really. (Respondent 8)

Honestly, I think that mentoring is one thing but another thing is the hard facts and the basic help you need with the things that matter for everyday life. Imagine people coming here with families... You really have to address these needs if people are going to really feel 'OK, we feel good here. We are happy here'. (Respondent 13)

I.5 Creating the environment for cultural diversity

The following section reflects on what Danvita's approach to diversity means for organizational members' perception of cultural diversity.

Not wishful thinking

The goal of Danvita's diversity strategy is to have non-locals in all senior management teams within five years. These intentions are welcomed by most of the employees for numerous reasons:

Diversity is something I have not felt until now. They are starting to think about diversity... Ok, we want to be international, so we have to show it also from inside to appear international. (Respondent 3)

If we have more and more international employees everywhere people will be more aware and not scared that either we [international employees] are taking their jobs or making their life more difficult. It is fine to have people from everywhere. We need also to send people from the headquarters to the affiliates and that we are doing more and more. So, both ways, we need to bring non-locals and we need to export Danes to the affiliates. (Respondent 2)

Of course, it is more demanding on you because you have to be aware: 'Oops, can't speak Danish now' but I think it enriches you as a person as well because when you talk to other people hopefully you benefit from it. They can teach me something. (Respondent 14)

Only a small number of the respondents perceive the change that is needed in terms of attitudinal, behavioural and structural changes:

It is very good, it is needed, but it is difficult just to say: 'This is what we are going to do and we have to do this' because I think it has to come naturally. You cannot force it on people. (Respondent 14)

> It is good when it comes from top management but still it's a long process. . . Again diversity should be more than just 'Now we will do this that, that and this'. It should be the mindset, but I know that that takes time. (Respondent 15)

Some of our informants perceive the diversity strategy as a matter of finally achieving fairness and had little sympathy with the locals:

> I was astonished to hear that Danes are saying, 'Ok, this means that we do not have a future in this company at all'. I say to them 'Welcome to our world!' If I were to face the barrier of nationality and then just give up, I would not be where I am today. Come on, get over it and work well, be competent in your job, perform well, and you'll be recognized. (Respondent 2)

Cultivating a diversity-valuing mindset

The corporate initiatives designed to raise awareness of cross-cultural differences among employees are the so-called 'Managing Across Cultures' seminars. During the seminars one can observe the same over-representation of non-local employees as we witnessed at so many other diversity events:

> I am aware of these things so it was not for me an eye-opener or whatever. It is always fun to discuss and there are of course some interesting points how Danes sometimes appear mute and about how we perceive foreigners but as such. . . I probably was not a target audience, but I think it is needed. (Respondent 16)

The fact that the majority of the locals choose not to attend the diversity-related corporate initiatives does not pass unnoticed in the eyes of many international employees. It arouses a wave of disappointment and disapproval. The international employees see participation of all organizational members without exclusion as crucially important for creating a good organizational climate for diversity where awareness, understanding and empathy prevail. Some of the international employees perceive this absence of locals as a sign of unwillingness to participate in the construction and support of a valuing diversity mindset, which they perceive as a common assignment for all organizational members:

> This seminar should be done for the Danish community. I think it was aimed for the Danish community but I do not know what has happened and in the end there are a lot of international people that are well aware. (Respondent 3)

> What I really see missing to make this piece work in particularly is actually engagement from everyone in the organization. These diversity issues do not only affect foreigners. We need to wake up in the organization and realize that it also

> affects our Danish colleagues as well. If we are going to be a global company, it is global together, not just the foreigners who have to roll their sleeves and work and assimilate... I do not see it working now. For example, when I attended the first cultural session there I was extremely disappointed to see that a lot of the management members who were invited from our organization and who are Danish did not show up. (Respondent 13)

In line with this perception, diversity is something that cannot be measured by numbers or achieved by fulfilling quotas or goals. Instead, acceptance and appreciation of people from different backgrounds are ingrained in the organizational way of thinking, as Respondent 15 expresses below:

> I do believe that diversity should be something that is penetrating what we are doing instead of saying: 'Ok, now we have to explore diversity for three days...' At some point we had diversity in our balanced scorecards and in some areas we have it as a kind of a tick-off exercise instead of really going in depth with what it means. (Respondent 15)

We observed that most of the local employees perceive the company Christmas dinner as an occasion for meeting colleagues. Despite its name – 'Christmas' dinner – most of the respondents from Denmark cannot see any religious connotation in this festivity. However, two of our respondents perceived this corporate tradition as unfair and excluding. These employees wondered why it could not be called a 'New Year' celebration in order to avoid any connection to religion.

When we discussed this issue with locals some of them argued that it is necessary to keep traditions. They further argued that the dinner has nothing to do with religion and that the international employees would have to adjust to the host country and its ways. It was often assumed by these locals that the two objectors to 'Christmas' dinner were Muslims. However, in reality, one was a Jehovah's Witness and the other a Jew.

Hiring the best

One key aspect to the diversity strategy at Danvita is that jobs are to go to the 'best' qualified candidate regardless of any other factors:

> The company will never promote anyone just because they are a woman or a non-Dane. We will not do that, but on the other hand we will not discriminate equal candidates for the same position because they are non-Danes or of the other gender. (Respondent 2)

However, what is understood by 'best' is not necessarily straightforward. For instance, being a manager from abroad and not being familiar with how things function in Denmark was referred to as a disadvantage by one of the respondents:

> If you go to marketing it is very diverse out there. Sometimes they even have problems that they are too diverse because it can be difficult for foreign managers if they do not know about Danish labour law and things like that... and nobody can help them because all around are non-locals. Then it can be a tough job for an HR partner to teach them how we do things here in DK. (Respondent 9)

However, few organizational members show any awareness that 'best' may be a matter of perception:

> Every time you hear about this strategy you also hear, 'But of course we should employ the best'. Try to remember that or try to be aware of this. (Respondent 15)

I.6 Why workforce diversity?

A number of respondents that we interviewed perceive cultural diversity as beneficial for organizational creativity and problem solving because it brings new perspectives and alternative views:

> [T]he fact that they are from different cultural backgrounds gives a new view of things. If we have another project, and are there people from different countries or from different educational backgrounds. Everybody has a different view of things and helps to generate ideas. (Respondent 12)

However, some respondents felt that it is only after the international employees have 'fit in' to the local working environment that they can become 'good' organizational members:

> I have heard from my own boss that he would not have hired me if I had not (fit in)... He told me that there were many good candidates – there are always many good candidates – and so he knew that I was very well qualified, but he just wanted to know whether my Danish was good enough... The social part in the working environment in Denmark is very important so you have to fit in. If you do not fit in there is not a good atmosphere at work... It was important that people should not have to switch in English during the lunch time and other events. It is just easier. (Respondent 17)

> [I]f you want to live in another country, work in another country, you have to do whatever you can to understand the language and speak the language. Not that I am

saying that it is not ok that they [international employees] do not do it, but please make an effort. (Respondent 11)

The economic rationale

In the empirical material we found that most of the respondents perceive the need for more balance between locals and non-locals, understand that it is a process that takes time, and express willingness to work in a more culturally diverse organization in the near future. Personal interest and motivation in working with people from all over the world as well as knowledge sharing are mentioned by Respondents 5 and 16 in the quotes below:

> It [more cultural diversity] will make it more interesting for me to be here. I would find it a more interesting place to work in if I could see that it is truly global. (Respondent 16)

> Our director told us that they would work on that more people would come from our affiliates to work for some time here in the headquarters so that we could learn from each other. It is a good way of in-house training, so we could learn about diversity, about language, about our affiliates and their challenges. (Respondent 5)

A number of the respondents also perceive the need for cultural diversity in the case company as directly connected to globalization of businesses where a large part of production and sales takes place abroad. Besides perceiving cultural diversity as enriching organizational processes with new perspectives, the need for human capital is also perceived as one of the reasons for having cultural diversity in the company:

> Everybody knows that it is not up for question that all resources cannot come from Denmark and from Danes alone. They simply have to include expertise from the outside world. Business relies on that and top management knows that. (Respondent 13)

The moral argument

While respondents' perceptions reveal adherence towards the economic rationale for cultural diversity, the moral underpinning, valuing and welcoming diversity in order to make it inclusive and fair for all organizational members is rather limited in the way employees talk about cultural diversity and reasons for it. Instead, a number of international organizational members perceive themselves and some of their colleagues as being excluded and thus treated unfairly from time to time. For instance, Respondents 17 and 3 refer to the occasions when local employees are not making an effort to be inclusive and speak Danish in presence of their international colleagues:

> I find it hard to believe that you do not notice that there is someone who does not understand for half an hour... It is the attitude like 'It is not my responsibility to make this person feel welcome'. (Respondent 17)

Respondent 17 is referring to a situation in which an Indian colleague sat isolated during a lunch break in the canteen, while the local employees were speaking the local language among themselves. The Indian colleague was thus simply excluded from the conversation.

Respondent 3 refers to his experience of meetings and the way he sometimes feels completely excluded when Danish takes over:

> Obviously I am not important for them. Do they really care about me? They only care about certain people in the team that are able to speak the language and if you are not one of them – good luck and that's it. Of course, it demotivates a whole lot. (Respondent 3)

To summarize, we noted several aspects to perceptions relating to cultural diversity. One was about being valued for whom one is as an individual rather than being identified with a group that possesses a set of ascribed qualities. Another concerned the issue of reverse discrimination. A third involved the stimulation of working with colleagues from diverse cultures. Finally, there was the rejection of responsibility by some of the employees for contributing to making diversity actually work.

I.7   Two employee stories

Despite the substantial tendency to operate with a divide between Danes and non-Danes, there are contrasting cases even within the same group. We have chosen two contrasting stories about being included and being excluded among the internationals.

The story of feeling valued and willingness to make others feel the same

> I spoke to my boss and we said: 'There are a lot of foreigners here right now. We need to do something so that we can all break down this imaginary wall of culture of oddness'. I think it was very odd that there was this sort of feeling in the air that we could not break and be able to walk and say: 'Hey, good morning! How are

> you? How is it going? How is your family?'... My boss asked, 'What do you know about Denmark? About us? Our traditions?' And I answered: 'Not much'. The first diversity training session started during a national holiday. Everyone who was Danish in the department took time to explain what that tradition was about, what they ate... It was in November. Out of this course I learnt so many things. I was really motivated and so I came back and more international employees were hired in December. I spoke to my boss again and then I said: 'Well, maybe we should bring this course to our whole department'. (Respondent 6)

Respondent 6 has been working in the company for several years and perceives the company as open towards foreigners. His employment interview was held by an American and a Turkish person and this expression of cultural diversity left a positive impression on him:

> I was interviewed by a girl from California and another lady from Turkey. So, just the very principle that it was not a Danish person. There were two foreigners as well that were interviewing me. One of them was from my own country. So, it made me feel more at home, made me feel: 'Ok, such diversity... I am not the only American running around in this building'. (Respondent 6)

Besides perceiving the case company as open and welcoming to international employees like himself, Respondent 6 expresses appreciation for the company's ability to welcome and value him, first of all as an individual with his skills and qualities, notwithstanding a different nationality and a gay sexual orientation. Respondent 6 feels valued and supported and is ready to support his colleagues when needed. He views his team, which comprises five nationalities, as somewhere he can acquire valuable knowledge and improve both his personal people skills but also his work performance. According to Respondent 6 he has developed in terms of adaptability, sensitivity, and tolerance and developed an acceptance of different viewpoints.

For Respondent 6 it has been important to learn Danish and to get to know Denmark. He takes private Danish lessons and practices his Danish every day: 'We can speak English, but it does not harm you to speak Danish and you live in Denmark, so...' (Respondent 6). In order to get to know his colleagues at the beginning he would every morning make a point of walking around his department to try to greet everybody. Respondent 6 wants to create a welcoming environment for all his colleagues and is proactive about doing that.

The story about feeling excluded

Respondent 3 has been living abroad for quite some time. First in the UK, then for a couple of years in Germany and for the last couple of years Respondent 3 has been working in Danvita in Denmark. Respondent 3 found it difficult to settle in Denmark and preferred to live in Sweden and commute across the border to work:

> When there are other people around and you are speaking a language they do not know (Danish) you are excluding. You are excluding them from communication, from belonging to the group; and when people use the language, they do not realize how much power is involved. (Respondent 3)

Respondent 3 does not perceive her working place as culturally diverse yet but acknowledges the importance for having diversity in the organization as a means to getting Danvita to live up to the image it is trying to project: 'We want to be international, so we have to show it also from inside' (Respondent 3). She experiences feelings of exclusion and not belonging to the group of her colleagues. Respondent 3 expresses a lot of emotion connected to those times when Danish colleagues revert to their local language. She finds it unfair, and it presents a real challenge for her that she has to cope with it on an everyday basis:

> My team is very Danish, which means if there is any excuse for not speaking English, people won't speak English. It is a problem for me. (Respondent 3)

Realizing that it is a problem for her, Respondent 3 used to make her colleagues aware that she could not understand what they were saying and felt excluded. Also, during larger events and department meetings Respondent 3 perceives resentment towards using English. Because these occasions of language-based exclusion have not become less frequent Respondent 3 is about to give up and tends to believe that the organization does not care about international people like herself. She is demotivated, disappointed and embarrassed because she believes that her colleagues find her annoying since she makes them switch from Danish into English:

> Well, what am I gaining from all this? I could be in the other country, or my country, or here and not having to go through all this that I have to cope with. (Respondent 3)

CASE DISCUSSION

1. Give a brief account of Danvita.
2. Describe the goals of the diversity strategy in Danvita and how HQ seeks to implement the strategy.

3   What are the main HR challenges HQ faces with respect to the cultural diversity strategy?
4   Discuss how HQ deals with these managerial challenges.
5   Relate the way in which HQ in Danvita deals with the challenges to the specific national culture that characterize Denmark (as measured by theories presented in the chapter).

REFERENCES

Allen, R., G. Dawson, K. Wheatley and C. White (2008), 'Perceived diversity and organizational performance', *Employee Relations*, **30**(1), 20–33.

Andersen, T.M. and M. Svarer (2007), 'Flexicurity – labour market performance in Denmark', *CESifo Economic Studies*, **53**(3), 389–429.

Blake-Beard, S.D., J.A. Finley-Hervey and C.V. Harquail (2008), 'Journey to a different place: Reflections on Taylor Cox, Jr.'s career and research as a catalyst for diversity education and training', *Academy of Management Learning and Education*, **7**(3), 394–405.

Cox, T., Jr. (1991), 'The multicultural organization', *Executive*, **5**(2), 34–7.

Cox, T.H. and S. Blake (1991), 'Managing cultural diversity: Implications for organizational competitiveness', *The Executive*, **5**(3), 45–56.

Litvin, D. (1997), 'The discourse of diversity: From biology to management', *Organization*, **4**(2), 187–209.

O'Reilly, C., D. Caldwell and W. Barnett (1989), 'Work group demography, social interaction, and turnover', *Administrative Science Quarterly*, **34**, 21–37.

Richard, O. (2000), 'Racial diversity, business strategy, and firm performance: A resource-based view', *Academy of Management Journal*, **48**, 164–77.

Richard, O., A. McMillan, K. Chadwick and S. Dwyer (2003), 'Employing an innovation strategy in racially diverse workforces: Effects on firm performance', *Journal of Management Issues*, **28**(1), 107–26.

Robinson, G. and K. Dechant (1997), 'Building a business case for diversity', *Academy of Management Executive*, **11**, 21–31.

Watson, W.E., K. Kumar and L.K. Michelsen (1993), 'Cultural diversity's impact on interaction process and performance: Comparing heterogeneous and diverse task groups', *Academy of Management Journal*, **36**(3), 590–602.

8
The institutional context

8.1 Introduction

In the previous chapter, we presented an overview of cultural distance. In this chapter, we turn our attention to another difference between home and host countries – the institutional context. Institutions are social structures that comprise laws and regulations (formal institutions) and cognitive and normative elements (informal institutions) (Hoffman, 1999). Institutions therefore have a degree of durability and it is generally accepted in the international business (IB) literature that they matter for MNEs. However, the discussion of why and how institutions matter for MNEs remains fragmented (see Aguilera and Grøgaard, 2019). A number of studies observe that institutional distance affects the strategic decisions of firms concerning internationalization, including entry mode (Hernández and Nieto, 2015). Gooderham et al. (2018) have also shown that institutional distance has an effect on choice of human resource management policies that is distinct from cultural distance.

8.2 Institutional distance

The focus on institutions in IB research is not new. As discussed in Chapter 2, institutions have played a central role for the advantages discussed in the OLI (ownership, location and internalization) framework (see, e.g., Dunning and Lundan, 2008) and for the concept of liability of foreignness (Zaheer, 1995, 2002). One common approach to understanding how the institutional context affects strategic decisions in MNEs involves a focus on the 'institutional distance' between the home and host countries.

In Chapter 1, we discussed Ghemawat's (2001) CAGE framework. The 'A' refers to administrative distance and is primarily about learning to deal with differences in national institutions including legal systems. It is now more usual to use the concept of institutional distance rather than administrative distance. In recent years, the IB field has had an increasing focus on institutional variations across countries (Meyer, Mudambi and Narula, 2011).

Within IB, it is common to distinguish formal from informal institutions, with the latter often viewed as referring to culture. Scholars who study formal institutions explore the influence that legal frameworks and regulatory systems have on business practices and strategies of both local firms (ibid.) and of foreign entrants. The conclusion is that firms, both local and the subsidiaries of MNEs, have to be responsive to formal institutions.

There are two dominant strands of institutional distance theory. One derives from institutional economics (North, 1990) and the other from sociology (DiMaggio and Powell, 1983; Scott, 1995). Both variants focus on formal as well as informal institutions. The two strands of theory differ in that while institutional economics emphasizes how rules and norms constrain what MNEs can do, the institutional theory with roots in sociology focuses on the normative and cognitive aspects of institutions – that is, what MNEs think they ought to do and what they take for granted as the proper way of acting. The sociological perspective is often labelled 'neo-institutional' theory, and it is emphatically a non-efficiency perspective. This implies that financial considerations are not considered the primary driver of managerial practices. Instead, the assumption is that organizations including firms are primarily driven to seek approval and thus are susceptible to social influence. Scholars within the sociological perspective argue that MNEs try to enhance or protect their legitimacy. Concern over legitimacy, in turn, induces MNEs to adopt practices that are 'socially valuable' within an institutional 'field' (i.e., an industry or even a country). The practices and strategic choices of MNEs cannot therefore be understood simply as efficient responses to opportunities or threats. Instead, scholars within the sociological perspective argue that the institutional environment is the key determinant of organizational structure and behaviour. The view is that a firm's action is not a choice among an unlimited array of possibilities determined by purely internal arrangements, but rather a choice among a narrowly defined set of legitimate options.

Whereas neo-institutional theory emphasizes cognitive (widely shared, stereotypical, taken-for-granted beliefs) and to a lesser extent normative aspects of institutions (notions of socially appropriate rather than optimal behaviour), economic institutional theory emphasizes the formal regulative aspects of institutions (laws underpinned by coercive sanctions) (Scott and Christensen, 1995). However, informal constraints also play a role. North (1990, pp. 3–6) defined institutions as 'the rules of the game in a society or, more formally, the humanly devised constraints that shape human interaction... Their major function is to reduce uncertainty by establishing a stable (but not necessarily efficient) structure to human interaction'. They comprise formal rules, including laws, contracts and judicial systems, but also informal constraints embodied in traditions and codes of conduct. MNEs will tend to avoid engaging in value-creating exchanges unless there are efficient institutional constraints that ensure that parties will live up to their side of an agreement. Rules do not solve all problems, but they do simplify them.

Different historical trajectories have led societies to diverge in terms of their institutions. These institutions have economic consequences. While developed countries such as the US have developed institutional frameworks that ensure competition and that incentivize firms to engage in productive activity, in many developing countries the institutional framework favours the creation of 'monopolies rather than competitive conditions' (North, 1990, p. 9). North argues that specific institutional frameworks are critical to national economic success and are hard to change.

Like the concept of cultural distance, institutional distance is useful for understanding cross-national differences in management practices. It is also an important consideration for MNEs entering a new country. For an MNE, the larger the institutional distance between it (i.e., its country of origin) and the host country of a subsidiary, the more challenging it is to achieve local legitimacy (Gooderham, Nordhaug and Ringdal, 2006; Kostova and Roth, 2002). Subsidiaries of MNEs experience pressure to adopt local practices and to resemble – that is, to become 'isomorphic' with – the local institutional context. Hereby lies a tension between the need for global integration on the one hand, and local adaptation on the other. For subsidiaries of MNEs, there are thus two sets of pressures. They are confronted by both an external host country institutional environment and by pressures from within the MNE to become isomorphic to the parent organization's norms (Harzing, 2002). Tension will be particularly acute when the MNE is trying to establish a subsidiary in an institutional context that is markedly different from its own and when it is not prepared to accept a multidomestic solution with comprehensive local responsiveness and little in the way of global integration.

8.3 Home country characteristics

Institutional distance can be used to assess the attractiveness of new markets and the choice of entry and establishment modes. It is also relevant for thinking about the home country characteristics of MNEs. MNEs, or EMNEs as we refer to them in Chapter 2, originating from countries with weak institutions or with considerable state ownership have received increasing attention as their international activities have increased. There are expressed concerns that such MNEs are less competitive (Madhok and Keyhani, 2012). According to mainstream IB theory, home country location advantages

(Rugman and Verbeke, 2001; Rugman, Verbeke and Nguyen, 2011) and state involvement in corporate governance (Cuervo-Cazurra et al., 2014) influence the development of firm-specific advantages (FSAs). MNEs from advanced markets can tap into location advantages and competitive contexts at home and thereby develop strong FSAs related to technology, marketing and managerial capabilities (De Beule, Elia and Piscitello, 2014; Madhok and Keyhani, 2012; Ramamurti, 2012).

This assumption of home country contextual influences is not without controversy. In IB research, FSAs are most commonly measured as market knowledge and technology development, which reflect FSAs that have traditionally served MNEs from advanced markets as they internationalize. Firms from home countries with weak institutions and strong government interference in markets are therefore expected to have weaker FSAs. Some scholars suggest that emerging market MNEs (EMNEs) primarily internationalize through acquisitions to access necessary FSAs in target firms, sometimes referred to as a springboard strategy (Yadong and Tung, 2007). However, other studies suggest that although EMNEs may not have developed traditional FSAs in their home markets, they develop different FSAs such as the ability to handle high levels of uncertainty and the capability to develop strong relationships with governments (Cuervo-Cazurra and Genc, 2008; Madhok and Keyhani, 2012). These alternative FSAs may also be valuable when internationalizing.

Host markets have also voiced concerns around MNEs originating from markets with weak institutions, particularly those with state ownership. For instance, at the end of 2012, Canada increased its scrutiny of M&As by state-owned firms in the oil and gas industry. The then Canadian Prime Minister, Stephen Harper, stated that 'going forward, the Minister [of Industry] will find the acquisition of control of a Canadian oil sands business by a foreign state-owned enterprise to be of net benefit, only in an exceptional circumstance' (Government of Canada, 2012). The concerns about state ownership are multiple. On the one hand, host markets fear undue political influence and possible security issues when business activities are closely tied to large (and sometimes opaque) governments such as China. On the other hand, historical research on state-owned enterprises has concluded that state-owned enterprises show weaker performance and tend to pursue non-economic motives (Goldeng, Grünfeld and Benito, 2008; Shapiro and Globerman, 2012).

While the non-economic motives and weaker performance may certainly characterize some EMNEs, more recent studies have emphasized the need to distinguish types of state ownership (Cuervo-Cazurra et al., 2014; Musacchio and Lazzarini, 2014; Musacchio, Lazzarini and Aguilera, 2015). In a recent study of investments into the Canadian oil and gas industry, Grøgaard, Rygh and Benito (forthcoming) empirically show that home country institutions influence the differences or similarities between firms with or without state ownership. Specifically, they find that state-owned enterprises do not differ from other firms when they originate from home markets with strong institutions. In contrast, state-owned enterprises with weak home institutions behave significantly differently from public or private firms, suggesting that it is primarily home country institutions, rather than ownership structures, that influence the behaviours of MNEs. This stream of research points to the importance of looking at specific home country institutions that influence the strategic behaviours of firms, particularly related to 'newcomers to the competitive landscape' (Beugelsdijk et al., 2018; Cui and He, 2017; Estrin et al., 2016; Kostova, Marano and Tallman, 2016).

8.4 Capturing the complexities of institutional contexts

For the past decade, IB scholars have been challenged to rethink their approach to institutions and employ methodological approaches that capture the complexities and richness of institutional influences (Jackson and Deeg, 2008). For instance, institutional distance measures have been criticized for oversimplifying the context when focusing on how particular institutional characteristics constrain firm-level decisions ('thin' approaches). This ignores complex configurations and interrelationships among institutional variables that can be of great importance for strategic decision making in MNEs and overlooks how institutions can influence firm-level capabilities as well as the ability of firms to influence institutions ('thick' approaches).

When thinking about 'thick' cross-national institutional differences, Hall and Soskice (2001) have developed an influential approach known as 'varieties of capitalism' (VoC). It distinguishes among developed capitalist economies by reference to the means firms and other actors use to coordinate their endeavours. Centred on the formal or 'rules' aspect of institutional context, the VoC approach clusters capitalist economies into two identifiable groups. Observing the extent to which firms rely on market or strategic (institutional) modes of coordination, Hall and Soskice distinguish between liberal market economies (LMEs) and coordinated market economies (CMEs). In LMEs, relations between firms and other actors are coordinated primarily by competitive markets. In contrast, in CMEs, firms typically engage in more strategic interaction with trade unions, suppliers of finance, and other external stakeholders. The VoC approach suggests that 'firms are not essentially similar across nations. On the contrary, firms in LMEs and CMEs develop distinctive strategies and structures to capitalize on the institutions available for market or non-market coordination in the economy' (Hall and Soskice, 2001, p. 56). In short, when faced by similar challenges, LME firms react differently from CME firms.

Using formal aspects to institutional context such as the legal protection of shareholders and collective bargaining rights, Hall and Gingerich (2004) developed a measure of coordination. The measure – see Table 8.1 – places 20 nations along a continuum between pure LMEs ('0') and pure CMEs ('1'). At one end of the continuum are the 'pure' LMEs and at the other end are the 'pure' CMEs.

Table 8.1 indicates that there is substantial 'institutional distance' between the Anglo-Saxon countries and Western European countries, particularly Austria and Germany but also the Scandinavian countries. These regulatory differences are reflected in other regulatory features of national context including employment legislation and industrial relations. They are both

Table 8.1 The coordination index

	Coordination Index	
Austria	1.00	('Pure' CME)
Germany	0.95	↓
Italy	0.87	
Norway	0.76	
Belgium	0.74	
Japan	0.74	
Portugal	0.72	
Finland	0.72	
Denmark	0.70	
France	0.69	
Sweden	0.69	
Netherlands	0.66	
Spain	0.57	
Switzerland	0.51	
Australia	0.36	
Canada	0.13	
United Kingdom	0.07	↑
United States	0.00	('Pure' LME)

Source: Hall and Gingerich (2004).

potent indicators of institutional distance. However, the two should be considered together because trade unions as well as courts are important guarantors of the enforcement of employment legislation (Gooderham et al., 2018). Employment legislation may be analysed in terms of: (1) the protection of permanent workers against (individual) dismissal length; (2) specific requirements for collective dismissals.

Applying these aspects to employment legislation, the OECD has developed a measure of employment protection that includes many LMEs and CMEs as well as countries that fall outside the 'VoC' index. Figure 8.1 provides an overview of employment protection in selected countries. If we compare the scores of the LME countries, the United States, the United Kingdom, Canada, Australia and (arguably) Ireland with their scores in Figure 8.1 we can readily observe relatively weak employment protection. Likewise, the 'pure' CME countries, Austria and Germany, both have strong employment protection.

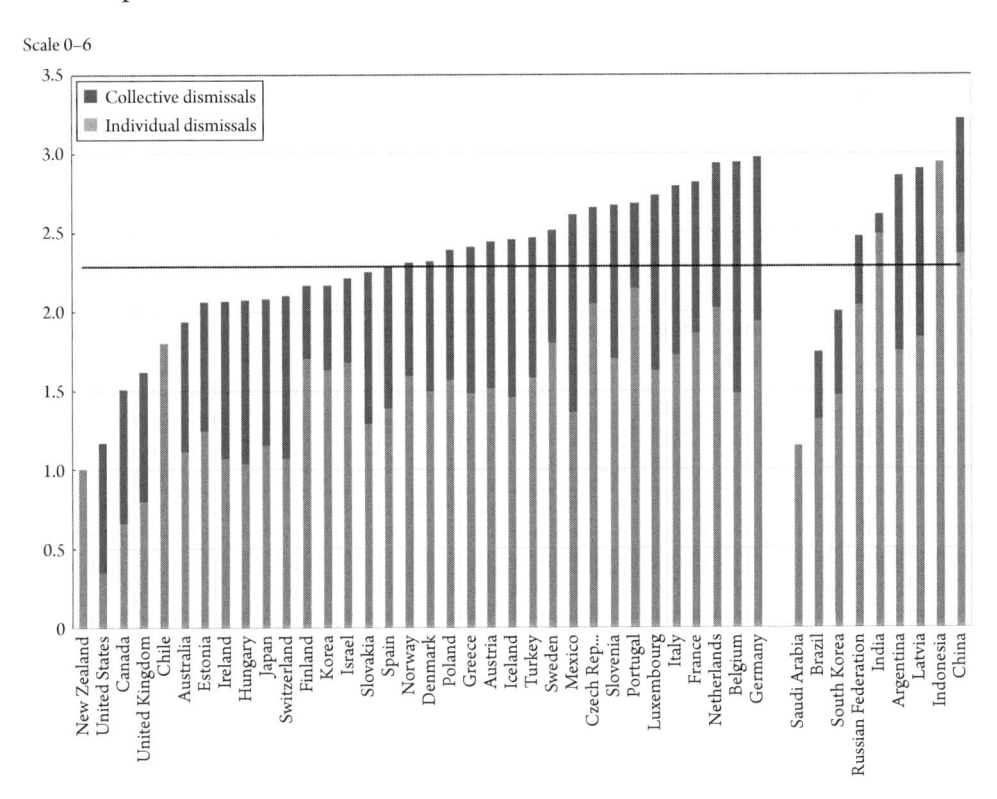

Source: OECD (n.d.), 'Indicators of employment protection', accessed 16 September 2018 at http://www.oecd.org/employment/emp/oecdindicatorsofemploymentprotection.htm.

Figure 8.1 Employment protection in 2015 – scale 0–6

Table 8.2 The influence of trade unions: Density and bargaining coverage 2015–16 (and 1994): percentages

Country	Union Density Rate	Bargaining Coverage
Denmark	67 (76)	84 (90)
Finland	65 (81)	89 (95)
Sweden	67 (91)	90 (93)
Norway	53 (58)	67 (74)
Belgium	54 (53)	96 (90)
Austria	27 (43)	98 (98)
Italy	34 (39)	80 (82)
Netherlands	17 (26)	79 (81)
Spain	14 (22)	73 (66)
France	8 (9)	99 (95)
Germany	18 (30)	56 (92)
UK	24 (36)	26 (47)
US	10 (16)[a]	12 (18)

Note: a. 1981: 35.4% of US manufacturing workforce were union members.

Source: ILOSTAT, 'Key indicators of the labour market', accessed 13 September 2018 at https://www.ilo.org/ilostat/faces/wcnav_defaultSelection?_adf.ctrl-state=10fqe8fven_25and_afrLoop=1473908585244832and_afrWindowMode=0and_afrWindowId=10fqe8fven_75#!.

Table 8.2 indicates that most European countries are more heavily unionized in terms of union membership than the United States.

However, in reality, trade union influence cannot be gauged adequately by focusing on trade union density rates. A more important issue is that of trade union recognition – that is, whether the employer deals with a trade union in a collective bargaining relationship that sets terms and conditions for all or most of the employees. It is in this respect that CME countries diverge to a considerable degree from the prototypical LME country, the United States. In countries such as France and the Benelux countries there is legislation in place requiring employers over a certain size to recognize unions for consultative purposes. In the case of Germany, there have been significant falls in trade union membership and bargaining coverage since the late 1980s. The issue is therefore whether Germany is undergoing institutional change and becoming more of an LME. However, it should be noted that Germany still has powerful unions within particular sectors of its economy and that they exert considerable influence in determining salaries and conditions. For example, the IG Metall engineering union represents 3.8 million German workers in annual industry-wide negotiations that have a significant impact on wage setting in Germany in general (Lauer, 2016).

In addition, works councils remain widespread. Thus, Germany remains a CME.

Differences among CMEs

While it is relatively straightforward to differentiate LMEs from CMEs, within the CME category there are nevertheless dissimilarities. One divide is between Southern and Northern European economies. More qualitative analysis indicates that the Southern countries tend to have a lower capacity for strategic coordination in labour relations than those in Northern Europe. Hall and Gingerich (2004) ascribe this to the nature of union movements. In Southern European countries, unions tend to be splintered along ideological or 'confessional' lines.

However, even among Northern European countries there are qualitative differences. Let us briefly compare the German and the Scandinavian models (see Gooderham, Nordhaug and Ringdal, 1999). The former employs relatively more detailed firm-level legislation than the latter. In practice, this means that the human resources (HR) function in German firms is largely restricted to providing legal advice to managers and to ensuring that the firm is not in breach of any of the numerous regulations that constitute national employment law and agreements. In Scandinavian countries, employment law is sufficiently general and trust between partners sufficiently high to permit the HR function to engage with employees and their unions on new practices. However, collaboration and flexibility has its limits. Changes in employment practices are subject to bipartite agreements and labour unions can withdraw their cooperation in the case of disagreement with management. This institutional framework contributes to a particular Scandinavian management style characterized by a 'democratic mentality' and by informal employee involvement in decision making (Lindeberg, Månson and Larsen, 2013). When designing their local human resource management (HRM) systems, MNEs respond to these differences between the German and Scandinavian institutional contexts (Gooderham et al., 2006).

8.5 Institutional voids

The VoC framework is limited to advanced economies. A fundamental aspect to such economies is that of 'effective, low-cost enforcement of contracts. [In these contexts] cheating, shirking, opportunism...are limited or indeed absent because they do not pay' (North, 1990, pp. 54–5). Property rights to material and immaterial assets are defined, protected and enforced by effective judicial systems. In broad terms, this feature of advanced economies is captured by the scores of countries in the annual Corruption Perceptions Index published by Transparency International (see Chapter 4). All the least corrupt countries are included in the VoC framework.

One criticism of VoC is 'its lack of attention to the developing world' (Wilkinson, Wood and Deeg, 2014, p. 2). The LME/CME framework includes a limited number of countries, and does not capture many of the emerging countries that are increasingly important to MNEs. One of the challenges with expansions of the framework into emerging countries is the lack of available data and difficulties getting insights into these markets. However, a few studies (see, e.g., Fainshmidt et al., 2018; Redding and Witt, 2009) have recently gathered qualitative institutional data on countries that were not initially included by Hall and Soskice (2001).

One concept that has been applied to emerging economies is 'institutional voids' – that is, 'the absence or underdevelopment of institutions that enable and support market activity' (Doh et al., 2017, p. 203). According to economic institutional theory, in these contexts the lack of legal and regulatory systems that effectively enforce property rights raises transaction costs – that is, it makes the cost of doing business, including enforcing contracts, protecting assets and raising capital, costly. Consequently, as Khanna and Palepu (2000) observe, in emerging countries such as India, firms engage in extensive diversification, forming business groups. Hence, we can observe in India business groups such as Tata and Reliance that are collections of publicly traded firms across various industries, with a significant amount of common ownership and control, typically exercised by a family. Khanna and Palepu's research suggest that diversified business groups add value by replicating the functions of institutions that are missing in emerging markets. Further, their size may also grant them privileged access to government. As was the case for BKT (Case E) and Uninor (Case D), MNEs that enter emerging economies 'often use strategic alliances with local firms to overcome the disadvantages resulting from institutional voids' (Kim and Song, 2017, p. 310).

Just as VoC differentiates between advanced economies, so there is an interest in differentiating between emerging economies. One attempt to do this is the 'varieties of institutional systems' (VIS) taxonomy (Fainshmidt et al., 2018). The VIS framework emphasizes the role of the state and the role of powerful families. *The Economist* (2014) reports that:

> [a]round 85% of $1 billion-plus businesses in South-East Asia are family-run, around 75% in Latin America, 67% in India and around 65% in the Middle East.

China (where the proportion is about 40%) and Sub-Saharan Africa (35%) stand out for their relatively low share of family firms, because in both cases many large firms are state owned.

As we noted above, extensive family-controlled business groups provide a means of coping with institutional voids.

VIS has a particular focus on different types of state influence. One variant is 'direct state dominance'. For example, in China, state companies make up 80 per cent of the stock market and in Russia 62 per cent. In the case of Russia and China, direct state dominance is supplemented by 'indirect intervention in the private sector'. For example:

> Russian oligarchs became wealthy not due to their acquisition of privatized means of production...but because Putin – in leading the Russian state – facilitated the accumulation of assets by these tycoons... [In China], the state often picks and chooses which IPOs [initial public offerings] are approved and promoted in the national stock exchanges. (Fainshmidt et al., 2018, p. 301)

Further, these state-led emerging economies have states that are 'predatory' in the sense of having elites who monopolize power and whose decision making is opaque.

In addition to China and Russia, VIS includes India, Pakistan and Bangladesh in a 'state-led' category of emerging economies. VIS distinguishes this category from emerging economies such as Iran, Saudi Arabia and Kuwait that have many of the same features, but have greater concentrations of family ownership. VIS labels these as 'centralized tribe' economies. VIS also distinguishes the state-led emerging economies from a category labelled 'fragmented with fragile state' such as Ethiopia, Sudan and Rwanda. VIS identifies relatively few emerging economies as 'emergent LME' (e.g., Chile, Israel and Singapore) or as emergent CME ('collaborative agglomerations'). All of the latter are Central European such as the Czech Republic, Hungary, Poland and Slovenia.

VIS is a snapshot taken at a particular point in time. Emerging economies are in transition and may shift category in ways that are difficult to foresee. However, VIS challenges any notion that most emerging economies are converging around LME/CME institutions. The challenge for MNEs operating in emerging economies is to adapt their local operations to the institutional context without suffering any loss to their legitimacy in their countries of origin. This challenge is not set to diminish.

8.6 Institutional distance versus cultural distance

Gooderham et al. (2018) have compared the impact of institutional distance and cultural distance on the adoption of a particular compensation system – individualized pay-for-performance systems (I-PFP). I-PFP is widespread in the United States but less common in many CME European countries. Their overall finding is that culture alone is insufficient to explain cross-national differences. Indeed, their study indicates that a country's institutions explain unique variance over and above the effect of culture on the use of I-PFP. Further, while culture plays some role in determining I-PFP use, this role is entirely mediated via institutions including labour regulations and the influence of trade unions. In other words, cultural distance does not directly explain cross-national differences in the adoption of I-PFP. Instead, while culture has some influence on institutional factors, it is institutional factors that explain the use of I-PFP.

While this is only one, albeit unique, study of the relative importance of cultural and institutional distance – we certainly need more studies before we can conclude – Gooderham et al.'s findings are a timely corrective to studies that exclusively focus on cultural distance. They argue that their:

> [...]findings imply significant consequences for researchers who use culture as their exclusive measure of cross-national differences. Cultural explanations of cross-national differences have dominated the field of international management, while institutional analysis has been underused especially in relation to large cross-national studies of management practices. An important implication for international management education is that institutional explanations of cross-national diversity in management practices should be given significantly greater attention. (Gooderham et al., 2018, p. 1499)

8.7 Summary

When reflecting on and attempting to understand cross-national differences in management practices, it is important to be able to distinguish institutional distance from cultural distance. Institutional distance is an important concern for MNE managers to take into account when they consider the types of management practices they aim to introduce to their foreign subsidiaries. For an MNE, the larger the institutional distance between it (i.e., its country of origin) and the host country, the more arduous it is to achieve local legitimacy using their country-of-origin approaches to management. Therein lies a dilemma. Should MNEs defy local institutional pressures or should they acquiesce? Domestic firms face a similar challenge when they attempt to introduce institutionally alien approaches to management. The case study that follows illustrates the institutional challenges experienced by a US MNE, Walmart, entering the German market.

REFERENCES

Aguilera, R.V. and B. Grøgaard (2019), 'The dubious role of institutions in international business. A road forward', *Journal of International Business Studies*, accessed 28 January 2019 at https://doi.org/10.1057/s41267-018-0201-5.

Beugelsdijk, S., T. Kostova and V.E. Kunst et al. (2018), 'Cultural distance and firm internationalization: A meta-analytical review and theoretical implications', *Journal of Management*, **44**(1), 89–130.

Cuervo-Cazurra, A. and M. Genc (2008), 'Transforming disadvantages into advantages: Developing-country MNEs in the least developed countries', *Journal of International Business Studies*, **39**(6), 957–79.

Cuervo-Cazurra, A., A. Inkpen, A. Musacchio and K. Ramaswamy (2014), 'Governments as owners: State-owned multinational companies', *Journal of International Business Studies*, **45**(8), 919–42.

Cui, L. and X. He (2017), 'Expanding near the home base or venture far? The influence of home country state on the economic distance of foreign direct investments', *Journal of Business Research*, **75**, 95–107.

De Beule, F., S. Elia and L. Piscitello (2014), 'Entry and access to competencies abroad: Emerging market firms versus advanced market firms', *Journal of International Management*, **20**(2), 137–52.

DiMaggio, P.J. and W.W. Powell (1983), 'The iron cage revisited: Institutional isomorphism and collective rationality in organizational fields', *American Sociological Review*, **48**(2), 147–60.

Doh, J., S. Rodrigues, A. Saka-Helmhout and M. Makhija (2017), 'International business responses to institutional voids', *Journal of International Business Studies*, **48**(3), 293–307.

Dunning, J.H. and S.M. Lundan (2008), *Multinational Enterprises and the Global Economy*, 2nd edition, Cheltenham, UK and Northampton, MA, USA: Edward Elgar Publishing.

Estrin, S., K.E. Meyer, B.B. Nielsen and S. Nielsen (2016), 'Home country institutions and the internationalization of state owned enterprises: A cross-country analysis', *Journal of World Business*, **51**(2), 294–307.

Fainshmidt, S., W.Q. Judge, R.V. Aguilera and A. Smith (2018), 'Varieties of institutional systems: A contextual taxonomy of understudied countries', *Journal of World Business*, **53**(3), 307–22.

Ghemawat, P. (2001), 'Distance still matters: The hard reality of global expansion', *Harvard Business Review*, **79**(8), 137–47.

Goldeng, E., L.A. Grünfeld and G.R.G. Benito (2008), 'The performance differential between private and state owned enterprises: The roles of ownership, management and market structure', *Journal of Management Studies*, **45**(7), 1244–73.

Gooderham, P.N., O. Nordhaug and K. Ringdal (1999), 'Institutional and rational determinants of organizational practices: Human resource management in European firms', *Administrative Science Quarterly*, **44**(3), 507–31.

Gooderham, P.N., O. Nordhaug and K. Ringdal (2006), 'National embeddedness and calculative human resource management in US subsidiaries in Europe and Australia', *Human Relations*, **59**(11), 1491–513.

Gooderham, P.N., M. Fenton-O'Creevy, R. Croucher and M. Brookes (2018), 'A multilevel analysis of the use of individual pay-for-performance systems', *Journal of Management*, **44**(4), 1479–504.

Government of Canada (2012), 'Statement regarding investment by foreign state-owned enterprises', accessed 28 January 2019 at https://www.ic.gc.ca/eic/site/ica-lic.nsf/eng/lk81147.html.

Grøgaard, B., A. Rygh and G.R.G. Benito (forthcoming), 'Bringing governance into internalization theory: State ownership, corporate governance and foreign entry strategies', mimeo.

Hall, P.A. and D.W. Gingerich (2004), 'Varieties of capitalism and institutional complementarities in the macroeconomy', *MPIfG Discussion Paper 04/5*, Berlin: Max Planck Institut für Gesellschaftsforschung.

Hall, P.A. and D.W. Soskice (eds) (2001), *Varieties of Capitalism: The Institutional Foundations of Comparative Advantage*, Oxford: Oxford University Press.

Harzing, A.W. (2002), 'Acquisitions versus greenfield investments: International strategy and management of entry modes', *Strategic Management Journal*, **23**(3), 211–27.

Hernández, V. and M.J. Nieto (2015), 'The effect of the magnitude and direction of institutional distance on the choice of international entry modes', *Journal of World Business*, **50**(1), 122–32.

Hoffman, A.J. (1999), 'Institutional evolution and change: Environmentalism and the US chemical industry', *Academy of Management Journal*, **42**(4), 351–71.

Jackson, G. and R. Deeg (2008), 'Comparing capitalisms: Understanding institutional diversity and its implications for international business', *Journal of International Business Studies*, **39**(4), 540–61.

Khanna, T. and K. Palepu (2000), 'Is group affiliation profitable in emerging markets? An analysis of diversified Indian business groups', *The Journal of Finance*, **55**(2), 867–91.

Kim, H. and J. Song (2017), 'Filling institutional voids in emerging economies: The impact of capital market development and business groups on M&A deal abandonment', *Journal of International Business Studies*, **48**(3), 308–23.

Kostova, T. and K. Roth (2002), 'Adoption of an organizational practice by subsidiaries of multinational corporations: Institutional and relational effects', *Academy of Management Journal*, **45**(1), 215–33.

Kostova, T., V. Marano and S. Tallman (2016), 'Headquarters–subsidiary relationships in MNCs: Fifty years of evolving research', *Journal of World Business*, **51**(1), 176–84.

Lauer, K. (2016), 'German construction workers agree two-stage wage rise', *Reuters*, 18 May 2016, accessed 12 February 2018 at https://www.reuters.com/article/us-germany-economy-wages/german-construction-workers-agree-two-stage-wage-rise-idUSKCN0Y90NM.

Lindeberg, T., B. Månson and H.H. Larsen (2013), 'HRM in Scandinavia – embedded in the Scandinavian model?', in E. Parry, E. Stavrou and M. Lazarova (eds), *Global Trends in Human Resource Management* (pp. 147–62), Basingstoke, UK: Palgrave Macmillan.

Madhok, A. and M. Keyhani (2012), 'Acquisitions as entrepreneurship: Asymmetries, opportunities, and the internationalization of multinationals from emerging economies', *Global Strategy Journal*, **2**(1), 26–40.

Meyer, K.E., R. Mudambi and R. Narula (2011), 'Multinational enterprises and local contexts: The opportunities and challenges of multiple embeddedness', *Journal of Management Studies*, **48**(2), 235–52.

Musacchio, A. and S.G. Lazzarini (2014), *Reinventing State Capitalism: Leviathan in Business, Brazil and Beyond*, Cambridge, MA: Harvard University Press.

Musacchio, A., S.G. Lazzarini and R.V. Aguilera (2015), 'New varieties of state capitalism: Strategic and governance implications', *Academy of Management Perspectives*, **29**(1), 115–31.

North, D.C. (1990), *Institutions, Institutional Change and Economic Performance*, Cambridge, UK: Cambridge University Press.

Ramamurti, R. (2012), 'What is really different about emerging market multinationals?', *Global Strategy Journal*, **2**(1), 41–7.

Redding, G. and M.A. Witt (2009), 'China's business system and its future trajectory', *Asia Pacific Journal of Management*, **26**(3), 381–99.

Rugman, A.M. and A. Verbeke (2001), 'Subsidiary-specific advantages in multinational enterprises', *Strategic Management Journal*, **22**(3), 237–50.

Rugman, A.M., A. Verbeke and Q.T.K. Nguyen (2011), 'Fifty years of international business theory and beyond', *Management International Review*, **51**(6), 755–86.

Scott, W.R. (1995), *Institutions and Organizations*, Thousand Oaks, CA: Sage.

Scott, W.R. and S. Christensen (1995), *The Institutional Construction of Organizations: International and Longitudinal Studies*, Thousand Oaks, CA: Sage.

Shapiro, D.M. and S. Globerman (2012), 'The international activities and impacts of state-owned enterprises', in K. Sauvant, L. Sachs and W.S. Jongbloed (eds), *Sovereign Investment: Concerns and Policy Reactions*, New York: Oxford University Press.

The Economist (2014), 'Business in the blood', 1 November 2014, print edition, accessed 10 June 2018 at https://www.economist.com/business/2014/11/01/business-in-the-blood.

Wilkinson, A., G. Wood and R. Deeg (eds) (2014), *The Oxford Handbook of Employment Relations: Comparative Employment Systems*, Oxford: Oxford University Press.

Yadong, L. and R.L. Tung (2007), 'International expansion of emerging market enterprises: A springboard perspective', *Journal of International Business Studies*, **38**(4), 481–98.

Zaheer, S. (1995), 'Overcoming the liability of foreignness', *Academy of Management Journal*, **38**(2), 341–63.

Zaheer, S. (2002), 'The liability of foreignness, redux: A commentary', *Journal of International Management*, **8**(3), 351–8.

Case J
Walmart in Germany

Kirsten Foss

J.1 Introduction

Walmart Corporation announced in 2006 that it would sell its holdings in Germany after eight years in the German retail market. During these eight years in Germany, Walmart had lost approximately US$200 million in each year of its operation and the divestment cost the company approximately US$1 billion (Christopherson, 2007).

There are many different explanations of the Walmart failure in Germany. Below is one account of the failure based on the research done mainly by Anders Knorr and Andreas Arndt (2003) and Susan Christopherson (2007). The case describes Walmart as an MNE and its markets (US and Germany) as they were in 2006.

J.2 Information about Walmart

Walmart is a US-based firm. By the 1990s, when it decided to enter Germany, it was the world's largest retailer by revenue. In the consumer market, Walmart has established its dominant position in the US using a strategy of 'everyday low prices' and 'excellent customer service'. Many of Walmart's shops are large stores that carry an assortment that allow customers to shop at one shop for a full range of household products and groceries.

Walmart's low-price strategy is supported by its power over suppliers and its cost-effective lean retailing system. In the US, Walmart is such a big customer that small suppliers as well as major producers of food, health and household products have to deal with the retail firm if they hope to reach the consumer market. Walmart is also known for its sophisticated 'lean retail' system that, for example, allows it to reduce product cost, time-to-market and inventory storage costs. Walmart locates its large retail stores close to distribution centres and uses sophisticated information technology (e.g., barcodes and hand-held computers) in the supply chain to optimize logistics. The IT system and its implementation represented best practices in supply chain management in the 1990s. In Walmart's home market the company was a market leader using its bargaining power to establish a cost-effective relationship with suppliers.

Walmart decided already in the 1980s to internationalize in order to maintain its high growth rates. The ambition was to have one-third of its total profits generated in foreign markets. Walmart was slow to internationalize, but at the time it entered into Germany it had already successfully entered other international markets. For example, approximately 22 per cent of Walmart's total profits obtained from non-US operations came from Canada and Mexico (Durand, 2007). Walmart's competitive strategy for gaining market shares in new international markets has been to pursue a cost leadership strategy in order to gain a large market share and reap benefit of economies of scale. In addition, as Walmart demonstrated in the US as well as in the UK, Canada and Mexico, it was able to move rapidly and autonomously in response to changes in market conditions. This ability stems from its understanding of the institutions that shape the business environments in these countries.

J.3 Walmart's home market

In the US, Walmart has been able to exploit the specific characteristics of the US labour market to drive down labour cost. The US labour market makes it possible for firms like Walmart to tap into a large flexible workforce, many of whom are willing to work in part-time jobs. Walmart pays its sales staff slightly above minimum wages, but because such a high proportion of the workforce is part-time, only 40 per cent of Walmart's employees are covered by the chain's health insurance package.

In the US labour market, trade unions are marginal to most private-sector firms. Hall and Gingerich (2004) classify the US as a pure liberal market economy (LME) – that is, relations between firms and their stakeholders (such as employees) are primarily coordinated by competitive markets. The norm in the US labour market is that firms act autonomously when implementing changes that influence workers in different job categories. For example, in the US, lean retailers have restructured work in retailing, eliminating skilled craft jobs such as butchers and bakers, replacing them with less skilled and non-unionized service workers. The unions do not necessarily accept such changes and one union, the US Food and Commercial Workers, responded to the retailers' actions by increasing their attempts to unionize meat cutters. Opposed to unions, Walmart simply eliminated these jobs and introduced pre-packaged meat products.

The LME characteristics are also present in the supplier markets. The suppliers compete for orders from retailers who assess the market for subcontractors and contract with those offering the lowest price. Concentration among the retailers increases competition among suppliers and allows the retailers, such as Walmart, to drive down prices and achieve continuous increases in profits despite 'the everyday low price strategy'. In the US model of lean retailing, the lead firm has the decision power and can move fast to exit markets and enter new markets in response to changes in customer demands. Information generated from the use of IT systems in supply chain management support the lead firm's decision power (Christopherson, 1999).

Walmart had, at the time it entered Germany, three main categories of retail outlets: the supercentres, which often carried 120 000 different product items in many different product categories; the discount stores with general merchandise and limited groceries; and neighbourhood markets with groceries and pharmacies. However, Walmart was mostly known for the shop concept called 'big box stores' where customers shop at one retailer for a wide range of consumer goods. US tax policy and economic development incentives in combination with limited land use controls have favoured large-scale, space-extensive, so-called 'gorilla' retailing, encouraging large-scale retailers who offer many goods at low prices.

J.4 Germany at the time when Walmart decided to enter the market

Germany was the third-largest retail market in the world (after the US and Japan) and accounted for fully 15 per cent of Europe's approximately US$2-trillion-a-year retail market. The German retail market consisted of about 80 million affluent consumers who spent about 30 per cent of their available income on retailers. In addition, the German market provided a gateway to many of the Eastern European markets. Although the market was large, the competition for customers was also intense, and the concentration of retailers was high, the ten largest representing around 84 per cent of sales. The dominant players were all 'hard discounters' that typically offered a range of 600–700 products, many of which were own-brands, at very low prices. Profit margins were as low as in the US, which is typically under 3 per cent. However, in the segment of hard discounters, profits were higher and the leading firm Aldi gained a return on investment of 2 per cent compared to the 0.5 per cent in other segments (Lewis, 2001). The retail-specific legislation does not allow firms to sell products at prices below costs for extended periods and in fact, in 2003, Germany's High Court ruled that Walmart's low-cost pricing strategy 'undermined competition' and ordered Walmart and two other supermarkets to raise their prices. Walmart won the appeal of the ruling, but the German Supreme Court overturned the appeal. Despite this strict regulation, many of the local hard discounters used price strategies centred on loss leaders (that is, selling a few products at prices below cost for a limited time span to attract customers to the stores).

The German *Länder* (states) use regulations that are significantly different from those in the US, thereby creating an unfavourable environment to big box store development. The aim in Germany is that retail business should not draw customers away from the city and local centres. The implication is that German retailing is carried out typically in neighbourhood locations in relatively small stores. German consumers also put more emphasis on price and value than on customer service. For decades, German shoppers were used to shopping in self-service, small-scale discount stores, which offer a narrow range of goods with special weekly offers.

Germany is a prototypical coordinated market economy (CME) and social norms emphasize consultation and collaboration in decisions with implications for all firm stakeholders, including employees and suppliers. This is noticeable in the labour market where the government and labour unions typically have cooperated in cases where major reorganization in the labour market eliminated particular occupational skills. However, this is gradually changing so that employment is based on the concept of 'competence' closer to that of the generally skilled worker who can fill a number of medium-level skilled positions. Both the occupational skills system and the industrial relations system provide for methods of adaptation to new technology that are absent in the US-type LME. For example, the industry, unions and government have introduced new training programmes upgrading labour to perform related tasks when technology and reorganization made existing occupational skills worthless.

Unions independent of any particular workplace have the research capacity and political influence to shape the development of new occupations through political pressure for training programmes and protection of career paths to protect traditional skilled craft occupations. The German retail sector mainly relies on skilled and semi-skilled labour, of which approximately 25 per cent are unionized.

In German lean retailing, there is a greater tendency to see logistics suppliers as strategic partners rather than as subcontractor-service providers, as was the case in the liberal market economy of the US. Moreover, in the German market, wholesaler intermediaries have a much stronger position compared to in the US. Part of the reason was that the structure of the retail sector with many relatively small firms influenced the structure of the supply chain. At the time when Walmart entered the German market, the logistics and distribution system was also much less sophisticated than that in the USA. Thus, there was less use of scanners and large-scale central distribution, with the implication that average warehouse inventory turns were lower than in the US (Dawson, 2009).

J.5   Walmart in Germany

In order to enter the German market, Walmart was forced to purchase two relatively weak chains, Interspar (74 stores) and Wertkauf (24 stores), which included stores of various sizes. The Interspar stores were in poor shape and in poor locations. With these acquisitions, Walmart was placed approximately 11th in overall German retail sales with a market share of about 3 per cent. Walmart intended to refurbish these stores – something they only succeeded in doing for some of the stores (Jui, 2011). After Walmart's entry, local German chains soon took steps to pre-empt Walmart from expanding further as they entered into a series of mergers, joint ventures and for one chain even a restructuring of ownership into a trust (Dawson, 2009).

In the US, Walmart cuts costs by dealing directly with factories and getting factory direct-delivery to its stores, bypassing wholesaler intermediaries. In Germany, they wanted to implement a similar strategy and invested in a 25 000 m^2 central depot in Kempen and later in Hockenheim. However, due to the large differences in US and German distribution systems the result was chaos. According to David Dawson (2009), individual store consignments were mixed up and there was an insufficient ability to trace the origins of damaged goods. Due to capacity problems, expediters delivering products to the distribution centre had to wait for hours to unload their cargo and, by comparison, did not meet the standards of the smooth efficiency characterizing its US operations. Walmart Germany had difficulty keeping its networks of stores adequately supplied, especially with fresh produce. In the end, Walmart had to accept the extra costs associated with the traditional German supply system. Walmart's approach to supplier relations was also similar to its US approach. Suppliers complained that they did not receive compensation for loss of time and revenue when Walmart failed to implement its centralized system. However, Walmart further aggravated its suppliers, expecting them to accept contractual terms that were unusual in Germany and highly favourable to Walmart. For example, Walmart unilaterally included in its vendor contract a right to inspect suppliers' premises without notice and claimed the right to return goods at suppliers' costs if quality criteria had not been meet (Dawson, 2009).

Walmart's major strategy to conquer the German market was its strategy of everyday low prices across categories. However, it did not succeed with this strategy. For example, the week that Walmart opened in Berlin, the Aldi store across the street from the new superstore offered the same loaf of bread that Walmart was selling for US$1.13 at US$0.34. In 2001, a consumer study showed that Walmart's prices on average were 11–25 per cent higher than that of its German rivals (Knorr and Arndt, 2003). In fact, Aldi was a tough competitor who benefitted from its low prices as well as from a high degree of consumer loyalty. In 2002, more than 75 per cent of all German consumers shopped at Aldi (Gerhard and Hahn, 2005).

Walmart apparently also failed in delivering on its other value proposition – customer service that was valued by local customers. Walmart tried to transfer many of the practices used in the US stores to the German stores. For example, it trained workers to greet customers and bag their groceries but German customers did not value these practices. German customers also felt overwhelmed by the number of products that Walmart carried (Geisler, 2012).

In dealing with its employees, Walmart implemented the same human resources management practices as in the US. For example, it utilized a marketing approach to create a feeling of personnel satisfaction (the Walmart 'cheer'). When employees started a shift they were required to engage in group chants and stretching exercises, chanting 'Walmart Walmart Walmart'. This practice was meant to create group loyalty, but this and other imported codes of conduct did not go down well with Germans. Many staff found it stupid and embarrassing and hid to avoid participating in the practice (Dawson, 2009). German courts deemed other practices illegal. For example, courts ruled that Walmart could not introduce a telephone hotline for employees to inform on their colleagues, nor could it ban flirting at work. The import of US practices created a resistance among workers who sometimes felt that these practices were unjust.

Walmart also experienced problems in its approach to collective bargaining as it refused to sign a nationwide wage union negotiated tariff contract. As a response, Ver.di, the largest union in the world, organized walkouts at 30 stores. The controversy escalated as the union filed a lawsuit against Walmart for breach of Germany's financial information disclosure regulations because of its refusal to release year-end figures. The lawsuit brought Walmart to the negotiation table and resulted in a salary increase that was 0.5 per cent higher than what was initially negotiated (Jui, 2011).

Adding to its problems with unions, Walmart also refused to recognize and deal with basic consultative organizations that are present in all German firms. The chains that Walmart had acquired were unionized by the major German commercial workers' unions, HBV and DAG, and each establishment had a work council with elected personnel representatives. Walmart's US managers, unfamiliar with the central role played by the work councils, consulted them only sporadically. Work councillors claimed that they were asked to replace their regular meeting with 'company barbecues' (Dawson, 2009). Walmart violated basic social norms when it rejected the cooperative and consultative nature of German labour and management policies. This resulted in German workers picketing the stores in July 2000 to force Walmart to join the employers' association and abide by collective agreements (HBV Gewerkschaft, 2000). The fact that workers wanted to strengthen management power by forcing Walmart to join an employer association completely surprised the company, who perceived labour and management relations as adversarial. The many controversies with unions did not help Walmart in gaining support with its staff problems, whether these stemmed from Walmart's relocation of head office, its desire to use cameras to supervise labour, or when laying-off labour to reduce costs. In fact, the German court system even got involved with issues that normally would be handled between managers and work councils (Geisler, 2012).

By 2001, Walmart Germany was the focus of concerted attacks in the press by unions, the employer or trade association membership, and farmers who attacked the company's everyday low prices strategy. Many German consumers would not shop at Walmart because of its violations of German law and bad press on how it treated its employees (ibid.). Walmart's shareholders began to lose patience that the firm's investment in Germany would produce a profit (Palmer, 2005). The result was Walmart's withdrawal from the German market in mid-year 2006 to look for other investment opportunities that would produce profits more quickly for Walmart's voracious investors.

J.6 Walmart after Germany

Walmart was not discouraged from international expansion after its withdrawal from Germany. In 2002, Walmart entered the Japanese market in a joint venture, which it took full control of by 2011. In 2011, Walmart opened stores in India and South Africa and by 2015 Walmart had over 11 000 retail units and more than 2 000 000 associates worldwide and a presence in 30 countries. It is difficult to determine what managers in Walmart learned from their experience in Germany. When Walmart entered China in 1996 (a year before it entered Germany), it did so over a ten-year period starting with a limited number of retail outlets and not until 2008 did it significantly expand its operation as it bought 108 Trust-Mart stores. While Walmart failed in Germany it is still present in China. Walmart also encountered difficulties in China, for example, with unions making it difficult for it to create a distribution system. However, in China such difficulties did not result in failure and withdrawal. Walmart has had some clear successes and failures in some markets, while in other markets it has been a bit of both. Brazil is an example of the latter. Walmart entered Brazil in 1995 and in 2015 it decided to close more than 10 per cent of its outlets, resulting only in a 5 per cent cut of the sales in the market (Hunt, Watts and Bryant, 2018).

CASE DISCUSSION

1. Identify the main motive behind Walmart's expansion into Germany.
2. Identify and discuss the various kinds of managerial challenges that Walmart faced entering into Germany.
3. Discuss if Walmart's firm-specific advantage (or owner-specific advantage) was transferable to Germany.

REFERENCES

Christopherson, S. (1999), 'Rules as resources: How market governance regimes influence firm networks', in T. Barnes and M. Gertler (eds), *The New Industrial Geography: Regions, Regulations and Institutions* (pp. 155–75), London: Routledge.

Christopherson, S. (2007), 'Barriers to "US style" lean retailing: The case of Wal-Mart's failure in Germany', *Journal of Economic Geography*, 7, 451–69.

Dawson, M. (2009), 'Wal-Mart Germany revisited', *German Retail Blog*, 20 August 2009, accessed 28 January 2019 at https://www.german-retail-blog.com/topic/past-blogs/wal-mart-germany-revisited-52.

Durand, C. (2007), 'Externalities from foreign direct investment in the Mexican retailing sector', *Cambridge Journal of Economics*, 31(3), 393–411.

Gerhard, U. and B. Hahn (2005), 'Wal-Mart and Aldi: Two retail giants in Germany', *GeoJournal*, 62, 5–26.

Geisler, M. (2012), 'International marketing and Walmart's missed opportunity', undergraduate thesis, University of Arkansas, Fayetteville.

Hall, P.A. and D.W. Gingerich (2004), 'Varieties of capitalism and institutional complementarities in the macro economy', *MPIfG Discussion Paper 04/5*, Berlin: Max Planck Institute für Gesellschaftsforschung.

HBV Gewerkschaft (2000), 'Tarifsitutionen bei Wal-Mart: Wir bleiben am Ball' [Tariff settlements at Wal-Mart: We stay on the ball] (labour union pamphlet), Berlin: HBV.

Hunt, I., A. Watts and S.K. Bryant (2018), 'Walmart's international expansion: Successes and miscalculation', *Journal of Business Strategy*, 39(2), 22–9.

Jui, P. (2011), 'Walmart's downfall in Germany: A case study', *Journal of International Management*,

16 May 2011, accessed 29 January 2019 at https://journalofinternationalmanagement.wordpress.com/2011/05/16/walmarts-downfall-in-germany-a-case-study/.

Knorr, A. and A. Arndt (2003), 'Why did Wal-Mart fail in Germany?', Vol. 24 of *Materialien des Wissenschaftsschwerpunktes 'Globalisierung der Weltwirtschaft'*, Universität Bremen.

Lewis, C. (2001), 'Muscling in', *Logistics Europe*, **9**(3), 22–4.

Palmer, M. (2005), 'Crossing threshold periods in the retail firm's life cycle: Insights from Wal-Mart International', *European Management Journal*, **23**, 717–29.

Part III

Fundamental managerial challenges

9
Social capital building and knowledge transfer

9.1 Introduction

The rise and fall of Nokia is a dramatic illustration of the difficulty in maintaining competitive advantage based on a particular technology. From 1998, it was the world's largest vendor of mobile phones. However, from 2007 it began to suffer a declining market share because of the growing use of smartphones. While at the end of 2007 it had been worth more than EUR110 billion, by April 2012 its market valuation was just EUR14.7 billion. For any MNE, both imitation and innovation by other MNEs are a constant threat. These forces drove Nokia out of mobile phones altogether and into an entirely different trajectory as a telecoms equipment manufacturer. Patents provide only a measure of protection. Research we conducted as long ago as the mid-1990s indicates that firms in general have been conscious of the fragility of technology, as well as financial resources, as a source of competitive advantage for some time (Nordhaug and Gooderham, 1996). Instead, it is the competencies and knowledge of their employees that they view as the most significant source of long-term competitive advantage.

The purpose of this chapter is to present a conceptual framework or model for analysing knowledge transfer and sharing within MNEs. One key aspect to our perspective on knowledge transfer in MNEs is the role social capital plays. In this chapter, we further develop the concept and discuss how social capital can be developed by MNEs. The model we develop clarifies the initiatives required for cultivating social capital in order to achieve knowledge synergies.

9.2 The MNE as a knowledge network

In Chapter 2, we discussed Dunning's (1981, 2009) eclectic approach or 'OLI theory'. To recap: the central idea of this approach is that three conditions (ownership, location and internalization) must hold for a firm to engage in foreign direct investment. In addition to the advantage of possessing superior competencies or other valuable and rare assets, there must be reasons why geographically separated production within the same firm is preferred to centralized production. The fundamental trade-off is between economies of scale on the plant level and potential decentralization advantages such as lower factor costs, transport costs or trade barriers. Finally, the firm needs to prefer internalizing production rather than, for example, licensing production to a local firm. This could be due, for example, to difficulties in writing a licensing contract that gives the parent firm sufficient protection.

However, as we discussed in Chapter 2, by the 1990s, Dunning (1997) was arguing that the OLI paradigm needed to be radically supplemented because firms are increasingly attempting to acquire knowledge-rich subsidiaries. In other words, MNEs are no longer simply developing products at home and transferring these innovations to foreign subsidiaries, they are increasingly seeking to optimize their global innovative capabilities by incorporating subsidiary-specific advantages in different countries (Andersson et al., 2015), sometimes engaging in major research at the subsidiary level (Davis and Meyer, 2004). Thus, while some subsidiaries have no more than a sales function, one can increasingly discern subsidiaries with a developmental capacity – that is, subsidiaries that not only have the capability to adapt products but that also have the resources to enhance them or even the capability to single-handedly develop new products (Kuemmerle, 1997). In these cases, the subsidiary is the centre of excellence for particular products and technologies (Birkinshaw, 1997). Consequently, it is no longer sufficient to analyse the competitive advantage of the MNE solely in terms of location advantages in its home country (cf. Porter's 'diamond' framework, 1990, also mentioned in Chapter 6).

Given that the essence of the competitive advantage possessed by MNEs lies in their potential to combine geographically distributed competencies, the management of these competencies is now regarded as a key challenge (Morris, Zhong and Makhija, 2015). Not only do these competencies have to be generated, but they also have to be transferred across spatial and national boundaries. There is now an increasing need to communicate with colleagues either in one's own department or in other departments or subsidiaries. Knowing whom one should approach to develop a solution to a problem is thus vital in order to create synergies across the operations of the MNE.

Managers of subsidiaries, for example, need both meta-competencies, such as communication skills and cooperative abilities, and intra-organizational competencies such as knowledge about informal communication channels and power structures together with knowledge about central persons in the company. The need to blend competencies may be triggered by the recognition on the part of the MNE that there is a need to integrate certain classes of complex and sophisticated knowledge. This requires employees who not only are highly competent in their own fields but who also concomitantly possess intra-organizational MNE competencies such as knowledge about the overall strategy as well as the MNE's organizational procedures and routines.

It should be borne in mind that for an increasingly significant proportion of MNEs, knowledge transfer is not necessarily unidirectional (from corporate headquarters to subsidiaries), but bi-directional or even multidirectional between knowledge-rich equals (cf. Cantwell, 1989, 1994). This notion of the MNE as a knowledge network has given rise to concepts such as 'heterarchy' (Hedlund, 1986) and some scholars have proposed an evolutionary theory of the MNE in order to better capture the knowledge-sharing aspect of MNEs.

9.3 Evolutionary theory of the MNE

Internalization theory explains the existence of MNEs in terms of firm boundary questions. For example, Buckley and Casson (1976) argued that because of market failure (see Chapter 4) in relation to knowledge-based assets, especially non-codifiable knowledge assets, the cost of internalization is less than the cost of using the market. In a similar way, Rugman (1980, p. 368) contends that internalization arises because there is no proper market, 'for the sale of the information created by the MNE and therefore no price for it. [Therefore] the MNE is driven to create an internal market of its own in order to overcome the failure of an external market to emerge for the sale of information'. Because of market failure, firms become MNEs as they internalize the markets for their knowledge assets in multiple locations. Internalization remains the solution as long as the cost of internalization is less than the cost of using the market (see also Chapter 4).

An alternative explanation of the existence of the MNE is the so-called 'evolutionary theory' of the MNE (Kogut and Zander, 1993, 1996). At the core of their theory of the MNE is the notion of the firm as specializing in the transfer and recombination of knowledge. 'The multinational corporation arises not out of the failure of markets for the buying and selling of knowledge, but out of its superior efficiency as an organizational vehicle by which to transfer this knowledge across borders' (Kogut and Zander, 1993, p. 625).

Further, '(the MNE) should be understood as a social community specializing in the speed and efficiency in the creation and transfer of knowledge' (Kogut and Zander, 1996, p. 503). That is, organizations have the potential to develop particular capabilities that enable them to share knowledge in a way that is superior to that of the market. Evolutionary theory challenges the notion that firms are internalized markets, viewing them instead as 'social communities' that unlike markets support the transfer and sharing of tacit, socially embedded knowledge. It challenges the assumption that market imperfections, not ownership advantages, explain the boundaries of the firm, asking, 'is it not possible that the nature of the firm's advantage, as resting in the cooperative rules among employees, will influence its scope of activities?' (Kogut and Zander, 1993, p. 638).

Evolutionary theory is controversial and has its critics (see, e.g., Love, 1995). Forsgren (2013, p. 71) is particularly scathing about the notion of 'social community'. In this sense:

> [. . .]the multinational firm is more like one big happy family. . . The somewhat extreme view adopted in internalization theory whereby human beings are considered to be 'cheaters and shirkers' is substituted by a similarly extreme view of them as 'altruistic' beings with no interest in maximizing their own interests at the cost of the organization as a whole.

In short, he views evolutionary theory as naive.

While our view is that the potential for 'market failure' is an important component in explaining the existence of firms, we do not dismiss the notion of the 'firm-specific advantage' (FSA). However, in order for the firm to exploit its FSAs (see Chapter 1) it must have a mechanism that promotes knowledge sharing. We now turn our attention to the kinds of capabilities and management-initiated practices managers of MNEs must develop in order to ensure effective knowledge transfer across the MNE.

9.4 Knowledge transfer in MNEs

While the possession of knowledge-based assets endows an MNE with the potential to derive advantageous synergies, a distinct ability to transfer knowledge and other competencies efficiently is also required. The application of social capital theory has contributed important insights into the processes underlying knowledge transfer within the MNE. However, this perspective needs to be supplemented in two ways. First, there is a need to take into account the influence of the external environment. Second, there is a need to specify the capabilities, in the form of management-initiated practices, required to promote and maintain social capital. The latter include transmission channels, socialization mechanisms and motivational mechanisms. These mechanisms represent the key modifiable elements in facilitating knowledge flows. In the following, we present a conceptual model for the study of intra-MNE knowledge transfer that embraces the various facets of social capital, the influence of the external environment and modifiable practices (Gooderham, 2007).

The possession by MNEs of these knowledge transfer capabilities cannot be taken for granted. This is of particular significance because a growing body of research argues that MNEs that have these knowledge transfer capabilities are more productive (Inkpen and Tsang, 2005; Tsai and Ghoshal, 1998). Thus, it is important to consider those practices or mechanisms that reduce the difficulties in transferring knowledge from one unit of an MNE to another. For successful knowledge transfer to occur there must be significant internal coordination in the sense of organizational capabilities that are consistent over time and that promote linkages across units. These capabilities consist of specific strategic and organizational commitments to particular practices and processes that enable the MNE to design and implement new resource configurations (Eisenhardt and Martin, 2000).

9.5 The concept of knowledge transfer

Four types of knowledge

Polanyi (1958 [1962]) distinguished explicit and tacit knowledge. The former is objective in the sense that it can be codified in, for example, scientific formulas and manuals, whereas the latter is subjective and experiential and therefore hard to formalize (Nonaka, 1994; Nonaka, Toyama and Nagata, 2000). Because explicit knowledge is easily transmitted, it is readily imitated by competitors and therefore unlikely to be a source of competitive advantage. In contrast, tacit knowledge, because it is non-codifiable, is difficult to assess from the outside and therefore has a stronger potential to generate distinctive competitive positions abroad. However, it is precisely tacit knowledge that is difficult to transfer, particularly when the knowledge overlap between the source and recipient is limited (Szulanski, 1996).

Kogut and Zander (1992, p. 386) employ a similar distinction. They use the terms 'know-what' for relatively articulable knowledge (i.e., explicit knowledge or information), and 'know-how' for 'the accumulated practical skill or expertise that allows one to do something smoothly and efficiently' (i.e., tacit knowledge). Gupta and Govindarajan (2000) have further elaborated this distinction by viewing 'know-how' as 'procedural' types of knowledge, including: (1) marketing know-how; (2) distribution know-how; (3) packaging-design technology; (4) product designs; (5) process designs; (6) purchasing designs; and (7) management systems and procedures. These contrast with 'declarative' types of knowledge such as monthly financial data. The focus in our context is effectively on these forms of 'procedural' or 'know-how' types of knowledge.

DiMaggio and Powell (1983) emphasize the socially embedded nature of knowledge. Knowing is a social act, the tools we use for thinking and acting, the categories available to us through which we know are the products of social action and negotiation. Thus, the social institutions in which we partake frame the ways we know. In this view, expertise is a property of social groups (Hakkarainen et al., 2004). In his knowledge-based theory of the firm, Spender (1996) proposed that in addition to distinguishing explicit and tacit knowledge one should distinguish individual from social knowledge. Spender refers to knowledge that is both tacit and social as 'collective' knowledge. Spender (ibid., p. 52) argues that in terms of organizational advantage 'it is collective knowledge [that] is the most secure and strategically significant kind of organizational knowledge'.

Collective knowledge is such that individuals can only be proficient once they are 'socialized' into the organization and 'have acquired much of the collective knowledge that underpins "the way things are done around here"' (ibid., p. 54). In other words, knowledge acquisition and its transfer within an organization are dependent on sustained exposure to that organization's collective knowledge.

Spender's knowledge-based theory of the firm results in four generic knowledge types (Figure 9.1). Drawing on Fenton-O'Creevy et al. (2011) we will now distinguish these four forms of knowledge.

Conscious knowledge is held by individuals and comprises established standards of practice that are a product of their technical training. *Automatic knowl-*

Figure 9.1 Different types of organizational knowledge

	Individual	Social
Explicit	Conscious	Objectified
Implicit	Automatic	Collective

edge is also held by individuals but is more psychological in the sense that it comprises the hunches, intuition and automatic skills of individuals. The *objectified knowledge* of a firm comprises its intellectual property such as its patents and registered designs, as well as its canonical knowledge embodied in forms, manuals, databases and IT systems. Finally, the *collective knowledge* of a firm comprises key aspects of its organizational culture that involve distinct, firm-specific processes of knowledge production underpinned by emergent idiosyncratic practices and rules. Such knowledge may be relatively unknown from individual actors but is accessible and sustained through their interaction (Spender, 1994).

For a given firm these four elements collectively constitute its intellectual capital. While these four elements are interdependent, Nahapiet and Ghoshal (1998) distinguish the two types of social knowledge in their analysis of what constitutes a firm's organizational advantage. Further, they argue that it is the two types of social knowledge that distinguish individuals working within an organization from individuals working at arm's length across a hypothetical market.

Knowledge transfer

In line with Bresman, Birkinshaw and Nobel (1999), we use the concept of transfer of knowledge to refer to the accumulation or assimilation of new knowledge in the receiving unit. However, like Minbaeva et al. (2003, p. 587), we would also specify that: '[t]he key element in knowledge transfer is not the underlying (original) knowledge, but rather the extent to which the receiver acquires potentially useful knowledge and utilizes this knowledge in its own operations'. In other words, for transfer to have taken place, not only has some change in knowledge or performance in the recipient unit occurred (Inkpen and Tsang, 2005) but through social interaction the underlying or original knowledge may have undergone profound change that affects both transfer and recipient. As such, 'knowledge sharing' rather than 'knowledge transfer' may be a more appropriate concept.

9.6 Determinants of knowledge transfer

Theorization on the determinants of knowledge transfer in MNEs has focused both on the MNE's external environment and on its internal environment. In terms of the latter, building on existing knowledge-based theories of the firm, Nahapiet and Ghoshal (1998) argue that social capital theory provides a sound basis for identifying the capabilities organizations are uniquely equipped to develop for the sharing of knowledge. Social capital, they contend, increases the efficiency of knowledge transfer because it encourages cooperative behaviour. They propose that differences between firms in terms of knowledge transfer may represent differences in their ability to create and exploit social capital. They distinguish three dimensions of social capital: the relational, the cognitive and the structural.

The *relational* dimension of social capital refers to facets of personal relationships such as trust, obligations, respect and even friendship that together increase the motivation to engage in knowledge exchange and teamwork. The significance of this dimension of social capital as a driver of knowledge flows has received empirical support through case studies conducted by Bresman et al. (1999) of three MNEs that had acquired companies with the main objective of gaining access to and utilizing the acquired companies' R&D knowledge. Their analysis indicates that in the early stages of an acquisition the lack of personal relationships between acquirer and acquisition made it very difficult for either party to trust in the abilities of the others. In this phase, knowledge transfer is limited to imposed, unidirectional knowledge transfer of a 'know-what' type from the parent to the subsidiary. It is not until the acquired company is fully integrated in the sense that trust has been established and that there is therefore a perception that 'the risk of opportunistic behavior is low' (ibid., p. 442) that a high level of reciprocal knowledge flow of a 'know-how' variety occurs.

This clearly underscores the significance of the relational dimension of social capital for knowledge transfer. Using data from the subsidiary units of a large multinational electronics company, Tsai and Ghoshal (1998) also indicate support for this relationship. Finally, Hansen and Løvås's (2004) research on knowledge transfer from new product development teams situated in a focal subsidiary of a large US high-technology MNE supports the notion that good informal relations are of critical importance for these teams to engage in competence transfers with subsidiaries without related competences. In short, the greater the degree of relational social capital that has been developed across the MNE, the greater the degree of knowledge transfer.

The *cognitive* dimension refers to shared interpretations and systems of meaning, and shared language and codes that provide the foundation for communication. Tsai and Ghoshal (1998) found empirical support for the idea that the role of the cognitive dimension of social capital lies in facilitating the development of the relational dimension of social capital rather than directly on knowledge transfer. In other words, sharing 'a view of the world' is a prerequisite for sufficient levels of trust to be developed, which in turn stimulates knowledge exchange. The greater the degree of cognitive social capital that has been developed between units, the greater the degree of relational social capital between them.

Nahapiet and Ghoshal's (1998) concept of social capital contains a third dimension, that of *structural* capital. The structural dimension of social capital refers to the presence or absence of specific network or social interaction ties between units of the MNE and the overall configuration of these ties. As such, it is not directly associated with the transfer of knowledge. Instead, its significance for the transfer of knowledge is through the ways in which it 'influences the development of the relational and cognitive dimensions of social capital' (ibid., pp. 251–2). Network ties facilitate social interaction, which in turn stimulates the development of the cognitive and relational dimensions of social capital. Thus, a precondition for the development and maintenance of relational and cognitive dimensions of social capital is that of sustained social interaction. Moreover, particularly rich patterns of interaction are important when the knowledge to be transferred is not codified.

Empirical support for the importance of social interaction ties can be found in the case studies conducted by Bresman et al. (1999). They found that technological know-how is best transferred through intensive communication, with many visits and meetings, because it facilitates the development of a common set of beliefs and values. In other words, social interaction is a key mechanism for the leveraging of knowledge because it effectuates the development of the cognitive and relational dimensions of social capital. Thus, the structural dimension of social capital is a necessary prerequisite for the emergence of the cognitive dimension of social capital, which in turn facilitates the development of the relational dimension of capital, which leads to the transfer and exchange of 'know-how'.

If it is the case that sufficient degrees of relational social capital must be in place to enable the transfer of 'know-how' and that this is dependent on a sufficient degree of cognitive social capital and structural social capital, the issue is then how best to develop these two latter forms of social capital. However, prior to examining this issue we shall consider the impact of the external environment on the formation of these two forms of social capital.

9.7 The external environment of the MNE

In terms of the external environment, Ghemawat's (2001) CAGE distance framework that we introduced in Chapter 1 distinguishes various dimensions that impact on the formation of inter-unit MNE social capital, including geographic distance, cultural distance and economic distance. Hansen and Løvås's (2004) study referred to above does indeed confirm that large spatial distance reduces the tendency for the facilitation of competence transfers even when the transferor and the receiver have related competences. Thus, it remains the case that because long-distance travel is expensive and time-consuming, geographical distance is a barrier to developing structural social capital.

Cultural distance, in the sense of a common language and a common administrative heritage (colony/colonizer), is also reported as a critical dimension for cross-border economic activity (Ghemawat and Mallick, 2003). In other words, there are initial steep costs involved in moving out of one's culturally proximate area because of the difficulties in creating a common language and shared interpretations. Thus, Bresman et al. (1999) found that in the early stages of an acquisition, the lack of cognitive social capital is accentuated by cultural distance. For US MNEs, the costs in terms of performance stemming from cultural distance appear to manifest themselves as an inverted J-curve (Gomes and Ramaswamy, 1999). This is because while initially US MNEs tend to locate foreign activities in Canada, the UK and Australia – that is, culturally proximate areas – a performance decline sets in when they move outside these areas. The curve appears to be different for Western European MNEs in that Ruigrok and Wagner's (2003) research indicates a U-form in terms of performance for German MNEs. German firms have only very limited culturally proximate areas to move into (Austria and parts of Switzerland) and are therefore immediately confronted by cultural non-proximity when engaging in foreign activities. As such, German MNEs expect to and therefore have experience of making the effort required for the development of a shared language and a common vision regardless of setting (McFadyen and Cannella, 2004). However, as cultural distance increases, the investment in creating social capital means that the first stage of the 'U' becomes steadily deeper and more prolonged.

Economic distance also appears to play a significant role concerning the formation of cognitive social capital. Gupta and Govindarajan's (2000) investigation of parent–subsidiary knowledge flows suggests that effectuating the flow is actually significantly more challenging when the subsidiary is an acquisition in a country with a relatively high per capita income. At first sight, this is a strange finding. However, given that high per capita income is usually associated with high levels of education and therefore self-confidence, it may be the case that the 'not-invented-here' syndrome kicks in in these locations.

9.8 The role of management-initiated practices

Given the impact of the external environment on inter-unit social interaction and the formation of cognitive social capital, having dynamic capabilities in the form of routines and practices that negate the impact of the external environment and that promote the development and maintenance of social interaction and the cognitive facets of social capital, is critical. Without such routines, knowledge synergies will be difficult, if not impossible, to achieve (Eisenhardt and Martin, 2000; Nonaka et al., 2000). Indeed, both Reger's (1997) and De Meyer's (1995) research indicated a considerable amount of effort by MNEs in developing mechanisms and practices that facilitate social interaction and the development of common sets of meaning. All in all, the research indicates three sets of practices or mechanisms that MNEs apply in varying degrees: transmission channels, socialization mechanisms and motivational mechanisms.

The first set of practices, *transmission channels*, features prominently in Gupta and Govindarajan's (2000) study of knowledge flows within MNEs and is of primary importance for social interaction. By transmission channels, they mean formal integrative mechanisms such as liaison personnel, inter-unit task forces and permanent international committees. Using the concept of formal proximity in the sense of units being formally grouped together and reporting to the same business or divisional manager, Hansen and Løvås's (2004) study also supports the significance of transmission channels in generating social interaction in the face of spatial distance.

Additionally, one may observe the use and significance of intranet systems as transmission channels. As early as 2000, Teigland's study of a multinational IT company noted the importance of intranet 'communities' as sources of knowledge for technical employees. He records that: '[t]his is a curious discovery because these "communities" exhibit many of the characteristics of communities of practice – reciprocity, identity, and so on – but the individuals have typically never met' (Teigland, 2000, p. 143). IBM (2004) has also documented the emergence of the intranet as a transmission channel. In 2003, 71 per cent of IBM's employees regarded the IBM corporate intranet, 'w3', as vital to their jobs as opposed to only 28 per cent in 1997 (ibid.). One effect of 'w3' is that it has spawned 'communities of practice' – that is, global communities of IBM professionals centred on particular domains of knowledge and focused on sharing both 'know-what' and 'know-how' across organizational boundaries. These are supplemented by 'BluePages' that list employees worldwide and their areas of expertise, 'World Jam Sessions' (virtual brain-storming events centred around a selected topic over a 72-hour period that employees are obliged to participate in), 'Buddy Networks' (virtual social communities), e-mail and telephone conferences. IBM also employs a number of more traditional communication channels such as global forums, face-to-face meetings and workshops. It is hence likely that the greater the magnitude of transmission channels between MNE parent and subsidiary, the greater the degree of structural social capital between them.

We have argued that the structural social capital dimension influences the cognitive dimension of social capital. However, social interaction ties in themselves may not be sufficient for a shared language and shared systems of meaning to emerge. The implication is that the development of the cognitive dimension of social capital requires particular attention by MNE managers. A number of researchers have observed the importance of mechanisms that promote the internalization of MNE-wide shared goals and mutual understandings (Reiche, Harzing and Pudelko, 2015). These *socialization mechanisms* have to be so potent that they are effective despite the impact of cultural distance and the 'not-invented-here' mentality MNEs often confront. One approach is to organize diversity training designed to help employees work effectively as part of a culturally heterogeneous workforce, to become aware of group-based differences among employees, and to decrease negative stereotyping and prejudice. Another involves training key employees in all host countries in the common language of the company (Caligiuri, Lazarova and Tarique, 2005). Gupta and Govindarajan (2000) identify vertical mechanisms such as job transfers to corporate headquarters and participation in corporate mentoring programmes as playing an important role in employee socialization into the MNE corporate culture. Tsang's (2001) case studies of Singapore-owned operations in China indicated the importance of Chinese managers not only spending time at corporate headquarters but also in other parts of the MNE. Supplementing these training initiatives is the design of performance appraisal that enables individuals to reflect on behaviours that are inconsistent with the shared corporate goals (Björkman, Barner-Rasmussen and Li, 2004; Minbaeva et al., 2003). Early mentoring of new employees by experienced veterans of the firm is also used by, for example, IBM.

Kyriakidou (2005, p. 112) cautions that:

> [d]eveloping integrating competencies and skills in a diverse group should not be an attempt to make it more homogeneous; rather these capacities should create a mechanism where individuals can retain their dimensions of diversity (which are inherently valuable for a variety of group tasks), while at the same

time avoiding such damaging processes as dysfunctional interpersonal conflict, miscommunication, higher levels of stress, slower decision making and problems with group cohesiveness.

Whereas socialization mechanisms involve occasional, formalized programmes and are aimed at groups of employees, *motivational mechanisms* are much more constant and are often aimed at individual employees. The motivational disposition of the sender and the receiver are key elements in successful knowledge transfer (Gupta and Govindarajan, 2000). By rewarding certain types of behaviour, motivational mechanisms contribute to a common understanding of what matters to the MNE. Motivational mechanisms may be divided into the use of extrinsic and intrinsic rewards. Several studies investigating the role of the use of extrinsic rewards (such as individual-level bonuses) for knowledge transfer indicate that they are counterproductive because they undermine the development of social capital (Bock et al., 2005; Frey, 1997). One explanation for this phenomenon might be that when pecuniary rewards are introduced, an incentive for the individual to withhold knowledge for future gains is also introduced. In terms of the recipient, extrinsic incentives may well encourage the adoption of transferred knowledge, but the transfer cost efficiency will be poor (Andersson et al., 2015). In short, the implication is that extrinsic incentives and knowledge sharing do not mix. Osterloh and Frey (2000) argue that only intrinsic motivation such as the expectation that knowledge contributions will be acknowledged by colleagues and superiors facilitates successful knowledge transfer. Gooderham, Minbaeva and Pedersen (2011) compared the impact of intrinsic and extrinsic rewards on social capital and knowledge transfer in MNEs. They found strong empirical support for the benefit for social capital of using intrinsic rewards, whereas extrinsic rewards had detrimental consequences.

However, it would be too simplistic to conclude that extrinsic rewards can never have positive consequences for knowledge sharing. One factor to take into consideration is the degree of global integration. In MNEs that are loosely integrated, extrinsic rewards may play a role, at least initially. Research by Dasí et al. (2017) makes an important distinction between knowledge sharing within business units and between business units. Business units comprise both global headquarters and subsidiaries. Their investigation of knowledge sharing in a multidomestic MNE with comparatively independent business units suggests that while intrinsic motivation is a relatively important driver of knowledge sharing within business units, extrinsic motivation is relatively more important for knowledge sharing across business units. However, they also found that those employees that had participated in corporate employee development – a socialization mechanism – were also more likely to share knowledge across business units. We may speculate that as more employees have the opportunity to partake in corporate employee development, extrinsic rewards will be of less importance. When initiating practices that have as their ultimate aim to enhance knowledge sharing across business units, it is critical that MNE managers have a realistic notion of the degree of global integration that exists. When there is very little integration, Dasí et al.'s findings suggest that extrinsic motivation could play a positive role.

9.9 Conceptual model

Figure 9.2 summarizes our discussion of knowledge transfer in MNEs. Although the model is conceived in linear terms, this is obviously somewhat simplistic. Undoubtedly one could posit a bi-directional effect between, for example, the transfer of knowledge and the degree of relational social capital and between the degree of cognitive social capital and the degree of relational social capital.

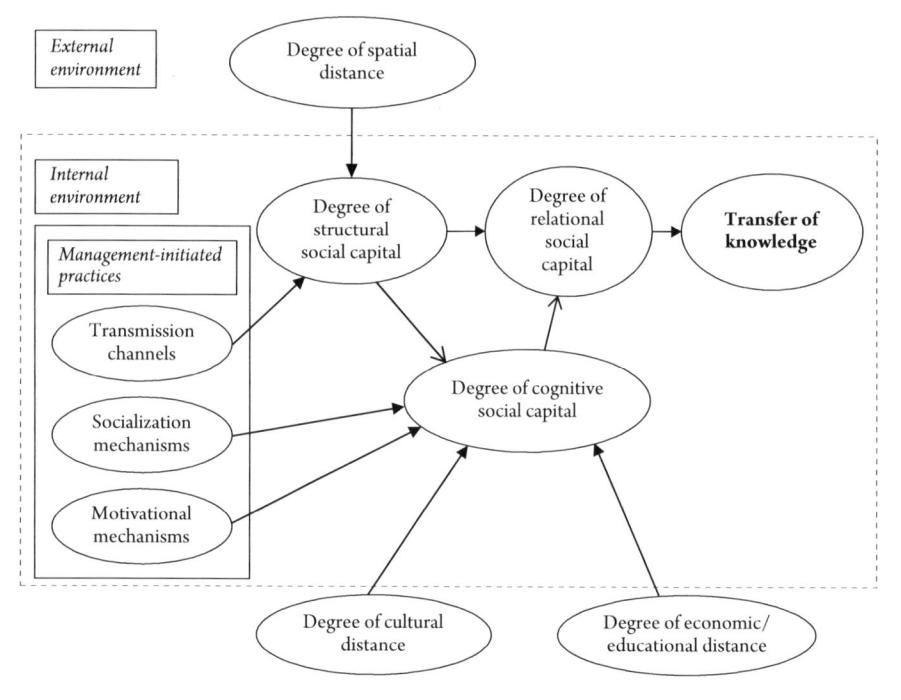

Source: Gooderham (2007).

Figure 9.2 A dynamic capabilities-driven conceptual model of the determinants of knowledge transfer in MNCs

The model proposes that successful leveraging of 'know-how' through its transfer across MNEs is directly dependent on the development of the relational dimension of social capital characterized not least by trust between units. The model further proposes that this relational dimension of social capital is in part a product of the degree of structural social capital and cognitive social capital that have been developed. This is largely congruent with the work of Nahapiet and Ghoshal (1998) and Tsai and Ghoshal (1998). However, the model also takes into account the impact of the external environment in relation to the formation of structural and cognitive social capital.

Finally, in order to augment the structural and cognitive dimensions of social capital the model also specifies a number of practices that can be developed and applied by managers. Thus, whereas the degree of parent–subsidiary cultural, spatial and economic distance is fixed, the model proposes that the selection and application of transmission channels, socialization mechanisms and appropriate motivational mechanisms are factors that can be influenced by managers. Not only can they determine the degree of social interaction and the development of a common language and set of meanings, they can also indirectly mitigate the impact of cultural, geographic and economic distance. Thus, a management perspective is at the core of the model in the sense that it is the purposeful design, selection and combination of transmission channels, socialization mechanisms and (primarily intrinsic) motivational mechanisms that are the key to developing the various dimensions of social capital that are key to knowledge transfer.

From a practitioner perspective, the model may, in an initial phase, be used as a means to identify and calibrate existing management-initiated practices aimed at creating the foundation for the transfer of 'know-how'. Thereafter practitioners can use it to guide them in their future efforts and investments for the achievement of those social capital foundations that research indicates are of significance for knowledge transfer within MNEs. This latter use of the model means that it has the added potential to function as a decision-making tool in relation to the acquisition of knowledge-rich subsidiaries by clarifying the initiatives required for knowledge synergies.

9.10 Summary

In this chapter, our focus has been on knowledge transfer in MNEs and their subsidiaries. We introduce a model that explains key sources of variation in the ability of MNEs to transfer and share knowledge in the face of spatial, cultural, economic and educational distance. The model not only considers the relationship between the three dimensions of social capital but also delineates the dynamic capabilities that condition the development of a social context that promotes knowledge transfer. The development of these dynamic capabilities is dependent on purposeful action and investment not least on the part of MNE managers. Thus, the model is not only a response to the need to understand variations in knowledge transfer but also a response to practitioner needs to augment their understanding of those organizational mechanisms and practices that enhance the efficient intra-MNE transfer of knowledge. The model may be used to analyse the case study that follows this chapter, that of the Scandinavian Food Company and its efforts to enhance sharing knowledge across its subsidiaries.

REFERENCES

Andersson, U., A. Gaur, R. Mudambi and M. Persson (2015), 'Unpacking interunit knowledge transfer in multinational enterprises', *Global Strategy Journal*, **5**(3), 241–55.

Birkinshaw, J. (1997), 'Entrepreneurship in multinational corporations: The characteristics of subsidiary initiatives', *Strategic Management Journal*, **18**(3), 207–29.

Björkman, I., W. Barner-Rasmussen and L. Li (2004), 'Managing knowledge transfer in MNCs: The impact of headquarters control mechanisms', *Journal of International Business Studies*, **35**(5), 443–55.

Bock, G., R. Zmud, Y. Kim and J. Lee (2005), 'Behavioral intention formation in knowledge sharing: Examining the roles of extrinsic motivators, social-psychological forces, and organizational climate', *MIS Quarterly*, **29**(1), 87–111.

Bresman, H., J. Birkinshaw and R. Nobel (1999), 'Knowledge transfer in international acquisitions', *Journal of International Business Studies*, **30**(3), 439–62.

Buckley, P.J. and M.C. Casson (1976), *The Future of the Multinational Enterprise*, London: Macmillan.

Caligiuri, P., M. Lazarova and I. Tarique (2005), 'Training, learning and development in multinational organizations', in H. Scullion and M. Lineham (eds), *International Human Resource Management: A Critical Text* (pp. 71–90), Basingstoke, UK: Palgrave Macmillan.

Cantwell, J. (1989), *Technological Innovation and Multinational Corporations*, Oxford: Blackwell.

Cantwell, J. (ed.) (1994), 'Introduction: Transactional corporations and innovatory activities', in *Transactional Corporations and Innovatory Activities*, London: Routledge.

Dasí, À., T. Pedersen and P.N. Gooderham et al. (2017), 'The effect of organizational separation on individuals' knowledge sharing in MNEs', *Journal of World Business*, **52**(3), 431–46.

Davis, L.N. and K.E. Meyer (2004), 'Subsidiary research and development, and the local environment', *International Business Review*, **13**(2), 359–82.

De Meyer, A. (1995), 'Tech talk', in J. Drew (ed.), *Readings in International Enterprise* (pp. 179–95), London: Routledge.

DiMaggio, P.J. and W.W. Powell (1983), 'The iron cage revisited: Institutional isomorphism and collective rationality in organizational fields', *American Sociological Review*, **48**(2), 147–60.

Dunning, J.H. (1981), *International Production and the Multinational Enterprise*, London: George Allen and Unwin.

Dunning, J.H. (1997), 'The sourcing of technological advantage by multinational enterprises', in K. Macharzina, M.J. Oesterle and J. Wolf (eds), *Global Business in the Information Age* (pp. 63–101), proceedings of the 23rd Annual EIBA Conference, Stuttgart.

Dunning, J.H. (2009), 'Location and the multinational enterprise: A neglected factor?', *Journal of International Business Studies*, **40**(1), 5–19.

Eisenhardt, K. and J.A. Martin (2000), 'Dynamic capabilities: What are they?', *Strategic Management Journal*, Special Issue, **21**(10/11), pp. 1105–22.
Fenton-O'Creevy, M., P.N. Gooderham, J.-L. Cerdin and R. Rønning (2011), 'Bridging roles, social skill and embedded knowing in multinational organizations', in M. Geppert and C. Dörrenbächer (eds), *Politics and Power in the Multinational Corporation* (pp. 101–38), Cambridge, UK: Cambridge University Press.
Forsgren, M. (2013), *Theories of the Multinational Firm*, 2nd edition, Cheltenham, UK and Northampton, MA, USA: Edward Elgar Publishing.
Frey, B. (1997), *Not Just for the Money*, Cheltenham, UK and Lyme, NH: Edward Elgar Publishing.
Ghemawat, P. (2001), 'Distance still matters: The hard reality of global expansion', *Harvard Business Review*, **79**(8), 137–47.
Ghemawat, P. and R. Mallick (2003), 'The industry-level structure of international trade networks: A gravity-based approach', *HBS Working Paper*, February 2003.
Gomes, L. and K. Ramaswamy (1999), 'An empirical examination of the form of the relationship between multinationality and performance', *Journal of International Business Studies*, **30**(1), 173–88.
Gooderham, P.N. (2007), 'Enhancing knowledge transfer in multinational corporations: A dynamic capabilities driven model', *Knowledge Management Research and Practice*, **5**(1), 34–43.
Gooderham, P.N., D.B. Minbaeva and T. Pedersen (2011), 'Governance mechanisms for the promotion of social capital for knowledge transfer in multinational corporations', *Journal of Management Studies*, **48**(1), 123–50.
Gupta, A.K. and V. Govindarajan (2000), 'Knowledge flows within multinational corporations', *Strategic Management Journal*, **21**(4), 473–96.
Hakkarainen, K., T. Palonen, S. Paavola and E. Lehtinen (2004), *Communities of Networked Expertise: Professional and Educational Perspectives*, 1st edition, London: Elsevier.
Hansen, M.T. and B. Løvås (2004), 'Leveraging technological competencies', *Strategic Management Journal*, **25**(8–9), 801–22.
Hedlund, G. (1986), 'The hypermodern MNC: A heterarchy', *Human Resource Management*, **25**, 9–36.
IBM (2004), *Corporate Responsibility Report*, accessed 1 August 2006 at http://www.ibm.com/ibm/responsibility.
Inkpen, A.C. and E.W.K. Tsang (2005), 'Social capital, networks and knowledge transfer', *Academy of Management Review*, **30**(1), 146–65.
Kogut, B. and U. Zander (1992), 'Knowledge of the firm, combinative capabilities and the replication of technology', *Organization Science*, **3**(2), 383–97.
Kogut, B. and U. Zander (1993), 'Knowledge of the firm and the evolutionary theory of the multinational corporation', *Journal of International Business Studies*, **24**(4), 625–45.
Kogut, B. and U. Zander (1996), 'What do firms do? Coordination, identity and learning', *Organization Science*, **7**(5), 502–18.
Kuemmerle, W. (1997), 'Building effective R&D capabilities abroad', *Harvard Business Review*, March–April, 61–70.
Kyriakidou, O. (2005), 'Operational aspects of international human resource management', in M. Özbilgin (ed.), *International Human Resource Management: Theory and Practice*, Basingstoke, UK: Palgrave Macmillan.
Love, J.H. (1995), 'Knowledge, market failure and the multinational enterprise: A theoretical note', *Journal of International Business Studies*, **26**(2), 399–407.
McFadyen, M.A. and A.A. Cannella (2004), 'Social capital and knowledge creation: Diminishing returns of the number and strength of exchange relationships', *Academy of Management Journal*, **47**(5), 735–46.

Minbaeva, D., T. Pedersen and I. Björkman et al. (2003), 'MNC knowledge transfer, subsidiary absorptive capacity, and HRM', *Journal of International Business Studies*, **34**(6), 586–99.

Morris, S.S., B. Zhong and M. Makhija (2015), 'Going the distance: The pros and cons of expanding employees' global knowledge reach', *Journal of International Business Studies*, **46**(5), 552–73.

Nahapiet, J. and S. Ghoshal (1998), 'Social capital, intellectual capital, and the organizational advantage', *Academy of Management Review*, **23**(2), 242–66.

Nonaka, I. (1994), 'A dynamic theory of organizational knowledge creation', *Organization Science*, **5**(1), 14–37.

Nonaka, I., R. Toyama and A. Nagata (2000), 'A firm as a knowledge-creating entity: A new perspective on the theory of the firm', *Industrial and Corporate Change*, **9**(1), 1–20.

Nordhaug, O. and P.N. Gooderham (1996), *Kompetanseutvikling i næringslivet* [Competence Development in Companies], Oslo: Cappelen Akademisk Forlag.

Osterloh, M. and B. Frey (2000), 'Motivation, knowledge transfer and organizational form', *Organization Science*, **11**(5), 538–50.

Polanyi, M. (1958 [1962]), *Personal Knowledge: Towards a Post-Critical Philosophy*, London: Routledge and Kegan Paul.

Porter, M.E. (1990), 'The competitive advantage of nations', *Harvard Business Review*, March–April, 73–93.

Reger, G. (1997), 'Internationalization and coordination of R&D of western European and Japanese multinational corporations', in K. Macharzina M.-J. Oesterle and J. Wolf (eds), *Global Business in the Information Age* (Vol. 2, pp. 573–604), Proceedings of the 23rd Annual EIBA Conference, Stuttgart, 14–16 December 1997.

Reiche, B.S., A.W. Harzing and M. Pudelko (2015), 'Why and how does shared language affect subsidiary knowledge inflows? A social identity perspective', *Journal of International Business Studies*, **46**(5), 528–51.

Rugman, A. (1980), 'Internalization as a general theory of foreign direct investment: A re-appraisal of the literature', *Weltwirtschaftliches Archiv*, **116**, 365–79.

Ruigrok, W. and H. Wagner (2003), 'Internationalization and performance: An organizational learning perspective', *Management International Review*, **43**(1), 63–83.

Spender, J.-C. (1994), 'Organizational knowledge, collective practice, and Penrosian rents', *International Business Review*, **3**(4), 353–67.

Spender, J.-C. (1996), 'Making knowledge the basis of a dynamic theory of the firm', *Strategic Management Journal*, **17**(10), 45–62.

Szulanski, G. (1996), 'Exploring internal stickiness: Impediments to the transfer of best practice within the firm', *Strategic Management Journal*, **17**(Special Issue), 27–43.

Teigland, R. (2000), 'Communities of practice', in J. Birkinshaw and P. Hagström (eds), *The Flexible Firm*, Oxford: Oxford University Press.

Tsai, W. and S. Ghoshal (1998), 'Social capital and value creation: The role of intrafirm networks', *Academy of Management Journal*, **41**, 464–76.

Tsang, E.W.K. (2001), 'Managerial learning in foreign-invested enterprises of China', *Management International Review*, **41**(1), 29–51.

Case K

SFC: From multidomestic to globally integrated – when local taste matters*

Paul N. Gooderham

K.1 Introduction

Multidomestic MNEs with structures that resemble federative rather than unitary organizations have been common particularly among European MNEs and above all in industries such as foodstuffs, where local taste matters (Bartlett and Ghoshal, 1989). Characteristic features of such MNEs are that their subsidiaries have a national focus and substantial latitude to forge locally oriented strategies. Present theory suggests that when multidomestic MNEs engage in making the transition to a globally integrated strategy they are confronted by the very conditions that enable them to maintain local taste – that is, the decentralization of decision making and the concomitant loose coupling of the organization. Consequently, extant theory points to a political and a social network challenge.

To illustrate this challenge, this case study features a Scandinavian multi-domestic MNE, Scandinavian Food Company (SFC), which has been engaged in the transition to a more integrated strategy for nearly a decade. More specifically, we focus on the attempts by the corporate centre to integrate the purchasing activities of its group of subsidiaries. We compare its early, and largely unsuccessful, initiative to achieve purchasing integration with its more recent, largely successful, initiative.

The case is structured as follows. First, we revisit extant theory that identifies two significant barriers to moving from a multidomestic to a global strategy. The first of these is political and the second concerns the lack of social networks across subsidiaries and the concomitant difficulty of facilitating knowledge transfer. We then present the case of SFC and its main subsidiaries, Voso (Norway), Pelecta (Poland) and Pitana (Czech Republic) (all names anonymized at the request of the company). We compare SFC's two contrasting efforts at integrating the purchasing activities of its subsidiaries.

K.2 Revisiting extant theory

For multidomestic MNEs, particularly those operating in industries where local adaptation continues to matter, product standardization is clearly problematic. Thus, for example, MNEs located within the food industry, where meeting local taste sensibilities is of critical importance, cannot disregard the issue of local responsiveness regarding their end products. To a significant extent, they must retain their ability to be experienced by local consumers as, to employ SFC's concept, 'local taste champions'. However, the integration and centralization of underlying activities such as purchasing and production is in principle viable. In practice though, the integration of such activities by multidomestic MNEs will involve having to confront two particular barriers that to a significant extent are products of their multidomestic heritage. The first derives from the polity of multidomestic MNEs and the second from the lack of social networks between subsidiaries. Either of these has the potential to block the transition from a multidomestic to a global strategy.

The political challenge

'Power (in MNEs) is far from being just a question of ownership' (Vahlne, Ivarsson and Johanson, 2011, p. 3). Indeed, it has been argued that MNEs may be conceived of as 'resembling highly political arenas in which power games continuously take place' (Bouquet and Birkinshaw, 2008, p. 492). As such, 'micro-politics and conflicts [are] an unavoidable social reality and a natural mechanism of social interactions in MNEs' (Dörrenbächer and Geppert, 2006, p. 261). In other words, actors within MNEs are intentionally and strategically attempting to advance their own interests, strengthen their influence and avoid conceding previous mandates. Mudambi and Pedersen (2007) distinguish two political theory pillars with which to understand decision making by managers in MNE subsidiaries: agency theory and resource dependency theory. Both theories suggest that the political character of the MNE will be particularly discernible when corporate headquarters seeks to move the MNE from a multidomestic to a global stance.

Agency theory assumes that the headquarters–subsidiary relationship in MNEs is founded on self-interest and opportunism so that 'the local interests of the subsidiaries may not always be aligned with those of the headquarters or the MNE as a whole' (Nohria and Ghoshal, 1994, p. 492). According to O'Donnell (2000), in order to counter this agency problem the corporate centre has two generic alternatives at its disposal. The first comprises control mechanisms in the form of centrally determined rules, programmes or procedures in order to obtain information about the behaviours and decisions of subsidiary management. The second involves the use of financial incentives that align subsidiary management goals with those of corporate headquarters. Given that outcome measurability is unproblematic, and as monitoring devices are unviable, financial incentives that reflect subsidiary performance are often the preferred governance device in the case of multidomestic MNEs (O'Donnell, 2000).

Typically, an MNE that has pursued a multidomestic strategy over time has institutionalized a semi-autonomous mode of governance characterized by substantial local strategic and operational discretion at the subsidiary level (Roth and Ricks, 1994). Furthermore, it has established incentives that reward local subsidiary managements based on their own outputs. A transition from the multidomestic to the global strategy constitutes a profound challenge to this local view and it will be resisted if subsidiary managers are unconvinced that it will confer benefits.

Resource dependency theory posits that power is based on the control of resources that are considered strategic within the organization (Pfeffer, 1981; Pfeffer and Salancik, 1977) and suggests another source of political strain in any move from the multidomestic strategy. Because the various national subsidiaries of a multidomestic MNE are confronted by different local markets, some of which will be larger and more munificent than others, over time subsidiaries will vary considerably in terms of their resource ownership and control. In other words, some subsidiaries will be relatively resource-strong while others will be relatively resource-weak. From a resource dependency perspective when a multidomestic MNE attempts to move to a global strategy, its various subsidiaries will attempt to acquire control over those resources that minimize their dependence on other subsidiaries while maximizing the dependence of other subsidiaries on themselves. In practice, this will mean that the most resource-powerful subsidiaries will seek to achieve the dominant role in the integrated MNE, while the weaker subsidiaries will resist, possibly through alliance-seeking with other similar subsidiaries.

The social network challenge

Social networks can be broadly defined as a web of personal ties and connections that enable individuals to secure favours such as access to novel information (Burt, 1992; Granovetter, 1973). In organizational settings such as MNEs, social network theory emphasizes how social relationships among subsidiaries and their managers within MNEs are necessary conditions for effective cross-subsidiary collaborations (Martin and Eisenhardt, 2010). In short: 'Coordination [between subsidiaries] requires communication, and for that communication to be effective a network of contacts between units has to be developed' (Vahlne et al., 2011, p. 5).

Because multidomestic MNEs comprise units that are locally responsive, a considerable proportion of knowledge development takes place locally. To the degree this knowledge is 'collective' (see Figure 9.1), it is not readily transferable across the MNE. A multidomestic MNE that is, for example, seeking to integrate its devolved, local approach to purchasing, needs to facilitate the exchange and combination of subsidiary-based collective knowledge in order to develop a purchasing approach that is relevant and viable across subsidiaries.

Subsidiaries are more likely to be connected to their external within-country social networks than to other units within the MNE (Forsgren, Holm and Johanson, 2005). A transition from the multidomestic to a global strategy will have to address the lack of inter-subsidiary social networks if knowledge exchange is to occur.

To summarize, extant theory posits significant barriers in making the transition from a multidomestic to a global strategy. On the one hand, there is a political barrier that stems from the self-interest subsidiaries have been rewarded for pursuing. On the other hand, there is a lack of social networks and bridging social capital that undermines the exchange of collective knowledge between subsidiaries. As we will argue, these were clearly factors in the initial unsuccessful attempt SFC made to integrate its purchasing operations. However, they do not provide any substantial insight into the success of SFC's second and successful attempt at purchasing integration.

K.3 Context

SFC's roots go back some 150 years. For most of the previous century and through until 2000 it was the corporate centre of a conglomerate spanning a number of unrelated industries including asphalt production and dry foods. At that point, it divested itself of all its businesses apart from those in the dry foods industry. In addition to its Norwegian subsidiary, Voso, this left SFC with a number of fully-owned foreign-based subsidiaries that it had acquired during the 1990s. The most important of these were Pelecta (Poland) and Pitana (Czech Republic). In addition, it had smaller operations in five other European countries and sales and market offices in a further six countries. In

2007, SFC owned 28 brands in 12 countries. Its workforce comprised nearly 4000 employees, of whom 1000 were located in Norway. Of its subsidiaries, while Voso (Norway) has for many years been highly profitable, its non-Scandinavian subsidiary units are markedly less so. In other words, like a significant proportion of other MNEs, SFC is for the most part achieving lower profitability from its operations abroad than from those in its home country (Gooderham and Nordhaug, 2003). In the specific case of SFC, differences in profitability have a number of explanations. In relation to Pelecta and Pitana, whose development was curtailed under communism, Voso has been developing its capabilities continuously since its establishment in 1933. Furthermore, while the Norwegian market Voso operates in is relatively protected from competition that is not the case for either Pelecta or Pitana, both of which operate within EU member countries. In addition, the spending power of Norwegian consumers is such that private labels as opposed to branded products are a less established alternative in Norway than in the Czech Republic or Poland.

When our research began in 2007 it would be reasonable to categorize SFC as a multidomestic MNE. Its approach to product development across its markets was summarized as that of being 'a local taste champion'. Despite the potential savings that could be realized by concentrating production to SFC's low-cost sites in the Czech Republic and Poland only 7 and 4 per cent of Pitana's and Pelecta's production volume respectively was for inter-subsidiary customers. Purchasing, the focus of this case study, was also largely uncoordinated. Just for Voso, raw materials were supplied by 268 different suppliers, 39 of which accounted for 70 per cent of raw materials by value. For packaging for Voso, the figures were 132 suppliers, of which 28 covered 95 per cent of packaging needs. The situation was repeated across Pelecta and Pitana with virtually no coordination of purchasing between any of the subsidiaries.

SFC has made two attempts to integrate its purchasing. The first, the Unification Project, spanned 2004–07, and is acknowledged by corporate and subsidiary managers and board members as having been largely unsuccessful. The second, the significantly more successful Programme Amalgamation, commenced September 2008 and was in the main completed by March 2010.

K.4 The Unification Project (2004–07)

In addition to their own brands, and their own product development and marketing specialists, in 2004 Voso, Pitana and Pelecta all had their own purchasing specialists. Given strong price growth in agricultural commodities worldwide SFC decided that the lack of inter-subsidiary synergies was an issue, particularly in regard to purchasing, that could no longer be ignored. Under the so-called 'Unification Project', during 2004–07, a number of activities were implemented in order to create purchasing synergies across subsidiaries. The approach was to harmonize raw material specification across subsidiaries and then for each category to allocate a central lead buyer with responsibility for sourcing across subsidiaries. For the most part these individuals were Norwegians located at Voso. In addition, the position of group purchasing director was established, whose task was to coordinate between the purchasing departments in the respective subsidiaries. This position was allocated to a senior Pitana manager. To support these initiatives, a number of supporting measures were undertaken: SAP software was introduced; inter-subsidiary networks for marketing and sales managers were formed; a common set of performance appraisal principles were introduced; annual two-day strategy meetings for subsidiary heads were organized.

A feature of the Unification Project was that no subsidiary was to be obliged to go against its business judgement and use the central lead buyers. In other words, each subsidiary had the latitude to decide the degree to which it was in their interest to employ the services of the central lead buyers. At its launch at a gathering of subsidiary managers the project and its core idea of using central lead buyers were generally greeted positively. However, despite this initial reaction, by the end of the project the subsidiaries had on the whole opted to continue to use local buyers. As a manager with product development engineering responsibilities at Pitana observed, because product development continued to be done locally, it was generally the case that she and others at Pitana decided that it was more efficient to use the local buyer rather than the central lead buyer. Not only were the communication opportunities significantly greater but mutual understanding was already established. According to another manager at Pitana with purchasing responsibilities, an important aspect to this mutual understanding was that local purchasers were significantly more cost conscious than central lead buyers based at Voso in affluent Norway.

This lack of confidence or trust in the central lead buyers based at Voso on the part of Pitana managers was experienced in reverse by one of the few central lead buyers located outside of Voso. Based at Pitana, his perception was that the view of managers at Voso was that 'anything that originated from the Czech Republic was by definition substandard'. As the Unification Project concluded, his experience was that rather than consulting with him, 'Voso managers would simply buy what they wanted behind my back'. However, as he himself recognized, this deficiency in trust was not just a matter of chauvinism. He acknowledged that one of the difficulties central lead buyers experienced was their lack of deep understanding of the end products of the other subsidiaries. He recalled that concerning one relatively large order for an ingredient he had placed on behalf of several subsidiaries, Voso vetoed it for what he came to accept were substantially objective reasons. The particular ingredient would have resulted in a taste that Norwegian consumers would have rejected. As a senior manager at SFC with long-term experience of purchasing for Voso emphasized, 'the challenge for a purchaser is to get the precise quality needs of the subsidiary right. Otherwise the brand suffers'. Furthermore, getting the quality right depends not only on understanding the needs of the subsidiary but also on communicating these to suppliers. His experience was that getting the supplier relationship to work could take as much as two years of steady interaction (see, e.g., Johanson and Vahlne, 2009).

The deficiency in trust across the group in the central lead buyers evolved into scepticism of the Unification Project. By the end of the project, this was understood not least by the group purchasing director. A Czech national and based at Pitana, he felt that the general attitude at Voso was that his position would eventually 'evaporate'. When it became clear that the position was actually going to be permanent, his Voso colleagues simply 'pretended to cooperate'. He experienced that it was significantly easier for him to gain respect and a measure of cooperation from the other subsidiaries such as Pelecta.

As the Unification Project ended, the view of managers at SFC was that the managing directors (MDs) of the various subsidiaries had failed to identify with its potential. One senior SFC manager stated that in the early phase of the project she and colleagues had calculated that savings from an integrated, group-wide approach to purchasing could have been in the order of NOK280 million. However, in her view, the subsidiary MDs failed to accord this group-level analysis any serious attention. She ascribed this in part to their lack of integration in the Unification Project and in part to the fact that their remuneration was exclusively calculated based on their local performance rather than on the basis of group-level performance. Like others, she acknowledged that by the end of the project the old local purchasing mentality had reasserted itself and that the Unification Project had achieved relatively little.

The view from the subsidiaries was similar. The Pitana-based group purchasing director viewed the Unification Project as having been a 'great idea' but 'old habits had quickly largely reasserted themselves'. Likewise, the MD of Pelecta concluded that a unified group mentality across SFC remained underdeveloped and that the process of integration had barely begun. In his view, one significant barrier had been the lack of willingness on the part of Voso to concede any significant purchasing responsibilities to the non-Norwegian operations. However, as he somewhat light-heartedly remarked, had Pelecta been as profitable as Voso he 'would not have voluntarily sacrificed anything for the greater good of the whole group'.

In short, after a flurry of top-down-initiated activities, SFC's group of subsidiaries still constituted very much a multidomestic MNE with not only predominantly locally evolved products and local production but also mostly local purchasing. The view that the Unification Project had been largely unsuccessful was one that was shared not least by the SFC board. Consequently, towards the end of 2007 it instructed SFC's CEO to leave the company.

In terms of the extant theory we have presented, the inability of SFC to move its approach to purchasing from a multidomestic to a global strategy was arguably predictable. Indeed, it would be reasonable to contend that SFC's experience with its Unification Project constitutes an almost perfect illustration of the existing theory. In line with agency theory, we observed that the corporate centre, SFC, was confronted by a fiefdom mentality. Given the critical importance of meeting local taste, SFC's approach was to accept that the subsidiaries should continue to determine which aspects of purchasing could be viably integrated. Likewise, it did not attempt to change the locally focused remuneration system. In line with resource dependency theory, Voso, the most powerful subsidiary, dominated the central lead buyer functions and undermined initiatives fronted by non-Voso employees. To the extent there was inter-subsidiary cooperation, this was between the non-Voso subsidiaries. Finally, in line with social network theory we observed the lack of inter-subsidiary social networks. Perceived as being too deeply embedded in their own respective subsidiaries and their particular notions of 'local taste', the central lead buyers failed to develop the degree of bridging social capital that would have facilitated critical knowledge exchange.

It should be noted though that the outcome of the Unification Project cannot readily be reduced to opportunism as intentional deceit (Williamson, 1985) from the outset. On the contrary, our informants insisted that at the outset the subsidiaries had been encouraging about their willingness to engage with the project. Instead, what we have observed is what Verbeke and Greidanus (2009, p. 1482) refer to as 'benevolent preference reversal associated with reprioritization'. That is, subsidiary managers had made ex ante commitments to the Unification Project in good faith. However, that commitment diminished over time in the face of pressure to focus on proximate events and as the costs of that commitment emerged. Thus, subsidiary priorities were reinstated at the expense of corporate centre priorities.

K.5 Post-Unification Project

The SFC board decided to engage in a second and what it signalled would be a final attempt at achieving group-wide purchasing integration. As a first step, it initiated a purchasing and supply management (PSM) analysis conducted by external consultants from McKinsey. The PSM analysis benchmarked the group's overall PSM performance against other companies in the same industry. The McKinsey analysis concluded that purchasing represented an unexploited cost savings potential of NOK300 million. Two-thirds of this derived from direct purchasing (raw materials and packaging materials) and one-third from indirect purchasing/operating (e.g., travel costs and office cleaning costs). This figure was almost identical to the calculation by corporate headquarters we referred to above.

Based on the McKinsey analysis, the board and the interim CEO took the decision to launch Programme Amalgamation starting early September 2008, some two weeks before the new CEO was due to start. The core aim of Programme Amalgamation was to integrate direct purchasing across the group. This would mean transforming the highly decentralized structure of the group. At the same time, the board reiterated the need for each subsidiary to be its respective country's 'local taste champion'.

Whereas the Unification Project had been loosely structured, the board was determined that Programme Amalgamation should have a clear structure from the outset. A working group comprising the group purchasing director who moved from Pitana to SFC, a Voso manager and a SFC corporate manager was formed to prepare the ground for Programme Amalgamation. Building on the work of the Unification Project the working group divided purchasing into 50 categories. It was then determined that the purchasing project should comprise four waves, with each wave accounting for 25 per cent of the total savings and roughly 25 per cent of the categories. The plan was that the project was to be completed by early 2010. Each purchasing category was to be assigned a team by the Programme Amalgamation project organization, which also had the responsibility for monitoring the progress of the category teams and reporting its findings to SFC corporate management. Each category team was to comprise about five category experts who would also have access to advice from an external purchasing consultancy. It was understood that the release of these experts by the subsidiaries would have to be based on cooperation between the Programme Amalgamation project organization and the subsidiaries. In terms of the category teams, we collected our data within the 'Flexible Foils' and the 'Traded Goods' teams.

The category teams were charged with defining the group-wide needs within each category and signing new group-wide contracts with new suppliers. Even before Programme Amalgamation commenced, the Voso member of the working group was deeply concerned that the category teams might fail to acquire sufficient understanding of the products for which they would be purchasing. His particular concern was that the precise quality needs of the Voso brand might be compromised. As Programme Amalgamation got underway in September 2008 under the leadership of the project director (formerly the group purchasing director) our research was to indicate that this scepticism was widespread across the group.

K.6 Programme Amalgamation (2008–10)

Initial reactions

One month after the launch of Programme Amalgamation, the project director was concerned that the MDs of Voso, Pelecta and Pitana viewed Programme Amalgamation as a top-down operation driven by a McKinsey analysis that was insufficiently anchored in the realities of their businesses. His impression was that 'things are moving too fast' for the subsidiaries and that there was a lack of common vision and trust in the project. He speculated that this would explain why subsidiary MDs had, in his view, resisted releasing their most qualified personnel to serve in the category teams. Instead of being composed of the 'best people' for the job, the project director characterized their nominees as being no more than 'somewhat above average'. He referred to one subsidiary MD as having said that, 'my best sales people should sell' and to another MD who had labelled the travel costs of his single employee thus far involved in Programme Amalgamation as a 'punishment'.

The project director had also observed that the category team members themselves had their concerns. He thought they were anxious that while they were involved in Programme Amalgamation their stand-ins either might harm the day-to-day business or, alternatively, might replace them on a permanent basis. Finally, he had no illusions about his own standing, remarking that '[s]ome don't see me as a sufficiently strong guarantor. If he's fired – well, life goes on'.

At highly profitable Voso, the view was that the McKinsey analysis was correct. However, scepticism was also voiced by its MD who commented: 'Our attitude to the issue of quality is different to that of Eastern Europe'. He pointed out that nearly 70 per cent of the (Norwegian) customer complaints Voso receives involve products emanating from Pitana, although Pitana accounts for no more than 10 per cent of the products Voso delivers to the Norwegian market. Likewise, attempts to get Pelecta to produce cake mixes on behalf of Voso had always been undermined by quality problems whose causes were impossible to determine. 'Therefore', he commented, 'we are sceptical as to "their" ability to deliver quality over time and [given Voso's long-term quality criticisms] "they" are browned-off with "us"'.

At Pelecta, the MD recalled that in the course of his six years' tenure he had seen a number of company-wide projects aimed at greater integration. However, he remarked that, 'few of these had been successful in the sense that they had delivered lasting, tangible, results'. They had been characterized by a lack of consistency and continuity. While he supported greater integration because it could ultimately lead to the greater use of Pelecta's production capacity, his immediate reaction to Programme Amalgamation was that it might prove to be 'just another time-consuming project'.

At Pitana, the initial reaction of the MD to Programme Amalgamation was even more sceptical. It was 'yet another so-called "improvement"' and one that could threaten Pitana's limited resources in a period of substantial improvement because of improved cost control and increased product focus. In short, the Pitana MD was concerned that Programme Amalgamation would distract critical personnel from their pressing Pitana responsibilities. He viewed the hazard posed by the demands inherent in Programme Amalgamation as relatively much greater for Pitana than Voso because the latter had significantly more 'slack'. In other words, potential suboptimality was not evenly distributed across SFC.

At this point, in line with overall extant theory, Programme Amalgamation appeared to be another unsuccessful attempt to move from the multidomestic to the global stance.

Concluding reactions

In March 2010, the initial misgivings to Programme Amalgamation had largely evaporated. The project director viewed Programme Amalgamation as having delivered on its targets and as being perceived as having done so by the subsidiary MDs. Not only had the category teams worked well together, but also they had 'created a lot of knowledge'. Furthermore, although Voso employees had constituted the largest contingent of category team members, in his opinion they had not been perceived by the other subsidiaries as having dominated the work of the category teams. Our other interviews confirmed that the view of the project director was shared by all the senior management team at SFC, including the CEO, and the subsidiary MDs. In the words of a senior manager at SFC: 'this good result had resulted in a good feeling around the whole of the company'. Furthermore, subsidiary MDs were actively discussing the development of products based on common platforms. A further measure of the success of Programme Amalgamation was the assertion by another senior manager at SFC that purchasing had moved from being a marginal function to 'being in the driving seat'.

One senior SFC manager had two caveats to the success of Programme Amalgamation. First, he pointed out that there is a time lag before one would see all the tangible profit and loss effects. Not only does it take time to get contracts signed, but old stocks must be disposed of – inattentive employees may continue to order the old materials and suppliers who are being phased out may renege on current contracts in terms of, for example, lower quality. Second, he had registered that SFC's competitors had in the meantime also improved their purchasing strategies. However, he also observed that Programme Amalgamation had been so successful that McKinsey regarded it as an exemplar of 'how things should be done'. Indeed, during the latter part of 2010 and early 2011 as the tangible profit and loss effects were fully realized and communicated to the markets there was a substantial increase in the value of SFC stock.

K.7 The distinctive elements of Programme Amalgamation

The contrast between the respective outcomes of Programme Amalgamation and the Unification Project is considerable. There is also a pronounced contrast between the initial reactions to Programme Amalgamation and the concluding reactions to it.

Governance reconfiguration: The general management team

When SFC's CEO joined the company in late September 2008, he was acutely conscious that the implementation of Programme Amalgamation was to be his key responsibility. Reflecting on the significance of Programme Amalgamation at the start of his tenure, his view was that it was a highly critical 'journey' for SFC's long-term success. For him the challenge was to get managers to develop a 'dualistic' view of their roles. On the one hand, they were to have a focus on the needs of their local markets, while on the other hand they were to have an equally strong commitment to the need for the integration of purchasing.

His first action in this 'journey' was during early October 2008 to conduct one-to-one meetings with each of the MDs of the main subsidiaries. He explicitly requested that they act on behalf of the whole business rather than their own subsidiaries. Late October 2008 he presented a two-page memo to subsidiary MDs, 'From a food conglomerate to an integrated food company'. This outlined a radical shift in the structure of the company. In it the new CEO stated that 'the history of SFC has been that of a conglomerate in which the performance of subsidiaries had been discretely measured with cooperation between subsidiaries. . .relatively voluntary. In 2009 we must take the step from a food conglomerate to an integrated food company to improve performance and efficiency'.

However, a much more substantial action by the new CEO was his decision to form an entirely new general management team (GMT) that, in addition to himself, the CFO, the head of human resources, the director of marketing and sales and the new supply chain director, included the MDs of the main subsidiaries. For the first time in the history of SFC, subsidiary managers were now integrated in the corporate centre. From December 2008, the GMT held monthly meetings in different locations supplemented by telephone conferences halfway through each month. At each GMT meeting the project director of Programme Amalgamation reported on the progress of the project, including any personnel issues that had arisen in the wake of staffing the category teams.

At its outset, the new GMT was a brittle entity. One senior manager at SFC recounted that there was a lack of understanding on how to cooperate in order to function as an effective top management team. She described the CEO's use of a variety of informal methods to develop the way in which GMT members interacted. The policy of the CEO was that critical views could be expressed at GMT meetings but once decisions had been taken those decisions should command collective loyalty. Another senior manager at SFC had a somewhat different recollection of the initial GMT phase. He recalled 'innumerable meetings' with the CEO 'hammering home Programme Amalgamation'. Unlike under the Unification Project it was now no longer the case that subsidiaries could use their local needs as 'an excuse for inaction'. Such was the pressure from the CEO that those who opposed Programme Amalgamation thought 'it wise to keep their scepticism to themselves'.

Indeed, as our 'Early Programme Amalgamation Interviews' indicated, that is precisely what the subsidiary MDs did. Nevertheless, according to this manager, the GMT, even in its initial phase provided a powerful mandate for Programme Amalgamation. He argued 'that none of the achievements of Programme Amalgamation would have been possible without this powerful mandate coming not just from the CEO but also from the collective voice of the GMT'.

Realignment of rewards

Coupled to the new GMT was a fresh approach to MD compensation. Whereas the former system had been primarily local in its orientation, rewarding subsidiary MDs on the basis of their unit's performance, the new CEO introduced a new rewards system that to a significant extent rewarded the subsidiary MDs on the basis of overall group performance. Thus, as the new GMT set to work on making Programme Amalgamation operational among the subsidiary MDs, this coincided with the introduction of a rewards package whose primary element reflected overall group performance. There would still be an element that reflected subsidiary performance, but for the first time in SFC's history, group performance as a metric was not just a metric, but the most significant metric.

Rolling measures of outcomes

A transition to a new centralized and integrated purchasing process challenges the local view of subsidiary MDs. As the Early Programme Amalgamation Interviews indicated, the adoption of an integrated approach to purchasing was initially viewed with some doubt by MDs. Part of the design of Programme Amalgamation comprised the regular monitoring by a controller of each category team in order to objectively identify tangible savings. Thereafter these unambiguous outcomes were immediately communicated to the GMT by the project director.

The communication of 'early wins' (i.e., immediate substantial savings) to the GMT not only persuaded subsidiary MDs that Programme Amalgamation was working but it even generated a conviction that further integration was both possible and desirable. Thus, by the end of Programme Amalgamation with profitability improving for the group as well as the subsidiaries as a consequence of the realized savings, the GMT had embarked on a discussion on how to develop 'common platforms' for products that could span several countries. The initial scepticism to Programme Amalgamation was converted into a belief in it and a greater commitment to making it work. The issue of which nationality dominated the category teams was transformed into a discussion of which individuals were most competent to lead and serve in them.

Mandated category teams

In terms of the overall task of the category teams, this was very similar to the task assigned to the central lead buyers of the Unification Project. It was to define the group-wide needs within each purchasing category and then to sign new contracts with suppliers on behalf of the group. However, in operational terms there were profound differences. The SFC approach to the operational integration of purchasing in the Unification Project was to appoint central lead buyers for the various purchasing categories and to provide them with authorization to invite cooperation from the purchasing managers based in the various subsidiaries. The approach of Programme Amalgamation to developing category teams was not to devolve the responsibility for forming them but to centralize it. Category teams were formed at the outset of each phase of Programme Amalgamation with designated team members covering a variety of relevant competencies, including production, product development, logistics and marketing. Furthermore, unlike the Unification Project where central lead buyers remained in their regular purchasing roles, category team leaders were designated on a full-time basis while the team members were to spend an average of 60 per cent of their working week on category team-related activities.

Initially, both category team leaders and their members were appointed by the project director based on nominations from the subsidiaries. The project director was not pleased with the outcome of this approach. As we have noted above, in his view, cost-conscious subsidiary MDs were not only trying to limit the number of nominees they forwarded, but more significantly they were resisting nominating their most qualified personnel for category team service. However, after the formation of the new GMT that included subsidiary MDs, both the nomination process and the category team appointments became subject to GMT scrutiny and monitoring. This scrutiny and monitoring effectively constituted a mandating and therefore legitimatization of the category teams by the GMT. Furthermore, the scrutiny and monitoring were also immediately applied to the category teams that had been formed shortly prior to the formation of the new GMT. As Programme Amalgamation concluded, the view of the project director was that the members of the category teams had been more than sufficiently qualified for their tasks. This was a view that was endorsed by a Pelecta manager who had herself participated in a category team. Finally, as the Voso MD pointed out, the boundaries of the category teams had in effect been buffered by the GMT against disruptive, competing tasks, thereby 'enabling its members to work outside of their normal functions and to work across both functions and geographies'. Effectively, the subsidiary MDs of the GMT had acted as 'sentries and guards' (Yan and Louis, 1999, p. 31).

Inter-subsidiary category teams

We have indicated that social network theory points to two salient features of multidomestic MNEs. First, because they comprise business units that must be responsive to local taste, product, and therefore purchasing, knowledge is both geographically distributed and locally embedded. Particularly that proportion of knowledge that is 'collective' – that is, knowledge that is both tacit and held by groups rather than individuals – is problematic to transfer across the MNE. Second, because of the lack of bridging ties there is little in the way of social capital between subsidiaries.

In terms of the first of these features, as we have observed, the Unification Project was spearheaded by central lead buyers who for the most part were Norwegians located at Voso. The view of non-Voso colleagues was that they failed to understand their idiosyncratic local needs. Equally, in relation to colleagues at Voso the central lead buyer located at Pitana fared no better. The approach to Programme Amalgamation was very different from that of the Unification Project in that it aimed to form inter-subsidiary category teams. In so doing, Programme Amalgamation created arenas for the exchange and sharing of locally embedded knowledge. Overall, according to the project director, these arenas worked well and resulted in 'a lot of knowledge' being created. A Pelecta manager referred to the category team she had belonged to as having consisted of 'a great mix of people'. The Voso MD also commented on the inter-subsidiary character of the category teams observing that 'the Norwegians [at Voso] had their fixation with quality questioned by the Czechs [at Pitana] and the Poles [at Pelecta] their focus on costs'. He further remarked that this had led 'to a much greater understanding of one another's thinking'.

Bridging category teams

In relation to the second salient feature of multidomestic MNEs underscored by social network theory, the lack of bridging ties, the category teams of Programme Amalgamation were specifically instructed to interact not just with suppliers but also with local stakeholders across the group. Furthermore, their success in doing this was monitored by the project director and the GMT. By contrast, bridging ties were not an explicit priority of the Unification Project.

The Voso senior manager in charge of the Traded Goods category team recounted that her team had consistently involved local purchasers drawing on their knowledge particularly concerning extant suppliers. This shared understanding created a 'buy-in' and a sense of common achievement when improved contracts with suppliers were achieved. Networks across the subsidiaries were developed that could be drawn on in the future. One of the Pitana managers that had had extensive dealings with the Traded Goods team concurred with this analysis. She added that because of the interaction both her purchasing competence and her inter-subsidiary contacts had increased significantly.

The Flexible Foils category team told a similar story. The Voso senior manager who led this team observed that in developing its new purchasing competencies the team had not only developed a strong internal network, but also a network across the company. A Pelecta manager who was a member of this team observed that when the team started its work 'not everybody was aware of what was going on and nobody really strongly believed in it'. The 'just-another-project-syndrome' ruled. However, at the conclusion of Programme Amalgamation she now observed a marked change of attitude and 'quite a high level of trust' in Programme Amalgamation. She ascribed this change to the extensive use the category team made of stakeholders and specialists across the company. In all, more than 20 people from product development, marketing, technical support, production and maintenance as well as controllers had been involved. It was not just a matter of consulting with these individuals but also 'lots of knowledge sharing'. She described the networking undertaken by the team as 'priceless', and emphasized the value of the interpersonal relations and the shared understanding that had been developed. She summed up her experience as: 'If you know people you can fix it' and referred to several 'fantastic experiences where new knowledge and insight had been created because the right people were in the right place at the right time'.

Overall, her account was validated by a senior manager at SFC who was also a member of the GMT and therefore had monitored the progress of the Flexible Foils category team. He remarked that these 'success stories' had functioned as 'change ambassadors' across the company. More substantially, he argued that by interacting with internal stakeholders across the subsidiaries, new purchasing knowledge was generated that enabled the category teams to favourably renegotiate with suppliers. Indeed, the savings were the double of the original aim. Likewise, he thought, the Traded Goods category team had also done 'an unbelievably good job'.

K.8 Summary

This case study illustrates an MNE attempting to make the transition from a multidomestic to a global strategy. The MNE experiences two fundamental challenges: a political and a social network challenge. These two challenges are so significant that achieving transition is a case of 'easier said than done'. In industries where 'local taste' continues to matter, integration is subject to limitations. A significant degree of purchasing integration may be achieved but the integration of product development is considerably more problematic. However, even in the case of purchasing integration the experience of SFC in conjunction with its unsuccessful Unification Project provides a potent illustration of the difficulty in surmounting the political and social network challenges.

Comparing and contrasting two initiatives to achieve purchasing integration within the same company at two different points in time is an approach that has its limitations in that both the company and its context are evolving. In the case of SFC one obvious difference in 2008 when it launched Programme Amalgamation was that the corporate centre and the subsidiaries had significantly more knowledge of one another than they had had in 2004 at the launch of the Unification Project. Not all this knowledge could be construed as constructive or positive. Indeed, in the wake of the failure of the Unification Project there was considerable mutual scepticism across the subsidiaries, borne out by the Pelecta MD's misgiving that Programme Amalgamation appeared to be 'just another time-consuming project'. In other words, the likelihood of Programme Amalgamation eliciting a response of 'benevolent preference' (Verbeke and Greidanus, 2009) was significantly lower than had been the case for the Unification Project. Indeed, as we observed, as Programme Amalgamation got underway, the project director was concerned that the attitude of the subsidiary MDs to staffing the category teams indicated resistance or what Williamson (1985, p. 47) refers to as 'calculated efforts to mislead'.

However, there were other differences. As we observed, in 2008 the SFC corporate board communicated a much greater sense of urgency to its subsidiaries than was the case in 2004. This had its roots in the benchmarking exercise conducted by McKinsey that revealed the extent of purchasing integration undertaken by competitors. Another difference was the amount of resources the board was prepared to commit to Programme Amalgamation. By 2008, the board had understood how time consuming and costly purchasing integration in the context of a multidomestic is.

Finally, we would add a footnote on how SFC might be categorized in the wake of Programme Amalgamation and how it might develop. A narrow focus on the integration of direct purchasing would suggest that SFC has moved from a multidomestic to a global strategy. However, in other important regards such as production, marketing and product development, as well as indirect purchasing, SFC undeniably remains a multidomestic. Thus, SFC was moving to a distinctly hybrid form.

CASE DISCUSSION

1. What were the goals that SFC headquarters wanted to achieve in the Unification Project and Amalgamation Project?
2. Describe the knowledge transfer that was required for SFC to reach its goals (e.g., describe the kind of knowledge and the sending and recipient units).
3. Use the dynamic capability model to describe and compare the way in which top management addressed the challenges of creating willingness and ability for knowledge transfer in the two projects.
4. In what ways did cultural, institutional, economic or geographic distances create specific challenges for SFC?

NOTE

* A version of this case study has been published as: Gooderham, P.N. (2012), 'The transition from a multidomestic enterprise in an industry where local taste matters', *European Journal of International Management*, **6**(2), 175–98.

REFERENCES

Bartlett, C.A. and S. Ghoshal (1989), *Managing Across Borders: The Transnational Solution*, Boston, MA: Harvard Business School Press.

Bouquet, C. and J. Birkinshaw (2008), 'Managing power in the multinational corporation: How low-power actors gain influence', *Journal of Management*, **34**(3), 477–508.

Burt, R.S. (1992), *Structural Holes: The Social Structure of Competition*, Cambridge, MA: Harvard University Press.

Dörrenbächer, C. and M. Geppert (2006), 'Micro-politics and conflicts in multinational corporations: Current debates, re-framing, and contributions of this special issue', *Journal of International Management*, **12**(3), 251–65.

Forsgren, M., U. Holm and J. Johanson (2005), *Managing the Embedded Multinational*, Cheltenham, UK and Northampton, MA, USA: Edward Elgar Publishing.

Gooderham, P.N. and O. Nordhaug (2003), *International Management: Cross-boundary Challenges*, Oxford: Blackwell.

Granovetter, M.S. (1973), 'The strength of weak ties', *American Journal of Sociology*, **78**, 1360–80.

Johanson, J. and J.E. Vahlne (2009), 'The Uppsala internationalization process model revisited: From liability of foreignness to liability of outsidership', *Journal of International Business Studies*, **40**, 1411–31.

Martin, J.A. and K.M. Eisenhardt (2010), 'Rewiring: Cross-subsidiary collaborations in multi-business organizations', *Academy of Management Journal*, **53**(2), 265–301.

Mudambi, R. and T. Pedersen (2007), 'Agency theory and resource dependency theory: Complementary explanations for subsidiary power in multinational corporations', *SMG Working Paper No. 5/2007*, Copenhagen Business School.

Nohria, N. and S. Ghoshal (1994), 'Differentiated fit and shared values: Alternatives for managing headquarters–subsidiary relations', *Strategic Management Journal*, **15**(6), 491–502.

O'Donnell, S. (2000), 'Managing foreign subsidiaries: Agents of headquarters, or an independent network?', *Strategic Management Journal*, **2**(5), 525–48.

Pfeffer, J. (1981), *Power in Organizations*, Marshfield, MA: Pitman.

Pfeffer, J. and G.R. Salancik (1977), 'Who gets power – and how they hold on to it: A strategic contingency model of power', *Organizational Dynamics*, **5**(3), 2–21.

Roth, K. and D.A. Ricks (1994), 'Goal configuration in a global industry context', *Strategic Management Journal*, **15**(2), 103–20.

Vahlne, J.-E., I. Ivarsson and J. Johanson (2011), 'The tortuous road to globalization for Volvo's heavy truck business: Extending the scope of the Uppsala model', *International Business Review*, **20**(1), 1–14.

Verbeke, A. and N.S. Greidanus (2009), 'The end of the opportunism vs trust debate: Bounded reliability as a new envelope concept in research on MNE governance', *Journal of International Business Studies*, **40**(9), 1471–95.

Williamson, O.E. (1985), *The Economic Institutions of Capitalism*, New York: Free Press.

Yan, A. and M.R. Louis (1999), 'Migration of organizational functions', *Human Relations*, **52**(1), 25–47.

10

Cross-national transfer of human resource management

10.1 Introduction

Because MNEs operate across national boundaries and must contend with different cultural and institutional contexts as well as geographic distances, they have to deal with human resource management (HRM) challenges that are distinct from those of domestic firms. International HRM (IHRM) explores the HRM challenges that are specific to MNEs. A key IHRM challenge involves achieving consistency and worldwide policies across the MNE. Cultural and institutional differences are constraints on the feasibility of achieving this. For example, a manager at a Southeast Asian subsidiary of a Norwegian MNE remarked in relation to recruitment and selection:

> [While in Norway] companies and society instinctively feel that it is not right that you hire your sister or your brother or your daughter, in our society you should definitely hire them because that's family, because that's the only people you can trust.

10.2 International human resource management (IHRM)

An important source of competitive advantage for MNEs is the utilization of their organizational capabilities on a worldwide basis through the leveraging of their management practices across their subsidiaries (Kostova and Roth, 2002). To get to grips with the substance of cross-national HRM we will first specify how it differs from domestic HRM. Thereafter, we will present a model for studying and analysing cross-national HRM within MNEs. The model differentiates between corporate and subsidiary-level factors and between macro- and micro-level forces to account for the degree of similarity of HRM systems between parent and subsidiary. The framework signals the need for international managers to develop not just an awareness of cultural distance but also an awareness of institutional distance.

A rapidly increasing number of firms are moving from being purely domestic players to being cross-national players. The majority are doing this through mergers and acquisitions. A major challenge for these firms is how to create a common identity across their operations. One response to this is to ensure that all HRM practices contribute to the overall strategy of the MNE. Schuler, Dowling and De Cieri (1993) define the MNE's IHRM system as the set of distinct activities, functions and processes that are directed at attracting, developing and maintaining an MNE's human resources. Thus, strategic IHRM (SIHRM) comprises 'human resource management issues, functions, and policies and practices that result from the strategic activities of multinational enterprises and that impact the international concerns and goals of those enterprises' (Taylor, Beechler and Napier, 1996, p. 961).

In a cross-national context, it is paramount that managers at corporate headquarters recognize that their ways of managing human resources have evolved in relation to the cultural and institutional conditions that are specific to their particular countries of origin. What is more, their particular, idiosyncratic style of management cannot readily be applied to subsidiaries operating in dissimilar cultures and institutional settings. Given this, it is important for these managers to fully accept that their HRM systems and practices are not necessarily superior. Furthermore, they must be sensitive not just to the cultural setting but also to the institutional setting of the subsidiary. It is also important for them to bear in mind that in many foreign contexts there is considerable risk attached to mismanaging human resources. This is because MNEs usually have a higher visibility and a higher exposure to both formal and informal monitoring than their indigenous counterparts. For instance, if a country has a policy requiring that host country personnel are to be preferred for specific positions, the MNE swiftly risks losing its legitimacy if it is perceived as having failed to adapt.

10.3 The substance of cross-national HRM

Managing human resources embraces a variety of tasks. These may be categorized into five broad but interrelated HRM areas: the acquisition of human resources, human resource development, compensation, design of work systems, and labour relations:

- Human resource acquisition encompasses both the internal and the external selection and recruitment of individuals to jobs. In addition,

it includes the hiring of temporary employees and the use of external consultants.
- Human resource development includes not only the development of competences among employees but also their maintenance.
- Compensation embraces a wide spectrum of employee rewards. In this chapter we focus on extrinsic or externally controlled rewards – that is, wages and employee stock ownership plans.
- The design of work systems refers to the ways in which tasks and responsibilities in the firm are structured and distributed, and the extent to which there are clear dividing lines between jobs.
- Labour relations span the negotiations with employees that are necessary in order to put into practice all of the above.

Although these areas are common to both domestic and cross-national HRM, foreign environments often make for a higher degree of complexity because of the cultural and institutional dissimilarities involved. One important consequence of this complexity is that it may be more difficult to specify tasks and define and reward performance levels than is the case in purely domestic environments. To succeed, managers with cross-national human resource responsibilities must be equipped with a broader cognitive perspective and more knowledge than their purely domestic counterparts. There is a need for managers who are capable of coping with uncertainty and ambiguity and who are equipped with the ability to develop negotiated solutions to problems that may even lack clear-cut definitions. Schuler and Jackson (2005, p. 28) contend that:

> [t]he practice [of SIHRM] involves the management of inter-unit linkages and internal operations (Bartlett and Ghoshal, 1989). Managing inter-unit linkages is needed to integrate, control and coordinate the units of a firm that are scattered throughout the globe... Internal operations, on the other hand, encompass the remaining issues. For example, internal operations include the way a unit operates in concert with the laws, culture, society, politics, economy, and general environment of a particular location.

Schuler and Jackson emphasize that this context for developing internal operations is much more complex and multifaceted than that of firms operating in a single country. Compared to domestic HRM, because of cultural and institutional differences, SIHRM involves more uncertainties and more variation in the external settings. Furthermore, SIHRM includes a wider array of functions and activities related to human resources. If these managerial challenges cannot be successfully addressed, the inter-unit linkages across the MNE may be critically weakened. For example, how can an MNE align subsidiaries with its strategies if all of them employ significantly different rewards systems and all have dissimilar perceptions of what talent is? As a starting point for addressing these challenges, Schuler and Jackson argue that MNEs need a SIHRM framework. In the next section, we will present a comprehensive SIHRM framework that encompasses both the management of inter-unit linkages and internal operations.

10.4 A framework for strategic international human resource management (SIHRM)

Adler and Ghadar (1990, p. 245) have argued that the 'central issue for MNEs is not to identify the best international HRM policy per se, but rather to find the best fit between the firm's external environment, its overall strategy, and its HRM policy and implementation'. Other researchers (e.g., Schuler and Jackson, 2005) caution that as neither the external environment nor the overall strategy are static there is a need for flexibility as well as fit. As discussed in Chapter 3, this often manifests itself as an ongoing tension between the need for MNE integration (i.e., inter-unit linkages) and differentiation (i.e., the need for each subsidiary to adapt to its local environment).

Taylor et al. (1996) have developed a model of the determinants of the SIHRM system of an MNE that we, with modifications, will adopt because of its sensitivity to this integration–local adaptation tension (Figure 10.1). The model enables us to analyse why the HRM systems at the subsidiary level may 'deviate' significantly from HRM at corporate headquarters.

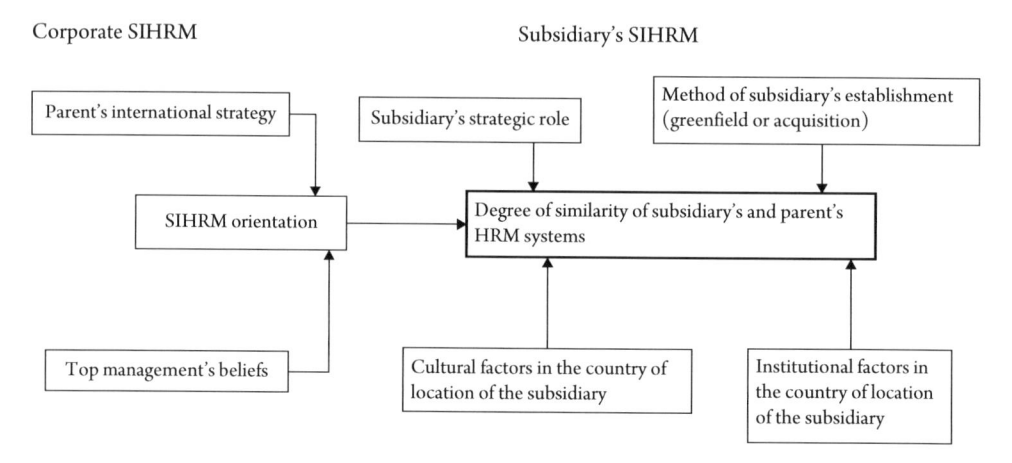

Corporate SIHRM   Subsidiary's SIHRM

- Parent's international strategy
- Subsidiary's strategic role
- Method of subsidiary's establishment (greenfield or acquisition)
- SIHRM orientation
- Degree of similarity of subsidiary's and parent's HRM systems
- Top management's beliefs
- Cultural factors in the country of location of the subsidiary
- Institutional factors in the country of location of the subsidiary

Source: Adapted from Taylor et al. (1996, p. 965) and reproduced with permission.

Figure 10.1 A model for analysing SIHRM

The principal dependent variable in Figure 10.1 is the degree of similarity between corporate parent company and subsidiary HRM systems. The first part of this two-fold model is at the level of the parent company and has as its focus the parent company's SIHRM orientation. By SIHRM orientation, Taylor et al. (1996, p. 966) mean 'the general philosophy or approach taken by top management of the MNE in the design of its overall IHRM system, particularly the HRM systems to be used in its overseas affiliates'. This approach will, for example, determine whether the MNE will have an IHRM director at headquarters or whether HRM will be decentralized. It will also determine whether there will be mechanisms designed to enable sharing of HRM policies and practices with and between subsidiaries. The MNE's SIHRM orientation determines its overall approach to managing the tension between the need for integration and the pressure for local adaptation.

Taylor et al. argue that the choice of SIHRM orientation is the product of the firm's international strategy coupled with top management's beliefs concerning the existence and context generalizability of its HRM competence. Let us start with the role of MNE strategy.

The role of MNE strategy

As we indicated in Chapter 3, it is common to differentiate four generic international strategies: the simple international, the multidomestic, the global and the transnational. In light of HRM in MNEs, it is helpful to contrast multidomestic and global strategies, as these represent diametrical opposites in terms of needs and challenges. Each is associated with specific forms of SIHRM.

MNEs pursuing local responsiveness grant considerable latitude to their subsidiaries not only to develop products but also to develop their own HRM practices in line with their local needs. Although there are indications that many MNEs are seeking to move away from an overtly multidomestic strategy to a more integrated strategy, any transition from the multidomestic strategy is usually a slow process (see Chapter 3). Subsidiary managers that are used to running local fiefdoms rarely willingly give up their prerogative to forge their own local strategies and HRM practices. This differs from HRM in firms with global strategies, as the major line of authority lies with the parent company. Subsidiaries are therefore largely managed according to the MNE's management principles.

The role of top management's beliefs

Taylor et al. (1996, p. 969) define top management's perception of HRM as 'the belief, expressed in corporate as well as personal communications, that the firm's way of managing its employees gives the company an advantage over its competitors'. However, in addition to this perception of HRM competence is the issue of whether top management believes that this competence is relevant beyond its national borders. A lack of such a belief would mean that there will be no attempt to apply its HRM competence in its subsidiaries. This is often a characteristic of multidomestic MNEs, just as a belief in the efficacy of its HRM applied beyond its borders is associated with global MNEs. In other words, top management beliefs will usually precede and determine strategy formulation.

The resultant SIHRM orientation

The interaction of top management's HRM beliefs and choice of strategy results in characteristic SIHRM orientations. Taylor et al. (1996) distinguish between three different forms of SIHRM orientation – adaptive, exportive and integrative:

- An *adaptive SIHRM* orientation is one in which top management of the MNE encourages the development of HRM systems that reflect subsidiary local environment (low degree of global integration and high degree of local responsiveness). In MNEs utilizing this approach there would be little or no transfer of HRM philosophy, policies or practices either from the parent firm to its foreign subsidiaries, or between its subsidiaries. It is an approach that is very much evident in multidomestic MNEs.
- An *exportive SIHRM* orientation is one in which top management of the MNE has a strong preference for a comprehensive transfer of the parent firm's HRM system to its foreign subsidiaries (high degree of global integration and low degree of local responsiveness). In effect, the aim is to replicate HRM policies and practices across subsidiaries with the parent determining those policies and practices. In short, unlike MNEs with an adaptive SIHRM approach, there is a high degree of control by the parent company over a subsidiary's system. In general, this is the approach adopted by global MNEs, particularly in their early phase.
- MNEs with an *integrative SIHRM* orientation attempt to take HRM 'best practices' regardless of whether they have originated in the parent firm or in the subsidiaries and apply them throughout the organization, while also allowing for some local differentiation, in the creation of a worldwide HRM system (high degree of global integration and high degree of local

responsiveness). Thus, transfer of HRM policies and practices occurs, but it is just as likely to occur between foreign subsidiaries as between the parent company and its subsidiaries. In other words, transfers can go in any direction. This SIHRM orientation is associated with the transnational MNE and involves moderate control by the parent company over the subsidiary's HRM system.

MNEs do not necessarily retain their SIHRM orientation throughout their lifespan. First, the beliefs of top management concerning the value and context specificity of parent company HRM competence can change because of international experience. Second, the firm may change its international strategy as a response to new technological opportunities or competitive pressures. Thus, for example, technology MNE ABB is today pursuing a global strategy rather than the transnational strategy it pursued in the early 1990s. However, with this proviso, SIHRM orientations are reasonably stable, not least because changes to strategy involve costs.

The subsidiary's HRM system

The second part of Taylor et al.'s SIHRM model is concerned with subsidiary-level influences. The main point to this part of the model is to point out that because of subsidiary-level influences the SIHRM orientation will not be applied uniformly to all subsidiaries. In Chapter 3, we distinguished subsidiaries in terms of their firm-specific advantages (FSAs) and their strategic importance for the MNE.

The resource dependence of the parent company on its subsidiaries is highest for those subsidiaries with the greatest outflow of resources to the rest of the MNE: strategic leaders and centres of excellence. At the same time, greater reliance by the parent company on the subsidiary will increase the power of the subsidiary over the parent company. Hence, the parent company will attempt to exercise high levels of control over these subsidiaries, but these subsidiaries will simultaneously have the power to resist these control efforts. In the case of powerful centres of excellence – powerful in the sense that there is little resource dependence on the parent company combined with resource dependence of the parent on the subsidiary – there will only be a moderate degree of similarity in subsidiary's and parent company's HRM systems.

In addition to the strategic role of the subsidiary, the degree of similarity between the parent company's and subsidiary's HRM systems will be influenced by a second subsidiary-level factor: the method of the establishment of the subsidiary. Because greenfield sites have no past and therefore no established HRM practices it is easier to introduce those HRM practices favoured by corporate headquarters than is the case for subsidiaries that have been acquired. Finally, Figure 10.1 includes macro-level factors that constrain what types of HRM practices an MNE can implement in its subsidiaries. One of these is the cultural context of the subsidiary: the national cultural differences we have discussed in Chapter 7 will impact on what types of HRM practices are readily acceptable in a subsidiary. In addition, institutional factors (Chapter 8) may inhibit what HRM practices an MNE can introduce to a subsidiary. We will now examine these macro influences in detail.

Calculative HRM

Gooderham, Nordhaug and Ringdal (1999) have noted that 'calculative' HRM practices such as individual performance-related pay and individual performance appraisals operate more easily in some national settings than in others: while it is generally accepted in UK business cultures, it is less widely accepted in Germany or Scandinavia. Particularly in Scandinavia, there is a resistance to the idea that individual members of the group should excel in a way that reveals the shortcoming of others. In addition, these countries have powerful trade unions and, in the case of Germany, work councils that narrow the scope for implementing calculative HRM practices. However, as we discussed in Chapter 8, although Scandinavia and Germany are institutionally more similar to one another than they are to the UK, there are also significant differences. In Scandinavia, despite the engrained assumption of divergent and conflicting interests between employer and employees and, therefore, an ongoing resistance to management-initiated calculative HRM practices, there is a greater latitude for experimentation than the more rigid German employment law permits.

When in Rome, do MNEs do as the Romans?

In their pursuit of being effective global competitors, MNEs will typically seek 'the unimpeded right to coordinate and control all aspects of the company on a worldwide basis' (Bartlett and Ghoshal, 1995, p. 119). That is, MNEs will attempt to apply the management practices they are most familiar with regardless of the location of their subsidiary. However, in order to maintain legitimacy MNEs also have to take into account the demands and expectations of their various host environments. These may necessitate the modification of their management processes.

The Cranet data set (www.cranet.org) enables us to contrast the use of calculative HRM practices by US MNEs in four different European contexts,

Source: Gooderham, Nordhaug and Ringdal (2006).

Figure 10.2 Deployment of calculative HRM practices among US subsidiaries in the UK, Ireland, Denmark/Norway (Den/Nor) and Germany and their indigenous counterparts, controlled for size, industry and age of establishment

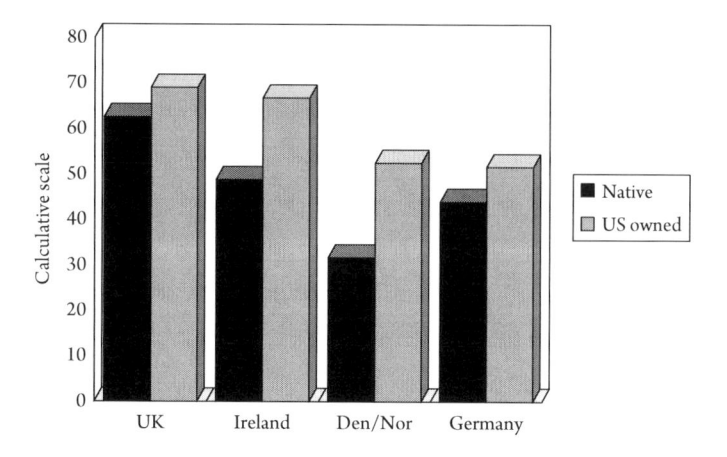

the UK, Ireland, Denmark and Norway combined and Germany. Figure 10.2 indicates that indigenous or native firms in the UK make significant use of calculative HRM particularly in relation to Denmark and Norway. The figure further indicates that the subsidiaries of US MNEs make significantly more use of calculative HRM practices in Denmark/Norway and Germany than their indigenous counterparts. However, their use is less than in the calculative HRM-friendly UK. In short, in Denmark/Norway and in Germany, US MNEs are succumbing to cultural and institutional pressures to moderate their use of calculative HRM practices. This process of semi-adaptation results in hybrid organizational practices that are partly rooted in practices emanating from headquarters, and partly rooted in local cultural and institutional conditions. Figure 10.2 also shows that for Ireland there is considerable divergence between native firms and subsidiaries of US MNEs. This is a product of the lack of institutional restrictions placed on MNEs that operate in Ireland.

10.5 Practical lessons

The environments that subsidiaries of MNEs operate in exert substantial influence on managerial decisions. This may undermine the efforts of managers in the individual MNE to make decisions they perceive as rational in relation to human resource acquisition, development, compensation, labour relations and in the design of work systems.

In practical terms, it is critical for the MNE to be able to identify and assess the significance of the conditions in the various environments in which it operates. The analytical model outlined in this chapter can be applied to environmental factors that influence the future operation of the subsidiary. Particularly before establishing a subsidiary or joint venture in a foreign environment, it is essential that information about environmental factors is compiled and that, on this basis, both possible and probable problems relating to HRM in this specific environment are clarified. Such an analysis may strengthen the MNE's ability to act proactively with regard to human resource issues.

Customization and internalization

So far, we have treated HRM practices almost as constants: they are either transferred or not. However, HRM practices may be subject to local customization by the subsidiary. As Lozeau, Langley and Denis (2002) have noted, in any transfer there is always some degree of customization necessary to the local context. Czarniawska and Joerges (1996) remind us that ideas are transformed as they are transferred. Given any significant degree of difference in context, transfer requires not just the encoding and movement of knowledge about practices, but making use of this knowledge and local knowledge to construct new practices that function in the context of local affordances.

Kostova and Roth (2002) have noted that the extent to which practices are fully internalized locally versus only superficially adopted, varies considerably – high internalization being more likely where the local institutional and cultural context is receptive to what is being transferred. Coercive pressures to adopt transferred knowledge and practice in the absence of a receptive local context lead most often to purely 'ceremonial adoption'.

Fenton-O'Creevy et al. (2011) have developed a categorization of outcomes of transfer attempts, as illustrated in Figure 10.3. Where the original context and the context of transfer are highly similar in salient features and where there is considerable exposure to shared cognitive social processes and

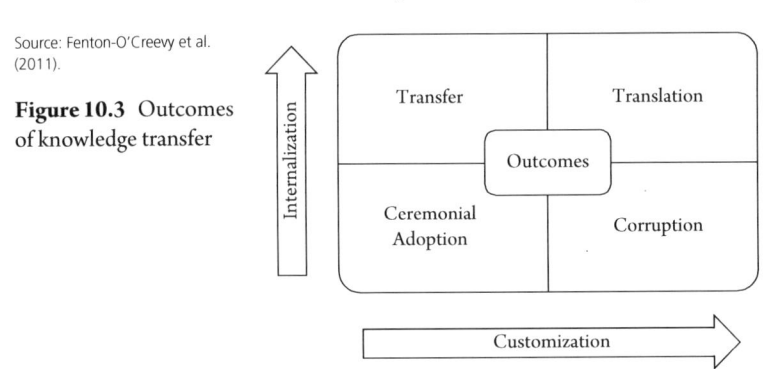

Source: Fenton-O'Creevy et al. (2011).

Figure 10.3 Outcomes of knowledge transfer

shared goals (i.e., social capital), we might expect that transfer of knowledge and practices could be achieved with little customization. While we would argue that there is always some reconstruction of practices in relation to local affordances, in practice two contexts may share such similarities and common assumptions that this work is quite small. Thus, for this case study we retain the term 'transfer'.

However, shared goals and effective mutual commitment across two geographically distinct parts of an MNE may, given that there is recognition that significant local customization of knowledge and practice is required, result in significant effort being made to translate knowledge and practice into the local context. We refer to this as 'translation', as what is implied is new meanings consistent with the original purpose of transfer. New practices are constructed with similar goals, drawing on both local knowledge and knowledge carried from the original context.

Either a lack of exposure to shared cognitive social processes or the absence of shared goals may lead to low internalization. This may lead to a purely ceremonial adoption, in a 'box-ticking' approach characterized by no real identification with or understanding of the knowledge or practice. Thus, the practice exists only on paper.

The low internalization case may also be marked by significant efforts at customization, but in this case, local efforts are largely directed at creating an impression that a serious effort has been made to ensure local customization. The reality is though that there is no change in practices and local objectives are reinforced. We follow Lozeau et al. (2002) in describing this as 'corruption' of the original intent of the practice.

10.6 Summary

In this chapter we have highlighted the fundamental differences between domestic and cross-national HRM. We explore SIHRM on the basis of a model that distinguishes the parent company's SIHRM orientation and subsidiary-level influences. Regarding the first part of the model we emphasized the parent company strategy. This is crucial to gaining an understanding of the degree of MNE-wide integration of HRM systems and practices. In the context of MNEs pursuing a multidomestic strategy we should expect to be able to observe many locally determined variants of HRM, whereas for MNEs with a global strategy there will be considerable MNE-wide integration of HRM. Furthermore, in multidomestic MNEs, corporate HR departments will be relatively small and there will be a more limited range of activities (Scullion and Starkey, 2000). This chapter has emphasized that to focus purely on the SIHRM orientation of the parent company is inadequate for an understanding of MNE-wide HRM. There are a number of subsidiary-level influences that must be taken into account. The first of these involves the resource dependence of the parent company on its subsidiaries: centres of excellence have the power to resist integration, whereas global offshores and servers do not. The second involves operating mode (see Chapter 4): acquisitions are generally considerably more of a challenge in terms of integration than greenfield subsidiaries. However, when MNEs design HRM systems for their subsidiaries, the model indicates that they invariably will have to consider host country culture and institutional constraints. Finally, in analysing the transfer of HRM to subsidiaries it is critical to distinguish 'genuine' transfer from other outcomes.

The case study that accompanies this chapter illustrates a Norwegian bank that attempted to import a set of HRM practices designed to stimulate sales from the US. The case shows how elastic the concept of translation is, and in doing so raises the issue of when practices have gone beyond translation to something fundamentally different.

REFERENCES

Adler, N.J. and F. Ghadar (1990), 'Strategic human resource management', in R. Pieper (ed.), *Human Resource Management: An International Resource Comparison* (pp. 235–60), New York: De Gruyter.

Bartlett, C.A. and S. Ghoshal (1989), *Managing Across Borders: The Transnational Solution*, Boston, MA: Harvard Business School Press.

Bartlett, C.A. and S. Ghoshal (1995), *Transnational Management: Text, Cases, and Readings in Cross-Border Management*, 2nd edition, Chicago, IL: Irwin.

Czarniawska, B. and B. Joerges (1996), 'The travel of ideas', in B. Czarniawska and G. Sévon (eds), *Translating the Organizational Change* (pp. 13–48), New York: Walter de Gruyter.

Fenton-O'Creevy, M., P.N. Gooderham, J.-L. Cerdin and R. Rønning (2011), 'Bridging roles, social skill and embedded knowing in multinational organizations', in M. Geppert and C. Dörrenbächer (eds), *Politics and Power in the Multinational Corporation*, Cambridge, UK: Cambridge University Press.

Gooderham, P.N., O. Nordhaug and K. Ringdal (1999), 'Institutional and rational determinants of organizational practices: Human resource management in European firms', *Administrative Science Quarterly*, **44**(3), 507–31.

Gooderham, P.N., O. Nordhaug and K. Ringdal (2006), 'National embeddedness and HRM in US subsidiaries in Europe and Australia', *Human Relations*, **59**(1), 1491–513.

Kostova, T. and K. Roth (2002), 'Adoption of an organizational practice by subsidiaries of multinational corporations: Institutional and relational effects', *Academy of Management Journal*, **45**(1), 215–33.

Lozeau, D., A. Langley and J.L. Denis (2002), 'The corruption of managerial techniques by organizations', *Human Relations*, **55**(5), 537–64.

Schuler, R.S. and S.E. Jackson (2005), 'A quarter-century review of human resource management in the U.S.: The growth in importance of the international perspective', *Management Revue*, **16**(1), 11–35.

Schuler, R.S., P.J. Dowling and H. De Cieri (1993), 'An integrative framework of strategic international human resource management', *Journal of Management*, **19**(2), 419–59.

Scullion, H. and K. Starkey (2000), 'In search of the changing role of the corporate human resource function in the international firm', *International Journal of Human Resource Management*, **11**(6), 1061–81.

Taylor, S., S. Beechler and N. Napier (1996), 'Toward an integrative model of strategic international human resource management', *Academy of Management Review*, **21**(4), 959–85.

Case L

SR-Bank: Gained in translation – the import, translation and evolution of a US sales and management concept

Martin Gjelsvik

L.1 Introduction

This case offers a detailed description on how a Norwegian organization, SpareBank1 SR-Bank, was suddenly confronted with a fundamental turnaround challenge brought about by profound changes to its external environment. The case tracks the adoption, translation and implementation by SR-Bank of a sales programme developed in the US, and how this initiative transformed over a period of 25–30 years. The programme – 'SESAM' – had strong implications for not only human resource management (HRM), but management in general, learning capabilities and organizational development.

The story goes back to the latter part of the 1980s when the institutional rules of Norwegian banks were turned upside down. The deregulation and liberalization of the financial markets swiftly and radically altered the rules of the game in the banking industry. This development coincided with a serious downturn of the economy, causing big losses for the banks. The case presented here deals with a bank and its people that survived what may be coined a close-to-death experience, as the bank was on the verge of bankruptcy in 1991. Since then, the bank, with its roots going back to 1839, has reinvented itself through a strong belief in linking its overall strategies to a human resource policy of continuously enhancing the knowledge and skills of the employees, close and long-term customer relations and a strong physical presence in the region. The bank is a learning organization where management consciously facilitates and encourages learning opportunities.

It is thus a story of an organization being forced to leave the shelter of strict, predictable government regulation and cartel-based non-competition to face and ride through the storms caused by deregulation. This story has repeated itself in many industries all over Europe, and during the financial crisis in 2008 it repeated itself for many financial institutions. Like other businesses exposed to dramatic changes, the bank had to learn how to compete more or less from scratch. The bank decided to base its turnaround on a redefinition of the roles of the employees and their managers through a comprehensive organizational development project. Developing its human resources became an integral part of the strategy. What was then conceived of as a programme or a project, is today a continuing process to leverage the knowledge and skills of all employees, and turning those competencies into sales and solid profits. The story centres on SESAM and how it eventually evolved and merged into a broader balanced scorecard system (Kaplan and Norton, 1996).

L.2 Cultural context

In this section we briefly describe the historical, cultural and institutional context SR-Bank operates in. It should be borne in mind that the Norwegian context is not static. In 2018, at the time of writing, there was a much greater acceptance of market-based solutions than was the case in 1990. Although Norway remains a relatively egalitarian society with a comprehensive welfare state, there are also increases in wealth disparity. The emphasis on equality has gone hand in hand with unionization. Powerful local and national unions have played, and still play, active parts in the public arena. Even in banks and insurance companies, unions have played a significant role and the principle of job security is defended, and wage differentials regarded with scepticism. Traditionally, unions have opposed individual performance assessments, and compensation has to a substantial degree been determined through collective bargaining.

Banks used to be among the most conservative work organizations in Norway. This was partly due to their shelter from competition through cartel agreements that determined interest rates and prices. In 1977, a new Savings Banks Act was implemented in which the savings banks such as SR-Bank were granted practically identical competitive conditions to the commercial banks. Furthermore, the savings banks were not obliged to keep mandatory capital ratios. There was no need for such requirements since losses were virtually non-existent. The lack of mandatory capital ratios turned the banks into vulnerable organizations when the bank crisis struck in the latter part of the 1980s. In addition, the banks had no systems for analysing or measuring the overall credit risk they were exposed to, leaving them unprepared for the turmoil the subsequent deregulation and the economic downturn would bring about. After the financial crisis, this has changed radically, and Norwegian banks now comply with strict EU regulations.

The post-1977 regime provided the foundation for a strong expansion in the savings banks' operations. The product range was substantially widened, and savings banks became full service banks for business and households. Compared to the rest of Europe, Norwegian savings banks command a unique position in their domestic market. However, the temptation to stretch for opportunities beyond the capabilities of the organization proved to be too great. The consequences of this dash for growth were exposed in the late 1980s and early 1990s when several banks went bankrupt.

L.3   SR-Bank's strategy

SR-Bank pursues a two-legged distribution strategy. Even today, after the introduction of internet banking and robots, the bank offers a strong physical presence. True, the number of offices has decreased from its peak of 50 to 35 in 2018, but they are devoted to being physically accessible for more complex financial services both for business and retail customers. The bank prides itself on providing a very high level of customer service accompanied by considerable investments in employees throughout the years, along with digitization of most routines. In parallel, the bank offers daily services through the internet, call centres and robots. Easy access to services and a high level of competent employees are an integral part of the strategy.

During the past 20 years, the bank has expanded geographically from the county of Rogaland to the whole of the south-western part of Norway. Recently, an office in the capital, Oslo, was established. The main office is located in Stavanger, the oil capital of Norway.

L.4   Key financial figures

We present the financial results of SR-Bank since 1989 in Table L.1. All figures are shown as a percentage of average total assets from the time of the introduction of SESAM.

We note the impact of the financial crisis that started in 1989 and that by 1991 had resulted in a disastrous performance. The long-term trend of slender interest margins had to be partly substituted by off-balance sheet sales (other than loans and bank savings). This trend has been a strong motivator for SESAM, which aims at supporting the bank's efforts to sell other products

Table L.1 Key financial figures (figures shown as a percentage of average total assets)

	2017	2011	2007	2000	1991	1989
Net interest margin	1.54	1.31	1.42	2.46	3.14	3.78
Other operating income	1.05	1.13	1.36	0.70	1.02	1.24
Total operating income	2.59	2.44	2.78	3.16	4.16	5.02
Total operating costs	1.06	1.22	1.44	1.76	3.56	3.43
Profit before losses and write-downs	1.54	1.22	1.34	1.40	0.60	1.59
Losses and write-downs	0.26	0.10	0.01	−0.18	3.96	1.50
Result of ordinary activities	1.27	1.12	1.33	1.58	−3.36	0.09

and services. We may also note the strong decrease in the operating costs since 1989–91, an indication of a considerable productivity gain achieved by the introduction and investment in state-of-the-art technology.

L.5 SESAM: The antecedents

Contrary to most banks, SR-Bank decided to keep and develop the branch network in the aftermath of the crisis in 1989–93. SR-Bank stayed with this strategy even with the introduction of internet banking. The strategy is costly and dependent on SR-Bank's ability to generate higher revenues. Back in 1989, this ability was lacking because bank employees were simply not salespeople. The most prevalent motive for seeking a job in a bank had been the desire to obtain a stable income and a secure job.

The decision to view the well-developed branch network as a part of the bank's strategy rather than as an unsustainable overhead was not an obvious decision. Indeed, in 1989, it was the subject of a heated debate. The introduction of ATMs (automatic teller machines) together with an electronic payment transfer system significantly reduced the customer's need to visit the bank in person. Consequently, there were good reasons for downsizing the branch network. The recommendations from the experts and consultants were also straightforward: get rid of the brick and mortar!

In the internal discussion, three points of view were present:

1. The bank needs to cut costs. Since the branch network incurs large costs, it must be reduced as much as possible. This is also in line with what our competitors are doing. The basis for this line of reasoning is purely cost

oriented. The contribution of bank employees to revenues was not taken into consideration.
2. The branch network, including both the physical and human resources it comprises, represents a unique competitive advantage. No competitor has a similar distribution system. Such an advantage must be developed and exploited, not dismantled.
3. Associated with the argument above, a humanistic point of view was present at that time: we are responsible for our employees and their jobs. The challenge is: how can we use these strategic resources more efficiently than in the past?

When the smoke subsided, points 2 and 3 surfaced as winners. However, the distribution network had to be modernized both physically and by enhancing the employees' communication skills and product knowledge. At this point in time, there was no appreciation on the part of employees that SR-Bank was facing a long-term crisis and a real need for change. The notion of improving the knowledge and competence of employees as well as providing high-quality service was easily agreed, but the process of transforming these ideas and intentions into practical actions gave rise to considerable differences of opinion. Different opinions surfaced as to whether there was a need for recruitment policy, career procedures and reward systems.

The case of lending is illustrative of the way things had been done. In determining the salary of employees working for the retail market (individuals and households), the traditional practice involved linking salary to the size of loans the employee was authorized to grant. Lending provided high internal status, leveraged authority and power with regard to the customer, and it meant more pay. Lending was associated with more status than deposits, which in turn ensured more status than working with payment transactions. 'Sales' was a four-letter word.

A common short-hand description of bank employees engaged in work with private customers was 'order takers'. This kind of reactive work behaviour was adequate as long as there was no reason for a customer to frequent more than one bank, as long as the customer, regardless of the service required, had to physically visit the bank. In addition, switching costs were high. But as the scale of the crisis became obvious and the awareness that the bank market had changed radically, the main questions were: How could a sales-oriented culture be developed? How could prevalent attitudes and work behaviour be changed? What kind of knowledge and skills do the employees and managers need? Do we have any tools or systems to aid us in this process?

For several years, the management had preached: 'We must get better at selling' and 'We must become better at understanding customers' needs'. There was no end to what the employees had to become better at doing. But can anyone be expected to improve without having the relevant tools or instructions indicating *how* this is to come about?

The first step was to stake out a path by formulating a special strategy for the retail market. This was outlined by the division's management as follows:

1. We shall turn profitable customers into *total* customer relations by:
   – providing a full range of financial services;
   – offering products and services for all phases of the life cycle;
   – being an active problem solver for the customer;
   – developing customer loyalty through cross-selling.
2. We shall develop our customer orientation through:
   – increased professional skills;
   – high service quality;
   – needs-oriented sales;
   – specifically focused market communication.
3. We shall provide speedy and efficient customer service through:
   – simplicity;
   – easy availability;
   – self-service.
4. We shall develop profitable customer segments through:
   – pricing;
   – needs orientation;
   – automation and standardization of mass-market products.

The notion of 'needs-oriented sales' was introduced to distance the employees from the common perception of an aggressive insurance salesperson, a salesperson more interested in his or her bonuses than in the customer's needs. 'Soft sell' was the buzzword – the starting point was always to meet the customer's actual needs. People had to be convinced that 'over-selling' would backfire in the form of complaints about poor and sloppy financial advice.

The human resources (HR) department assumed responsibility for arranging sales courses, typically one-day or weekend courses aimed at teaching the employees various sales techniques. However, this approach was unsuccessful. The reasons were plenty. The courses were not specifically directed at sales in banks: the ideals and techniques were copied from traditional retail business. The concepts of 'soft sell' and the focus on long-term customer relations were not at the forefront. Moreover, courses not part of a larger organizational context would easily result in only short-term enthusiasm among the participants, at best. The need for structural changes that could facilitate learning with lasting effects through organizational capabilities such as improved routines and revised computer programs became increasingly evident. No system existed to indicate what had been learned and if performance in any substantial way had actually improved.

L.6 SESAM: The initial steps through knowledge import

In 1989, during a business trip to the US, the manager of the retail market happened to come across a sales training programme that seemed to offer a solution to the issue of how to develop the skills needed to create a sales culture. The programme had an excellent track record in US financial institutions and the designer of the programme managed to convince him that what worked in the US could work in Norway.

On his return to Norway he attempted to convince colleagues that the programme was the way forward for SR-Bank. This turned out to be rather difficult. Comments such as 'this will be expensive' and 'the US is different from Norway' were indications of a profound scepticism. On the other hand, colleagues did accept that the programme was tailor-made for banks with a proven track record. Furthermore, it was based on practice, not abstract theory.

After a year of internal discussions, a contract was finally signed with the American developer of the programme. A pivotal condition was that the programme was not only to be translated into Norwegian, but also adapted to SR-Bank's culture and strategy. The latter point proved to be a great challenge.

American businesses, not least in the banking industry, are characterized by a high degree of management by directive compared to the more participative Scandinavian model. Therefore, bank employees in the US typically have less autonomous jobs than their Norwegian counterparts. Employee behaviour is directed more through detailed manuals and hierarchy than through development-oriented, cooperative projects, as is the case in Norway where empowerment has a long tradition. In addition, the gap between Norwegian managers and employees in terms of both salaries and mentality is smaller than in the US. This is illustrated by the fact that SR-Bank's management were far more active and visible participants at all stages of the project than had been the case for US banks. Through their involvement in the training programmes, they disseminated the 'new sales language' and discussed further developments of the project in the top management team.

There was another important reservation regarding the original US version of the programme. SR-Bank management and several employees observed that the programme was explicitly based on behaviouristic theory and assumptions. This provided considerable opportunity for managerial manipulation of employees. A prominent organizational psychologist was asked to consider the ethical implications of the programme. He advised that the programme was ethically sound given that the employees were informed about the measures taken and the tools to be used.

A new position as coordinator for the entire programme was established on a contract basis. The coordinator, an external consultant, and the bank manager in charge of the retail market division completed an intensive two-week training session in the US. They then 'Norwegianized' it. A translation from English to Norwegian is, of course, standard procedure. The challenge was to redefine the role expectations of employees into the Norwegian culture. Norwegian bank employees are more empowered to make decisions, work is more horizontally coordinated and team oriented. This transformation and redefinition was carried out by the group mentioned above, in addition to managers from the marketing and HR department.

L.7 SESAM: The explicit face

Having been 'Norwegianized', the programme was implemented for all employees in the retail market division, including managers at all levels. More than 500 employees were involved. The programme thus constituted a comprehensive organizational development process.

The primary objective was to offer a tool and a learning environment that provided understanding and opportunities to utilize the process of communication between the customer and the bank employees providing services to the customer. The aim was to develop the skills to determine the customer's present and future needs and to suggest the right products and services to fulfil these needs.

The sales and organizational development project was labelled SESAM, the Norwegian acronym for *salg er samarbeid* (sales is cooperation). The emphasis on the collaborative aspect was related to the customers' tendency to perceive the bank branches as one single bank. The customer wants to be recognized, regardless of whom they approach in the bank. It became crucial to stress the significance of intra-organizational cooperation, also across departmental boundaries. The SESAM project had a long-term perspective. The organization was to be transformed from an 'order-taking station' into a 'proactive sales train'. The process consisted of a number of training manuals defining the new roles of employees and managers combined with two-to-three-day training sessions. The new roles and the related necessary skills were explicitly formulated in manuals. The training sessions were designed to transform this explicit knowledge into practice. The employees were expected to learn the content in the manuals in two ways – by repeating their contents and by internalizing the content through learning by doing.

Below we offer detailed descriptions of two of the new roles, the one for tellers and the one for the manager of the retail division. Thus, we illustrate their complementarities. Each individual employee's role was defined through the so-called 'winning plays'. All levels of management were also equipped with winning plays, from the first-line managers ('sales leaders' in the new language) to the managing director. The sales leader of a bank outlet (for instance, the local branch manager) was familiar with his or her subordinates' winning plays. Conversely, employees also knew their superior's winning play. Thus, the different levels could check each other, and measures were generated so that everybody could continuously perfect his or her role performance. Box L.1 illustrates how the new role for the teller was defined.

The winning play revealed a very important and previously controversial point for the tellers' role. The tellers themselves were not asked to cross-sell, they were asked to refer the customer to a financial advisor if an opportunity for cross-selling arose. However, the tellers had previously responded negatively to any suggestion that they assume a more proactive attitude towards sales. They claimed that sales activity would 'only lead to queues at the counters'. The management had until now been unable to provide any specific suggestions as to how these two seemingly conflicting demands, prompt service and active cross-selling, could be met simultaneously. The paradox had finally been resolved, and the tellers' attitudes towards sales became more positive.

The second example of a winning play was designed for the general manager of the Retail Market division, as illustrated in Box L.2. Note the hierarchical system of roles and their complementarity.

Considerable emphasis was placed on measurable behaviour. Behavioural change was to be observed and reinforced through various forms of rewards: attention, praise and prizes. Reinforcing positive behaviour was a priority. During the first year, managers were instructed not to react negatively towards employees that did not succeed. The first year was designated to be a

BOX L.1

THE NEW ROLE FOR TELLERS IN SR-BANK

Winning play for tellers

Greeting and presentation
Greet the customer politely so that he or she feels important and welcome
Look up, smile and establish eye contact
Even if you are busy with something else, greet the customer by saying something, nodding or waving
Ask how you may be of assistance

Carry out the customer's wishes
Deal with the customer's requests in a competent and polite fashion
Use your knowledge to deal with requests, be precise and effective
Address the customer by name
Draw the customer into conversation – establish contact

Uncover needs
Discover what PNOs[a] a customer may have, show interest and consideration
Comment as you serve the customer
Listen for sales opportunities in what the customer says

Give recommendations
Find out which service best suits the customer and recommend it
Explain the solution
Use brochures actively
Recommend that the customer talk with a member of the customer service personnel

Refer the customer to relevant colleagues
Use a customer presentation card
Write the customer's name, the services you suggested and your name on the card
Enclose your business card and any other relevant documents
Refer the customer to the right person
If possible, escort the customer and introduce him or her
If you are unable to escort the customer, explain who he or she is to see and give the customer the customer presentation card

Conclusion
Thank the customer politely, using his or her name
If possible, shake hands
Welcome the customer back and offer your help in the future

Note: a. PNO: Problems, Needs and Opportunities. The rationale is that the customer comes to the bank with a problem that may be transformed into a need, which is a sales opportunity for the bank.

> **BOX L.2**
>
> ## THE NEW ROLE FOR GENERAL MANAGERS IN THE RETAIL MARKET DIVISION OF SR-BANK
>
> **Winning play for the division general manager**
> *Define and communicate the results you expect from each manager*
> Establish 'Winning plays for sales managers' as a standard for sales management and training
> Set targets together with the managers
> Obtain acceptance for expected actions and set targets, both for superiors and subordinates, so that the desired behaviour is measurable
>
> *Be a good example*
> Practice what you preach
> Be optimistic and enthusiastic
> Practice the three Cs (Competence, Courtesy and Consideration)
> Demonstrate correct customer service when you are involved in sales yourself
> Use the winning play
> Be consistent
>
> *Empower your employees*
> Share information
> Arrange monthly follow-up meetings with your managers
> Give your managers opportunities for individual development
> Delegate authority and responsibility
> Remove sales barriers
> LISTEN! LISTEN! LISTEN!
>
> *Build team spirit*
> Set goals for the region
> Communicate goals and results
> Map progress in the region
> Don't forget the humorous side of things
>
> *Check on your expectations*
> Execute hands-on management by visiting the local banks and branches
> Review the local bank's results monthly with each manager, using the sales reports
> Ask the customers if they are satisfied with the bank
> Go through customer messages, letters etc.
>
> *Reward and recognize*
> At your monthly meetings, reward and recognize those who have achieved good results
> Reward and recognize both individual employees and teams
> Express your approval for a well-done job on a daily basis
> Catch your employees doing a good job

trial-and-error period. Employees unable to adjust were helped to overcome their problems in their current job or transferred to another job.

'Catch your employees doing a good job' expressed the positive team spirit the organization sought to nurture. This proved to be a great challenge, especially for managers. Contrary to the US, Norwegians are introvert and seldom brag about their peers, let alone themselves. Employee sentiments were mixed. Many wanted to demonstrate and visualize their own skills, for example as expressed in sales figures. Others, particularly the more union oriented, were sceptical. They partly expressed concern with the assumed 'weak' performers, and partly argued on the basis of their legal right to stick to the main provisions of the National Bank Agreement, which prohibited individual performance measurements. Evaluations at the group level were accepted, on the condition that nothing could be traced back to the individual employee. The bank's management contested this formal argument, however, since the point in question was included under the main section in the National Bank Agreement dealing with *electronically* based systems. The management claimed that registration using an electronic medium was forbidden, while manual recordings and measurements were allowed.

Many possible avenues to compromises were attempted. One suggestion was that manual measurements of individual employee performance could be carried out at the workplace and the results then collected by the closest line manager. Union representatives opposed this suggestion, even though the employees in many divisions found this solution desirable. However, the management was not interested in letting the issue evolve into an open conflict. A project that otherwise had been so positively received was not to be spoiled by a feature not considered vital to the success of the project.

Ultimately, the following agreement was reached: each individual employee should manually record his or her own sales figures every week. These were in turn registered on a form without specifying the actual persons. The sales leader added up the figures and calculated the results of the branch/department. The individual employee could then benchmark him- or herself against the average sales scores.

SESAM did not challenge the organizational hierarchy as such, but it did change roles at all levels. Whereas the requirements and expectations previously had been diffuse and ambiguous, clear instructions about what was expected and how it was to be accomplished were now provided. Demands were now explicit, measurable and precise.

The responsibility for training employees at the operational level was assumed by their immediate superior, the sales leader. An external consultant trained the 60 sales leaders. He was also in charge of training 20 bank employees to act as on-the-job instructors. These instructors assisted the sales leader in training their personnel.

L.8 Branches and departments: The new learning communities

The most important and encompassing learning process took place in the local branches and support departments. The sales leaders were responsible for arranging weekly personnel meetings, held in the morning before the bank opened for customers. They typically lasted for half an hour. The meeting followed a fixed pattern in one-month periods. Two meetings were designated for service improvement, one meeting for product knowledge, and one for presentation and discussion of sales targets. The cycle was repeated every month. This responsibility was a new challenge for the sales leader, and the quality and results of the meetings varied greatly, but no deviation from the plan was accepted. Management simply required that these arrangements were part of the sales leaders' job, something he or she was committed to through SESAM.

The weekly meetings were regarded as an appropriate vehicle to institutionalize the learning process at the organizational level as well as with the individual employee and manager. It was an important tool for the transition from project to organization, from experiment to organizational routine. Learning was to be an organizational capability to leverage the competitive position of the bank.

The weekly meetings were always based on *local* experiences. Employees were encouraged to present good or bad examples of customer service or responses. These examples served as the basis for a discussion of improvements, changes, needs for new system solutions and advertising material. This institutionalized arena for learning through experience transfer was also important for political and ethical reasons. Local learning based on the team's own experience could serve as an important counterbalance to the more centralized and behaviourist learning model on which the project was originally founded. This local learning, which became increasingly significant, led to a 'democratization' of the organizational development that took place, and successful agendas for weekly meetings were exchanged among the sales leaders.

The weekly meetings represent a telling example of what Nonaka and Takeuchi (1995) have coined the 'socialization' process in the knowledge-creation spiral. At the individual level, explicit knowledge (the SESAM manuals and the winning plays) was internalized through learning by doing in their respective jobs and communications with customers and peers. Explicit knowledge becomes embodied in new skills and attitudes, and gradually part of the individual's automatic routines, and thus made tacit. Since tacit knowledge is context specific and difficult to formalize, transferring tacit knowledge requires sharing the same experience through joint activities and spending time together. The weekly meeting became a supplement to the formal training sessions. The combined learning arenas facilitate the blend of internalization and socialization processes that allow for leveraging both from the explicit and tacit knowledge potential.

As we will see in the following sections, learning from experience became the dominant knowledge-creation method in the bank. Gradually, the explicit and formal manuals were replaced with broad socialization processes across all levels of the bank.

The first test of the viability of the programme came with the new CEO of the bank in 1991. The main structure of the programme was then in place and likewise the outcome of the rather cumbersome negotiations with the union as to performance measurements and the policies towards those employees that did not want to change their roles. The new CEO was recruited from outside the banking industry. At the time of his arrival SR-Bank was close to bankruptcy (see Table L.1).

Contrary to the development at other banks in similar situations he reiterated the commitment to keep all branch offices as part of a strategy to stay close to the customer. He quickly became convinced of the potential of the SESAM programme and dedicated much of his time to being visible at training sessions. He made it clear that without increased sales efforts and tangible results, bank offices would have to shut down and employees laid off.

The position as SESAM leader became a two-year assignment with high status and high visibility. The candidate was handpicked from the highest ranks in the bank. Sales improved and with it the bank's financial results.

L.9 SESAM 12 years later: Best practice in practice

In 2001, SESAM was still very much alive. It had survived three CEOs, all of whom had been very enthusiastic about the programme. The programme initially included only the retail bank, but by 2001 the entire bank was included.

Figure L.1 The training arm

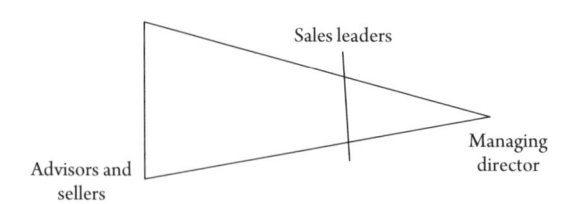

[Figure: triangle diagram showing "Sales leaders" at top, "Advisors and sellers" at left, and "Managing director" at right]

SR-Bank had outperformed every savings bank in Norway and it regarded SESAM as a critical element to this success.

When SESAM was first introduced, the aim was to transform bank employees from order takers to proactive salespeople. In 2001, this was no longer an issue. The employees had learned how to sell, and leaders at all levels knew how to motivate their employees to do just that. The objective in 2001 was to improve the performance of the existing roles, not to create new ones. The winning play outlined above was no longer in use as an explicit template, as the routine had become an internalized competence. Instead, learning focused on learning from practice – positive and negative experiences. SESAM had contributed to developing a common experience across the bank and therefore a common culture. All bank managers were expected to perform as sales leaders. Withdrawal to their paperwork in secluded offices was no option. These middle managers were all a vital part of SR-Bank's 'training arm', as illustrated in Figure L.1.

The arm may look like a modest attempt to demolish the traditional pyramid and hierarchical order. We have all encountered the advice of consultants to turn the pyramid on its head. Such advice is often embraced, but seldom implemented beyond window dressing. According to the bank in 2001, however, its sales organization actually worked horizontally. The managing director, the sales leaders and the advisors/sellers supported and served each other throughout the value chain.

Sales leaders were evaluated on an annual basis. Two dimensions were significant: (1) sales results over time; (2) feedback from the employees, by means of an annual internal appraisal and analysis. The analysis included leadership and organizational qualities like climate, job satisfaction, openness, and trust. In addition, a score of individual capacity was provided.

In other words, the sales leader's performance was evaluated in terms of quantitative sales statistics and more qualitative dimensions at both the organizational as well as the individual level. If the sales leader did not perform as expected, he or she would be offered other opportunities in the bank.

The CEO actively supported the programme, took part in the training sessions, and challenged the employees to propose chores for him to support them. He frequently asked, 'What can I do to make you perform a better job?' And the employees were responsive: 'We want better systems, we need more people, and we want a more visible leader'. The CEO took care not to control the process. He put his head on the block in the same way as the sales leaders and employees in their common efforts to improve their sales capabilities and relational processes. This was the logic of the 'training arm', the strength of the arm is dependent on everybody playing their respective roles to serve the customers.

In 2012, the programme had been managed by a series of dedicated SESAM leaders and the two-year position remained highly regarded. For some, the position had been a stepping stone to top jobs in SR-Bank, for others it had been a time out from their normal careers.

L.10 The issue of performance measurement

Ever since SESAM was introduced, performance measurement has been a significant issue. In the early years, any form of performance measurement was at odds with the SR-Bank culture. Not only did the unions make their demands, but management was uncomfortable with what it also regarded as a US approach to management.

The negotiations with the union ended in a compromise: measuring sales at the branch level was accepted, but not at the individual level. A selection of products was to be measured. In accordance with the principles of the 'training arm' (see Figure L.1) the branch offices were, after consultations with the marketing department and the top management group, to decide on which products were to be measured. The range of products was narrow because SR-Bank wanted to focus on prioritized initiatives. Typically, these coincided with marketing campaigns, seasonal sales or the utilization of new technologies such as internet banking. The mix of products could change from one quarter to another and the relative weighting of products could also change.

Compared with the original US programme, the connection between sales performance and economic incentives was intricate and definitively not pitched at the individual level. On a monthly basis, branches that reached their sales budgets would receive 50 euros per employee. Branches that achieved their quarterly budgets were granted a bonus of 200 euros per employee. An internal competition was introduced between the branch offices by rewarding the five best-performing branches with 400 euros per employee and the subsequent five best branches (numbers 6–10) 70 euros per employee. In addition to these regular bonuses, economic incentives were used for certain campaigns. Overall, the employees in the superior sales branches could pocket an added 10 per cent to their annual wages.

To avoid complacency, the bank implemented various schemes for benchmarking at three levels:

- internally between the branches of SR-Bank;
- between SR-Bank and the other member banks of the savings bank alliance;
- nationally through Gallup Polls.

The effects of this performance measurement system were indisputable. In relation to comparable banks, SR-Bank had the superior sales organization. Within the bank, it was noted that products and services included in the SESAM measurement scheme outperform those not included. This raised a new issue: economic incentives produced a short-term motivation. Remove a product from the basket of measured products and sales performance declines. This was at odds with SR-Bank's desire to achieve long-term motivation in line with its ambition to have long-terms customers.

The management was surprised that economic, external incentives were such powerful motivators. Performance measurement set in motion powerful emotional and competitive forces. Management made efforts to balance these unintended consequences by stressing ethics and norms as the most viable basis for good customer relations. SESAM was instrumental in transforming the bank from a passive 'order taker' to an active sales organization. Although the department manager knows individual scores, the agreement with the union is that the results are only ever to be published on the team/department level. The scores are actively used by departments to benchmark themselves against other departments and therefore to learn from one another.

As you will recall, for many years any open recognition or rewarding of individual performance was blocked by the union. In more recent years, as SR-Bank employees have developed a liking for being measured and for competing internally, the union has responded by withdrawing its objections. There are now even monthly celebrations of the top ten individual sales performers. In the Scandinavian institutional context, this degree of change is not particularly unusual. At the firm level, HR departments are not burdened with having to administer the mass of legislative detail that, for example, their German counterparts have to deal with. Employment law is sufficiently general to permit HR departments to experiment with and implement novel local HRM practices accepted by employees. Concomitantly, the law preserves the rights of unions to withdraw their cooperation in the case of disagreement with local management.

This collaborative and local nature to Scandinavian HRM is particularly discernible in another innovation that is specifically about fostering team spirit. Not only are 'goals' registered but also 'goal-creating passes' are registered. SR-Bank has introduced the term 'passes' (i.e., recommendations) in order to record and measure collaboration between the branches. A branch gets a credit when it recommends a customer to another part of the bank, and the receiving branch records the recommendation as a pass.

L.11 Yet another transformation: The balanced scorecard

Around 2000, after ten years' experience with SESAM, the bank introduces the balanced scorecard (Kaplan and Norton, 1996). The implementation was based on the broad experiences and learning from SESAM and may be seen as a path-dependent evolutionary process. The implication is that history matters. To understand the successful use of the balanced scorecard and how it co-evolved with the overall strategies of the bank, one needs to appreciate the transformative role of SESAM.

SESAM measured sales. The bank management wanted a *broader* measurement tool, and a more general management and communication system. The balanced scorecard offered these features. Monthly, the balanced scorecard measures four dimensions:

- the relations with customers and the market;
- the quality of internal processes;
- the quality of management and employees;
- financial results.

The SESAM-generated sales figures were integrated with the broader scorecard.

Currently (2018), SR-Bank has become a transparent organization with pervasive performance measures. Employees have developed a taste for measurements and celebrations of results, also at the individual level. However, it remains an organization with a strong union that is entitled to be consulted.

Interestingly, in the midst of encompassing and long-lasting performance measurements, the bank has realized that 'what counts most, cannot be measured'. Developing long-term, trustful customer relations, tacit knowledge, a sharing culture and so on does not lend itself to direct measurements.

Many organizations have introduced the concept of the balanced scorecard, often as lip service. SR-Bank has taken it very seriously, for several reasons. First, SESAM had proved highly successful with tangible results and represented a training ground. Second, banks are permeated by easily accessible data, so the balanced scorecard is reliably produced at the beginning of each month. Third, it functions as a communication platform across the organization, presenting both achievements and challenges. The bank organization represents an internal labour market. As the scores are open for everyone to see, the scorecard functions as a signal for employees. The most talented employees are attracted to the branches and departments that display superior performance. For top management the scorecard is further used as an evaluation tool of managers, as the content of the scorecard expresses clearly what is expected of managers and their teams. Simultaneously, the scorecard may support a democratic management style, as standardized and agreed-upon information is distributed to all levels of the organization. Potential conflicts may be mitigated as the scores represent objective and commonly accepted measures of issues that otherwise might be ambiguous.

Like SESAM, the scorecard is a platform for shared learning through experience. It has revealed a 'learning paradox', the fact that learning capabilities are unevenly distributed. The performance difference between comparable branches increased in periods, and it is recognized as a formidable challenge to sort out why that happens. Learning is also related to the scorecard as such. The content of the scorecard (what is being measured) changes over time, and measurements have been further developed. Some performance measures show not only absolute numbers, but how the bank's performance compares to competitors. Efforts are presently made to measure the impact and value of new innovations and projects on customers. Thus, the learning process goes on and on, as it has through almost 30 years. This is illustrated by the fact that SESAM and the balanced scorecard have survived four CEOs. The case has demonstrated that learning and transformations unfold in an evolutionary, path-dependent way, where culture and history always count.

CASE DISCUSSION

Give a short presentation of SR-Bank and the strategic challenges it faced and then discuss the following:

1 What did SR-Bank want to achieve by implementing a new sales and management concept?

2 Explain how institutional and cultural distance between the US and Norway could have impacted the way the programme was modified and implemented.
3 What general lessons can be learned from the SR-Bank case that are relevant for managers in multinational firms?

REFERENCES

Kaplan, R.S. and D.P. Norton (1996), *The Balanced Scorecard: Translating Strategy into Action*, Boston, MA: Harvard Business School Press.

Nonaka, I. and H. Takeuchi (1995), *The Knowledge-creating Company: How Japanese Companies Create the Dynamics of Innovation*, Oxford: Oxford University Press.

11
International career development as global strategy

11.1 Introduction

Moving the right people across national borders is a significant generic challenge for MNEs. Expatriation may be necessary either for safeguarding control of a subsidiary or for ensuring knowledge transfer. However, expatriation is expensive. The selection and training of expatriates, and their remuneration, are therefore key international human resource management (IHRM) concerns. Another is repatriation to capture the valuable experiences from international assignments. The head of global talent management at a Scandinavian MNE commented:

> [W]e are sending people out for one to two to three years but there is absolutely no idea or thoughts about how we will utilize the experiences that these people have gained. We leave it to the individual expat to take the risk of having something sensible to come back to after being out for a few years. We don't have any systematic follow through.

11.2 What is expatriation and why invest in it?

Expatriation is a term used when MNEs assign human resources to foreign locations for a set period of time, typically lasting three to five years (Shaffer et al., 2016). The expatriates become embedded in the daily business of their assigned foreign location, which sets this cross-border interaction apart from shorter-term business travel and project work. Our definition of expatriates also differs from an increasingly recognized group of self-initiated expatriates, where individuals independently seek new employment in a foreign location and are hired as locals (Andresen, Biemann and Pattie, 2015). With the increased focus on globalization of business, firms' investments in expatriates have become more common and increasingly important for the MNE's success (Bolino, 2007; Shortland, 2016).

MNEs utilize expatriation for a variety of reasons and the lengths of assignments vary according to the purpose and internal needs. The reasons for expatriation are typically grouped into three main categories: (1) filling a position when local talent is lacking; (2) developing the organization; and (3) developing future leaders (Brock et al., 2008; Edstrom and Galbraith, 1977; Shay and Baack, 2004; Shortland, 2016). Filling a position for immediate business needs requires individuals with specified competencies and skills who can transfer these to the local business context. Expatriates with such roles and responsibilities are usually expected to invest significant time in supporting and training the local organization by contributing with their specific knowledge (e.g., technical or process knowledge). Expatriates are also used for organizational development purposes to improve internal coordination by facilitating the transfer of organizational systems, processes and technologies across the geographically dispersed organization. Expatriates can furthermore enhance direct control through behaviour and outcome monitoring as well as indirect control by fostering shared values and culture. The use of expatriates for knowledge sharing or control purposes has increased as MNEs grow their distributed network of organizational units (Lee, 2016). Many MNEs also use expatriation as a tool to develop future managers by exposing them to cross-cultural situations and thus develop a stronger understanding of global business needs and the complexities of cross-border organizations.

Just as the reasons for investing in expatriates differ, the ideal candidates and expected long-term effects also vary. For instance, the objective of filling a position targets specific competencies and skills. While this reason for using expatriates is critical to meet immediate business demands, learning opportunities for the individual expatriate may be limited. The strategic importance of such experience for long-term career development may also be lower than when expatriation is motivated by organizational- or leadership-development. When the MNE wants to achieve organizational learning, the expatriates' technical skills should ideally be balanced with social skills. This balance can better support long-term benefits through the development of shared values and a strengthening of internal networks. Similarly, expatriation motivated by leadership development requires that the identified individuals possess necessary business, cognitive and social skills to learn from the organization.

Research on the actual value creation from expatriation is inconclusive despite estimates that the cost of an expatriate can be two to ten times higher than if the position was filled locally (Black and Gregersen, 1999; Carraher, Sullivan and Crocitto, 2008). Nowak and Linder (2016) propose that MNE value creation from expatriation should be examined in the same manner as other investments, calculating an expatriate return on investment (eROI). They further argue that MNEs should break down expenses into three categories: before, during and after the expatriation in order to discount cash flows properly. Costs are often incurred long before benefits are realized. Depending on the motive for expatriation, expected benefits could be measured both at an individual (e.g., career advancement) and organizational (e.g., knowledge transfer) level.

Studies suggest that CEOs with experience from international assignments tend to be more effective and perform better than those who were not expatriated (Bolino, 2007; Shay and Baack, 2004; Tan and Mahoney, 2007). There is no clear empirical support, however, for the relationship between the number of expatriate managers and degree of knowledge transfer from subsidiaries to other corporate units (Björkman, Barner-Rasmussen and Li, 2004). For foreign subsidiaries experiencing growth, hosting expatriates has been found to increase headquarters' attention (Plourde, Parker and Schaan, 2014). This can benefit both headquarters and the subsidiary by ensuring sufficient visibility of the subsidiary and increase headquarters' understanding of the local needs and opportunities, thus reducing bounded rationality at headquarters.

Mobility can also add value for recruitment and retention of employees. Mobility is not limited to the assignment of headquarters personnel to foreign subsidiaries, but also includes assignments from foreign subsidiaries to the home country as well as between foreign units. Some distinguish between expatriation and inpatriation where expatriation entails sending people from headquarters to foreign subsidiaries and inpatriation entails sending people from the foreign subsidiaries to headquarters (Harzing, 2001). Although inpatriation can also be driven by similar motives, it will likely exhibit few control motives. In this chapter, the term expatriation will be used for both forms of foreign assignments.

11.3 The importance of repatriation

Repatriation occurs when employees return from their foreign assignments and reintegrate into the organization in their home country. This process is extremely important for MNEs to ensure that the organization taps into, and makes use of, the valuable experience and expertise gained during the expatriation period. The repatriates become important vehicles for knowledge transfer and organizational learning (Lazarova and Cerdin, 2007).

Despite its importance, however, many employees are disappointed when repatriated. This dissatisfaction is rooted almost entirely in the repatriation process (Jassawalla and Sashittal, 2009; Reiche, Harzing and Kraimer, 2009). The expectations of repatriates are often unfulfilled and there is no clear link identified between an expatriate assignment and subsequent career success (Bolino, 2007). Some repatriates have even claimed that they would have been better off career-wise without the expatriate experience, as the positions are often not left open during their absence and some experience a loss of their internal connectivity.

Organizations that have invested in expatriates are also often dissatisfied (ibid.). The dissatisfaction from both the individual and organization can be seen in the dismal statistics suggesting that as many as 20–50 per cent of repatriates leave the firm within a year of their return (Jassawalla and Sashittal, 2009). In their ground-breaking study of 750 MNEs from the EU, Japan and the US, Black and Gregersen (1999) found that the average turnover within three months after repatriation was 25 per cent. As many as 75 per cent of repatriates felt that their permanent position when returning home was a demotion from their position abroad, and 61 per cent felt they lacked opportunities to put their experiences to work. More recent research shows that the individual's perceived 'return on investment' in terms of career development is particularly important when an expatriate assignment is considered (Shortland, 2018).

Successful repatriation requires planning and preparation prior to the actual return of the individuals, and retaining people becomes one of the greatest HRM challenges. When repatriates leave the MNE, the organization not only loses valuable knowledge and skills, but also potentially loses it to a competitor. Disappointed repatriates may also deter other employees from wanting to take on international assignments.

11.4 Enabling the expatriate

Accepting a foreign assignment exposes the individual to many new challenges such as a new work environment as well as differences in both organizational and national cultures (Shay and Baack, 2004). The expatriate must thus overcome a number of challenges to achieve anticipated career advancements and opportunities for personal development associated with foreign assignments. There has been extensive research on how expatriates can increase their effectiveness and suggestions for how to ensure their assignments are successful. One of the most important areas to clarify early is the alignment of expectations. Organizational and personal expectations do not always align. It can be helpful for an expatriate to understand the motivations behind the foreign assignment to better align expectations (ibid.). If the assignment is motivated by filling an immediate business need, fewer expectations will be placed on learning and contributing to informal control mechanisms. At the same time, filling an immediate business need may provide less of a boost for the individual's career advancement than the expatriate might be expecting (Bolino, 2007).

Most research to date has focused on adjustments at the individual level without linking it to performance outcomes. The performance of the individual undoubtedly has a huge impact on the organization's value creation. Knowledge transfer, for instance, is highly contingent on the expatriate's ability and motivation to accumulate and share knowledge (Reiche et al., 2009). Achieving satisfactory embeddedness in both the home organization and the local organization to enable valuable knowledge transfer is challenging. MNEs can support individuals by establishing formal communication channels. These should ideally enable the expatriate to communicate and transfer knowledge throughout the assignment and not be limited to repatriation (Carraher et al., 2008). The role of expatriates' local social networks also impacts adjustment and performance. A study of expatriates in China found that successful interactions with host-country nationals play a significant role in the success of expatriate assignments (Bruning, Sonpar and Wang, 2012). Repatriation adjustment assistance and engaging with the expatriate in career development plans also supports successful outcomes. Many expatriates express concerns of losing touch with the home country as they fear being 'out of sight, out of mind' might affect their career opportunities when repatriating (Reiche et al., 2009).

Since the roles and responsibilities of many expatriates require extensive experience and expertise, individuals are often at a stage of life with family situations where partners and children are also directly affected by the foreign assignment. Adjustment difficulties among family members have long been recognized as one of the most common reasons for expatriate dissatisfaction and shortened assignments, supported by a meta-analysis identifying the spouse's adjustment as the most important predictor for adjustment of expatriates in their new assignments (Bhaskar-Shrinivas et al., 2005). Later studies have also identified that how expatriates perceive the support for their parent organizations also explains why some expatriates adjust well and meet performance expectations in their new assigned locations while others 'fail' (Abdul Malek, Budhwar and Reiche, 2015). In a study of women expatriates in the global oil and gas industry, Shortland (2018) found that providing services to find suitable accommodation was one of the most valued types of support from the parent organization, followed by the coverage of their children's educational expenses and spousal support. However, theoretical and empirical research on predictors of expatriate success remain limited.

The previous discussion of managerial mindsets is naturally not limited to managers making staffing decisions. Mindsets of the individual expatriates also impact the success and outcomes of an assignment. The ability to accumulate and share information is critical, requiring openness and appreciation for information that is perceived as 'foreign' and difficult to grasp. Expatriates with strong ethnocentric mindsets may exhibit less willingness and ability to recognize valuable local knowledge. As previously discussed, clarifying the reasons behind the assignment may enable the expatriates to better understand their roles and responsibilities and create an opportunity to build on strengths and develop weaknesses to better meet communicated expectations. Many MNEs also work with potential expatriate candidates to assess individual mindsets and develop a plan for building necessary skills and capabilities to tackle the expatriate assignment (Javidan, Teagarden and Bowen, 2010).

11.5 Capturing the value of repatriates

Since the expatriate's accumulated knowledge and experience is believed to have high value for the organization, the ability to transfer knowledge and reintegrate repatriated individuals is critical (Reiche et al., 2009). One of the key managerial challenges is thus related to minimizing repatriation failure rates. Although the estimated costs and failure rates of expatriation vary across studies (Carraher et al., 2008), there is nevertheless agreement that the costs of expatriates are significantly higher than the costs of local hires, with empirical evidence supporting concerns about failure rates.

Repatriates frequently express dissatisfaction with unfulfilled expectations regarding their career opportunities upon their return (Bolino, 2007). So why have decades of debate and research on the topic not resulted in significantly lower failure rates? MNEs are characterized as 'too focused on expatriation instead of repatriation, too ad hoc and opportunistic instead of strategic in their behaviors, and too disorganized to implement post repatriation-related programs scholars recommend' (Jassawalla and Sashittal, 2009, p. 770).

To fully capture the value of repatriates, MNEs must recognize that cross-cultural transfers of human resources generate added complexities compared to domestic transfers. The accumulated knowledge is often perceived as 'foreign' and difficult to understand by the home organization, requiring organizational capabilities to receive such information (Oddou, Osland and Blakeney, 2009). But as Lazarova and Tarique point out, 'not all knowledge is easy to capture...individuals and organizations do not necessarily have coinciding goals with respect to using knowledge as a basis for developing a competitive advantage' (2005, p. 362). This requires a fit between the repatriate's type of knowledge and motivation and the organizational capability to capture knowledge and create appropriate incentives for repatriates to share their knowledge. The re-socialization process may also be more extensive due to geographical and cultural distances. This is an area that is frequently overlooked by human resource departments.

Selecting the right individuals for foreign assignments can have a huge impact on the outcomes. MNEs should therefore send people on foreign assignments 'for the right reasons'. A good technical track record in the home country may not serve as a good success recipe for future international leaders. Technical skills do not necessarily reflect the ability to understand business at a global level, whether the person is open to new ideas and experiences, or has the ability to build trusting relationships in cross-cultural settings (Javidan et al., 2010). In a study of Japanese expatriates, intercultural personality traits identified before the assignment were positively related to the expatriates' abilities to acquire competencies when expatriated and subsequent abilities to transfer these competencies when repatriated (Furuya et al., 2009).

Many firms, such as Siemens, also try to avoid expatriation becoming financially motivated and focus on setting fair conditions that enable employees to maintain equivalent living standards but not 'gain economically' from it (Russwurm et al., 2011). In general, there is not one specific type of person that is most suitable for expatriation. Different people fit with different reasons for expatriation. Consequently, resourceful organizations such as Royal Dutch Shell invest tremendously in HRM systems that will enhance the selection and fit between individual characteristics and needs and the organization's immediate and long-term needs (Sucher and Corsi, 2011). Clarifying the reasons for an expatriation will thus enable the organization to ensure best fit with potential candidates.

There is an inherent assumption that if expats are well adjusted, they will also be effective (Shay and Baack, 2004). Mentoring has been identified as a tool to enhance the adjustment and effectiveness of expatriates. The mentorships should ideally be connected to both the home country and host country (Carraher et al., 2008). Accordingly, host-country mentors are particularly helpful with cultural adaptation while home-country mentors create important links back to the organization in the home country and ease various repatriation issues. Formal mentoring programmes can thus be beneficial to avoid negative outcomes of international assignments.

The knowledge acquired during expatriation (such as procedures, ideas, experiences, models developed over time that guide actions and decisions) is particularly valuable in a global business environment where learning generates competitive advantages. If MNEs fail to capture value from their repatriates, they miss opportunities for competitive advantages and risk 'losing their investment' if repatriates leave (Oddou et al., 2009). There are two key reasons why MNEs have problems retaining repatriates. First, repatriates become dissatisfied when their organizations do not express any interest in utilizing their newly acquired expertise. Second, repatriates may also be proactive in managing their own careers and evaluate career opportunities outside the company (Suutari and Brewster, 2003). This turnover does not merely reflect dissatisfaction with the repatriation process and career opportunities. Expatriates may also be assessing the overall attractiveness of future opportunities (Lazarova and Tarique, 2005). A study of Finnish expatriates found that 65 per cent received external job offers while still expatriated and 60 per cent received external job offers after repatriation (Suutari and Brewster, 2003).

11.6 What can we learn from best practices?

With the dismal statistics discussed earlier showing dissatisfaction with outcomes both at the organizational and individual level, learning from best practices can be valuable. Despite the many reasons for expatriation, filling immediate business demands has long represented the most common driver for expatriation (Black and Gregersen, 1999). While this addresses immediate business needs, it may not result in long-term effective human resource management or organizational development. MNEs continuously need to consider their long-term goals in terms of knowledge creation and leadership development. This requires an investment in structured repatriation. Just as the reasons behind expatriation differ, the type of knowledge accumulated will vary depending on the nature of the responsibilities and degree of interaction involved in the position (Lazarova and Tarique, 2005).

Successful companies have been found to emphasize three key practices for international assignments. First, knowledge creation and global leadership development is emphasized to ensure that the assignment creates long-term value for the MNE. Although filling an immediate business need with an expatriate may not be motivated by learning, the MNE should strive to use expatriation foremost as a learning opportunity. Second, MNEs must invest in identifying the right candidates by ensuring that any technical skills are matched or exceeded by cross-cultural abilities. The ability to absorb and transfer knowledge in cross-cultural contexts requires cognitive and social capabilities. Selection processes should thus value specific technical skills as one of many necessary expatriate qualities. Finally, successful MNEs have deliberate and well-prepared repatriation processes that start well in advance of the physical repatriation (Black and Gregersen, 1999).

11.7 How managerial mindsets impact staffing policies

The MNE characteristics and approach to staffing is often rooted in the managerial perceptions and mindsets. We commonly refer to three distinct mindsets to help us understand strategic decisions in MNEs and their approaches to staffing policies: ethnocentric, polycentric and geocentric (Perlmutter, 1969; Reiche et al., 2009). Although these mindsets are distinct they may to some extent coexist within the same MNE, especially if the success of a geographically spread organization requires internal differentiation in the approach to managing and staffing foreign operations.

Ethnocentric mindsets

Ethnocentric mindsets reflect a management approach that is deeply rooted in the home-country culture and 'ways of doing things'. Top management seeks to project competencies and capabilities (including processes and procedures) from headquarters to the rest of the organization, reflecting a unidirectional flow of resources and information (Johnson, Lenartowicz and Apud, 2006). Staffing policies in ethnocentric MNEs are characterized by extensive use of expatriates to manage foreign subsidiaries and transfer knowledge throughout the organization. Local employees in foreign subsidiaries are typically viewed as the recipients of knowledge and often find it difficult to excel into higher management positions as these are entrusted to expatriates from headquarters.

The benefits of ethnocentric mindsets include a greater degree of control in geographically dispersed organizations by staffing key management positions with expatriates and directly influencing 'ways of doing things' in the foreign subsidiaries. This can also enable the development of a shared organizational culture that largely reflects the home-country organizational culture. The benefits are greatest when host markets lack qualified managers or employees to fill positions or when competencies and capabilities have tacit characteristics that are otherwise difficult to codify and transfer.

Ethnocentric mindsets can trigger resistance in the foreign subsidiaries. If expatriates rather than locals continuously fill top management positions, local employees may feel disgruntled by perceived limitations to their career development. This may result in lower productivity and high turnover, and at worst lead to self-fulfilling prophecies that reinforce headquarters' perceptions that key positions can only be trusted to individuals with close ties and proven loyalty to the parent organization. Furthermore, inherent limitations to headquarters' ability to identify and understand local needs may result in lost business opportunities and management decisions that are not well adapted to the local business context. A lack of recognition of competencies and capabilities outside headquarters can also influence repatriation by creating barriers to receptivity (Oddou et al., 2009).

Polycentric mindsets

Polycentric mindsets, in contrast, value local adaptation and seek to develop the foreign operations to 'think locally'. These MNEs value localized 'ways of doing things' and management positions in foreign subsidiaries are preferably filled by locals. The polycentric mindset is compatible with multidomestic strategies where foreign operations experience greater levels of autonomy. Communication across organizational boundaries is lower, often limited to financial and accounting reports from the subsidiaries to headquarters, rather than transfers of competencies and capabilities. Staffing policies in polycentric MNEs are characterized by more restrictive use of expatriates since cross-border organizational and leadership development is less emphasized.

Many of the advantages of polycentric mindsets address the identified disadvantages of ethnocentric mindsets. Local employees see better opportunities for local career advancement, which also positively influences the attractiveness when recruiting new talent. The local organization can more easily develop important local networks and communicate better both internally and externally as managers are fully embedded in the local culture. It hinders the danger of 'cultural imperialism' that may clash with local traditions. The local management is also better able to identify and respond to local business challenges and opportunities. Additional benefits include less resistance locally (both politically and socially) when the organization is perceived as 'local', and avoiding the high costs of large numbers of expatriates.

The main disadvantages of polycentric mindsets include the difficulties of achieving synergies and efficiencies in geographically dispersed organizations' globalization of markets. The increased globalization of markets has pushed many MNEs to become more cost efficient by tapping into location advantages such as low-cost labour and build scale economies through geographically dispersed but closely integrated value chain activities. Localizing activities with minimal control and coordination hinders such competitive advantages and the MNE may suffer from inefficiencies in the organization. Limiting the use of expatriates can make the foreign subsidiaries more detached from headquarters, resulting in managers and employees that lack an understanding of 'global business' and overlook opportunities for cross-border value creation. In addition, opportunities for local employees to gain international experience through foreign assignments or work with headquarters, qualities that often make MNEs attractive, may be limited.

Geocentric mindsets

Contrary to ethnocentric and polycentric mindsets that emphasize the importance of a specific geographical location, geocentric mindsets seek to build on best practices from all parts of the organization. Geocentric mindsets thus reflect multidirectional transfers of resources and capabilities (Reiche et al., 2009). Staffing policies using this approach are characterized by selecting the best candidates for the positions, regardless of organizational or geographical origin. As such, subsidiary managers may be staffed by expatriates from anywhere in the organization, based on the alignment of organizational needs and individual qualifications.

Key advantages of geocentric mindsets include the ability to tap into a larger pool of resources for expatriation and thereby make better use of the organization's human resources. It can also facilitate the development of internal networks, transfer of core competencies and build a unified organizational culture that is not perceived imposed by headquarters. This should ideally reduce the resistance to perceptions of 'cultural imperialism' while also recognize needs for local adaptation. Geocentric mindsets can thus facilitate the development of a greater pool of future leaders with a sound understanding of global business needs, as the selection criteria and international appointments are not rooted in geographical considerations. Individuals may also more easily transfer from assignment to assignment across organizational units, extending their expatriate careers while ensuring cross-border value creation in the MNE.

One could ask why not all MNEs strive to become geocentric, with the apparent benefits it can generate. First, true geocentric mindsets require extensive coordination and an ability to identify both organizational needs and individual qualifications. The diversity of international assignments can also result in difficulties when developing compensation structures, training programs and development plans. This is particularly challenging as dual-career families make longer expatriate assignments increasingly difficult. Further, challenges in the foreign subsidiaries may still exist if key management positions are continuously filled by expatriates from other parts of the organization rather than locally recruited individuals.

Can managerial mindsets change?

Some argue that managerial mindsets are influenced by the MNE's home-country national culture. Japanese firms in particular, have been examined extensively to determine if they exhibit ethnocentric mindsets and invest in expatriates primarily to exert home-country 'ways of doing things' (Brock et al., 2008). While Japanese firms do use expatriation extensively for top management positions in foreign subsidiaries, the reasons for this are inconclusive. Mixed effects of ethnocentrism and a contingency approach have been identified in Japanese firms where decisions are also contingent upon strategic issues such as the emphasis on inter-firm ties or the local market orientation and perceived strategic importance of the foreign subsidiary (Belderbos and Heijltjes, 2005).

Some MNEs purposefully hire top managers with different experiences and perspectives to infuse different mindsets into the organization. This is particularly visible in MNEs with polycentric mindsets that feel increasing competitive pressures as markets become more globalized and competitors tap into low-cost countries to achieve efficiencies. Increasing the investment in expatriates for the purposes of organizational and leadership development can also gradually influence the managerial mindsets as a new generation of managers with extensive international experience takes on key positions. Ownership structures also influence managerial mindsets. It may be more fitting for state-owned enterprises, for instance, to maintain ethnocentric mindsets where the hiring of foreigners into top management positions can generate resistance among key stakeholders. International joint ventures and mergers will also likely influence managerial mindsets, making ethnocentric mindsets more difficult to maintain.

11.8 Summary

In this chapter, we have addressed the challenges related to global mobility. Expatriation is costly, and the success rates are discouraging. This poses the question of whether we need to consider alternative forms of global mobility as well as reconsider how we define successful expatriation (Lazarova and Cerdin, 2007). We tend to assume that retention implies positive organizational outcomes and that individual benefits translate into organizational benefits. When re-examining the three main reasons for expatriation, however, one could argue that not all turnover is negative as assignments vary in their long-term strategic importance for the organization.

It should also be recognized that despite their individual qualities and leadership potential, not all individuals are interested in or able to accept international assignments. Dual-income families are frequently referred to as one of the main challenges of expatriation, although the reasons are many. In some instances, these barriers to accepting foreign assignments can be addressed by the length of the assignment. Firms, such as Walmart and Samsung, are increasingly focusing on shorter assignments to enable people who are earlier in their careers or who have difficulties moving for longer periods to gain global experience (Russwurm et al., 2011). Shorter assignments are by no means new, but have received greater attention lately as a strategic tool to reduce costs and expose attractive candidates to international experiences (Bonache et al., 2010).

In addition to revisiting the length of assignments, the following alternatives have been identified as interesting alternative approaches to consider: self-initiated expatriates, commuter assignments/flexpatriation, frequent travelling and virtual working (Bonache et al., 2010; Shortland, 2016). Studies on self-initiated expatriation show many similarities in terms of education backgrounds and career ambitions, but that more women tend to choose self-initiated expatriation (Andresen et al., 2015). This opens opportunities for MNEs to hire qualified self-initiated expatriates in foreign subsidiaries to reduce the cost of expatriation and overcome potential gender biases, particularly when the motive is to fill a position. The effectiveness of expatriation versus more centralized control as well as investments in training, diversified projects and task forces have also been debated without clear empirical evidence. Some of the proposed alternatives may better address certain aspects of organizational development, however, rather than satisfy the needs for knowledge transfer or management development (Harzing, 2001). Clarifying the reason behind a proposed expatriation assignment will help managers when comparing the costs and benefits of alternative arrangements. To date, such non-traditional categories of expatriates have received scant attention in research (Guttormsen, 2018).

Finally, as MNEs increasingly grow through mergers and acquisitions (UNCTAD, 2011, 2018), new challenges may arise for expatriation. Most research to date has primarily focused on expatriation in wholly-owned MNEs, while the international ownership structures increasingly exhibit variations of joint ventures and strategic alliances. MNEs must carefully consider how the role of expatriates fits with their international strategies and ownership structures (Harzing, 2001).

The case study that accompanies this chapter focuses on LVMH, an MNE that strategically uses global mobility to remain competitive and develop future managers.

REFERENCES

Abdul Malek, M., P. Budhwar and B.S. Reiche (2015), 'Sources of support and expatriation: A multiple stakeholder perspective of expatriate adjustment and performance in Malaysia', *International Journal of Human Resource Management*, **26**(2), 258–76.

Andresen, M., T. Biemann and M.W. Pattie (2015), 'What makes them move abroad? Reviewing and exploring differences between self-initiated and assigned expatriation', *International Journal of Human Resource Management*, **26**(7), 932–47.

Belderbos, R.A. and M.G. Heijltjes (2005), 'The determinants of expatriate staffing by Japanese multinationals in Asia: Control, learning and vertical business groups', *Journal of International Business Studies*, **36**(3), 341–54.

Bhaskar-Shrinivas, P., D.A. Harrison, M.A. Shaffer and D.M. Luk (2005), 'Input-based and time-based models of international adjustment: Meta-analytic evidence and theoretical extensions', *Academy of Management Journal*, **48**(2), 257–81.

Björkman, I., W. Barner-Rasmussen and L. Li (2004), 'Managing knowledge transfer in MNEs: The impact of headquarters control mechanisms', *Journal of International Business Studies*, **35**(5), 443–55.

Black, S.J. and H.B. Gregersen (1999), 'The right way to manage expats', *Harvard Business Review*, **77**(2), 52–63.

Bolino, M.C. (2007), 'Expatriate assignments and intra-organizational career success: Implications for individuals and organizations', *Journal of International Business Studies*, **38**(5), 819–35.

Bonache, J., C. Brewster, V. Suutari and P. De Saá (2010), 'Expatriation: Traditional criticisms and international careers: Introducing the special issue', *Thunderbird International Business Review*, **52**(4), 263–74.

Brock, D.M., O. Shenkar, A. Shoham and I.C. Siscovick (2008), 'National culture and expatriate deployment', *Journal of International Business Studies*, **39**(8), 1293–309.

Bruning, N.S., K. Sonpar and X. Wang (2012), 'Host-country national networks and expatriate effectiveness: A mixed-methods study', *Journal of International Business Studies*, **43**(4), 444–50.

Carraher, S.M., S.E. Sullivan and M.M. Crocitto (2008), 'Mentoring across global boundaries: An empirical examination of home- and host-country mentors on expatriate career outcomes', *Journal of International Business Studies*, **39**(8), 1310–26.

Edstrom, A. and J.R. Galbraith (1977), 'Transfer of managers as a coordination and control strategy in multinational organizations', *Administrative Science Quarterly*, **22**(2), 248–63.

Furuya, N., M. Stevens and A. Bird et al. (2009), 'Managing the learning and transfer of global management competence: Antecedents and outcomes of Japanese repatriation effectiveness', *Journal of International Business Studies*, **40**(2), 200–215.

Guttormsen, D.S.A. (2018), 'Does the "non-traditional expatriate" exist? A critical exploration of new expatriation categories', *Scandinavian Journal of Management*, **34**(3), 233–44.

Harzing, A.W. (2001), 'Of bears, bumble-bees, and spiders: The role of expatriates in controlling foreign subsidiaries', *Journal of World Business*, **36**(4), 366–79.

Jassawalla, A.R. and H.C. Sashittal (2009), 'Thinking strategically about integrating repatriated managers in MNEs', *Human Resource Management*, **48**(5), 769–92.

Javidan, M., M. Teagarden and D. Bowen (2010), 'Making it overseas', *Harvard Business Review*, **88**(4), 109–13.

Johnson, J.P., T. Lenartowicz and S. Apud (2006), 'Cross-cultural competence in international business: Toward a definition and a model', *Journal of International Business Studies*, **37**(4), 525–43.

Lazarova, M.B. and J.-L. Cerdin (2007), 'Revisiting repatriation concerns: Organizational support versus career and contextual influences', *Journal of International Business Studies*, **38**(3), 404–29.

Lazarova, M. and I. Tarique (2005), 'Knowledge transfer upon repatriation', *Journal of World Business*, **40**(4), 361–73.

Lee, J.M. (2016), 'Managing complex MNEs: Structural attributes of the MNE and expatriation strategies', *Academy of Management Annual Meeting Proceedings*, **2016**(1), 846–51.

Nowak, C. and C. Linder (2016), 'Do you know how much your expatriate costs? An activity-based cost analysis of expatriation', *Journal of Global Mobility*, **4**(1), 88–107.

Oddou, G., J.S. Osland and R.N. Blakeney (2009), 'Repatriating knowledge: Variables influencing the "transfer" process', *Journal of International Business Studies*, **40**(2), 181–99.

Perlmutter, H.V. (1969), 'The tortuous evolution of the multinational corporation', *Columbia Journal of World Business*, **4**(1), 9–18.

Plourde, Y., S.C. Parker and J.-L. Schaan (2014), 'Expatriation and its effect on headquarters' attention in the multinational enterprise', *Strategic Management Journal*, **35**(6), 938–47.

Reiche, B.S., A.-W. Harzing and M.L. Kraimer (2009), 'The role of international assignees' social capital in creating inter-unit intellectual capital: A cross-level model', *Journal of International Business Studies*, **40**(3), 509–26.

Russwurm, S., L. Hernández, S. Chambers and K. Chung (2011), 'Developing your global know-how', *Harvard Business Review*, **89**(3), 70–75.

Shaffer, M.A., B.S. Reiche and M. Dimitrova et al. (2016), 'Work- and family-role adjustment of different types of global professionals: Scale development and validation', *Journal of International Business Studies*, **47**(2), 113–39.

Shay, J.P. and S.A. Baack (2004), 'Expatriate assignments adjustment and effectiveness: An empirical examination of the big picture', *Journal of International Business Studies*, **35**(3), 216–32.

Shortland, S. (2016), 'The purpose of expatriation: Why women undertake international assignments', *Human Resource Management*, **55**(4), 655–78.

Shortland, S. (2018), 'What seals the deal? How compensation and benefits affect women's decisions to accept expatriation in the oil and gas industry', *Personnel Review*, **47**(3), 765–83.

Sucher, S.A. and E. Corsi (2011), 'Global diversity and inclusion at Royal Dutch Shell (A) and (B)', *Harvard Business School Case*.

Suutari, V. and C. Brewster (2003), 'Repatriation: Empirical evidence from a longitudinal study of careers and expectations among Finnish expatriates', *International Journal of Human Resource Management*, **14**(7), 1132–51.

Tan, D. and J.T. Mahoney (2007), 'The dynamics of Japanese firm growth in U.S. industries: The Penrose effect', *Management International Review*, **47**(2), 259–79.

UNCTAD (2011), *Non-Equity Modes of International Production and Development: World Investment Report 2011*, accessed 1 February 2019 at https://worldinvestmentreport.unctad.org/wir2011/chapter-3-non-equity-modes-of-international-production-and-development/.

UNCTAD (2018), *World Investment Report, 2018: Investment and New Industrial Policies*, New York and Geneva: UNCTAD.

Case M
LVMH: Career development through international mobility

Jean-Luc Cerdin

M.1 Introduction

Headquartered on the Avenue Montaigne in Paris, LVMH Moët Hennessy Louis Vuitton (LVMH) is the world's largest luxury goods maker. Globally, it operates over 2400 stores and offers products under 70 brands, including Louis Vuitton (leather goods & fashion), Moët & Chandon (champagne), Bulgari (jewellery) and Guerlain (perfumes). Each one of its brands has its unique history and culture: for example, Château d'Yquem was founded in 1593, Moët & Chandon in 1743, Hennessy in 1765, Guerlain in 1828 and Louis Vuitton in 1854. Since its creation in 1987, following a merger between Louis Vuitton with Moët Hennessy, LVMH has experienced spectacular growth. By 2013, it had grown ten-fold (*The Economist*, 2014). At the beginning of 2018, LVMH posted yet another set of impressive results, including a 13 per cent increase in revenue to EUR42.6 billion (US$52.9 billion) for 2017 – a record figure (Economist Intelligence Unit, 2018). It currently employs more than 145 000 people, of whom only 30 per cent work in France. Figure M.1 presents the key figures for LVMH by geographic region of delivery in 2017.

From its formation, LVMH was an international business. There was a recognition early on that its human resources were sometimes lacking in international experience. Competing in a global environment, LVMH was under pressure to attract, develop and retain managers with global competence.

Today the group defines its core values as 'being creative and innovative', 'aiming for product excellence', 'promoting our brands with passion', 'acting as entrepreneurs' and 'striving to be the best in all we do'.

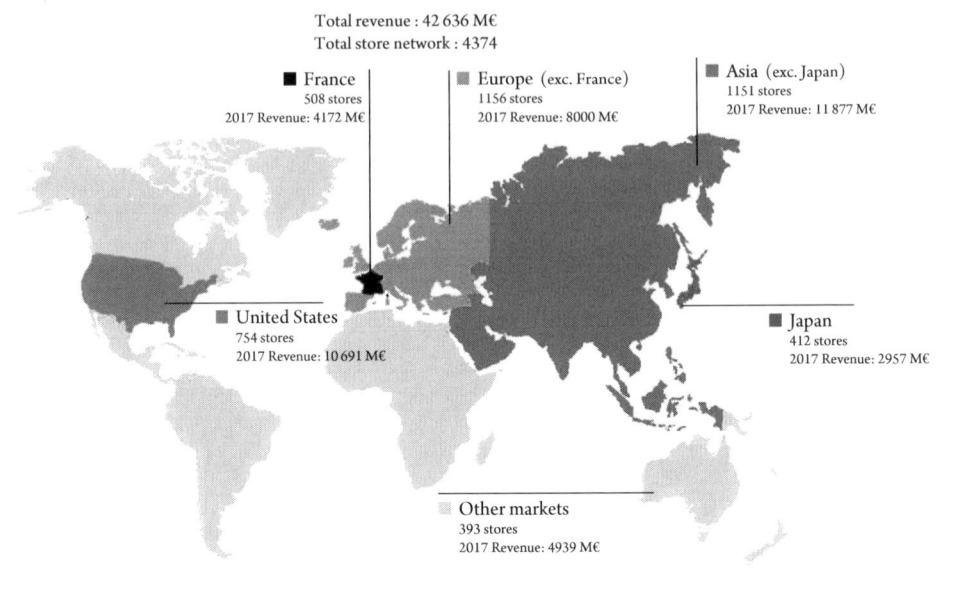

338 · Global strategy and management

LVMH
MOËT HENNESSY · LOUIS VUITTON

2017 key figures by geographic region of delivery

Total revenue : 42 636 M€
Total store network : 4374

- **France** — 508 stores — 2017 Revenue: 4172 M€
- **Europe** (exc. France) — 1156 stores — 2017 Revenue: 8000 M€
- **Asia** (exc. Japan) — 1151 stores — 2017 Revenue: 11 877 M€
- **United States** — 754 stores — 2017 Revenue: 10 691 M€
- **Japan** — 412 stores — 2017 Revenue: 2957 M€
- **Other markets** — 393 stores — 2017 Revenue: 4939 M€

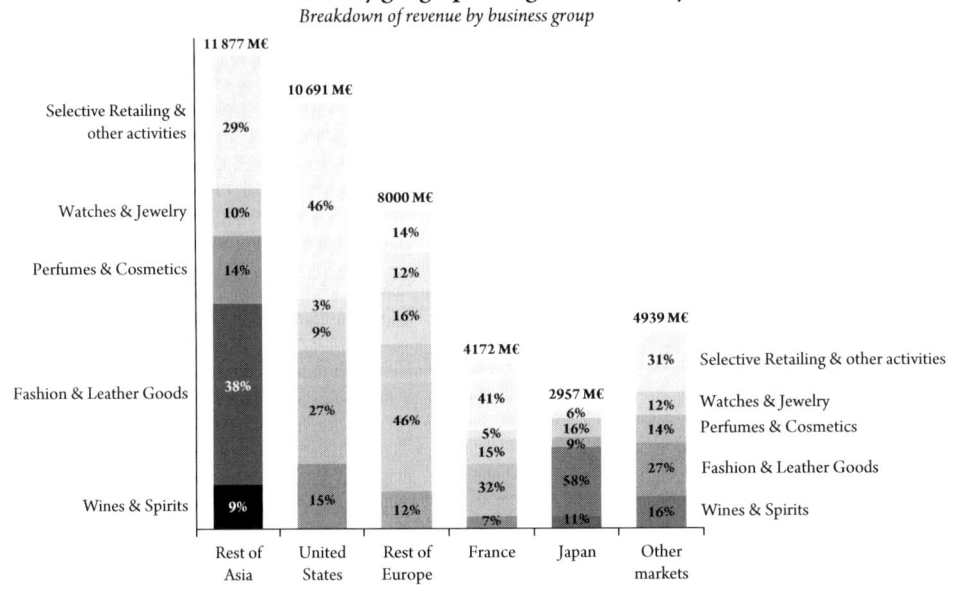

2017 revenue by geographic region of delivery
Breakdown of revenue by business group

Business group	Rest of Asia (11 877 M€)	United States (10 691 M€)	Rest of Europe (8000 M€)	France (4172 M€)	Japan (2957 M€)	Other markets (4939 M€)
Selective Retailing & other activities	29%	46%	14%	41%	6%	31%
Watches & Jewelry	10%	3%	12%	5%	16%	12%
Perfumes & Cosmetics	14%	9%	16%	15%	9%	14%
Fashion & Leather Goods	38%	27%	46%	32%	58%	27%
Wines & Spirits	9%	15%	12%	7%	11%	16%

Source: LVMH group, accessed 15 November 2018 at https://www.lvmh.com/investors/profile/key-figures/#groupe.

Figure M.1 2017 key figures by geographic region of delivery in EUR millions (top); 2017 revenue by geographic region of delivery in EUR millions (bottom)

M.2 LVMH's history and structure

The creation of Moët Hennessy in 1971 was a first step towards the creation of a larger group in 1987 under the name LVMH. The group's roots are French. Most headquarters of LVMH's companies are located in France. Yet, from the outset LVMH believed that its management had to be multicultural.

We explore the genesis of LVMH's approach to career development through international mobility and in doing so we revisit the company as it was in its early years.

M.3 Understanding international mobility through a retrospective lens

We take a retrospective look at LVMH to understand the company's focus on international mobility. Our narrative is located in the period before and around 2001 when we conducted our research. At this point, LVMH already had 260 expatriates and 650 other employees working in a country not their own. Much of our description in this early phase of LVMH remains broadly applicable today. In particular, what LVMH developed in terms of approaches to international HRM in general and international mobility in particular, in this period remains its approach to operating as a global company.

In 2001, the group was structured around five business groups, Wines & Spirits, Fashion & Leather Goods, Perfumes & Cosmetics, Selective Retailing, and Watches & Jewellery as well as a grouping of other businesses. Each business group was a collection of several strong brands. For example, Wines & Spirits contained Hennessy and Krug and Watches & Jewellery contained TAG Heuer and Christian Dior. The strength of each brand stems from a unique culture that translates into relatively autonomous brand management. In all, the LVMH group or federation comprised 50 companies managing 450 subsidiaries. These companies were the foundation of the group. As is the case in 2018, each company had its president and its executive committee. Each company had its subsidiaries that reported directly to it either through the president or through an international director in charge of supervising the activities of the company's subsidiaries.

From its inception, LVMH's leadership was based on its balanced presence in several key sectors of luxury goods and an even geographical split of its activities between Europe, Asia and the Americas. LVMH was pursuing an aggressive growth strategy based on a high level of innovation, control over distribution and sustained advertising and promotion. We now turn to LVMH's human resources (HR) structure as it was in 2001.

M.4   HR structure

LVMH organized its human resource management around five main world zones, namely, France, Europe, the Americas, Pacific Asia and Japan. France and Japan were regarded as country/zones because of the size of their markets. See Figure M.2.

Corporate HR policy went beyond compulsory rules imposed on the business groups and on the companies. Through adaptable guidelines, it also provided management support to the companies. The role of corporate HR was to normalize certain procedures, to define strategy and to give an impetus to companies' HR teams. Regarding guidelines, corporate HR proposed but seldom imposed.

An employee dealt directly with the company he or she worked for; this company in turn dealt with the business group that reported to corporate headquarters. Roughly 50–60 per cent of moves were handled by companies, the others being managed by the business groups or corporate.

There were four types of HR managers at LVMH. Following the group's structure, they operated on four levels: corporate, regional, business group and company level. The subsidiary HR director, or the person acting as

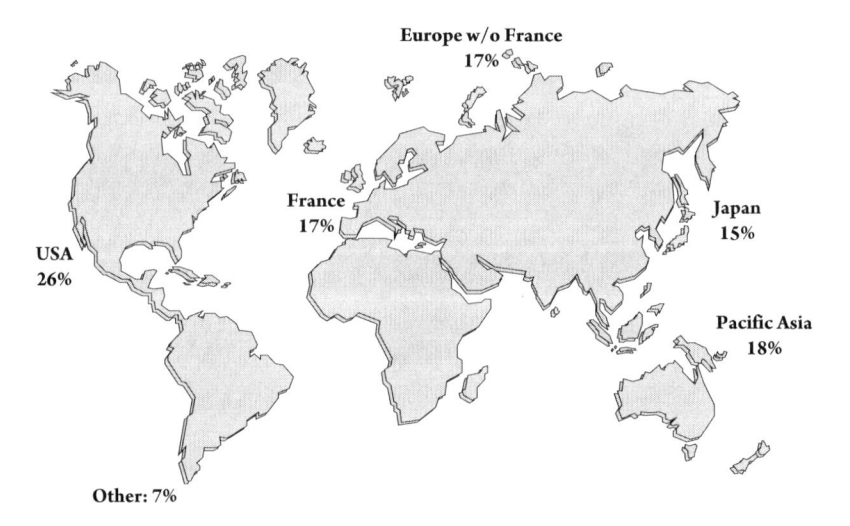

Europe w/o France 17%
France 17%
Japan 15%
USA 26%
Pacific Asia 18%
Other: 7%

Figure M.2   World sales in 2001

such, reported to the subsidiary's president. The subsidiary's HR director got advice and support from his or her company. The business group's HR director coordinated his or her companies' HR directors through monthly meetings. The purpose of these meetings was to identify vacant positions throughout the world and to study the list of the potential candidates for these positions, amongst which are the 'Ready to Move'. Being a 'Ready to Move' did not mean that a candidate had formally expressed a desire to move, but that the organization had identified him or her as having the potential to progress through a new assignment within the year.

The main goal of corporate HR management was to ensure information flow and to harmonize procedures, while leaving final decisions to the company, up to a point. The regional HR director ensured that internal rules were coherently applied within his or her zone. For subsidiaries with no HR director, recruitment was done by the regional HR director.

M.5 Career development and international mobility

LVMH was a global business from the start. However, it soon realized that its human resources often lacked international skills. In 1987, too many managers were not fluent in English. Since then, LVMH has sought to create a pool of global managers, with a working knowledge of international markets. The head of LVMH's Compensation & Benefits (C&B) defines a global manager as a person with the training or the experience needed to manage a global business. He or she can perform from any place in the world thanks to a global vision and skills in managing multilingual and multicultural teams. To achieve such abilities, one must have worked in several countries so that his or her potential can be released, and noticed.

LVMH believes that the best way to develop its employees is not formal training but mobility. This includes vertical, horizontal and geographical moves within the organization. In order to facilitate mobility, employees' seniority is valued at the group level. International mobility is but one form of mobility – it accounts for one out of five moves.

M.6 Basic principles of LVMH's policy for international mobility

LVMH prefers to use the term 'international mobility', rather than expatriation. Contrary to the concept of international mobility that suggests perpetual movement, the term expatriation suggests systematic repatriation. For example, a Dane leaving a Danish subsidiary of 15 people to take on an international assignment will not be expatriated. He or she will sign a local contract in the country of his or her assignment. He or she will be considered 'internationally mobile' because it is most unlikely that he or she will ever work again in Denmark for LVMH. The skills he or she will have acquired abroad will largely surpass the competence needed in Denmark.

The international mobility policy is part of a career development scheme that requires the training of global managers on a limited time basis. LVMH does not want to create a legion of expatriates who live out their careers outside their home base, often in the same country, maintaining their benefits. In such cases, expatriates are disconnected from their home base. Moreover, such practices are not cost effective.

LVMH strives to attract managers to international assignments through exciting career development prospects and not through economic incentives, even though its incentive programme is competitive. HR convinces a manager to become 'internationally mobile' by offering him or her a more challenging job with more freedom to perform his or her task than at home.

LVMH does not dispatch expatriates because of a lack of local talent. Most of its expatriates fit two profiles: those sent out by the corporate HQ to control its subsidiaries and protect its interests (internal auditors and financial staff) and those sent out to develop their skills. Organization development accounts for a quarter of expatriates while the rest are part of a management development scheme. Most expatriates are in charge of small subsidiaries for three years on average; very few of them stay longer. They are senior expatriates whose role is to manage the local business, train the host-country nationals and transfer corporate culture. Clearly, some expatriations result from specific needs. For example, certain designers in leather goods are very hard to find and must be expatriated.

M.7   International talents

International mobility is an integral part of each high potential's career path. International mobility mainly aims at developing managers. Many expatriates are high potentials. International mobility is likely to entail a radical functional move. The head of HR development recalls the case of a French insurance specialist in the fashion business unit who was sent to Romania to head a shoe factory. LVMH recognizes the need to take risks in order to develop high potentials. It wants to put them in new situations to help them develop new skills and prove their mettle.

LVMH's career development goal is to make the mobility process smoother, particularly international moves. Indeed, HR is well aware that top management is somewhat ethnocentric. In 2001, half of LVMH's senior executives and 40 per cent of its managerial staff were French, whereas the French accounted for 37 per cent of the group's global workforce. HR's ambition was to develop more foreign global managers so that they could in turn globalize top management.

LVMH defines two types of high potentials: HP1 and HP2. An HP1 is an individual likely to achieve a top management position such as a member of board committees, regional president or subsidiary president. An HP2 is an employee likely to go up one or two steps in the hierarchy. LVMH's performance appraisal system is not only based on results but also on the ability to propose and implement new ideas. The group's growth and financial might allow these projects to come to life. LVMH has a career management process called Organizational and Management Review (OMR). This annual process aims at reviewing HR objectives and results. The OMR is an essential tool for LVMH's human resource planning, taking into consideration the organization's needs for the next three years. It defines succession planning and HP and 'Ready to Move' lists. Employees identified on these lists are given developmental experiences that include international assignments, in order to prepare them for top management positions. The OMR particularly looks back on the previous year's objectives for HPs and those 'Ready to Move' and assesses their current development. LVMH manages to staff internally two out of three executive positions.

The typical career path includes showing one's mettle in France, moving from position to position within France in order to master the corporate culture. Once these conditions are met, the employee could be expatriated. More recently, LVMH has been willing to make expatriation happen earlier. It recognizes the risks involved in such a policy but believes that these risks are offset by the development of a young and adventurous global workforce.

M.8 International recruitment

In order to build a pool of global managers, LVMH is committed to having a worldwide recruiting process and to sending its employees on global assignments. LVMH is a very attractive company for French prospects; however, it is not as successful on international labour markets. LVMH's natural labour market is France. LVMH is a very attractive company for early career professionals and is very active on French business campuses. An early career professional is an individual with less than five years of professional experience.

In 2001, roughly 70 per cent of early career professionals at LVMH were recruited in France.

LVMH continues to aim at expanding its labour source to a more international level. Being a decentralized organization, its website is its main source of candidates along with on-campus job fairs. Through this website, candidates from any country can apply directly to any of LVMH's subsidiaries in a country not their own and obtain a local employment contract.

LVMH wants to recruit more individuals with international profiles. The ideal candidate is a person who has been immersed in several cultures, has travelled extensively, speaks at least three languages and has an open mind.

By 2001, the number of expatriates at LVMH was 260; 79 per cent of them were French. Inpatriates (foreigners in France) represented 5.5 per cent and third-country nationals 15.5 per cent of employees on international assignment. The average age of expatriates was 36 years, and 48 per cent were under 35. General managers, area managers and brand managers accounted for 35.5 per cent of expatriates, finance and audit staff for 17.5 per cent, marketing for 12 per cent, store managers and HR staff each account for 4 per cent of expatriates, and the remaining 27 per cent includes other positions.

In addition to these expatriates, 650 other employees had a home-based salary in a country not their own – that is, they had a local employment contract. For example, an Australian recruited in France, and still working there, is not an expatriate and is not on global assignment.

M.9 The international transfer policy

The International Transfer Department operates at the corporate level to provide support to the group's companies. It defines its role through five main functions:

- determining international mobility packages in order to guarantee internal equity between the group's various companies;
- helping the group's companies address specific issues regarding international transfers;
- providing information and advice on the evolution of 'external rules' that govern international transfers – that is, labour laws;
- conducting, spreading and explaining LVMH's internal mobility policy;
- monitoring of international mobility data.

Corporate HR's purpose is to define clear and simple principles that can be applied to all subsidiaries in all countries. In order to facilitate mobility within the group, LVMH is trying to harmonize its practices to allow for a more global workforce. The prime condition for achieving this goal is to make equity a priority, between both countries and employees. LVMH did not choose to set up an international corporation that would centralize HRM and would dictate the compensation policy of the entire organization. The organization aims to avoid situations where line managers are confronted with the frustrations of expatriates earning less than their colleagues in the same position. LVMH has chosen to maintain a decentralized organization where corporate HR defines general principles.

LVMH's corporate policy of international mobility is relatively recent. Before 1987, each company proceeded according to its own international transfer policy. The foundation of the corporate policy was laid out at the group's creation. The companies gradually adopted this policy that was eventually formalized in July 2000. By 2001, each company HR possessed a copy of the 'International Transfer Policy' charter that covers all main aspects of international mobility. The charter does not focus on career development but rather on the formal procedures related to international mobility. It encompasses all the aspects pertaining to an expatriate package. It is meant to be used by company HR directors. Some technical annexes are for the use of the companies' C&B staff so as to facilitate communication with the International Transfer Department and to provide answers to potential expatriates' concerns. Indirectly, this charter helps expatriates understand their package.

M.10 International mobility

In 2001 LVMH was not aiming to attract expatriates through high compensation levels. The group was striving for cost efficiency. It was aware that a 'good' package is necessary, but that it is not the main incentive to go abroad. Research on French expatriates shows that compensation is not the main motive for accepting an international assignment, as shown in Table M.1.

The basic balance-sheet approach for compensation package was based on the principle that expatriates should neither lose nor gain from their move. LVMH's Compensation & Benefits (C&B) department has retained this approach as a guide for its compensation package policy.

The home-based salary is marked up at the time of departure according to the international assignment. It will increase during the length of the assignment.

Table M.1 French managers' motives for expatriation

Motive	Rank	%
Desire for change	1	77.7
Personal experience in another culture	2	75.3
Increased prospects of future promotion	3	49.8
Compensation	4	37.8
Immediate promotion	5	18.3
Desire to escape home country's economic and social environment	6	16.2
To distance oneself from certain personal problems	7	6.2

Note: Ranking of French managers' motives for expatriation (293 expatriates working for 12 organizations in 44 countries were asked to express their motives to go and work abroad).

Source: Cerdin (2002).

It is used as a base for the calculation of social security and pension contributions. The mobility salary is compared to local labour market averages in compatible countries. LVMH delineated two types of countries: the 'compatible' countries, roughly including OECD countries, and the 'incompatible' countries.

In order to calculate an expatriate's gross salary in local currency, that is, the mobility salary, LVMH's C&B department first considers his or her home-based gross salary in parent-country currency, then it calculates his or her net salary (by deducting theoretical home tax, social security and compulsory pension contribution). Then a cost of living allowance (COLA) and various family allowance differentials are added to or subtracted from this net salary in parent-country currency. A foreign premium service can also be granted. The net figure obtained is then expressed in local currency. The net salary is then 'grossed up' by adding taxes and social contribution of the host country. See Figure M.3 for an overview:

Figure M.3 Basic balance-sheet approach

Home-based gross salary in parent-country currency → Home-based net salary in parent-country currency → Net salary in local currency ← Host-country gross salary in local currency + Housing

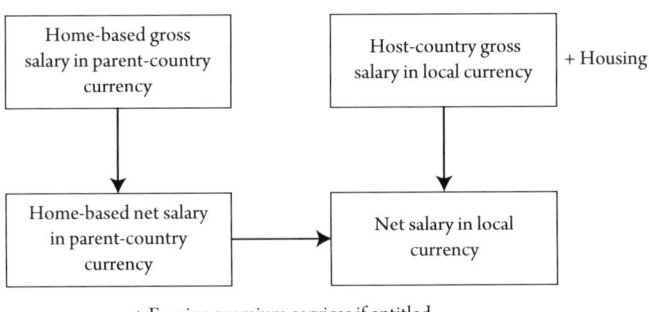

+ Foreign premium services if entitled
+/− COLA
+ Family allowance differentials

LVMH's C&B department has adapted the balance-sheet approach for its housing policy. A consultancy provides them with the housing market rate for the host country. LVMH's local correspondents verify this information. Potential expatriates may also have their own knowledge of market rates. As a rule, all the parties involved are honest, but they might not always understand each other perfectly. HR put it in the following way:

> Having local correspondents is one thing, understanding each other is another one. For instance, an apartment of 125 square metres in Hong Kong refers to the surface area of the apartment itself plus a proportion of the communal parts area. This is less than 125 square metres of living space. The same apartment surface might appear smaller to a person used to areas where only living space is taken into account.

Once the local market rate is agreed on, LVMH will compensate the expatriate but he or she must contribute 15 per cent of his or her home-based gross salary. For example, a French expatriate in New York will be paid an amount in US dollars equal to the average monthly market rate times 12, minus an amount in dollars equal to 15 per cent of his or her yearly gross salary in France as expressed in euros. This 15 per cent contribution is based on the assumption that a French employee's housing cost amounts to roughly 15 per cent of his or her gross salary. LVMH believes that this estimate is below the cost effectively paid by most employees. The rationale behind this contribution is that the employee must pay a percentage of his or her salary on housing at home and must also do so abroad. LVMH can directly provide housing to the expatriate or it can grant him or her an allowance by using the above principle. This housing allowance is also 'grossed up'. The expatriate is responsible for the cost of utilities, while granted a relocation allowance equivalent to one month's worth of gross salary upon arrival and upon repatriation.

LVMH works with consulting firms specialized in overseas COLA calculations. It uses a positive index to protect its employees from losing money when they move to a country with a higher cost of living. It uses a negative index when they move to a country with a lower cost of living. Here the balance-sheet approach is strictly applied. C&B relies on the internal exchange rate used by the corporate finance department, in order to avoid any complaints from financial expatriates. The calculation of the cost-of-living differential is based on the assumption that all employees, regardless of their family situation, save 30 per cent of their home-based net salary. The COLA is set at the time of departure.

C&B does not rely on outside consultancies to determine its incentive allowances. A foreign service premium is calculated by taking into account four criteria, namely, the environment (health facilities, pollution, climate), personal security, social amenities and the everyday quality of life. The granted premiums range from 0 to 30 per cent depending on the home country and the host country. For instance, for an expatriate from France, whatever his or her nationality, the premium is null when the move is within the European zone or towards the US. It achieves its maximum, 30 per cent, for a host country such as India.

LVMH's appeal to global managers does not rely mainly on its mobility salary but on its home-based salary, from which the mobility salary is calculated. This appeal is also greatly increased by the role of international mobility in career paths. International mobility is like an investment – the return on investment for the expatriate will be the high future incomes generated by a promotion achieved through successful international assignments.

The mobility salary also includes other aspects such as compensation for other social benefits (like family support). It also compensates for the possible loss of profit-sharing benefits resulting from a move from one successful subsidiary to a less successful one. Indeed, no profit-sharing schemes exist at the corporate level.

Expatriates are also entitled to additional benefits such as paid education for children, paid home-leaves, temporary housing for up to 30 days, loans for housing deposits or for purchasing a vehicle. Costs of moving are also covered. According to French labour laws, in addition to their five-week vacation, French managers, except top executives, are entitled to have more days off. Some countries are far less advantageous in terms of vacation time. LVMH grants four-week vacations in the US and five-week vacations elsewhere.

The expatriate package is prepared at the corporate level but the final decision is left up to the companies. As the companies are the ones that must pay the expatriates, they have some leeway. For instance, as expressed by a C&B manager:

> Some of them are going to give higher housing allowances, they may offer more generous home-leave allowances than those favoured by the group, such as business-class air fare instead of less expensive economy-class ones.

The International Transfer Department defines clear procedures; however, implementing them requires some flexibility. At the company level, policies often end up being tailor-made to cope with expatriates' specific concerns.

The group's policy is to treat expatriates as locals when they are sent to compatible countries. Nevertheless, when it wishes to send an employee on an international assignment, it may have to meet his or her specific needs. A corporate manager recalls the concerns of some expatriates:

> My children have a French culture and education, and I want them to be in an international school.
>
> My wife has health problems, so I'd like to get this particular kind of health insurance.
>
> I was used to a 180 square metre apartment in Rome and for the same price, I can only afford a 35 square metre one in New York.

Negotiation with expatriates might appear time-consuming and much too focused on details for a company's HR staff. Indeed, international assignments often entail specialized, strategic and key positions, for which the company must be more flexible. This is also due to the HR structure that allows potential expatriates to negotiate, in rare instances, some non-technical aspects of the compensation package at the company level.

Harmonizing the package in the group's various companies remains a high priority. Each company is responsible for its budget. The companies can rely on the group's expertise to address certain issues, but they are the ones that implement the policies.

Expatriate compensation policies of other multinational companies may appear more advantageous than the one defined by LVMH, particularly with respect to housing allowances, car allowances and club membership allowances. The package facilitates mobility, as far as it avoids having employees cling to a country in the hope of keeping favourable benefits. It is also a cost-effective practice and has not yet failed to attract the needed talents.

Home-based salaries may differ between individuals depending on the country and on the business group they come from. As reported by an HR manager:

> Global cash compensation for equivalent positions vary depending on the business group and on the country. Some business groups offer historically higher or lower wages than others. The purpose of LVMH's compensation policy is to reduce these differences between the various companies in the same country. Some countries offer higher wages than others because of specific labour market conditions. As a

result, the salary for a specific international assignment may vary according to the expatriate's previous position.

LVMH is very sensitive to international compensation market rates. It is striving to offer competitive compensation with regard to local practices. For equal qualifications, wages in the US are much higher than in France. Relying solely on the balance-sheet approach to determine the salary of a French employee sent to the United States would result in a low salary, not at all competitive on the American market. LVMH takes into account the local market, but does not always align its compensation with it. The reverse situation of an American sent to France is equally problematic for LVMH. The balance-sheet approach implies that he or she must accept a lower gross salary according to the cost of living differential; buying power is maintained for a lower salary. Compensation first follows the balance-sheet approach but then illustrates a hybrid approach in order to combine cost of living, exchange rate, housing and labour market conditions.

M.11 Managing benefits

LVMH will not compromise over its expatriates' peace of mind concerning security benefits. The principle is that the chosen schemes will not penalize expatriates – that is, they will have access to security benefits as good as those available in their home country.

Many countries have, because of their own social history, unique retirement plans. This requires the security benefits aspect of the compensation package to take into account the retirement plans expatriates have contributed to. Building compensation packages for French expatriates is particularly difficult due to the unique nature of the French retirement system.

The French retirement system is partly linked to the social security system. It is not based on capitalization like a self-funded pension scheme, but rather on a principle of wealth sharing with a contributory 'pay-as-you-go' pension scheme. Employees and employers on the French territory have a legal obligation to contribute to the retirement system. In order to be eligible for full retirement benefits, a French worker must contribute to the system for 40 years. Provided that they contribute, French workers believe they are guaranteed good retirement at no risk. A French expatriate may wish to stick to the French system, particularly if he or she is to experience but one international assignment within the group. This is especially the case for older employees who have been contributing to the French system for many years. Things are different for a young graduate who is about to begin contributing to the

French social security system. In compatible countries, he or she can opt for another, more satisfactory system.

Maintaining continuity between the different systems is a priority for expatriates. LVMH deems it its own responsibility. When no agreement exists between the French social security system and the host country's social security system, such as in Japan, a double contribution has to be paid. LVMH pays the French contribution to maintain the expatriates' right to retirement in France and must pay the contribution in Japan, because the Japanese system does not recognize the French one.

Most third-country nationals are dealt with differently, because many countries have implemented pension funds. LVMH analyses the employer's contribution to a retirement fund before an expatriation. It then compares it to the retirement plan of the host country. When it can find neither a solution to maintain the expatriate within the parent-country system, nor a solution in the host-country, it uses an 'off-shore' system. This 'off-shore' or international fund has no anchor in the countries involved in the move. LVMH acknowledges that there is no ideal response to the retirement issue. Generally, the parent-country scheme is maintained.

LVMH is attentive to its employees' health benefits. As a rule, the group will opt for the insurance schemes available in the host country only if they offer coverage as wide as those prevailing in the parent country. When in doubt, it provides expatriates and their families with international insurance. Many of the group's companies have adopted this scheme. Roughly 95 per cent of the group's expatriates are covered by it. According to a C&B manager:

> Our plan is very competitive. Besides, because health is part of daily expenses and because expatriates exchange information, having various reimbursement levels would create pointless frustrations.

For life insurance and disability protection, LVMH also ensures that the level of protection is at least as good as the one before the move.

Unemployment insurance benefits reveal some intricacies. Within Europe, because of European regulation, it is not possible to maintain the system of the parent country. An employee is only entitled to receive unemployment compensation from the country he or she is working in. For a move from Europe to another country, options will depend on the host country's regulations. The group has not yet ruled on a common private scheme for all of its employees.

M.12 Logistical support

International transfer policy provides expatriates with acceptable logistical support needed to ensure smooth relocation. This amounts to support in housing search, administrative procedures, such as the lease, utilities and hook-up, and so on. Relocation services also help families find schools and help them with the enrolment procedures.

International transfer experts are now working to expand their relocation services offering. Indeed, expatriates need help in finding good, experienced suppliers, such as furniture movers. It aims to provide more than financial support. These experts are writing up requirements for relocation services suppliers in order to assist companies.

M.13 Spousal support

Very few employees turn down an international assignment. Nevertheless, LVMH acknowledges that certain employee characteristics impede their mobility. Indeed, some are hesitant to accept a move. LVMH puts out feelers to assess employee willingness to take on international assignments. It prefers not to offer international mobility when it anticipates reluctance or potential problems.

The issue of dual careers has become increasingly critical for any organization willing to expatriate employees. The willingness of the French to go and work abroad is rather weak compared to other nationalities in Europe. In order to cope with this issue, LVMH has agreements with other French multinational companies, which include résumé exchanges. However, it does not integrate the spouse in one of its companies to avoid any problems.

The process of identifying potential expatriates does not take into account marital and family status. Young graduates, mostly single, are keen to accept international assignments because they understand its developmental purpose. In 2001, most senior expatriates were males married to a non-working spouse. LVMH was well aware of this. It has since encouraged women to commit to expatriate careers.

M.14 Intercultural training

As a rule, when a candidate is sent on an international assignment, he or she has had some previous international exposure, for instance through his or her studies, or through earlier professional experience. In the early years, intercultural training was not perceived as a priority because of the international profile of the expatriates. By 2001, LVMH was increasingly feeling the pressure to prepare its expatriates for its international assignments in order to facilitate cross-cultural adjustment. However, intercultural training was more of a project than a reality with both pre-departure and post-arrival training comprising language courses. One reason for this was that an international position usually has to be filled very quickly, which leaves little time for intercultural training. Therefore, very little training was or is provided, even for 'culturally tough' countries like Brazil or Mexico where people are expected to adjust on their own. However, they are not pressured to perform as quickly as if they had had rigorous training. Preparatory field trips are paid for and, in some cases, subsidiaries provide help to newcomers. Often, the size of the subsidiary does not allow for HR staff devoted to helping newcomers. The attitude is that informal learning is valuable. The view of a human resource manager in 2001 was that:

> [o]n international assignments, French expatriates are most likely to find other French or European expatriates, particularly in the North America, Asia and Japan zones. To some extent, the expatriates can rely on the experience of other already adjusted expatriates.

M.15 Repatriation

Regardless of the nature of an employee's international assignment, be it an expatriation per se or a local contract, there is always the intentional limitation of the length of the assignment. LVMH has always warned its companies not to create permanent expatriates. These expatriates tend to lose contact with their home country, which makes their repatriation difficult. In order to facilitate the next move or repatriation, assignments are customarily limited to a period of two to three years.

When someone begins a career within the LVMH group, in most cases, he or she is anchored to a home base. Throughout this career and in spite of many international moves, the home base country usually remains the same.

Even when expatriates are compensated like locals, they have a theoretical home-based salary in order to facilitate their return home. Expatriates are clearly informed that LVMH will use this theoretical home-based salary as a basis for the calculation of the return compensation. The home-based anchor is upgraded each year. Upon returning home, the compensation of the international assignment is not a referent. When a promotion is granted, the home-based salary is upgraded accordingly. The theoretical home-based salary acts as a minimum guarantee referent. The repatriation process begins at least six months to one year before the return home. It chiefly tackles career issues by addressing expatriates' concerns about return positions and career progression.

Sometimes, the anticipated return is altered to another move toward a third country. Such a situation is captured by the following example from 2001:

> The Business Group Perfumes & Cosmetics recently transferred a young French expatriate from Givenchy in Sydney to manage the business group in Hong Kong. He will be on the Givenchy payroll, because the business group has no legal entity.

The times when each company would send their employees only to their own subsidiaries were well over even then. Thanks to the 'Ready to Move' list, moves have become more frequent within a business group or between business groups. For instance, transferring employees from Veuve Clicquot France to Louis Vuitton Pacific exemplifies this inter-business group mobility. The corporate level ensures that the prevalent logic is group strategy.

M.16 The view of the future in 2001

In 2001, in spite of its young age, LVMH had already acquired an impressive expertise in international assignment policy. The International Transfer Department relied on the information flowing from LVMH's vast international networks to better determine the needs of HR decision makers. International transfer experts could then provide a helpful framework of reference that HR companies can rely on. Corporate HR hoped to build a global HR information system designed to provide updated and upgraded information and guidelines for HR staff around the world.

As the number of international assignments rises, the group is considering its future needs. It is looking for ways to strengthen its expertise and its ability to assist companies' HR teams. LVMH is pondering over the future of its corporate HR structure that has to cope with the group's growth and with the rising number of expatriates.

By 2001, international transfer policy had become an integral part of LVMH's management philosophy. It had a clear mandate to spread the group's key values that are about preserving autonomy and encouraging entrepreneurship. It was and is part of the process by which LVMH tries to define its future policy of career development.

CASE DISCUSSION

After giving a short presentation of the LVMH group, discuss the following:
1. What were LVMH's strategic goals and what role does expatriation play in fulfilling these goals?
2. What kind of procedures did LVMH have in place for recruiting and selecting candidates for expatriation?
3. What kind of managerial challenges did LVMH face with respect to reaching its HR goals?

REFERENCES

Cerdin, J.-L. (2002), *L'expatriation*, Paris: Éditions d'Organisation, p. 65.

The Economist (2014), 'Beauty and the beasts: Think global, act artisan', 11 December 2014, accessed 1 February 2019 at https://www.economist.com/special-report/2014/12/11/beauty-and-the-beasts.

The Economist Intelligence Unit (2018), 'LVMH's revenue rises 13% to US$53bn in 2017', 30 January 2018, accessed 9 July 2018 at http://www.eiu.com/industry/article/1796361363/lvmhs-revenue-rises-13-to-us53 billion-in-2017/2018-01-30.

Index

ABB 86–7, 295
Accenture 7
achievement motivation 195–6
Ackermann, F. 145
active management of assets 3, 5
adaptive SIHRM orientation 294
Adecco 100
Adler, N.J. 292
administrative distance 8–9, 30
After-Sales Services 131
agency theory 270–71, 276
Aggarwal, R. 34
Airbnb 5
Aldi store 245
Allen, D.B. 171, 172
Allen, R. 207
Amazon 5, 63
American pharmaceutical companies 89
Ang, S. 125
antecedents, SESAM 305–8
Apple 4, 35, 113, 176–9
    definition of MNEs 5
Argosy Energy International 62
Arndt, A. 240
Arnold, D. 112
Articles of Association 126
Asante, Ebenezer 49
ATMs, SR-Bank 305

Baksaas, Jon Fredrik 95, 98, 102
balanced scorecard 319–20
Bansal, P. 171
Bartlett, C.A. 3, 4, 80, 86–8
BBC 177
Beamish, P.W. 3, 4, 117, 125
behavioural cultural intelligence (CQ) 125
Benedict, Ruth 187
Benito, G.R.G. 229
Ben & Jerry's 168–9
Berger, I. 147
Bharti Airtel 96, 97

Bhati Dilwan case, Nestlé 182–3
big box stores 242
Bird, Alan 10
Birkinshaw, J. 257
BKT 121, 234
BKT joint ventures 126
    boundary spanners in 128
    Bremen 127, 128, 131, 132
    Dalian-JV 129
    formal governance structure 127
    global operations in Sweden 126
    Lübeck 127–31
    Shanghai-JV 131–2
    virtual boundary spanner 133
black holes subsidiaries 88, 89
Black, S.J. 325
BluePages 261
Body Shop 168–9
Boko Haram 49
Bond, M.H. 193
bonding cost 32
bottom-of-the-pyramid (BOP) 94, 104
    challenge 89–91
    Group Industrial Development transfer from 103–4
    markets 75, 89–91
        business model innovation in 90
        products and marketing strategies 90
    transfer of practices from 105–6
boundary spanners, in BKT joint ventures 128
boundary-spanning 124–5
Bowen, H.P. 162
box-ticking approach 299
BP 58, 60
Brabeck, Peter 78, 79
Bradley, F. 124
Brekke, Sigve 98, 103–5
Bremen 127, 128, 131, 132
Bresman, H. 257–60
Bretaña oil discovery 71, 72
bridging category teams 284–6
Brouthers, K.D. 114

Buckley, P.J. 36, 253
Building Workers International (BWI) 157
Bulcke, Paul 13
business and business needs, Danvita 209
business, globalization of 6–8
business model innovation 90

CAGE distance framework 8, 84, 259
calculative HRM practices 296
Canon 33
Cantwell, J. 5
career development, LVMH 341
Carroll's pyramid 166
Casson, M.C. 253
causality, culture 199
CEM *see* contract equipment manufacturer (CEM)
Cement Wage Board Agreement 156, 157
CEOs 11, 12, 24, 50, 324
Challinor, John 183
Chen, D. 115, 117
Chevron 60
China
    FDI recipient 8
    foreign investors 30
    global vehicle sales 35
    outward FDI 36
Choi, C.B. 117
Christmann, P. 171
Christopherson, S. 240
claimant stakeholders 144
cluster-based operating model 99
CMEs *see* coordinated market economies (CMEs)
CNBC 24
CNOOC (the Chinese National Offshore Oil Corporation) 60
Coca-Cola 33
Coffield, Dana 55, 62, 66, 68, 73
cognitive cultural intelligence (CQ) 125
Colgate-Palmolive 76
collaborator stakeholders 145
collective bargaining 154, 156–9, 303
    relationship 232
    rights 230
    Walmart 245
collective knowledge 256, 257
    exchange in subsidiaries 272
collectivism 191–3, 197, 200
common organizational psychology 87
Compensation & Benefits (C&B), LVMH 341, 345, 347

competitive advantage 77, 81, 83–5, 91, 114, 147, 255, 328, 332
    MNEs 82, 252, 289, 329
competitive strategy
    international strategies and 81–2
    Walmart 241
ConocoPhillips 58, 60
conscious knowledge 256
contingency perspective criticism 198–9
contingency theory 198–9
contract equipment manufacturer (CEM) 113
contract manufacturing 113–14
contract workers 153–4
    LafargeHolcim 155–9
contributor subsidiaries 88–9
Cook, Tim 178
Coon, H.M. 192
coordinated market economies (CMEs) 229–34, 243
corporate social responsibility (CSR) 177
    defining 162–3
    local/global 171
    in MNEs 160, 171–3
    short- and long-term benefits 168–9
    stakeholder theory applied to 164–8
    strategies 146
    win–win possibilities 169–71
corporate structure and organization, MNT 44–5
Corruption Perceptions Index 114, 115, 234
cost–benefit calculus 32
cost leadership 81
Cranet data set 296–7
'Creating Shared Value' business strategy 181–2
Crilly, D. 172, 173
cross-national HRM 290–92
cultural distance 8, 30, 200–201, 260
    institutional distance *vs.* 236
    and MNE performance 185–7
    see also administrative distance
cultural diversity
    case study 221–3
    diversity-valuing mindset 217–18
    economic rationale 220
    employee stories
        feeling excluded 223
        feeling valued and willingness 221–2
    language as exclusion mechanism 213–14
    moral argument 220–21
    as perceived by organizational members 207
    segregation, preventing 215–16

as social construct 210–13
as strategic resource 206
wishful thinking 216–17
see also Danvita
cultural imperialism 331, 332
cultural intelligence (CQ) 125
cultural values 199
culture
concept of 187–8
equating nations with 201
Hofstede's four dimensions of see Hofstede's four dimensions
other dimensions of 202
stability of 201
validity and causality 199
Cunningham, P. 147
customer-focused strategy, MTN Group Limited 43–4
customization, HRM 298–9
Czarniawska, B. 298

Dahlsrud, A. 162
Dalian-JV 128–31, 133–5
Danish language, as exclusion mechanism 213–14
Danvita
business and business needs 209
case study 221–3
Danish 207
Denmark 207
diversity
as perceived by organizational members 207
as strategic resource 206
employees 208
equality 209–10
guiding principles 208–9
hiring the best employees 218–19
inclusion 210
reverse discrimination 214–15
segregation, preventing 215–16
supporting initiatives 209
see also cultural diversity
Das, B.K. 158
Dasí, A. 263, 264
Davoine, E. 12
Dawson, D. 244
De Cieri, H. 290
De Meyer, A. 261
Denis, J.L. 298, 299
differentiation strategy 81

digital firms 5
DiMaggio, P.J. 256
diversity
cultural see cultural diversity
of top management 12–13
workforce 206
diversity-valuing mindset 217–18
Donnalson, L. 198
Dowling, P.J. 290
downstream (refining and marketing) 60
Drumwright, M. 147
dual-income families 334
Dulac, T. 135
Dunning, J.H. 5, 8–9, 31, 251, 252
'dynamic pricing' concept, Uninor 98–9

Earley, C. 185
Earley, P.C. 125
'Early Programme Amalgamation Interviews' 282
EBITDA (earnings before interest, tax, depreciation and amortization) 101
eclectic approach 251
eclectic paradigm see OLI framework
economic distance ('E') 9, 89, 260, 265
economic institutional theory 226
economic rationale, for cultural diversity 220
Economist, The 12, 29, 234
Ecopetrol 62
Eden, C. 145
Eden, Martin 56, 68
Eells, R. 167
efficiency-seeking motives 28
Elkington, J. 165
Elter, F. 9
emerging market MNEs (EMNEs) 36, 228–9
as challenge for Uppsala model 36
internationalization strategy of 36
employment protection 231
energy industry see oil and gas industry
entry modes see operating modes
equal cultural distance 199–200
equality, Danvita 209–10
equity entry modes 109, 111
Ericsson 129, 131–4
allied with Uninor 97
esteem motivation 196
ethnocentric mindsets 330–31
European pharmaceutical companies 89
evolutionary theory of MNE 253–4

exceptional global leaders 11, 16
    see also Ghosn, Carlos
expansion strategy, MTN Group Limited 43–4
expatriate return on investment (eROI) 324
expatriation
    defined 322
    dual-income families 334
    enabling 325–7
    importance of 324–5
    investments in 322–4
    knowledge transfer 326
    learning from practices 329–30
    mobility 324
    organizational learning 323
    staffing policies 330–33
    value of repatriates 327–9
explicit knowledge 255–6, 310, 315
    see also tacit knowledge
exporting 111–12
    through third party distributors 111
exportive SIHRM orientation 294
extant theory 270–72
    threat by MNEs 35–7
external environment 259–60
Extractive Industries Transparency Initiative (EITI) 170
ExxonMobil 60

Facebook 5
Fair Labor Association 177
Fang, M. 201
FDI see foreign direct investment (FDI)
femininity 194–7
Fenton-O'Creevy, M. 256, 298
Financial Times 12, 22, 24–5
firms 60
    active management of foreign assets 3, 5
    cost–benefit calculus 32
    cost leadership 81
    differentiation 81
    digital 5
    exporting 111–12
    generic positioning strategies 81
    governance cost 32
    internationalization of 27–8
        motives 28
    knowledge spillovers 4
    MNE qualifications 3
    multidomestic strategies 83

productivity spillovers 4
reputation 85
resources 84–5
service, value chain 6
sourcing agreement with foreign firms 4
strategic alliances with local partners 114
substantial direct investment 3, 5
in supporting industries 60
Uppsala model 32–3, 35
    see also multinational enterprises (MNEs)
firm-specific advantages (FSAs) 31, 34, 75, 76, 80, 82, 88, 228, 254
    identifying 83–5
    international strategies and 82–3
    location-bound 83
    OLI framework 83–5
    transferable 83
Flexible Foils category team 285–6
Flextronics 33, 113
foreign affiliates 6, 27
foreign direct investment (FDI) 7, 31, 36, 114–15, 119, 252
    in China 8, 36
    growth rate 7
    indicators and, international production 7
    recipients of 7–8
foreign markets 77
foreign operating modes 108–11
    equity and non-equity modes of entry 109, 111
    firms
        agency costs 110
        and market contract 110
        MNE's choice of 108
        ownership over resources 109
        transaction cost theory 109
foreign subsidiaries 30, 76, 87, 88
formal governance structure
    BKT joint ventures 127
    IJVs 126–7
Fortune Global 500 list 35, 36
Foxconn 35, 177–9
franchise contract 110
franchising 112–13
Freeman, R.E. 141, 142, 164
Freeman, R.W. 142
Frey, B. 263
Friedman, M. 165
Frooman, J. 145
FSAs see firm-specific advantages (FSAs)

Gao, J. 171
Gap 146, 164
Gazprom 60
General Electric 12, 77
general management team (GMT) 280–85
General Motors 24
geocentric mindsets 332–3
geographic distance ('G') 9, 260
geographically distributed organizational units 85–7
    ABB 86–7
    integration–responsiveness framework 85–6
Gerhart, B. 201
German retail market, Walmart in 242–7
Ghadar, F. 292
Ghana, MTN Group Limited in
    '21 days of Y'ello Care' 48–9
    corporate social investment initiatives 48–9
    Ghana Telecom 46
    mission 48
    Scancom Limited 45
    Tigo 46
    unique services 48
Ghana Telecom 46
Ghemawat, P. 8, 225, 259
Ghoshal, S. 80, 86–8, 257–9, 265
Ghosn, Carlos 16, 25
    allegations of false accounting 16
    analysis of Nissan 21
    as chairman of Mitsubishi Motors 22
    fall of 23–5
    as 'le cost killer' 19
    at Michelin factory 18–19
    move to Japan 20–22
    Nissan–Renault alliance 22
    Nissan Revival Plan 21–2
    Nissan's allegations against 23–4
    in North America 18–19
    return to Brazil 18
    rise of 17–23
    upbringing and education 17–18
    work reforms 23
Gibson, C.B. 199
GID *see* Group Industrial Development (GID)
Gingerich, D.W. 230, 241
Global Alliance for Workers and Communities 113
global international strategies 77
global leaders 10
    'exceptional' 11
    expatriation 11

global leadership 10
    CEOs 11
    international managers exercising 11
    relationship complexities 10
    task complexities 10
global replication, of BOP innovations 101–2
global system for mobile communications (GSM) 45
global union federations (GUFs) 154–7, 159–60
global value chains 4
Gooderham, P.N. 9, 225, 236
Google 5
gorilla retailing 242
governance cost 32, 118
governance reconfiguration 280–82
Govindarajan, V. 256, 260–62
Grameen Bank 94
GrameenPhone 94
Gran Tierra Energy Inc. 55
    Argentine base 61–2
    average daily production (2006–12) 71
    background of 55–6
    in Brazil
        assets 66–7
        challenges 67
        decision to enter 63, 66
        experience 67–8
        offshore agreements 67
        Recôncavo basin 66, 69
    Bretaña oil discovery 71, 72
    business plan 58
    capital allocation budget 68–9
    capital expenditures (2006–12) 72
    in Colombia 62, 63
    consolidated statements of cash flows 70
    current stock price 73
    executive team 56, 63
        global experience 57
    financial balance sheet 69
    financial situation 68
    high-risk opportunities for 67
    initial markets 63, 64–5
    investments in Peru 55
    local business units 61
    in Marañon basin 62–3
    net after royalties 68
    oil and gas industry 58, 59–60
    portfolio 61–3, 68, 70
    potential asset valuation summary 73
    return on investment 58

in South America 63
strategy 56–61
total employees (2006–12) 72
total reserves 71
greenfield 6
  investments 114, 119, 120
Gregersen, H.B. 325
Greidanus, N.S. 276
Griffith, D. 186
GRI G3 Sustainability Reporting Guidelines 163
Group Industrial Development (GID) 102–3
  corporate purchasing solutions 103
  with global sourcing 102
  outsourcing customer service 104
  Scandinavian and European markets 104
  transfer from bottom-of-the-pyramid 103–6
GUF stakeholder relations 147–50
Gupta, A.K. 256, 260–62

Hall, P.A. 229, 230, 233, 234, 241
Hansen 129–31, 133
Hansen, M.T. 258, 260, 261
Hardy, David 56
Harper, Stephen 228
Hart, S.L. 90, 91, 104
Harzing, A.-W. 197, 120
health, safety and environmental (HSE) standards 157
Hennart, J.F. 36
Hillemann, J. 36
Hillman, A.J. 168
Hofstede, G. 185–202
Hofstede's four dimensions, of culture
  causality 199
  contingency perspective criticism 198–9
  critique of 197–201
  equal distance 199–200
  IBM as source of data 197–8
  illusion of symmetry 199–200
  individualism–collectivism 191–3
  level of analysis 199–200
  masculinity-femininity 194–7
  motivation 195–6
  power distance 188–9
  stability of culture 201
  uncertainty avoidance 189–91
  validity 199
home country characteristics 227–9
home country institutions 227–9

Honda 12
HR structure, LVMH 340–41
HRM *see* human resource management (HRM)
human resource management (HRM)
  cross-national 290–92
  customization 298–9
  internalization 298–9
  international 289–90
  practical lessons 297–9
  strategic international 292–7
  systems 233
Husted, B.W. 171, 172
Hutzschenreuter, T. 185, 186
Hymer, S.H. 27, 29

IBM 33, 197–8, 262
IG Metall 232
IJV *see* international joint venture (IJV)
IKEA 8, 77
illusion of symmetry 199–200
implementer subsidiaries 88
independent oil and gas firms 60
individualism 191–3
individualized pay-for-performance systems (I-PFP) 236
IndustriALL 155, 156, 158
industry standards 154
influencer stakeholders 144
informal constraints 226–7
inimitable resources 85
institutional context
  complexities 229–33
  home country characteristics 227–9
  institutional distance 225–7
  institutional voids 233–5
institutional distance 225–7
  between Austria and Germany 230
  coordination index 230
  vs. cultural distance 236
institutional economics 226
institutional voids 233–5
integrated oil and gas companies (IOCs) 60
integration–responsiveness framework 75–6
  geographically distributed organizational units 85–7
  global strategy 77
  multidomestic strategy 78–80
  simple international strategy 76
  transnational strategy 80–81

integrative SIHRM orientation 294–5
Intel 33
intercultural training, LVMH 352–3
internalization
   HRM 298–9
   OLI framework 32
   theory 108, 253–4
international business (IB) 225–6
International Club 215
international diversification, performance and 35–6
international framework agreements (IFAs) 154–5
international HRM (IHRM) 289–90
internationalization
   of firms 27–8
      efficiency-seeking motives 28
      market-seeking motives 28
      resource-seeking motives 28
      strategic asset-seeking motive 28
   MNEs 31–2, 37
      regionalization thesis 34–5
      region bound 33–4
   process of 32–5
   Uppsala model 32–3
internationalization strategy, of emerging market MNEs 36
international joint ventures (IJVs) 114–18, 124–6
   agendas 116
   benefits of 116
   case setting 126
   Chinese partner 116–17
   establishment of 115
   formal governance structure 126–7
   local participation 115–16
   MNEs and local partners 117
   negotiations 116
   trust between partners 118
   see also BKT joint ventures
International Labour Conference 158
International Labour Organization (ILO) 149, 154
international management 8
international managers 10–11
international mobility, LVMH 339–42, 345–50
international recruitment, LVMH 343–4
international strategies 75–6
   BOP challenge 89–91
   and competitive strategy 81–2
   firm-specific advantages enabling 82–3
   geographically distributed organizational units 85–7

   global 77
   integration-responsiveness framework 75–81
   multidomestic 78–80
   simple 76
   subsidiary roles 87–9
   transnational 80–81
   types 76
   see also firm-specific advantages (FSAs)
international talents, LVMH 342–3
International Transfer Department 354
international transfer policy, LVMH 344–5
internet banking, SR-Bank 305
Interspar stores 244
inter-subsidiary category teams 284
IOCs *see* integrated oil and gas companies (IOCs)
iPhone 176
ISO 26000 Guidance on Social Responsibility 163

Jackson, S.E. 291, 292
Jamali, D. 172
Jobs, Steve 178
Joerges, B. 298
Johanson, J. 34, 37
Jorgensen, S. 165

Kanematsu, Y. 179
Keim, G.D. 168
Kemmelmeier, M. 192
Kempen 244
Khanna, T. 234
Kim, C. 173
Kirkman, B.L. 200
KitKat 79
KMIS *see* knowledge management information system (KMIS)
Knorr, A. 240
knowledge
   collective 256, 257
   conscious 256
   explicit 255–6, 310, 315
   objectified 257
   organizational 256
   tacit 118, 255–6, 315
knowledge-based resources 84
knowledge-based theory 256
knowledge management information system (KMIS) 102
knowledge network, MNE as 251–3

knowledge transfer 326
  determinants 257–9
  in MNEs 254–5
  types 255–7
Kogut, B. 255
Kostova, T. 86, 298
Kraft 76
Kramer, M.R. 168, 169
Kroll, M. 11
Kyriakidou, O. 262

LafargeHolcim 155–6
  chronology of dispute 157–9
  in India 156–7
Lafont, Bruno 155
Langley, A. 298, 299
Larsen 128, 133–5
Lazarova, M. 328
Le, S. 11
lean retail system 240
learning communities 314–15
lending 306
Leung, K. 202
Levinson, Daniel 187
Levitt, Theodore 77
liability of foreignness (LoF) 29–32, 37
  discrimination of foreign companies 30
  domestic companies 29
  lack of institutional and cultural insight 30–31
liability of outsidership (LoO) 35
liberal market economy (LME) 229–34, 241–2
licensing 112
Lieberthal, K. 90
Linder, C. 324
LME *see* liberal market economy (LME)
location advantages, OLI framework 31–2
logistical support, LVMH 352
London, T. 90, 91, 104
LoO *see* liability of outsidership (LoO)
Löscher, Peter 12
Løvås, B. 258, 260, 261
low-price strategy, Walmart 240, 242
Lozeau, D. 298, 299
Lübeck 127–31
Lundan, S.M. 5
Luo, Y. 36
Lutz, Bob 24
LVMH 33
  balance-sheet approach 345–7, 350

career development 341
expatriate package 348–9
future in 2001 354
history and structure 339
home-based salary 345, 349, 353–4
human resource structure 340–41
intercultural training 352–3
international mobility 339–42, 345–50
international recruitment 343–4
international talents 342–3
international transfer policy 344–5
logistical support 352
managing benefits 350–51
mobility salary 346
policy, basic principles of 341–2
'Ready to Move' 341
repatriation 353–4
spousal support 352
unemployment insurance benefits 351

Madam Tan 131–5
Madhok, A. 117, 118, 135
Malik, Yogesh 98
management-initiated practices, role of 261–4
managerial mindsets 333
  change of 333
  ethnocentric 330–31
  geocentric 332–3
  polycentric 331–2
managers
  distance types 8–9
  international 10–11, 86
'Managing Across Cultures' seminars 217
managing benefits, LVMH 350–51
mandated category teams 283–4
Manpower 100
manufacturing
  advantage of 6
  foreign affiliates in 6
Marañon basin 62–3
Margolis, J.D. 166, 168
market capitalization 42
market contract 110
market failure 110, 253, 254
marketing strategies 90
market-seeking motives 28
Marsman, I. 12
M&As *see* mergers and acquisitions (M&As)
masculinity-femininity 194–7

Maslow's hierarchy of needs 195
McDonald's 8, 33, 113
McKinsey 96, 277, 278, 280
McSweeney, B. 198
McWilliams, A. 168
Mead, Margaret 187
mentorships 328–9
Menzer, John 30
Merchant, B. 177, 178
mergers and acquisitions (M&As) 28, 119
　advantage of 119
meta-competencies 252–3
microfinance programmes 170
Microsoft 12
Middle East and North Africa (MENA), MTN Group Limited 44–5
midstream (transportation and trading) 60
Miles, S. 143–5
Millicom International Cellular 46
Minbaeva, D.B. 257, 263
Mitsubishi 17, 22
MNE Telenor 9
MNEs see multinational enterprises (MNEs)
mobile phone vendors 113
mobile subscriber growth 52
'Mom and Pop stores' 100, 103
Monaco Telecom 52
moral underpinning 142, 220
Moreira, Julio 66
Morris, M.W. 202
Mosakowski, E. 185
motivation 195–6
　achievement 195–6
　security and esteem 196
　social 196
motivational cultural intelligence (CQ) 125
motivational mechanisms 263
Motorola 113
MTN Dubai 45
MTN Foundation 48–9
MTN Group Limited (MTN) 41
　corporate structure and organization 44–5
　customer-focused strategy 43–4
　expansion strategy 43–4
　geographical locations 42
　in Ghana see Ghana, MTN Group Limited in
　international joint ventures 43
　long-term vision 43–4
　management of 43–4
　market capitalization 42
　markets, institutional development of 47
　Middle East and North Africa 44–5
　organization structure 46
　products and services 42–3
　South Africa 45
　Southern, East Africa & Ghana 44
　telecommunication industry 52
　unique local challenges 45–52
　West and Central Africa 44
MTN International, operational vs. ownership structure 45
MTN Mauritius 45
MTN Nigeria 45, 49–52
　average revenue per user 51
　fine of $5.2 billion 49–51
　market share by mobile operator 51
　one-year share price 49
　registration of SIM cards 50
　sale of Cyprus unit 52
MTN Swaziland 45
Mudambi, R. 270
Muller, A. 172
multidomestic international strategies 78–80, 91
multidomestic MNEs
　bridging category teams 284–6
　concluding reactions 279–80
　general management team 280–82
　governance reconfiguration 280–82
　initial reactions 278–9
　inter-subsidiary category teams 284
　mandated category teams 283–4
　realignment of rewards 282
　rolling measures of outcomes 282–3
multinational enterprises (MNEs) 3, 35
　Apple's definition of 5
　BOP markets 89–91
　boundary of 5
　challenge 235
　competitive advantage 82, 252, 289, 329
　conceptual model 264–5
　control and coordination mechanisms 83
　coordination with supply chains 6
　corporate social responsibility in 171–3
　cost leadership 81
　cultural distance and 185–7
　definition 3–6
　developing managers 10
　drivers of global value chains 4

Dutch 12
evolutionary theory 253–4
extant theory 35–7
external environment 259–60
foreign affiliates 27
foreign subsidiaries 88
geographic distribution of organizational units 86
global international strategies 77
greenfield *vs.* acquisition 120
home country characteristics 227–9
host markets 82, 228
institutional context affecting 225
integration–responsiveness framework 75–6
internal consistency 10
international executive boards of 12–13
internationalization 31–2, 37
international joint venture 116, 117
as knowledge network 251–3
knowledge transfer 254–5
as lead firms 4
legitimacy 226
'liability of foreignness' 29–31
management-initiated practices 261–4
managers, distance types 8–9
market contract 110
multidomestic *see* Scandinavian Food Company (SFC)
multidomestic international strategies 78–80, 91
multiple embeddedness of 87
multiple pressures for global integration 82
national identities 12
price leadership 82
qualifications for firms 3
region bound 33–4
regionalization thesis 34
scrutiny 228
selling innovative products 33–4
SIHRM in 293
simple international strategies 76
Spanish 12
strategic leaders 88
subsidiaries 227
subsidiaries role 87–9
Swiss 13
transnational strategy 86
use of contracts 113–14
value-creating exchanges 227
multiple embeddedness 86
Mycoskie, B. 168

NAFTA *see* North American Free Trade Agreement (NAFTA)
Nahapiet, J. 257, 259, 265
National Bank Agreement 313
national culture
 concept of 187–8
 cultural distance 185–7
 Hofstede's four dimensions 188–202
 situated dynamics framework 202
national diversity 13
National Iranian Oil Company 60
national oil companies (NOCs) 59–60
needs-oriented sales 307
neo-institutional theory 226
Nescafé 79
Nestlé 13, 30, 78, 164
 Bhati Dilwan case 182–3
 commitment to decentralization 78
 'corporate business principles' 181
 'creating shared value' goals for water 181–2
 expansion 78
 in New Zealand 78–9
 Ontario case 183–4
 purchasing 79
 'Pure Life' product 182–3
 role in society 181
 subsidiaries 181
Neuhaus 129–31, 133
Newburry, W. 115
Nexen (Canadian IOC) 60
NGOs, stakeholders relationships to 146–7
Nhleko, Phuthuma 41
Nielsen, B.B. 13
Nielsen, S. 13
Nigerian Communications Commission (NCC) 50
Nike 113, 143, 146, 164
Nikkei Asian Review 178
Nissan 16, 17, 20
 cost reduction plan 22
 Ghosn analysis of 21
 joint venture arrangement with Renault 20
 Nissan–Renault alliance 22
 plan for rebuilding 21
Nissan Leaf 22
Nissan–Renault alliance 22
Nissan Revival Plan 21–2
Nobel, R. 257
NOCs *see* national oil companies (NOCs)
Nokia 33, 251

Nonaka, I. 314
non-equity modes of entry 109, 111
North American Free Trade Agreement (NAFTA) 33
North, D.C. 9, 226
Norwegian MNE Telenor's subsidiary 91
Nowak, C. 324

objectified knowledge 257
O'Donnell, S. 270
OECD *see* Organisation for Economic Co-operation and Development (OECD)
OFII *see* Organization for International Investment (OFII)
oil and gas industry 59–60
   reserve replacement 59
O'Leary, Shane 56, 66, 68
OLI framework 31, 36
   firm-specific advantages 83–5
   internalization 32
   location advantages 31–2
   ownership advantages 31, 36
   vertical expansion 31
OLI theory 251–2
One Device: The Secret History of the iPhone, The (Merchant) 177
Ontario case, Nestlé 183–4
operating modes 108
   contract manufacturing and service provision 113–14
   exporting 111–12
   foreign 108–11
   foreign direct investments 114–15
   franchising 112–13
   international joint ventures 115–18
   licensing 112
   wholly-owned subsidiaries 118–20
Organisation for Economic Co-operation and Development (OECD) 6–7, 149–50, 154, 159
Organization for International Investment (OFII) 30
organizational knowledge 256
organizational learning 323
organized resources 85
Orlitzky, M. 168
Orunesu, Rafael 61
Osegowitsch, T. 34, 37
Osland, J. 10, 11, 16
Osterloh, M. 263
over-selling 307
ownership advantages, OLI framework 31

ownership, location and internalization (OLI) framework 225
Oyserman, D. 192

Pacific Rubiales 58
Pakapath, Aranya 158
Palepu, K. 234
Park, S.H. 115
Parola, F. 36
Pedersen, L.J. 165
Pelecta 272–4, 276, 278, 279, 284, 285
PEMEX 60
perceived benefit and price, Uninor 98–9
performance measurement issue, SESAM 317–19
Persico, L. 36
Persson, M. 270
Petrobras 60, 63, 66, 67, 73
Petronas 60
Pfizer 89
Philips 33
Phillips, R.A. 142
Pitana 272–5, 277–9, 285
Polanyi 255
polycentric mindsets 331–2
Porter, Michael 119–20, 168, 169
possible reserves 59
Post-Unification Project 277–8
Powell, W.W. 256
power distance 188–9
Pragatisheel Cement Shramik Sangh (PCSS) 155–9
Prahalad, C.K. 90
'premium service' business model, Telenor 96
price leadership 82
PricewaterhouseCoopers (PwC) 7
private employment agency (ILO) 153
private regulation 149
probable reserves 59
Procter & Gamble 76
productivity spillovers 4
products and services, MTN 42–3
products strategies 90
Programme Amalgamation (2008–10)
   bridging category teams 284–6
   concluding reactions 279–80
   general management team 280–82
   governance reconfiguration 280–82
   initial reactions 278–9
   inter-subsidiary category teams 284
   mandated category teams 283–4

realignment of rewards 282
rolling measures of outcomes 282–3
property rights 126, 233, 234
   theory of firm 109
proved reserves 59
purchasing and supply management (PSM) 277
'Pure Life' product 182–3

Ramamurti, R. 36
rare resources 84–5
Ravasi, C. 12
R&D 6
recipient stakeholders 145
Recôncavo basin 66, 69
Reger, G. 261
regionalization thesis 34–5
Reiche, B.S. 10
Reitzle, Wolfgang 155
Reliance 234
Renault 16, 17, 19, 24
   joint venture arrangement with Nissan 20
   Nissan–Renault alliance 22
repatriates 327–9
repatriation, LVMH 353–4
re-socialization process 328
resource dependency theory 271
resources 84
   inimitable 85
   organized 85
   rare 84–5
   valuable 84
resource-seeking motives 28
retail sales executives (RSEs) 100, 101
return on investment 242, 325
reverse discrimination 214–15, 221
rewards system 282
Roth, K. 298
Royal Dutch Shell 143, 146, 328
RSEs see retail sales executives (RSEs)
Rugman, A. 33, 34, 253
Rugman, A.M. 8–9
Russell, C. 186
Rygh, A. 229
Rynes, S.L. 168

Saikawa, Hiroto 16, 24
Sammartino, A. 34
Samsung 337
Sande, Olav 103

Sarin, Arun 9
Satta, G. 36
Savings Banks Act 303
Scancom Limited 45
Scandinavian Food Company (SFC) 269–70
   context 272–3
   extant theory 270–72
   political challenge 270–71
   Post-Unification Project 277–8
   Programme Amalgamation 278–86
   social network challenge 271–2
   Unification Project 273–7
Schmidt 131, 132, 134
Schmidt, F.L. 168
Schotter, A. 125
Schuler, R.S. 290–92
security and esteem motivation 196
service provision 113–14
SESAM
   antecedents 305–8
   balanced scorecard 319–20
   explicit face 309–15
   knowledge importation 308–9
   learning communities 314–15
   learning paradox 320
   local learning 314
   performance measurement issue 317–19
   practice 315–17
   programme 302
   sales leader's performance 316
   weekly meetings 314–15
   winning plays 310–13
SFC see Scandinavian Food Company (SFC)
Shanghai-JV 129, 131–2
Shapiro, D.L. 200
Shell 60, 164
short- and long-term benefits 168–9
Shortland, S. 326
Siegel, D. 168
Siemens 12
SIHRM see strategic international human resource management (SIHRM)
Silva, S. 124
simple international strategies 76
situated dynamics framework 202
social capital theory 254–5, 257–65
social construct, cultural diversity as 210–13
social embeddedness 91
socialization mechanisms 262–4

social motivation 196
social network challenge 271–2
social norms 8, 243, 246
Social Policy and Development Centre (SPDC) 183
social trust 118, 124
sociology 226
soft sell 307–8
Sony 30, 33, 77
Soskice, D.W. 229
Sousa, C.M.P. 124
South Africa and Nigeria, MTN Group Limited 45
Southern, East Africa & Ghana (SEAGHA), MTN Group Limited 44
Spender, J.-C. 256
spousal support, LVMH 352
SR-Bank 302–3
  ATMs 305
  cultural context 303–4
  human resources department 307–8
  internet banking 305
  key financial figures 304–5
  lending 306
  retail market 307
  SESAM *see* SESAM
  strategy 304
staffing policies 330–33
Stahl, G.K. 186
stakeholders 141–3
  claimant 144
  collaborator 145
  GUFs 147–50
  influencer 144
  legitimacy 146
  MNEs' relevant 143–6
  NGOs 146–7
  power 145–6
  recipient 145
  trade-offs 142
  urgency 146
stakeholder theory, in corporate social responsibility 164–8
state-owned enterprises (SOEs) 62, 127, 228, 229, 333
Statoil 60, 67, 68
Steel, P. 193
strategic asset-seeking motive 28
strategic international human resource management (SIHRM) 290–92
  analysing 292
  calculative HRM practices 296

  framework 292–3
  in MNEs 293
  orientations 294–5
  subsidiary-level influences 295–6
  top management's perception 294
strategic leaders 88
Strike, V.M. 171
structural trust 118, 124–5
subsidiary roles 87–9
  foreign subsidiaries 88–9
  MNEs 87
  research on 87–8
subsidiary's HRM system 295–6
substantial direct investment 3, 5
substantial foreign direct investment (FDI) 3, 5
super majors 60
suppliers
  Apple 176–9
  challenges 176–9
  competitive situation 176–9
  Foxconn 177–9

tacit knowledge 118, 255–6, 315
Takeuchi, H. 314
Taras, V. 193
Tarique, I. 328
Tata 234
Tayeb, M. 198, 201
Taylor, S. 292–4
telecommunication industry 52
  see also MTN Group Limited (MTN); MTN Nigeria
Telenor 9, 94, 104
  in Asian markets 95, 103
  in Bangladesh 94
  business model 98
  Central European operations 95–6
  Group Industrial Development 102–3
  in India 94, 95
  knowledge management information system 102
  as multidomestic MNE 101–2
  new management team 98
  in Pakistan 94
  'premium service' business model 96
  transfer of practices from BOP 105
  see also Uninor
Templeton Global Performance Index 29
Terry Gou 178
'The True Story of Carlos Ghosn' 22
Tigo 46

Tihanyi, L. 186
TOMS Shoes 168
top management diversity 12–13
top management's beliefs, role of 294
Total 60
Toyota 12, 33
trade agreements 9, 111
Traded Goods category team 285, 286
Trade Union Advisory Committee (TUAC) 149
trade unions 148, 231–2
transaction cost 38, 234
  theory 109
transmission channels 261
transnational international strategies 80–81
transnational private labour regulation (TPLR) 154
transnational strategy 80–81, 86
Transparency International 114
triple bottom line 165
Tsai, W. 258, 265
Tsang, E.W.K. 262
Tung, R.L. 36, 186

Uber 5, 10, 84
Ulset, S. 9
uncertainty avoidance 189–91
UNCTAD *see* United Nations Conference on Trade and Development (UNCTAD)
unemployment insurance benefits 351
Unification Project (2004–07) 273–7
Unilever 30, 33
Uninor 91, 94, 95, 104, 234
  allied with Ericsson 97
  business model 96
  in call-centre industry 97
  cluster-based operating model 99
  cost cutting efforts 99–100
  cost-effective distribution system 100
  declining growth of 97–8
  'dynamic pricing' concept 98–9
  failure and turnaround of 95–8
  global replication of BOP innovations 101–2
  Group Industrial Development 102–3
    transfer from BOP 103–4
  implementation phase 96
  initial market positioning 96
  innovative distribution system 99, 100
  perceived benefit and price 98–9
  retail sales executives 100, 101
  value capture and value creation 101
  value delivery 99–101
  value proposition 101
  see also Telenor
United Nations Conference on Trade and Development (UNCTAD) 5
Uppsala internationalization process 32–3, 35
upstream (exploration and production) 60
Uribe, Álvaro 62

Vahlne, J.E. 34, 37
validity, cultural 199
valuable, rare, inimitable and organized (VRIO) 84
valuable resources 84
value capture, Uninor 101
value chains 6, 28
  global 4, 148
value creation, Uninor 101
value delivery, Uninor 99–101
value proposition, Uninor 101
Van Oudenhoven, J.P. 189
Van Veen, K. 12
varieties of capitalism (VoC) 229–31, 233–4
varieties of institutional systems (VIS) 234–5
Verbeke, A. 33, 276
vertical expansion 31
virtual boundary spanner, in BKT joint ventures 133
VIS *see* varieties of institutional systems (VIS)
VoC *see* varieties of capitalism (VoC)
Vodafone 9, 97
Voll, J.V. 185, 186
Voso 272–80, 284, 285
VRIO *see* valuable, rare, inimitable and organized (VRIO)

Walmart 30, 337
  after Germany 246–7
  collective bargaining 245
  competitive strategy 241
  enter into the market 242–4
  in Germany 244–6
  home market 241–2
  information about 240–41
  in Japanese market 246
  lean retail system 240
  low-price strategy 240, 242
  shareholders 246
  US labour market 241
Walsh, J.P. 166, 168
Walton, C. 167

Wang 129–31, 133, 134
West and Central Africa (WECA), MTN Group Limited 44
wholly-owned subsidiaries (WOSs) 114, 118–20, 126
  greenfield investment 120
  mergers and acquisitions 119
Wick, A.C. 142
win–win possibilities, by CSR investments 169–71
Wipro 97, 99–100
workforce diversity 206

World Bank's Worldwide Governance Indicators 45
World Commission on Environment and Development (WCED) 163
World Economic Forum 148
World Jam Sessions 261

Yaziji, M. 146

Zander, U. 255
Zellmer-Bruhn, M.E. 199
Zhang, S. 202